CRITICAL CONSCIOUSNESS

Critical consciousness represents the analysis of inequitable social conditions, the motivation to effect change, and the action taken to redress perceived inequities. Scholarship and practice in the last two decades have highlighted critical consciousness as a key developmental competency for those experiencing marginalization and as a pathway for navigating and resisting oppression. This competency is more urgent than ever given the current sociopolitical moment, in which long-standing inequity, bias, discrimination, and competing ideologies are amplified. This volume assembles leading scholars to address some of the field's most urgent questions: How does critical consciousness develop? What theories can be used to complement and enrich our understanding of the operation of critical consciousness? How might new directions in theory and measurement further enhance what is known about critical consciousness? It offers cutting-edge ideas and answers to these questions that are of utmost importance to deepen our critical consciousness theory and measurement.

Luke J. Rapa is Assistant Professor in the Department of Education and Human Development at Clemson University, USA. He is coeditor of *Developing Critical Consciousness in Youth: Contexts and Settings* (2023) and *Disproportionality and Social Justice in Education* (2022). He was Clemson University's College of Education Junior Researcher of the Year in 2022.

Erin B. Godfrey is Associate Professor of Applied Psychology in the Steinhardt School of Culture, Education, and Human Development at New York University, USA. She is coeditor of *Developing Critical Consciousness in Youth: Contexts and Settings* (2023) and an editorial board member for the *Journal of Youth and Adolescence*. She won NYU Steinhardt's W. Gabriel Carras Research Award in 2013 and NYU Steinhardt's Griffiths Research Award in 2018.

## Contemporary Social Issues

General Editor: Brian D. Christens, *Vanderbilt University*

*Contemporary Social Issues* is the official book series of the Society for the Psychological Study of Social Issues (SPSSI). Since its founding in 1936, SPSSI has addressed the social issues of the times. Central to these efforts has been the Lewinian tradition of action-oriented research, in which psychological theories and methods guide research and action addressed to important societal problems. Grounded in their authors' programmes of research, works in this series focus on social issues facing individuals, groups, communities, and/or society at large, with each volume written to speak to scholars, students, practitioners, and policymakers.

### Other Books in the Series

*Developing Critical Consciousness in Youth: Contexts and Settings*
Erin Godfrey and Luke Rapa, editors

*Critical Consciousness: Expanding Theory and Measurement*
Luke Rapa and Erin Godfrey, editors

# Critical Consciousness

## *Expanding Theory and Measurement*

*Edited by*
Luke J. Rapa
*Clemson University*

Erin B. Godfrey
*New York University*

Shaftesbury Road, Cambridge CB2 8EA, United Kingdom

One Liberty Plaza, 20th Floor, New York, NY 10006, USA

477 Williamstown Road, Port Melbourne, VIC 3207, Australia

314–321, 3rd Floor, Plot 3, Splendor Forum, Jasola District Centre, New Delhi – 110025, India

103 Penang Road, #05–06/07, Visioncrest Commercial, Singapore 238467

Cambridge University Press is part of Cambridge University Press & Assessment, a department of the University of Cambridge.

We share the University's mission to contribute to society through the pursuit of education, learning and research at the highest international levels of excellence.

www.cambridge.org
Information on this title: www.cambridge.org/9781009153775

DOI: 10.1017/9781009153751



First published 2023

*A catalogue record for this publication is available from the British Library.*

*Library of Congress Cataloging-in-Publication Data*
NAMES: Rapa, Luke J., editor. | Godfrey, Erin B, editor.
TITLE: Critical consciousness : expanding theory and measurement / edited by Luke J. Rapa, Clemson University, South Carolina, Erin B Godfrey, New York University.
DESCRIPTION: 1 Edition. | New York, NY : Cambridge University Press, [2023] | Series: Contemporary social issues series | Includes bibliographical references and index.
IDENTIFIERS: LCCN 2022057092 | ISBN 9781009153775 (hardback) | ISBN 9781009153768 (paperback) | ISBN 9781009153751 (ebook)
SUBJECTS: LCSH: Critical psychology. | Transformative learning.
CLASSIFICATION: LCC BF39.9 .C734 2023 | DDC 150.19/87–dc23/eng/20230201
LC record available at https://lccn.loc.gov/2022057092

ISBN 978-1-009-15377-5 Hardback
ISBN 978-1-009-15376-8 Paperback

*For Sarah, my model in the pursuit of love, humanity, and justice. Thank you for leading the way – not only for me, but for our children as well. We are better because of you.*

LJR

*This book on critical "consciousciousnes" is for you, Jada, and for DD, Mali, Kian, Bijan, Carson, and all my other honorary children. May you always recognize what is unfair and fight for what's right.*

EBG

# CONTENTS

# FIGURES

# TABLES

# CONTRIBUTORS

LAUREN ALVIS, PHD, Meadows Mental Health Policy Institute, USA

SHEREEN ASHAI, University of Maryland, College Park, USA

CANDICE W. BOLDING, Clemson University, USA

CARI ALLYN BROOKS, Clemson University, USA

RIANA M. BROWN, New York University, USA

ESTHER BURSON, PHD, Bronfenbrenner Center for Translational Research, Cornell University, USA

KELLY D. CHANDLER, PHD, Oregon State University, USA

AUTUMN DIAZ, University of Washington, Tacoma, USA

MATTHEW A. DIEMER, PHD, University of Michigan, USA

SARAH ESSNER, Boston College, USA

FLÓRA FARAGÓ, PHD, Stephen F. Austin State University, USA

LINDA J. FENSKE, Oregon State University, USA

KEVIN A. FERREIRA VAN LEER, PHD, California State University, Sacramento, USA

MATTHEW N. GEE, Tufts University, USA

ERIN B. GODFREY, PHD, New York University, USA

MACKENZIE HART, University of South Carolina, Columbia, USA

AMY E. HEBERLE, PHD, Clark University, USA

MANUEL TERAN HERNANDEZ, University of Maryland, College Park, USA

RACHEL HERSHBERG, PHD, University of Washington, Tacoma, USA

NOAH HOCH, Clark University, USA

DEANNA A. IBRAHIM, PHD, New York University, USA

SARA K. JOHNSON, PHD, Tufts University, USA

BRIAN KEUM, PHD, University of California, Los Angeles, USA

MARIAH KORNBLUH, PHD, University of South Carolina, Columbia, USA

GABRIELLE KUBI, University of Michigan, USA

YUN LU, PHD, Zhejiang University, China

KARA MCELVAINE, Oregon State University, USA

SARAH E. MCKELLAR, PHD, Learning Research and Development Center (LRDC), University of Pittsburgh, USA

SVEA G. OLSEN, Oregon State University, USA

ANDRES PINEDO, University of Michigan, USA

JASON A. PLUMMER, University of California, Los Angeles, USA

LUKE J. RAPA, PHD, Clemson University, USA

RICHARD Q. SHIN, PHD, University of Maryland, College Park, USA

SARA SUZUKI, PHD, CIRCLE (Center for Information and Research on Civic Learning and Engagement), Tisch College of Civic Life, Tufts University, USA

SHAUNA L. TOMINEY, PHD, Oregon State University, USA

CORINE P. TYLER, Oregon State University, USA

JENNIFER WATLING NEAL, PHD, Michigan State University, USA

LAURA WRAY-LAKE, PHD, University of California, Los Angeles, USA

# ACKNOWLEDGMENTS

A project like this cannot materialize without the contributions of so many people. We are grateful to all who supported this work – in big and small ways, and in seen and unseen ways.

To all who contributed chapters to this volume, thank you for engaging with us in this project and for trusting us with your ideas and your scholarship. Your contributions truly are the sine qua non of this work; without your commitment to participate in conversations, writing groups, idea exchanges, and peer review processes – not to mention doing the hard work of writing and revising your own chapters – this volume would not be what it is today. We are eternally grateful for your participation in this project and we are honored to be a part of a scholarly community with you, sharing in your intellectual, academic, and critically reflective spaces.

To colleagues who offered guidance, support, and encouragement along the way, thank you for your commitment to us and for your care about our work, our ideas, and our successes.

To our families, thank you for your love, encouragement, patience, and support. We are only able to do what we do because of you.

To Erin, I (Luke) am so grateful for your collaboration in this endeavor. This project is much richer for your involvement, and I cannot say emphatically enough how rewarding this work and our partnership has been for me. Our efforts on this began as many aspects of prepandemic life subsided; connecting with you in the midst of such disruption fostered hope and restoration. It is my privilege to call you a colleague and a collaborator – thank you for your commitment to our shared vision and for your friendship. Perhaps we will have the good fortune to do this again someday.

Dr. Brian Christens, we offer you our most sincere gratitude for your assistance and your guidance over the course of this project. We appreciate the trust and confidence you placed in us, and your willingness to allow us to engage in this work as we did. The volume would surely not be what it is today without your support of the vision we had for this book.

Janka Romero and Rowan Groat, at Cambridge University Press, thank you for your expert hands in guiding us through the process, from initial proposal development through manuscript completion. Your insights and care were invaluable to us, and this volume could not have come to fruition without you. Your patience and your speedy replies to our queries are greatly appreciated.

This project was funded in part by Clemson University's R-Initiative Program. We are grateful to the Clemson University Division of Research for the generous funding provided to support a portion of Luke's work on this volume. This project was also funded in part by New York University's University Research Challenge Fund and the NYU Steinhardt School of Culture, Education and Human Development Faculty Challenge Grant. We thank NYU and NYU Steinhardt for their generous support of this scholarship.

We dedicate this book to the young people everywhere, and to those who love, teach, support, guide, and learn with, from, and alongside them. Your activism, creativity, passion, and strength inspire us to try every day to make the world we live in worthy of you.

# Introduction

## Critical Consciousness Theory and Measurement

### *Mapping the Complexity of the Terrain*

LUKE J. RAPA AND ERIN B. GODFREY

Structural oppression and systemic inequity are interwoven into the fabric of American society. One need only reflect on the past decade to see the continued pernicious influence of racism, sexism, classism, ableism, nativism, heterosexism, transphobia, and multiple other forms of marginalization on the rights, freedoms, and humanity of large segments of our society. We live in a system of white supremacy and patriarchy that patterns not only our history, but our current society, institutions, interactions, and beliefs about each other and ourselves (Bonilla-Silva, 2006). To be Black, Brown, Indigenous, immigrant, differently-abled, gay, gender-expansive, female-identified – among many other identities – means being subjected to systems and structures that, at best, limit access to the resources and privileges others take for granted and, at worst, take away fundamental rights to life, liberty, and choice. To be white, straight, able-bodied, male-identified, and more (e.g., Christian Protestant) means wielding privilege one may or may not know one has, but that contributes to the maintenance of these inequities. These unfair, unjust, and inequitable social conditions shape all our lives in multiple seen and unseen ways and have effects across all developmental domains (Brown et al., 2019; Ruck et al., 2019).

Social scientists have amassed considerable evidence on how oppressive systems shape people's development, adaptive functioning, and general well-being (Heberle et al., 2020), showing deleterious effects on multiple life outcomes across multiple populations. It is only relatively recently, however, that scholars have begun to consider people's own beliefs and actions regarding the fairness and legitimacy of the systems in which they live. This shift in perspective recognizes that individuals can be formidable assets in the fight against injustice, and treats them as active agents in the construal and transformation of systems of oppression. Central to this area of inquiry is critical consciousness (Freire, 1968/2000; Watts et al., 2011), which relates to how individuals critically "read" social conditions, feel empowered to change those conditions, and engage in action toward that goal. Alongside allied perspectives such as sociopolitical development, culturally relevant pedagogy, critical theory, and antiracist perspectives, critical consciousness theory has emerged as a particularly useful framework for interrogating how people understand, navigate, and resist social injustice and inequity.

## WHAT IS CRITICAL CONSCIOUSNESS AND WHY DOES IT MATTER?

Critical consciousness was originally conceptualized by Paulo Freire (1921–1997) as a pedagogical method to foster the ability of marginalized people to analyze the economic, political, historical, and social forces that contribute to inequitable social conditions and become empowered to change these conditions (Freire, 1973, 1968/2000). Freire termed this process *conscientização* – translated into English as "conscientization" – and described it as a dialectical process of reflection and action in which people engage with others about their experiences of oppression and marginalization and attend to their historical, social, and economic sources. Through discussion and dialogue – core elements of Freirean pedagogy – people become critically aware of the causes of their marginalization at the hands of historical and societal forces, take action to address this marginalization, and further deepen their understanding of the causes of oppression based on this experience.

Critical consciousness is considered to be especially potent for those who experience marginalization and structural oppression first-hand, in their daily lives and across their lived environments. It has even been called the "antidote to oppression" (Watts et al., 1999) because of its ability to arm marginalized youth with the insight, agency, and engagement needed to navigate and change oppressive systems (Watts et al., 2011). Yet, critical consciousness is also important for those experiencing relative privilege, as they work to understand systems of power, and their own power and privilege within those systems, and ally with others to bring about social change.

Building on Freire's theory of conscientization, and his pedagogical approach, developmental scientists typically conceptualize critical consciousness as three distinct, but overlapping components (e.g., Diemer et al., 2015; Watts et al., 2011). The first component, critical reflection, refers to an individual's ability to analyze current social realities critically, and recognize how historical, social, economic, and political conditions limit access to opportunity and perpetuate injustice. The second component, critical motivation (also referred to as sociopolitical or political efficacy), encompasses an individual's motivation and perceived ability to act to change these social, economic, and political conditions. The third component, critical action, is the extent to which individuals participate in action, individually or collectively, to resist, challenge, or disrupt social inequity. While the first component concerns increased awareness of and deepening reflection on unjust circumstances and their causes, the latter two involve the translation of this critical reflection into behaviors and action. The process of gaining critical awareness and acting to change conditions is self-perpetuating and reciprocal. That is, scholars conceptualize critical reflection as leading directly to action, but they also see critical action as reinforcing and deepening critical reflection and analysis, creating a virtuous cycle starting from either reflection or action. The role of critical motivation in this cycle is the subject of continued conceptual (i.e., theoretical) and empirical debate, but it is often thought of as a mediator through which reflection is linked to action or as a moderator that changes the way reflection and action influence each other or interrelate (e.g., Diemer & Rapa, 2016). Scholars are just beginning to delve more deeply into how these components interact and/or pattern together to characterize different types, levels, and/or processes of critical consciousness development (Christens, et al., 2013; Diemer & Rapa, 2016; Godfrey et al., 2019). This is the case, at least in part, because measures incorporating all three dimensions of critical consciousness are just emerging (e.g., Diemer et al., 2022; Rapa et al., 2020; see also Rapa et al., Chapter 7 [this volume]).

Critical consciousness is important from a societal perspective as it can play a central role in addressing unjust systems, challenging marginalization in society, and promoting positive community development. It is also an extremely important developmental competency for individuals, as it promotes positive growth and development. As mentioned earlier, it can function as an “antidote to oppression” or a form of “psychological armor” (Watts et al., 1999) for individuals experiencing and navigating oppressive systems. Indeed, we now have considerable evidence, primarily for Black, Brown, and low-socioeconomic status (SES) youth, that higher critical consciousness is connected to better educational outcomes (e.g., Seider et al., 2020); higher occupational aspirations and attainment (e.g., Rapa et al., 2018); greater political, civic, and community participation (e.g., Bañales et al., 2020; Diemer & Rapa, 2016; Tyler et al., 2020); and enhanced well-being across a range of dimensions (e.g., Godfrey et al., 2019; Zimmerman et al., 1999) (for excellent reviews, see Diemer et al., 2016; Heberle et al., 2020; Maker Castro et al., 2022). Although less scholarship to date has examined critical consciousness among individuals holding ethnic/racial, class, and/or other forms of privilege, developing a critical stance toward the status quo is also important – and doing so should not be the sole responsibility of those who are marginalized or oppressed. As many authors in this volume argue, it is also important for those who hold power and privilege to recognize it, and then use that power and privilege to engage in efforts to dismantle systems that reify, uphold, or perpetuate injustice and inequity. Indeed, recognizing privilege and its sources, and learning how to work in allyship and solidarity with those individuals and groups experiencing oppression, is a critical developmental competency for those who hold more privilege as well (Spanierman & Smith, 2017).

## WHY THEORY AND MEASUREMENT?

While critical consciousness scholarship has matured in recent years (Heberle et al., 2020), no comprehensive collection brings together the voices of leading scholars working in this area to address – through careful (re)consideration of theory and measurement – some of the field's most pressing questions: How does critical consciousness develop? What theories can be used to complement and enrich our understanding of the development and operation of critical consciousness? How do various measurement approaches align with or diverge from theory? How might new directions in theory and measurement further enhance what is known about the development, operation, and effects of critical consciousness? These questions are of great importance. Answering them seems more urgent now than ever, especially in light of the current sociopolitical moment – a moment in which long-standing racial inequity, structural oppression, bias, discrimination, marginalization, and competing ideologies are not only evident but also have been amplified.

*Critical Consciousness: Expanding Theory and Measurement* addresses these questions and more. This edited volume – along with the complementary volume, *Developing Critical Consciousness in Youth: Contexts and Settings* (Godfrey & Rapa, in press) – stems from our engagement with leading scholars in the field to identify topics and content considered most necessary to meaningfully advance critical consciousness scholarship. This volume represents the most exhaustive compendium to date attending to issues related to the theory and measurement of critical consciousness. In the chapters that follow, readers will find contributions that push the boundaries of critical consciousness theory, along with contributions that carefully explore existing and new measurement approaches. Some contributions do both. We expect the ideas presented here to shape research and inform dialogue about critical consciousness theory and measurement for years to come.

In short, this volume: (1) provides novel insights about critical consciousness theory itself, and articulates new links between critical consciousness and other related, but distinct developmental theories and frameworks; (2) fosters deeper understanding of critical consciousness and, in places, offers new empirical evidence about how critical consciousness develops and operates over the life course; and (3) highlights the complexity of this field of study while offering innovative ways that critical consciousness might be theorized about and measured. Ultimately, through this volume, our aim is to examine and expand critical consciousness theory and measurement in order to elucidate anew – by way of an incisive and groundbreaking collection of chapters – issues germane to theory and measurement and to set new directions for future research in this area.

## THE ORGANIZATION OF THIS VOLUME

This volume is organized into two parts. Part I contends with issues more salient to and is more explicitly focused on critical consciousness theory, while Part II summarizes, highlights, and attends to issues more relevant to measurement. Of course, the close interplay between theory and measurement means that chapters appearing in the measurement section also address issues relevant to theory, even while the chapters appearing in the theory section point to and address issues relevant to measurement.

### Part I: Theory

In Chapter 1, Andres Pinedo, Gabrielle Kubi, and Matthew Diemer examine critical consciousness theory alongside the theory of identity-based motivation in order to explicate how the psychological experiences of youth of color shape the way they navigate oppressive societal conditions, particularly those resultant from racial capitalism. Through their explication of critical consciousness and identity-based motivation theories, Pinedo et al. offer a new framework for assessing how various contextual and motivational factors interact with critical consciousness to shape adaptive development and support social mobility among youth of color.

In Chapter 2, Sara Suzuki, Sara Johnson, and Kevin Ferreira van Leer situate critical consciousness theory alongside developmental systems theory – highlighting the phenomenological variant of ecological systems theory (PVEST), in particular – to suggest the expansion of critical consciousness theory to account more fully for how critical consciousness functions within developmental systems. They also highlight how individual's meaning-making processes might serve as a primary mechanism supporting the development of critical consciousness, suggest the importance of considering broader chronosystemic (time-related) impacts on the development and operation of critical consciousness, and call attention to dynamic and collective characteristics of critical consciousness. Consequently, new research questions are envisioned that consider how individuals contend with marginalization and resist marginalizing systems over the course of their development.

In Chapter 3, Luke Rapa, Candice Bolding, and Cari Allyn Brooks present a new framework that integrates critical consciousness with social empathy, which itself is tied to people's ability to understand, connect with, and empathize with others who face marginalizing conditions and contend with structural inequities. After introducing an integrated critical consciousness–social empathy framework, the authors test that framework within the context of an exploratory study, highlighting the ways in which social empathy may complement critical consciousness, both in terms of theory and in terms of measurement.

In Chapter 4, Amy Heberle, Flóra Faragó, and Noah Hoch push theoretical boundaries by exploring the ways that children in early, middle, and late childhood exhibit developmental competencies that equip them to understand social inequities, feel empowered to promote social change, and actually engage in action to address injustice. As a matter of great practical benefit to the reader, while they engage in this expansion of critical consciousness theory, Heberle et al. provide both very specific examples of how critical consciousness may manifest across preadolescent developmental periods and details about how measurement approaches may need to be adapted to assess critical consciousness during childhood. In this way, they offer a blueprint for – and reveal the urgency of – the explicit examination of critical consciousness in children.

In Chapter 5, Laura Wray-Lake, Jason Plummer, and Lauren Alvis integrate relational developmental systems theory, critical race theory, and intersectionality theory to highlight processes tied to critical consciousness development among both youth of color and white youth. They then explore how variation among youth in critical consciousness dimensions, in light of the contextual realities tied to oppression and privilege, can elucidate – both empirically and theoretically – how critical consciousness develops and operates.

In Chapter 6, Esther Burson, Erin Godfrey, Riana Brown, and Deanna Ibrahim examine how critical consciousness theory encapsulates more than what current critical consciousness measures typically capture. Specifically, Burson et al. contend that the structural and historical thinking that is central to critical consciousness, from a theoretical perspective, has not been sufficiently accounted for in its instrumentation. In this chapter, the authors explicate critical consciousness theory to make the case for expanding measurement approaches in order to account more fully for structural and historical thinking in critical consciousness scales. Serving as somewhat of a bridge between this volume's two parts, this chapter suggests that new measures tied to structural thinking about and historical attributions for inequity should be incorporated into the measurement of critical reflection.

## Part II: Measurement

In Chapter 7, the first chapter of the measurement section, Luke Rapa, Sarah McKellar, and Erin Godfrey review the history of critical consciousness measurement and provide an overview of its current status within developmental and applied research. The authors suggest that critical consciousness measurement has emerged through four distinct phases: (1) proxy measurement; (2) scale development; (3) scale expansion and (re)specification; and (4) scale refinement and adaptation. Using this review to highlight thorny conceptual, theoretical, and practical measurement issues, Rapa et al. also point to a number of opportunities for the advancement of critical consciousness measurement, highlighting new directions for measurement work and previewing some of the innovative approaches that are suggested in the other chapters appearing within this part.

In Chapter 8, Mariah Kornbluh, Jennifer Watling Neal, and Mackenzie Hart argue that the analytical approach known as social network analysis (SNA) might provide new pathways to study and measure the development and operation of critical consciousness among youth. Kornbluh et al. provide an introduction to SNA and specify how SNA can be used to quantify relational power dynamics that manifest within youths' developmental contexts (e.g., the school classroom), and ultimately suggest SNA as a new measurement approach to assess precursors to and specific aspects of critical consciousness at multiple levels: individuals, dyads, and settings.

In Chapter 9, Corine Tyler, Kelly Chandler, Shauna Tominey, Svea Olsen, Linda Fenske, and Kara McElvaine present a conceptual model and outline a preliminary research agenda for examining how youth engage in critical consciousness and related processes on a daily basis. Tyler et al. offer a roadmap for using daily diary studies to capture more fine-grained, "micro" assessments of critical consciousness. Such an approach, they argue, better accounts for the temporal nature of critical consciousness's development and operation and captures intraindividual variability in important ways – ways that current measurement approaches do not. The authors contend that the expansion of critical consciousness measurement to include "micro" assessments will serve as a necessary complement to the more "macro" assessments that are typical of current instrumentation. Implementing such a two-pronged measurement approach would have clear implications for advancing theory, as new insights gleaned about in-the-moment manifestations of critical consciousness would inform – and may necessitate reappraisal of – current knowledge and theorization about critical consciousness's development and operation.

In Chapter 10, Sara Johnson, Matthew Gee, Autumn Diaz, and Rachel Hershberg consider the complexity of critical consciousness measurement as related to multiple, intersecting, and interlocking forms of marginalization and oppression, as well as related to individuals' self-perceptions and understandings of the marginalizing and oppressive forces that operate in their lives. Like a few other chapters in this volume, Johnson et al. provide very specific recommendations for advancing critical consciousness measurement – in this case, in light of what they refer to as the complexity of "systems" and "selves" and the interaction between them. New insights emerging from their analysis lead Johnson et al. to suggest a number of practical steps for researchers to follow to enhance future quantitative critical consciousness measurement.

Finally, in Chapter 11 Richard Shin, Shereen Ashai, Manuel Teran Hernandez, Yun Lu, Brian Keum, and Sarah Essner present a new brief measure of critical reflection that emanated from the integration of their two previously developed measures. The new measure, the Contemporary Critical Consciousness Measure-Short (CCCM-S), reflects the kind of refinement and adaptation that Rapa et al. (Chapter 7 [this volume]) highlight as reflective of the most recent phase of critical consciousness measurement research. The new 24-item CCCM-S provides its users both a general measure of critical consciousness and measures of critical consciousness linked to five specific forms of modern-day oppression: racism, classism, heterosexism, ableism, and sexism/cis-sexism. Drawing on intersectional theory (e.g., Crenshaw, 1989), Shin and colleagues push the boundaries of critical consciousness measurement by developing instrumentation aiming to assess multiple forms of marginalization and oppression as well as tap understanding of the sociohistorical and sociopolitical foundations of marginalization and oppression faced by many within contemporary American society.

## NAVIGATING THE CONTENTS OF THIS VOLUME (AND OTHER SCHOLARSHIP ON CRITICAL CONSCIOUSNESS)

As we have discussed, and as the chapters of this volume further illustrate, the literature on critical consciousness is diverse and expansive. There has been tremendous growth in this area of scholarship over the past few decades (Heberle et al., 2020), and this trajectory of growth does not appear to be slowing. Beyond this, there is great complexity within the landscape of critical consciousness scholarship. While not unique to this area of study, there is wide variation in what scholars have attended to in terms of critical consciousness theory within their work. This variation also manifests in how critical consciousness and its subdimensions have been operationalized and measured.

Through this volume, we hope to make the terrain of critical consciousness scholarship more easily navigable, even while adding to its complex landscape. We do this through a collection of chapters that: (1) name complexities as they exist; (2) clarify core issues related to those complexities; and (3) contribute new insights, advance new knowledge, and set new directions for future research.

To punctuate this, within this last section of our introduction, we briefly present "schema" that foregrounds some of the most complex issues in the field – issues related to both theory and measurement – and provides a few waypoints that might guide readers through the complex terrain of critical consciousness research. We hope this schema is useful to hold in mind while engaging with the contents of this volume (and other critical consciousness scholarship). The complex issues we call out are represented in our schema as five different axes, or continua, with each axis holding implications for theory and measurement. We view these axes as orthogonal. That is, scholarship that is close in some respects – theoretically aligned or similar with respect to one axis or another – may not necessarily be close or theoretically aligned on other axes.[1] We frame these axes as: (1) unidimensional–multidimensional; (2) individual–collective; (3) person-focused–systems-focused; (4) domain specific–domain general; and (5) singular axis of oppression–manifold axes of oppression.

## Axis 1: Unidimensional–Multidimensional

One complex issue in the landscape of critical consciousness scholarship is variation in the representation of dimensionality – that is, the extent to which critical consciousness is theorized about, operationalized, and/or measured as unidimensional versus multidimensional (for helpful discussion of this issue, see Jemal, 2017). As of this writing, and as noted earlier, the field seems to have matured to the point where the general consensus is that critical consciousness comprises three distinct, but interrelated dimensions: critical reflection, critical motivation, and critical action (Heberle et al., 2020; Watts et al., 2011). While consensus is building theoretically about what critical consciousness entails, measurement has not yet caught up with theory in terms of dimensionality (see Burson et al., Chapter 6, [this volume]; Rapa et al., Chapter 7 [this volume]). For example, most critical consciousness instruments only account for one or two of critical consciousness's canonical dimensions, and only two instruments include all three (i.e., Diemer et al., 2022; Rapa et al., 2020). Notably, even if a study is grounded theoretically in the multidimensional nature of critical consciousness (or if a researcher holds the position that critical consciousness has tripartite dimensionality), a given study may be directed empirically toward the examination or measurement of just one or two dimensions. This reality is not inherently problematic, but our field of study is made more complex by – and even more so when we fail to acknowledge – this continuum of dimensionality. Recognizing where on this axis of unidimensional–multidimensional a given study falls (or where a set of studies fall, or even where an instrument falls) can be useful in accounting for how it aligns with prior research and/or critical consciousness theory, or how it does not.

## Axis 2: Individual–Collective

Another complex issue in the landscape of critical consciousness scholarship is variation in the extent to which critical consciousness is foregrounded as a characteristic or attribute of, or a process related to, an individual versus a collective. As we have noted elsewhere (Heberle et al., 2020), most critical

1 While the focus of his writing was entirely different, we acknowledge Philips (1995) for insights that inspired our consideration of these various "axes" as pertaining to critical consciousness.

consciousness scholarship focuses on the individual level; virtually all measurement is targeted at the individual level as well. However, many have highlighted the need to reexamine how critical consciousness may also be a characteristic or attribute of a group or may be more of a collective phenomenon (e.g., Sánchez Carmen et al., 2015). As highlighted within a number of chapters of this volume, scholars are just beginning to contend more directly with this individual–collective axis, both in terms of theory (e.g., Suzuki et al., Chapter 2 [this volume]) and in terms of measurement (e.g., Kornbluh et al., Chapter 8 [this volume]).

### Axis 3: Person-Focused–Systems-Focused

Complexity also manifests in terms of an axis we characterize as person-focused–systems-focused. Most scholarship to date has focused squarely on marginalized individuals (or, perhaps, individuals experiencing marginalization; see Causadias & Umaña-Taylor, 2018) as opposed to marginalizing systems (Godfrey & Burson, 2018). Yet, as Godfrey and Burson (2018) have argued, there is the need for increased attention on examination of the systems that marginalize as opposed to continued focus (solely) on individuals themselves. This, they contend, is more in line with critical consciousness theory's focus on the systemic, structural nature of inequity, and the resultant marginalization and oppression faced by people and people groups. Johnson et al. (Chapter 10 [this volume]) clearly bring this issue to the fore in their chapter on the complexity of "systems" and "selves" in critical consciousness research. Expanding the focus of critical consciousness scholarship toward systems in addition to individuals may prompt further reformulation of critical consciousness theory and measurement as, again, all existing measures of critical consciousness are person-focused. Heberle et al. (2020) also call for renewed focus on consciousness-raising systems in order to better align critical consciousness scholarship with theory (see also Godfrey & Rapa, in press). Expansion to critical consciousness measurement must follow. Kornbluh et al. (Chapter 8 [this volume]) are among the first to detail how this might be done, as they provide specific ways to advance critical consciousness measurement to better account for critical consciousness at the systems level. As new measurement approaches are developed, to align better with critical consciousness theory, continued attention to this person-focused–systems-focused axis will be merited.

### Axis 4: Domain Specific–Domain General

Another complex issue in the critical consciousness landscape relates to how critical consciousness is theorized about, characterized, or accounted for along the domain specific–domain general continuum. This issue has been acknowledged within the field for some time (e.g., Diemer et al., 2016), as empirical research has suggested that development of critical consciousness in one domain (e.g., gender inequity) does not always translate to corresponding critical consciousness in another domain (e.g., racial inequity). Theoretically, one's awareness of and action to address certain types of inequity may prompt reflection, motivation, and action related to other types of inequity, but this is not necessarily always the case. One may be critically conscious of sexism or genderism but less so of racism, classism, ableism, or other forms of marginalization or oppression. Instruments measuring critical consciousness vary along these lines (Rapa et al., Chapter 7 [this volume]). That is, some instruments capture more general, overarching critical consciousness while others capture more domain-specific forms. Theory, empirical research, and measurement work must continue to bear out the domain specific versus domain general nature of critical consciousness.

### Axis 5: Singular Axis of Oppression–Manifold Axes of Oppression

One final complexity within the critical consciousness landscape manifests because scholarship is varied in the extent to which it is focused on or addresses a single form or system of oppression versus multiple, interlocking systems of oppression – what we characterize as the singular axis of oppression–manifold axes of oppression continuum. Theoretically, critical consciousness is concerned with the multiple, interlocking, structural forms of marginalization and oppression individuals and groups experience (Godfrey & Burson, 2018). However, studies are often carried out in ways that focus on single forms of oppression rather than manifold forms.[2] Depending on the purpose of an individual study – and the theoretical foundations on which that study is built – it may be perfectly appropriate to focus inquiry in this way.

Measurement tools themselves also vary along the singular axis of oppression–manifold axes of oppression continuum. For example, the

[2] There are some conceptual similarities between the previous axis, domain specific–domain general, and this one, singular axis of oppression–manifold axes of oppression. However, we view them as distinct. One relates to composition and the other to focus. Regarding composition – namely, what "is" critical consciousness – whether or not one can be "generally" critically conscious or critically conscious only of "specific" forms of marginalization and oppression is something that is theorized about and something that can and should be further examined empirically. This is distinct from the issue of focus – that is, whether a study (or an instrument) attends to a "single" versus "manifold" axis of oppression. An example illustrates the distinction: The CCCM captures both general and specific critical reflection across multiple axes of oppression (due to its bifactor structure). The CCS captures only general critical reflection but, similar to the CCCM, it does so across multiple axes of oppression.

Measure of Adolescent Critical Consciousness (McWhirter & McWhirter, 2016) is focused on racial marginalization and oppression, a *singular axis of oppression*. Contrarily, other instruments have been built to capture *manifold axes of oppression*. For example, the Critical Consciousness Scale (CCS; Diemer et al., 2017) and its derivatives (Diemer et al., 2022; Rapa et al., 2020; see also Rapa et al., Chapter 7 [this volume]) capture critical reflection of inequities manifesting across race, class, and gender. In a similar way, the Contemporary Critical Consciousness Measure (CCCM; Shin et al., 2016), the Contemporary Cortical Consciousness Measure II (Shin et al., 2018), and the newer Contemporary Critical Consciousness Measure-Short (Shin et al., Chapter 11 [this volume]) all account for various forms of oppression. Even these instruments, however, which are designed to assess manifold axes of oppression, are not yet fully intersectional in ways that capture reflection, motivation, and/or action at the nexus of these manifold axes of oppression.

Adding even more complexity to this issue, some measures that account for manifold axes of oppression only address those unidimensionally (i.e., with a focus on one of critical consciousness's canonical dimensions). For example, the CCS's critical reflection measure accounts for numerous forms of oppression (i.e., manifold axes of oppression) – assessing critical reflection on inequities across ethnic/racial, class, and gender lines – but it does not account for motivation or action regarding manifold axes of oppression in the same way. That is, it does not attend to manifold axes of oppression across all dimensions of critical consciousness.

## Interplay Between Axes

Additional complexity is introduced when considering one or more of these axes alongside the other axes. As a more straightforward example, consider the axes of unidimensional–multidimensional and individual–collective. We observe that unidimensional scholarship focused on critical action as the (singular) dimension of interest can more readily fall on the collective end of the individual–collective continuum. That is, scholarship focused on critical action may have an easier time operationalizing and measuring that critical consciousness dimension at the collective level. Critical reflection and motivation, however, are much more difficult to represent in a collective manner. Critical action thus lends itself more to a collective conceptualization (i.e., theorization) and a collective measurement – though we expect innovations in measurement may help clarify whether and how critical reflection and critical motivation may also be theorized about and measured in collective ways, extending beyond the intrapsychic toward communal or multilevel measurement (e.g., Kornbluh et al., Chapter 8 [this volume]). As another example, to illustrate this point further, consider what might need to change in conceptualization and measurement if scholarship using a multidimensional approach also tried to account for manifold axes of oppression. The instrumentation would quickly become lengthy and unwieldy, and so, likely, would the conceptualization and resultant interpretation. Even more complexity is introduced when we imagine accounting for even more axes at one time. Nonetheless, considering these axes as representations of issues germane to critical consciousness theory and measurement – and assessing how scholarship accounts for theory and measurement along these axes – may help support further understanding and advancement within our field.

## CONCLUDING THOUGHTS

The axes we have highlighted herein represent the range of theory- and measurement-related complexities manifesting within critical consciousness scholarship. We hope that naming these complexities explicitly, and providing a schema to navigate them, helps the field contend with some of the more complex aspects of studying – of theorizing about and measuring – critical consciousness. In the pages that follow, new insights are offered about critical consciousness. New links are established between critical consciousness and other theories, and new empirical evidence is presented about critical consciousness's development, operation, and instrumentation. Indeed, the complexities of the field are on full display. Yet, through the field's engagement with this volume, we hope that knowledge of critical consciousness will be deepened and innovation will be sparked to delve further into new and nuanced aspects of critical consciousness theory and measurement.

## REFERENCES


Bañales, J., Hoffman, A. J., Rivas-Drake, D., & Jagers, R. J. (2020). The development of ethnic-racial identity process and its relation to civic beliefs among Latinx and Black American adolescents. *Journal of Youth and Adolescence*, *49*(12), 2495–2508.

Bonilla-Silva, E. (2006). *Racism without racists: Color-blind racism and the persistence of racial inequality in the United States*. Lanham, MD: Rowman & Littlefield Publishers.

Brown, C. S., Mistry, R. S., & Yip, T. (2019). Moving from the margins to the mainstream: Equity and justice as key considerations for developmental science. *Child Development Perspectives*, *13*(4), 235–240. https://doi.org/10.1111/cdep.12340.

Causadias, J. M., & Umaña-Taylor, A. J. (2018). Reframing marginalization and youth development: Introduction to the special issue. *American Psychologist*, *73*(6), 707–712. https://doi.org/10.1037/amp0000336.

Christens, B. D., Collura, J. J., & Tahir, F. (2013). Critical hopefulness: A person-centered analysis of the intersection of cognitive and emotional empowerment. *American Journal of Community Psychology*, *52*(1), 170–184.

Crenshaw, K. (1989). Demarginalizing the intersection of race and sex: A Black feminist critique of antidiscrimination doctrine, feminist theory and antiracist politics. *University of Chicago Legal Forum, 140*(1), 139–167. http://chicagounbound.uchicago.edu/uclf/vol1989/iss1/8.

Diemer, M. A., Frisby, M. B., Pinedo, A. et al. (2022). Development of the Short Critical Consciousness Scale (ShoCCS). *Applied Developmental Science, 26*(3), 409–425. https://doi.org/10.1080/10888691.2020.1834394.

Diemer, M. A., McWhirter, E., Ozer, E., & Rapa, L. J. (2015). Advances in the conceptualization and measurement of critical consciousness. *The Urban Review, 47*, 809–823. https://10.1007/s11256-015-0336-7.

Diemer, M. A., & Rapa, L. J. (2016). Unraveling the complexity of critical consciousness, political efficacy, and political action among marginalized adolescents. *Child Development, 87*, 221–238. https://doi.org/10.1111/cdev.12446.

Diemer, M. A., Rapa, L. J., Park, C. J., & Perry, J. C. (2017). Development and validation of the Critical Consciousness Scale. *Youth & Society, 49*(4), 461–483. https://doi.org/10.1177/0044118X14538289.

Diemer, M. A., Rapa, L. J., Voight, A. M., & McWhirter, E. H. (2016). Critical consciousness: A developmental approach to addressing marginalization and oppression. *Child Development Perspectives, 10*(4), 216–221. https://doi.org/10.1111/cdep.12193.

Freire, P. (1968/2000). *Pedagogy of the oppressed.* Continuum.

Freire, P. (1973). *Education for critical consciousness.* Continuum.

Godfrey, E. B., & Burson, E. (2018). Interrogating the intersections: How intersectional perspectives can inform developmental scholarship on critical consciousness. *Envisioning the Integration of an Intersectional Lens in Developmental Science. New Directions for Child and Adolescent Development, 161*, 17–38. https://doi.org/10.1002/cad.20246

Godfrey, E. B., Burson, E. L., Yanisch, T. M., Hughes, D., & Way, N. (2019). A bitter pill to swallow? Patterns of critical consciousness and socioemotional and academic well-being in early adolescence. *Developmental Psychology, 55*(3), 525–537. https://doi.org/10.1037/dev0000558.

Godfrey, E. B., & Rapa, L. J. (in press). *Developing Critical Consciousness in Youth: Contexts and Settings.* Cambridge University Press.

Heberle, A. E., Rapa, L. J., & Faragó, F. (2020). Critical consciousness in children and adolescents: A systematic review, critical assessment, and recommendations for future research. *Psychological Bulletin, 146*(6), 525–551. https://doi.org/10.1037/bul0000230.

Jemal, A. (2017). Critical consciousness: A critique and critical analysis of the literature. *The Urban Review, 49*, 602–626. https://doi.org/10.1007/s11256-017-0411-3.

Maker Castro, E., Wray-Lake, L., & Cohen, A. K. (2022). Critical consciousness and wellbeing in adolescents and young adults: A systematic review. *Adolescent Research Review.* Advanced online publication. https://doi.org/10.1007/s40894-022-00188-3.

McWhirter, E. H., & McWhirter, B. T. (2016). Critical consciousness and vocational development among Latina/o high school youth: Initial development and testing of a measure. *Journal of Career Assessment*, *24*(3), 543–558. https://doi.org/10.1177/1069072715599535.

Phillips, D. C. (1995). The good, the bad, and the ugly: The many faces of constructivism. *Educational Researcher*, *24*(7), 5–12.

Rapa, L. J., Bolding, C. W., & Jamil, F. M. (2020). Development and initial validation of the Short Critical Consciousness Scale (CCS-S). *Journal of Applied Developmental Psychology*, *70*, 101164. https://doi.org/10.1016/j.appdev.2020.101164.

Rapa, L. J., Diemer, M. A., & Bañales, J. (2018). Critical action as a pathway to social mobility among marginalized youth. *Developmental Psychology*, *54*(1), 127–137. https://doi.org/10.1037/dev0000414.

Ruck, M. D., Mistry, R. S., & Flanagan, C. A. (2019). Children's and adolescents' understanding and experiences of economic inequality: An introduction to the special section. *Developmental Psychology*, *55*, 449–456. https://doi.org/10.1037/dev0000694

Sánchez Carmen, S. A., Domínguez, M., Greene, A. C. et al. (2015). Revisiting the collective in critical consciousness: Diverse sociopolitical wisdoms and ontological healing in sociopolitical development. *The Urban Review*, *47*(5), 824–846. https://doi.org/10.1007/s11256-015-0338-5.

Seider, S., Clark, S., & Graves, D. (2020). The development of critical consciousness and its relation to academic achievement in adolescents of color. *Child Development*, *91*(2), e451–e474. https://doi.org/10.1111/cdev.13262.

Shin, R. Q., Ezeofor, I., Smith, L. C., Welch, J. C., & Goodrich, K. M. (2016). The development and validation of the contemporary critical consciousness measure. *Journal of Counseling Psychology*, *63*, 210–223. https://doi.org/10.1037/cou0000137.

Shin, R. Q., Smith, L. C., Lu, Y. et al. (2018). The development and validation of the contemporary critical consciousness measure II. *Journal of Counseling Psychology*, *65*, 539–555. https://doi.org/10.1037/cou0000302.

Spanierman, L. B., & Smith, L. (2017). Roles and responsibilities of white allies: Implications for research, teaching, and practice. *The Counseling Psychologist*, *45*(5), 606–617. https://doi.org/10.1177/0011000017717712.

Tyler, C. P., Olsen, S. G., Geldhof, G. J., & Bowers, E. P. (2020). Critical consciousness in late adolescence: Understanding if, how, and why youth act. *Journal of Applied Developmental Psychology*, *70*, 101165. https://doi.org/10.1016/j.appdev.2020.101165.

Watts, R. J., Diemer, M. A., & Voight, A. M. (2011). Critical consciousness: Current status and future directions. In C. A. Flanagan & B. D. Christens (Eds.), Youth civic development: Work at the cutting edge. *New Directions for Child and Adolescent Development*, *134*, 43–57. https://doi.org/10.1002/cd.310.

Watts, R. J., Griffith, D. M., & Abdul-Adil, J. (1999). Sociopolitical development as an antidote for oppression—theory and action. *American Journal of Community Psychology*, *27*, 255–271. https://doi.org/10.1023/A:1022839818873.

Zimmerman, M. A., Ramirez-Valles, J., & Maton, K. I. (1999). Resilience among urban African American male adolescents: A study of the protective effects of sociopolitical control on their mental health. *American Journal of Community Psychology*, *27*(6), 733–751.

# PART I

# THEORY

1

# Synthesizing Critical Consciousness and Identity-Based Motivation to Clarify How Youth of Color Navigate and Challenge Racial Capitalism

ANDRES PINEDO, GABRIELLE KUBI, AND MATTHEW A. DIEMER

The United States is rife with racist inequality. European settlers' violent dispossession of Native people and these settlers' accumulation of enormous wealth from the labor of enslaved Black people set the foundation for contemporary racial disparities (Baptist, 2014; Dunbar-Ortiz, 2014; Tuck & Yang, 2014). A racial capitalism analysis illuminates that capitalist growth for white European settlers came with the destruction of life-forms for Native peoples and the violent, perpetual exploitation of Black people and other racialized people in the United States and globally (Jenkins & Leroy, 2021; Robinson, 1982). Today, racial inequality is reinforced through several mechanisms, including racist violence, economic deprivation, mass incarceration, and cultural hegemony (Gilmore, 2007; Hall, 2001). These historical injustices, along with the mechanisms developed to maintain racial hierarchy, have contemporary ramifications for the social position of people of color (Du Bois, 1935; Ray, 2019; Santiago-Rivera et al., 2016). Racial inequality within the contemporary United States, a country that offers few public and accessible forms of material assistance (e.g., housing) and that is heavily segregated (Orfield & Lee, 2005), is reinforced at the structural and individual levels (Bonilla-Silva, 2001; Lewis, 2021).

Exposure to racism shapes youth of color's prospects for social mobility, specifically through the availability of material resources and via psychological processes such as ethnic/racial socialization, cognitive load, and processes related to identity that guide youth's goal-directed behaviors (Destin, 2019; Steele, 1997; Wang et al., 2020). Materially, youth of color are more likely to attend underfunded schools with less experienced teachers. Their schools tend to be underfunded as public school funding in the United States is largely determined by local communities' property taxes (Derisma, 2013; Turner, 2016; Treskon, 2017). Such funding policies and mechanisms are problematic considering that government policies kept Black people and other people of color out of middle- and upper-class white communities during the majority of the twenty-first century (Rothstein, 2017). Psychologically, exposure to high levels of social inequality shapes marginalized youth's[1] beliefs about social mobility or "what is possible for people like me" (Destin, 2020). In turn, these beliefs and related psychological processes shape goal-directed behaviors and, ultimately, school and life outcomes (Browman et al., 2019; Oyserman & Destin, 2010).

The means by which social inequality affects psychological processes and behavior is termed identity-based motivation (IBM; Oyserman, 2009). Identity-based motivation is a social psychological theory of goal pursuit that attempts to predict when and how social identities motivate behavior (Oyserman, 2013). While there is a plethora of studies documenting IBM processes (see Oyserman & Lewis, 2017), less research has explored how youths' beliefs about – and actions to challenge – inequality affect IBM processes.

Relatedly, few studies have analyzed points of convergence between IBM and critical consciousness theory. Critical consciousness theory conceptualizes how youth come to form beliefs about and resistance to inequality. This theory suggests that marginalized youth's analysis of inequality and whether they feel capable of challenging inequality has important implications for how they navigate inequitable contexts (Heberle, et al., 2020; Watts et al., 2011). Critical consciousness refers to a structural-historical analysis of inequality (i.e., critical reflection), perceived efficacy and motivation to enact social change (i.e., critical motivation), and participation in sociopolitical action to challenge the status quo (i.e., critical action; Burson & Godfrey, 2020). Originally, critical consciousness was theorized as a tool that enables marginalized people to overcome their oppression and self-determine their futures (Freire, 1970). More recent work in psychology suggests critical consciousness facilitates youth's ability to traverse inequitable social contexts in ways that afford them beneficial developmental capacities (Diemer et al., 2016; Heberle et al., 2020). Indeed, greater critical consciousness is associated with beneficial outcomes such as academic gains, but *how* critical consciousness promotes academic and other benefits remains unclear (Seider & Graves, 2020). Examining critical consciousness and IBM in tandem may help to clarify the processes through which critical consciousness benefits racially marginalized youth and to illuminate how contextual affordances link critical consciousness to social mobility.

Therefore, the aims of this chapter are to articulate: (1) the racialized basis of economic inequality in the United States; (2) the psychological effects of this inequality on racialized youth; and (3) the interplay of context and psychological processes, as this interplay either encourages or discourages the challenging of inequality. We draw on the framework of racial capitalism

[1] In this chapter, "marginalized youth" refers to youth of color (primarily Black, Latinx, and Native American youth, but the term can also include Asian American, Middle Eastern, and multiracial youth) from poor and working-class backgrounds who experience marginalization due to racialized economic exploitation.

(Gerrard et al., 2021; Jenkins & Leroy, 2021) to illuminate the historical and structural basis of oppression that youth contend with. We focus primarily on racial capitalism's operation in the educational and occupational experiences of Black, Chicanx, and Native students specifically. We do so not because these are the only groups constrained by racial capitalism, but because they are the groups most studied in the literature and because their status in the racial hierarchy has remained relatively unchanged (Bonilla-Silva, 2001; Heberle et al., 2020; Oyserman & Lewis, 2017). We then draw on IBM theory and critical consciousness theory to elucidate the individual-level reproduction and/or challenging of social inequities. Our focus on linkages between structural inequality and individual-level processes should not be misrepresented to communicate that the means of countering injustice should be changing marginalized youth as individuals, but rather to highlight the ways that contexts can more greatly support youth on an environmental, systematic level. Finally, we synthesize IBM and critical consciousness within the context of racial capitalism. In doing so, we detail youth's experiences in navigating racialized inequality and potential areas of intervention to improve their experiences.

## RACIAL CAPITALISM AND THE EXPERIENCES OF RACIALIZED YOUTH

Although Black people's resistance to and emancipation from slavery in the United States held the promise of a future multiracial democracy in which all people were afforded the full rights of citizenship, this future was never realized (Glaude, 2020). White society, with the backing of the US government, employed legally sanctioned, racist violence and terror; instituted policies that prevented Black people from exercising their political rights; and initiated a media campaign that depicted Black people as inferior and subhuman to maintain racial hierarchy. These same practices were used against other racialized groups, such as Native Americans and Mexicans (Du Bois, 1935; Dunbar-Ortiz, 2014). As the cotton empire of the south dwindled, the white settler elite coordinated with the US government to export their monocrop economic policies and industrialization to the southwest (Karuka, 2021). During westward expansion, the settler class and the US government forcefully dispossessed Indigenous peoples, including but not limited to the Quechan, Navajo, Apache, Yaqui, and Cahuilla. In so doing, the US government turned land into private property to profit from (Dunbar-Ortiz, 2014). Selective government intervention on behalf of the white settler elite helped concentrate the major industries of the region – agriculture, cattle ranching, and mining – in the hands of a few large corporations (Du Bois, 1935). As economic and political power became concentrated among the white settler class, the white elite solidified a racial hierarchy in the emerging country, whereby white workers tended to receive the best jobs while Black, Chinese, Mexican, and Native workers received irregular, poorly paid, and often the most difficult jobs (Anderson, 1978; Karuka, 2021). These divisions signaled the early makings of the contemporary racialized economic landscape of the United States. Within this landscape, white settlers carved out decent, livable conditions for themselves, while people of color were economically, socially, and politically oppressed.

Youth of Color in the United States are thus born into a racialized economic system that relegates them to a position in which they serve as exploitable laborers and consumers in the economy (Jenkins & Leroy, 2021; Joseph, 1995; Melamed, 2015). The overrepresentation of people of color in the most exploited rungs of the economy has been preserved and naturalized via racial ideology rooted in white supremacy (Feagin, 2009; Salter et al., 2018). The United States rendered racialized people as subhuman for the sake of exploitation and profit. Racialized people's false inferiority was reified through laws, policies, and violence. Consequentially, the United States gave and continues to give rise to a racial ideology and material reality that limits the possibilities of racialized youth. Today, people of color face structural barriers in access to preschool, healthy food, well-funded schools, good teachers, and safe neighborhoods. These barriers exist because people of color are continually denied control of material and political resources that would improve their conditions by white supremacy (Bell, 1987; Benson & Dumas, 2021; Cameron & Heckman, 2001; Orfield & Lee, 2005). As such, youth of color are more likely to occupy the bottom of the social hierarchy and experience stigma due to their place therein (Oyserman & Lewis, 2017).

In all, racial capitalism fostered conditions wherein youth of color have few opportunities for social mobility and are stigmatized for their social position. Such stigmatization may manifest psychologically, via stereotypes that may encourage perceptions of one's self as lacking academic ability, and/or through perceptions of difficulties as insurmountable impossibilities. Susceptibility to the negative stereotypes about one's racial group is a result of a culture of white supremacy, in which Black people and other people of color are deemed less intelligent and capable than white people (Du Bois, 1935; Salter et al., 2018). This culture of white supremacy and the inequity it breeds continue to organize people's social worlds and beliefs. Stigma also undermines youth's perceptions that their decisions and efforts matter because their exploitation and marginalization communicate that they have less control over their lives. Such perceptions may reduce the likelihood that they will exert effort to improve their social position (Oyserman, 2013). As structural and psychological factors interact and reproduce social inequalities, it is essential to clarify how these factors unfold and shape the experiences of youth of color to better understand how to support their social mobility.

## IDENTITY-BASED MOTIVATION

Identity-based motivation theory posits that identity-based social inequality (e.g., gender- or race-based inequality) serves as a cue for individuals that suggests whether success or failure in a domain is likely for them based on their identity. Such suggestions have consequences for their motivation and behavior in the domain (Oyserman, 2009). Accordingly, IBM explicates the ways in which macrolevel processes (e.g., racialized economic inequality) affect microlevel processes (e.g., individual goal pursuit), and the ways in which situations in relation to individuals' identities can encourage or undermine action to attain their goals (Oyserman & Lewis, 2017). According to IBM, social identity is dynamic, which means that an identity's bearings on meaning-making and action are dependent on the cues in the immediate context (Oyserman, 2009). In this way, small changes to the environment can have large implications for how an individual's identity implicates their meaning-making and action. For example, a Chicanx student whose counselor suggests they not enroll in college preparation courses, saying that these courses are too difficult, will likely experience incongruence between their identity and school achievement and feel that their identity is not congruent with a desired outcome like school success. Given that Chicanx students are negatively stereotyped in the academic domain (Hudley & Graham, 2001), they may interpret the counselor's words to mean too difficult *for students like them*, thus undermining their motivation. However, if the counselor encouraged this Chicanx student to enroll in college preparation courses because they have seen many students like them succeed and go on to college, then the student may experience congruence between their identity and school achievement. Feelings of congruence and incongruence are thus dependent on the *dynamic construction* of identity – one of the three main components of IBM. Dynamic construction shapes the other two main components of IBM: *procedural readiness* (i.e., making meaning of experiences from the lens of one's identity), and *action readiness* (i.e., being inclined to act in ways that are congruent with one's identity; Oyserman, 2009; Oyserman & Destin, 2010).

Another central postulation of IBM is that occupying a low status in the social hierarchy (e.g., being a Black student living in poverty) reduces individuals' sense of control and their belief in their ability to control their life outcomes (Kraus et al., 2009; Oyserman & Lewis, 2017). For example, poor and working-class Black students may regularly witness other Black students working hard yet being mistreated and discriminated against in school (Carter Andrews et al., 2019; Dumas, 2016). Thus, these students may believe that matriculating to college is unlikely for them or incompatible with their ethnic/racial identity. Barriers to Black students' social mobility are

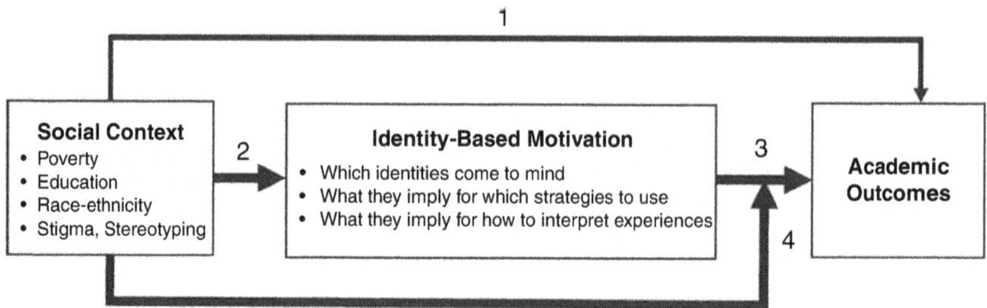


FIGURE 1.1 The identity-based motivation process. Figure recreated from Oyserman and Lewis (2017). Reprinted with permission.

hypothesized to undermine their sense of control, seeing as these barriers limit the extent to which their individual actions can facilitate success. Thus, sense of control mediates the relationship between social inequality and identity incongruence, leading to an understanding of their identity that minimizes the role of school success (Oyserman & Lewis, 2017). In the following paragraphs, we will review how each component of IBM is linked to student academic outcomes (see Figure 1.1).

The first component of IBM, dynamic construction, refers to how cues in people's immediate context shape which identities are salient in the moment. Students of Color who grow up in difficult economic circumstances are not only hindered by a lack of actual material supports (e.g., nutritious food, internet access), but are more likely to witness contextual cues that indicate that people like them are not capable of educational success. For instance, students in low-income communities of color have less access to college-graduated adults who serve as role models than youth in white middle- and high-income communities (Adelman & Gocker, 2007). These contextual cues signal to low-socioeconomic status youth of color that academic success may not be congruent with their identity (Lewis & Sekaquaptewa, 2016). This incongruence shapes their perceived possible future selves (Markus & Nurius, 1986) and, ultimately, their motivation in the academic domain.

In one study, poor and working-class Black and Latinx students were presented with graphs showing that future career earnings were either tied to greater educational attainment (education-dependent condition) or unrelated to educational attainment (education-independent condition; Destin & Oyserman, 2009). In the education-dependent condition, students were six times more likely to complete an extra-credit assignment than students in the education-independent condition (Destin & Oyserman, 2009). This result can be explained by the education-dependent condition cuing an academic identity amongst students, whereas the education-independent condition did not. Accordingly, students in the education-independent condition did not link the extra-credit assignment to their future identity and therefore did not see it as important. Unfortunately, for racially and/or economically marginalized students, environments often communicate messages that do not link education to their future identities. Such messages make the experience of disconnect between present academic tasks and one's future all too common. In another study, Native American high school students were presented with role models who were self-relevant (shared their ethnic/racial identity) or were not (did not share their ethnic/racial identity or were ambiguous). Students in the self-relevant condition reported greater school belonging than students in the other conditions (Covarrubias & Fryberg, 2015). Thus, the self-relevant condition highlighted to Native American students that their Native American identity can be congruent with academic success and therefore fostered greater belonging in school.

Youth's dynamic construction of their identity influences procedural readiness, which suggests that individuals have a readiness to make sense of information through the lens of their identity. That is, thinking actively about a certain identity shapes one's present-moment thinking and consequently implicates one's behavior. One specific area where meaning-making is particularly important is in the context of encountering difficulty and challenge (Fisher & Oyserman, 2017). Most students will encounter difficulty along their educational trajectory. Difficulty can either motivate students to work hard to overcome challenges or it can demotivate students and lead them to stop trying (Fisher & Oyserman, 2017). Procedural readiness suggests that the identity that is on a student's mind in the midst of difficulty – and what that identity implies for meaning-making – will determine said student's persistence. In the case of a Latinx student, if their ethnic/racial identity is cued, difficulty may suggest that school success is unlikely for them because of the stigma associated with this identity in the school context (Hudley & Graham, 2001; Oyserman & Lewis, 2017). They will then be more likely to disassociate a task's difficulty from its importance, which will shape their actions. In one experiment, students who were encouraged to believe that important things are often difficult performed better on a difficult task, compared to both students who were led to believe that impossible things are often difficult and to students who received no message (Elmore et al., 2016). Thus, students' identities shape their interpretation of difficulty and these interpretations have consequences for action.

The final component of IBM is action readiness: an inclination to act in congruence with one's currently activated identity(ies). When youth perceive education-related outcomes, such as attending college, to be incongruent with their identity, they are less likely to exert effort to pursue a college preparatory path (Oyserman, 2009). For example, middle school students from low-income families who were exposed to the high costs of college indicated that they planned to spend less time reading and doing homework than students who were told about need-based financial aid (Destin & Oyserman,

2010). This study primed a social-class identity such that incongruence arose between students' low-SES identities and the prospect of college enrollment given the conveyed unaffordability of enrolling in college. In another study, girls who saw a graph depicting that girls graduate high school at higher rates than boys were more likely to focus on school-related possible identities and persisted longer on a difficult math task than girls who saw a graph depicting graduation rates left unaggregated by gender (Elmore & Oyserman, 2012). In this study, seeing the "girls are more successful than boys" condition made school success feel congruent with their identity as girls, and so these girls did better on academic tasks. On the other hand, boys in the "girls succeed" condition were less likely to focus on school-related possible selves and persisted less on a math task than did boys in the "boys are more successful condition" or the neutral condition (Elmore & Oyserman, 2012). Moreover, in a separate study, African American middle school students were asked to answer questions about their ethnic/racial identity either before (treatment condition) or after (control condition) completing a novel math task. Students were then asked what it meant to them to be African American and to provide examples from their lives. Asking students about their identity mattered for performance on the math task when they were asked prior to completing the task, but not when they were asked after completing the task. Even more, students who linked African American identity to school achievement performed better on the math task than students who did not. Their improved performance was due to perceiving achievement as part of their African American identity (Oyserman et al., 1995).

In all, IBM theory clearly articulates pathways through which exposure to racial capitalism and the inequality it facilitates shape psychological processes related to identity and goal pursuit. Specifically, this literature suggests that chronic cues associated with living at the bottom of the racial hierarchy limit sense of control and elicit stigma. These limitations may lead to identity incongruence and other psychological processes that negatively affect school outcomes. Identity-based motivation theory is useful for understanding how structural factors (e.g., economic deprivation) interact with individual-level factors to shape outcomes for marginalized youth. However, it does not attend to youth's agency and their beliefs and actions in response to inequality, or how these factors may interact with IBM processes. A greater appreciation of the ways marginalized youth develop and act on their agency in the face of oppression and racial capitalism is necessary to more fully understand the variety of their experiences. Youth are not simply and passively affected by social inequality. Youth also resist inequality, and the ways they do so can shed light on important channels for supporting their social mobility (Rogers & Way, 2021). Critical consciousness theory delineates how youth understand, feel motivated to challenge, and contest oppression.

## CRITICAL CONSCIOUSNESS

Critical consciousness refers to the process through which individuals develop a structural-historical awareness of the root causes of social inequality, along with efficacy, commitment, and action to challenge said inequality (Freire, 1970; Watts et al., 2011). Scholars posit that critical consciousness can be protective and adaptive for marginalized youth in the United States (Diemer et al., 2016; Heberle et al., 2020). Critical consciousness is composed of three components: (1) critical reflection: the awareness of how historical and structural processes shape contemporary inequalities; (2) critical motivation: individuals' beliefs about their ability and responsibility to enact social change, and (3) critical action: sociopolitical action taken to rectify inequality (Diemer et al., 2020). These components are theorized to be interrelated, and to develop in a reciprocal manner (Gutiérrez, 1995; Watts & Hipolito-Delgado, 2015). For example, as youth perceive and critically analyze social inequalities, they will feel motivated to act to challenge perceived inequalities. These feelings will foster greater growth in critical reflection and, in turn, further critical action. In the same way, youth's successes and setbacks when challenging inequality can foster and diminish their critical motivation, respectively.

Social psychological theory on attributions is helpful for understanding critical reflection (Watts et al., 2011). People are inclined to make sense of the world in a causal manner, such that they ascribe causes to outcomes as well as to differences that exist in the world (Brewer & Kramer, 1985; Kelley, 1973). The attributions people make for social disparities are captured via critical reflection. That is, people higher in critical reflection are those who make structural attributions for social disparities and acknowledge that historical factors, like discriminatory policies, shape contemporary racial disparities (Bañales et al., 2020). On the other hand, people who primarily attribute racial disparities to individual-level characteristics, like a group's intelligence or work ethic, demonstrate less critical reflection. Attribution theory has been applied to understand educational outcomes among marginalized youth (see Graham, 1991; Weiner, 1972). However, research on attributions largely ignores the role of structural attributions in making sense of social disparities and these attributions' consequences for motivation and achievement in school.

Given that racial capitalism has hindered many of marginalized youth's opportunities for social mobility, their critical consciousness regarding social barriers seems key to their ability to effectively negotiate said barriers. An accumulating body of research that links youth's critical reflection to positive outcomes (Heberle et al., 2020) suggests that such reflection is indeed beneficial for marginalized youth. In ethnographic work, Black youth with a more sophisticated understanding of the structural basis of racial inequality were found to be some of the highest achieving students in high school (Carter, 2008; O'Connor, 1997). In fact, some of these students highlighted their keen awareness of racism as a motivating factor in their academic pursuits (O'Connor, 1997). For low-income Latinx students, greater critical reflection correlated with higher academic motivation, educational outcome expectations, and academic achievement (Luginbuhl et al., 2016). Further, in a longitudinal study with Black and Latinx adolescents, baseline critical reflection was positively associated with SAT scores, while growth in critical reflection over the course of high school was associated with higher GPAs at the end of high school (Seider et al., 2020). While these positive outcomes can be potentially explained by a third variable, such as higher-achieving youth being more likely to think critically about inequality and thus to develop critical consciousness, the current evidence suggests that GPA and standardized achievement measures are only weakly related to later critical consciousness, if at all (Diemer, 2009; Diemer et al., 2010). Altogether, these findings suggest that a critical analysis of inequality can be empowering, rather than disempowering, for youth.

Critical reflection of social inequality, though, may be most beneficial to youth who also hold greater critical motivation – those who are motivated and believe they have the capacity to enact social change. Possessing critical reflection without critical motivation may be demotivating to some youth if they do not believe that they can effectively challenge inequality (Godfrey et al., 2019). In Godfrey and colleagues' study, critical motivation (termed "sociopolitical efficacy") was the key predictor of positive academic and mental health outcomes when examined in combination with critical reflection and critical action. Similarly, among low-SES Black and Latinx youth, only critical motivation was positively related to educational motivations and educational preparation. Critical reflection and critical action were unrelated to educational motivations among these youth (Uriostegui et al., 2021). Furthermore, O'Connor (1997) posited that the major factors distinguishing the high-achieving Black youth with a keen awareness of structural inequality from those with a similar awareness but lower achievement were dual awarenesses of the importance of struggle and the possibility for social change. Thus, critical motivation may be catalytic in linking critical reflection to outcomes that are beneficial to youth.

Finally, critical action is also related to beneficial developmental and academic trajectories for marginalized youth (Diemer et al., 2021). Critical action refers to individual or collective action youth take to combat oppression (Heberle et al., 2020). Among Black and Latinx youth, increased engagement in critical action during high school was positively associated with their grades at the end of high school (Seider et al., 2020). Similarly, two studies with nationally representative samples of youth of color from working-class backgrounds uncovered that greater participation in critical action was associated with greater occupational expectations in high school and better occupational attainment in adulthood (Diemer, 2009; Rapa et al., 2018). It is theorized that these positive outcomes arise because engaging in critical action leads youth to feel more agentic in their ability to navigate structural constraints that limit their opportunities (Rapa et al., 2018). In other words, critical action helps youth to see that they can change the conditions that constrain them, pushing them to strive for success in multiple domains, such as school and work. Thus, critical action can alter social inequality's impact on youth's agency and possible identity incongruence.

Examining the role of critical action in the developmental trajectories of marginalized youth takes us away from damage-centered research, which examines the outcomes of marginalized youth from a deficit perspective (Clonan-Roy et al., 2016; Ginwright & Cammarota, 2007; Tuck, 2009). Much of the research examining the life outcomes of youth of color makes the implicit assumption that the youth themselves are simply passive recipients of oppression, failing to acknowledge the ways in which youth resist oppression (Rogers & Way, 2021). Attending to critical action broadens our understanding of what engenders beneficial outcomes in the context of racial capitalism. Is success for marginalized youth limited to upward social mobility or success in school? Or are there other or additional avenues of engagement, such as efforts to transform community conditions, that should also be deemed beneficial? Shedding light on how marginalized youth engage in action to challenge oppression can push the field of psychology to consider the full range of marginalized youth's experiences. In turn, the literature can then paint a more complete picture of how youth engage with their contexts to foster change and achieve their goals.

## INTEGRATING CRITICAL CONSCIOUSNESS AND IDENTITY-BASED MOTIVATION

IBM theory and critical consciousness theory have both contributed to our understanding of how macrolevel factors (e.g., racial capitalism) interact with microlevel processes (e.g., psychological processes) to shape marginalized youth's experiences and the ways they challenge injustice. Yet, while both theoretical frameworks examine the implications of social inequality for youth's academic and broader life trajectories as well as factors that can foster successful trajectories, they are yet to be examined in tandem. It is constructive for researchers to examine critical consciousness together with IBM because critical consciousness provides youth with a frame for understanding inequality in their contexts, which can shape IBM processes. IBM theory is primarily concerned with how one's identity and the context one is in shape psychological processes, but is less concerned with how youth actively

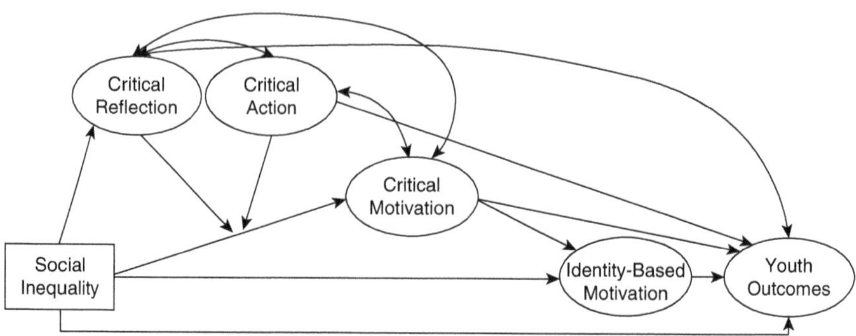


FIGURE 1.2 Integrated Critical Consciousness and Identity-Based Motivation Model.

negotiate inequality. On the other hand, critical consciousness theory considers how the psychological impact of inequality is moderated by how people understand it, whether they feel motivated to challenge it, and whether they take action to combat inequality. Contemporary theorizations about critical consciousness, however, have undertheorized the ways that specific situations foster critical consciousness and the processes by which critical consciousness transmits beneficial outcomes. Insights from IBM, which theorizes how situations shape psychological processes, can shed light on these factors. In the following pages, we consider how integrating these two perspectives may help clarify the processes through which critical consciousness benefits racially marginalized youth and illuminates the role youth play themselves in resisting inequality within IBM theory (see Figure 1.2).

While a fast-growing body of research links greater critical reflection to positive outcomes (Heberle et al., 2020), less is known about the psychological mechanisms that mediate this link. What is it about being critically aware of the structural roots of inequality that fosters positive academic and later life outcomes for marginalized youth? Oyserman and colleagues (2006) posit that chronic images of the ingroup as low achieving that stem from racial oppression (Bell, 1987) undermine academic possible selves. The undermining of these academic possible selves is consequential because possible selves facilitate the self-regulatory action needed to achieve academic goals (Markus & Nurius, 1986; Oyserman et al., 2006). Greater critical reflection can potentially provide youth of color with a constructive frame for interpreting the racial disparities that they chronically encounter. For example, low-SES youth of color who identify residential segregation and underfunded schools as a cause of educational disparities between white students and Students of Color may be less likely to conclude that "school isn't for people like me" than students who believe there is something essential about people of color that prevents them from securing educational success. This is because the disparity represents a broader, deeper societal problem rather than their group's inherent educational capabilities. Instead of believing that people like them cannot achieve in school, they may conclude that they have made quite a bit of progress considering the barriers that their group has faced and that success is also a possibility for themselves. In coming to this latter conclusion, youth can maintain their academic possible selves, which may mediate the link between critical reflection and positive academic outcomes.

An issue with this, however, is that IBM posits that what an identity means for action and meaning-making is dependent on the context in which it is cued (i.e., dynamic construction). If identity is constructed in context, how do prior beliefs about inequality (i.e., critical reflection) come to affect this process, particularly considering that beliefs are not consistently related to behavior (Ross & Nisbett, 2011)? There are a couple of possibilities. One is that once youth develop a critical understanding of the structural roots of inequality, all cues that highlight disparities between racial groups will be interpreted from this perspective. That is, once youth believe that disparities are due to structural factors, it will become the default frame from which they interpret disparities, or at least a particular type of disparity (e.g., racial), and thus any cue to racial disparities will be interpreted from a structural perspective. Research examining beliefs about inequality supports this perspective because, once formed, metatheories about the causes of inequality become the cognitive framework for interpreting disparities (Smith & Stone, 1989). Thus, critical reflection will be particularly important for reconciling with chronic cues that are present in marginalized communities, where racialized class disparities continuously color the ways in which youth understand their identities and the likelihood that they can be successful.

Another possibility is that individuals can hold a critically consciousness perspective but can still fall back on individualist notions of merit when making sense of disparities (Godfrey & Wolf, 2016). In this case, people may be more likely to come to a structural interpretation of disparities when critical consciousness is also cued. This would mean that contexts must encourage critical consciousness to cue critical reflection among youth. Recent calls in the critical consciousness literature, in fact, task researchers to examine critical consciousness at the contextual level and as characteristic of consciousness-raising systems (Heberle et al., 2020). The IBM framework suggests that the immediate context can either encourage or diminish critical consciousness by shaping what comes to mind. These contextual details likely have implications for how critical consciousness operates among youth and may help reconcile instances where expected relationships between critical reflection and academic outcomes failed to emerge (Uriostegui et al., 2021). Critical reflection may be most likely linked to beneficial outcomes when features of the immediate context link a critical analysis of inequality to successful behaviors or highlight how successful role models also exert critical consciousness. Recent research suggests that experienced mentors, with whom youth can build critical consciousness, are instrumental in fostering longer-term beneficial outcomes (Monjaras-Gaytan et al., 2021). In short, contexts that link critical reflection to success may strengthen relations between critical reflection and beneficial outcomes (Watts & Flanagan, 2007).

Critical motivation is sometimes described as essential for moving youth from being critical of inequality to engaging in sustained action aimed at improving the conditions of their community – in other words, for moving the needle from critical reflection to critical action (Anyiwo et al., 2018; Watts et al., 2003). Indeed, Black youth with greater beliefs in their ability to enact social change engaged in more civic activities (e.g., protesting, working on political campaigns; Hope & Jagers, 2014). Insights from IBM can clarify whether and how critical motivation links critical reflection to critical action (Burson & Godfrey, 2020). For example, IBM theory suggests that sense of control shapes interpretations of difficulty (Oyserman & Lewis, 2017). Critical motivation may shape how youth interpret difficulty: marginalized youth who feel capable of effecting individual and community change may reach different interpretations of difficulty than students who feel like change is impossible. Those with more critical motivation may see difficulty and challenge as necessary to make progress, whereas those with less critical motivation may not conclude the same. Therefore, when challenges arise in social change efforts, youth with more critical motivation may be more willing to persist.

Another area in which theorizations around critical motivation can be sharpened by IBM theory is in drawing on the link between possible selves and effective strategies for attaining possible selves. As evidenced by IBM research, academic possible selves are most beneficial when they are tied to effective strategies, making them "plausible possible selves" (Oyserman et al., 2006; Oyserman & Fryberg, 2006). Critical motivation can be considered a form of future possibility (social change being the possibility), and so IBM theory would suggest that critical motivation will be most beneficial for youth when it is tied to effective strategies for creating change. Accordingly, critical motivation may be most beneficial to youth when they are presented with effective strategies for engaging in social change efforts – reaffirming the importance of context and opportunity structures for channeling youth critical consciousness (Seider & Graves, 2020; Watts & Flanagan, 2007).

Regarding critical action, IBM theory suggests mechanisms by which youth with varying degrees of critical reflection and motivation can become engaged in action. According to IBM, regardless of people's individual differences (e.g., levels of efficacy or reflection), all people can be encouraged to engage in future-relevant action (e.g., critical action) if they are in a context where the future and the present feel relevant to what one is doing in the moment. That is, when youth find themselves in contexts that connect future possibilities (e.g., their communities having better-resourced schools and parks) to available avenues for achieving these aims (e.g., lobbying local politicians), they may be motivated to act even when they do not yet possess high levels of critical reflection or motivation. Given this potential lever for spurring action, critical consciousness theory should specifically consider how connecting the future to the present facilitates action.

Lastly, critical action is a pathway through which social inequality is ultimately reduced. Considering that IBM and critical consciousness theories are concerned with youth development in the context of inequality, it is of utmost importance to understand how youth themselves act to create more equitable contexts that are conducive to their development. Several historical examples, such as the American Indian Movement, the Black Power Movement, and the Chicano Movement, illustrate how youth have played key roles in improving conditions for marginalized communities. Through the 1968 East Los Angeles walkouts, for example, Chicano youth were able to change school policies in which Chicanx students were being tracked into remedial classes and not given college preparation opportunities (Garcia & Castro, 2011). Critical action is essential for minimizing the extent to which inequity seeps into educational practices, which may otherwise signal to youth that they do not belong and cannot be successful. Such signals ultimately shape the psychological processes that motivate adaptive outcomes. Importantly, critical action also provides crucial contextual supports (e.g., a community of committed activists) and effective strategies that IBM suggests are crucial for connecting youth cognitions to successful behaviors (Oyserman & Lewis, 2017). Thus, as youth engage in critical action, they alter the impact of social inequality on their development.

## OPPORTUNITIES FOR INTERVENTION

One space where the dynamic between critical consciousness and IBM processes can be examined is in classrooms that utilize critical pedagogy. Critical pedagogy centers issues from the perspective of marginalized groups through a problem-posing ethic, fostering students' drive to transform their world in pursuit of justice (Freire, 1970; Pinedo et al., 2021). Courses which foreground this pedagogy, such as ethnic studies courses, aim to foster critical consciousness. By fostering their critical consciousness, youth come to challenge racial capitalism and settler colonialism in their local contexts (Sleeter & Zavala, 2020). In this way, these classrooms cue critical consciousness among youth and can trigger healthy dynamic construction and interpretations of difficulty. Previous studies demonstrate that when compared to students not enrolled in ethnic studies, those who are enrolled showed improved attendance and grades. These effects held true or were particularly apparent even among students who significantly struggled in school (Cabrera et al., 2014;

Cammarota, 2007; Dee & Penner, 2017). Gains associated with ethnic studies appear to persist throughout high school and predict postsecondary enrollment (Bonilla et al., 2021).

Seeing as ethnic studies curricula explicitly aim to raise students' critical consciousness, and as these curricula directly engage ethnic/racial identities, ethnic studies likely have implications for both students' critical consciousness and their IBM. For example, in realizing how education can be leveraged to improve their communities, students may be more likely to feel congruence between their identities and their school tasks. A longitudinal study could potentially uncover how students' baseline critical consciousness and growth in critical consciousness, following a year-long ethnic studies course, relate to their academic possible selves and changes therein. In short, classrooms that implement critical pedagogy provide a promising context to investigate how critical consciousness and IBM processes unfold to shape the academic outcomes of racially marginalized youth. More importantly, critical pedagogy is ultimately concerned with transforming the status quo and redistributing power in society. As such, critical pedagogy encourages concrete social change, which can ameliorate the racial inequity that constrains youth.

## CONCLUSION

In this chapter, we have illuminated the structural-historical basis for youth of color's overrepresentation among the poor and working-class in the United States. Specifically, we posit that racial capitalism, which highlights contemporary globalized capitalism's emergence from racist and violent exploitation, has continuously evolved to maintain racial hierarchy and to constrain youth's school and life chances. In this chapter, we contend that a structural-historical awareness of inequality, along with critical motivation and action to challenge it, can be beneficial for marginalized youth. Specifically, we argue that critical consciousness has implications for IBM processes, which have well-documented consequences for youth outcomes. Further, we argue that the processes articulated by IBM can be fruitful for better understanding the psychological mechanisms that explain the positive links between critical consciousness and positive youth outcomes. In particular, IBM's emphasis on the immediate situation suggests attending to immediate environments can shed light on the way critical consciousness unfolds among youth. Our understanding of complex human phenomena is never complete through scientific investigations, but we hope that in articulating connections and tensions between these two theories, we can better understand how marginalized youth chart their social mobility within contexts that are most often opposed to their success.

## REFERENCES

Adelman, R. M., & Gocker, J. C. (2007). Racial residential segregation in urban America. *Sociology Compass, 1*, 404–423.

Anderson, J. (1978). Northern foundations and the shaping of Southern black rural education, 1902–1935. *History of Education Quarterly, 18*, 371–396. https://doi.org/10.2307/367710.

Anyiwo, N., Bañales, J., Rowley, S. J., Watkins, D. C., & Richards-Schuster, K. (2018). Sociocultural influences on the sociopolitical development of African American youth. *Child Development Perspectives, 12*, 165–170.

Bañales, J., Aldana, A., Richards-Schuster, K. et al. (2021). Youth anti-racism action: Contributions of youth perceptions of school racial messages and critical consciousness. *Journal of Community Psychology, 49*(8), 3079–3100. https://doi.org/10.1002/jcop.22266.

Bañales, J., Mathews, C., Hayat, N., Anyiwo, N., & Diemer, M. A. (2020). Latinx and Black young adults' pathways to civic/political engagement. *Cultural Diversity and Ethnic Minority Psychology, 26*(2), 176.

Baptist, E. E. (2016). *The half has never been told: Slavery and the making of American capitalism.* Hachette UK.

Bell, D. (1987). *And we are not saved.* Basic Books.

Benson, J. , & Dumas, M. J. (2021). Building out the edges: Reading racial capitalism into jean anyon's political economy of urban education. *Teachers College Record.* https://doi.org/10.1177/01614681211063966.

Bonilla, S., Dee, T. S., & Penner, E. K. (2021). Ethnic studies increases longer-run academic engagement and attainment. *Proceedings of the National Academy of Sciences, 118*(37), e2026386118.

Bonilla-Silva, E. (2001). *White supremacy and racism in the post-civil rights era.* Lynne Rienner Publishers.

Brewer, M. B., & Kramer, R. M. (1985). The psychology of intergroup attitudes and behavior. *Annual Review of Psychology, 36*(1), 219–243.

Browman, A. S., Destin, M., Carswell, K. L., & Svoboda, R. C. (2017). Perceptions of socioeconomic mobility influence academic persistence among low socioeconomic status students. *Journal of Experimental Social Psychology, 72*(9), 45–52.

Browman, A. S., Destin, M., Kearney, M. S., & Levine, P. B. (2019). How economic inequality shapes mobility expectations and behaviour in disadvantaged youth. *Nature Human Behavior, 3*(3), 214–220.

Burson, E., & Godfrey, E. B. (2020). Intraminority solidarity: The role of critical consciousness. *European Journal of Social Psychology, 50*(6), 1362–1377.

Cabrera, N. L., Milem, J. F., Jaquette, O., & Marx, R. W. (2014). Missing the (student achievement) forest for all the (political) trees: Empiricism and the Mexican American Studies controversy in Tucson. *American Educational Research Journal, 51*(6), 1084–1118. https://doi.org/10.3102/0002831214553705.

Cameron, S., & Heckman, J. (2001). The dynamics of educational attainment for Black, Hispanic, and White males. *Journal of Political Economy, 109*, 455–499. https://doi.org/10.1086/321014.

Cammarota, J. (2007). A social justice approach to achievement: Guiding Latina/o students toward educational attainment with a challenging, socially relevant curriculum. *Equity and Excellence in Education*, *40*, 87–96.

Carter, D. (2008). Achievement as resistance: The development of a critical race achievement ideology among Black achievers. *Harvard Educational Review*, *78*(3), 466–497.

Carter Andrews, D. J., Brown, T., Castro, E., & Id-Deen, E. (2019). The impossibility of being "perfect and White": Black girls' racialized and gendered schooling experiences. *American Educational Research Journal*, *56*(6), 2531–2572. https://doi.org/10.3102/0002831219849392.

Clonan-Roy, K., Jacobs, C. E., & Nakkula, M. J. (2016). Towards a model of positive youth development specific to girls of color: Perspectives on development, resilience, and empowerment. *Gender Issues*, *33*, 96–121. https://doi.org/10.1007/s12147-016-9156-7.

Covarrubias, R., & Fryberg, S. (2015). The impact of self-relevant representations on school belonging for underrepresented Native American students. *Cultural Diversity and Ethnic Minority Psychology*, *21*, 10–18.

Dee, T. S., & Penner, E. K. (2017). The causal effects of cultural relevance: Evidence from an ethnic studies curriculum. *American Educational Research Journal*, 54(1), 127–166.

Derisma, M. (2013). Opposing views: The divide in public education funding – Property tax revenue. *Children's Legal Rights Journal*, *34*(1), 122–124.

Destin, M. (2019). A path to advance research on identity and socioeconomic opportunity. *American Psychologist*, *74*, 1071–1079.

Destin, M. (2020). Identity research that engages contextual forces to reduce socioeconomic disparities in education. *Current Directions in Psychological Science*, *29*(2), 161–166.

Destin, M., & Oyserman, D. (2009). From assets to school outcomes: How finances shape children's perceived possibilities and intentions. *Psychological Science*, *20*(4), 414–418.

Destin, M., & Oyserman, D. (2010). Incentivizing education: Seeing schoolwork as an investment, not a chore. *Journal of Experimental Social Psychology*, *46*(5), 846–849.

Diemer, M. A. (2009). Pathways to occupational attainment among poor youth of color: The role of sociopolitical development. *The Counseling Psychologist*, *37*(1), 6–35.

Diemer, M. A., Frisby, M. B., Pinedo, A. et al. (2022). Development of the Short Critical Consciousness Scale (ShoCCS). *Applied Developmental Science*, *26*(3), 409–425. https://doi.org/10.1080/10888691.2020.1834394.

Diemer, M. A., Pinedo, A., Bañales, J., et al. (2021). Recentering action in critical consciousness. *Child Development Perspectives*, *15*(1), 12–17. https://doi.org/10.1111/cdep.12393.

Diemer, M. A., Rapa, L., Voight, A., & McWhirter, E. H. (2016). Critical consciousness: A developmental approach to addressing marginalization and oppression. *Child Development Perspectives*, *10*(4), 216–221. https://doi.org/10.1111/cdep.12193.

Diemer, M. A., Wang, Q., Moore, T., et al. (2010). Sociopolitical development, work salience, and vocational expectations among low-SES African American, Latin American, and Asian American youth. *Developmental Psychology*, *46*(3), 619–635.

Du Bois, W. E. B. (1935). *Black reconstruction in America 1860–1880*. Harcourt, Brace, and Company.

Dumas, M. J. (2016). Against the dark: Antiblackness in education policy and discourse. *Theory Into Practice, 55*, 11–19. https://doi.org/10.1080/00405841.2016.1116852.

Dunbar-Ortiz, R. (2014). *An Indigenous peoples' history of the United States.* Beacon Press.

Elmore, K. C., & Oyserman, D. (2012). If "we" can succeed, "I" can too: Identity-based motivation and gender in the classroom. *Contemporary Educational Psychology, 37*(3), 176–185. https://doi.org/10.1016/j.cedpsych.2011.05.003.

Elmore, K., Oyserman, D., & Novin, S. (2016). When the going gets tough: Implications of reactance for interpretations of experienced difficulty in the classroom. *AERA Open, 2*(3). https://doi.org/10.1177/2332858416664714.

Feagin, J. R. (2013).*The white racial frame: Centuries of racial framing and counter-framing.* Routledge.

Fisher, O., & Oyserman, D. (2017). Assessing interpretations of experienced ease and difficulty as motivational constructs. *Motivation Science, 3*(2), 133–163. https://doi.org/10.1037/mot0000055.

Freire, P. (1970). *Pedagogy of the oppressed.* Continuum.

Garcia, M. T., & Castro, S. (2011). *Blowout!: Sal Castro and the Chicano struggle for educational justice.* University of North Carolina Press.

Gerrard, J., Sriprakash, A., & Rudolph, S. (2021). Education and racial capitalism. *Race Ethnicity and Education, 25*(3), 425–442. https://doi.org/10.1080/13613324.2021.2001449.

Gilmore, R. W. (2007). *Golden gulag: Prisons, surplus, crisis, and opposition in globalizing California.* University of California Press.

Ginwright, S. A. (2010). Peace out to revolution! Activism among African American youth: An argument for radical healing. *Young, 18*(1), 77–96. https://doi.org/10.1177/110330880901800106.

Ginwright, S., & Cammarota, J. (2007). Youth activism in the urban community: Learning critical civic praxis within community organizations. *International Journal of Qualitative Studies in Education, 20*, 693–710. https://doi/org/10.1080/09518390701630833.

Glaude, Jr., E. S. (2020). *Begin again: James Baldwin's America and its urgent lessons for our own* (1st ed). Crown.

Godfrey, E. B., Burson, E. L., Yanisch, T. M., Hughes, D., & Way, N. (2019). A bitter pill to swallow? Patterns of critical consciousness and socioemotional and academic well-being in early adolescence. *Developmental Psychology, 55*(3), 525–537. https://doi.org/10.1037/dev0000558.

Godfrey, E. B., & Wolf, S. (2016). Developing critical consciousness or justifying the system? A qualitative analysis of attributions for poverty and wealth among low-income racial/ethnic minority and immigrant women. *Cultural Diversity and Ethnic Minority Psychology, 22*, 93–103. https://doi.org/10.1037/cdp0000048.

Graham, J. W. (1991). An essay on organizational citizenship behavior. *Employee Responsibilities and Rights Journal, 4*(4), 249–270.

Gutiérrez, L. M. (1995). Understanding the empowerment process: Does consciousness make a difference? *Social Work Research, 19*(4), 229–237. https://doi.org/10.1093/swr/19.4.229.

Hall, S. (2021). Why Fanon? [1996]. In *Selected writings on race and difference* (pp. 339–358). Duke University Press.

Heberle, A. E., Rapa, L. J., & Faragó, F. (2020). Critical consciousness in children and adolescents: A systematic review, critical assessment, and recommendations for future research. *Psychological Bulletin*, *146*(6), 525–551.

Hope, E. C., & Jagers, R. J. (2014). The role of sociopolitical attitudes and civic education in the civic engagement of Black youth. *Journal of Research on Adolescence*, *24*(3), 460–470. https://doi.org/10.1111/jora.12117.

Hudley, C., & Graham, S. (2001). Stereotypes of achievement striving among early adolescents. *Social Psychology of Education*, 5, 201–224.

Jenkins, D., & Leroy, J. (2021). *Introduction: The old history of capitalism.* In D. Jenkins & J. Leroy (Eds.), *Histories of Racial Capitalism* (pp. 1–26). Columbia University Press.

Joseph, J. (1995). *Black youths, delinquency, and juvenile justice.* Greenwood Publishing Group.

Karuka, M. (2021). The counterrevolution of property along the 32nd parallel. In D. Jenkins & J. Leroy (Eds.), *Histories of racial capitalism* (pp. 135–168). Columbia University Press.

Kelley, H. H. (1973). The processes of causal attribution. *American Psychologist*, *28*(2), 107–128. https://doi.org/10.1037/h0034225.

Kraus, M. W., Piff, P. K., & Keltner, D. (2009). Social class, sense of control, and social explanation. *Journal of Personality and Social Psychology*, *97*(6), 992–1004. https://doi.org/10.1037/a0016357.

Lewis Jr., N. A. (2021). Can we achieve "equality" when we have different understandings of its meaning? How contexts and identities shape the pursuit of egalitarian goals. *Psychological Inquiry*, *32*(3), 155–164.

Lewis, N. A., Jr., & Sekaquaptewa, D. (2016). Beyond test performance: A broader view of stereotype threat. *Current Opinion in Psychology*, *11*, 40–43.

Luginbuhl, P. J., McWhirter, E. H., & McWhirter, B. T. (2016). Sociopolitical development, autonomous motivation, and education outcomes among low income Latina/o adolescents. *Journal of Latina/o Psychology*, *4*, 53–59.

Markus, H., & Nurius, P. (1986). Possible selves. *American Psychologist*, *41*(9), 954.

Monjaras-Gaytan, L. Y., Sánchez, B., Anderson, A. J., et al. (2021). Act, talk, reflect, then act: The role of natural mentors in the critical consciousness of ethnically/racially diverse college students. *American Journal of Community Psychology*, *68*(3–4), 292–309. https://doi.org/10.1002/ajcp.12517.

O'Connor, C. (1997). Dispositions toward (collective) struggle and educational resilience in the inner city: A case analysis of six African-American high school students. *American Educational Research Journal*, *34*(4), 593–629.

Orfield, G., & Lee, C. (2005). *New faces, old patterns? Segregation in the multiracial south.* Cambridge, MA: The Civil Rights Project at Harvard University.

Oyserman, D. (2009). Identity-based motivation: Implications for action-readiness, procedural-readiness, and consumer behavior. *Journal of Consumer Psychology*, *19*, 250–260.

Oyserman, D. (2013). Not just any path: Implications of identity-based motivation for disparities in school outcomes. *Economics of Education Review*, *33*, 179–190.

Oyserman, D., Bybee, D., Terry, K., & Hart-Johnson, T. (2004). Possible selves as roadmaps. *Journal of Research in Personality*, *38*, 130–149.

Oyserman, D., & Destin, M. (2010). Identity-based motivation: Implications for intervention. *The Counseling Psychologist, 38*, 1001–1043.

Oyserman, D., & Fryberg, S. A. (2006). *The possible selves of diverse adolescents: Content and function across gender, race, and national origin.* In C. Dunkel & J. Kerpelman (Eds.), Possible Selves: Theory, Research, and Application (pp. 17–39). Nova.

Oyserman, D., Gant, L., & Ager, J. (1995). A socially contextualized model of African American identity: Possible selves and school persistence. *Journal of Personality and Social Psychology, 69*, 1216. https://doi.org/10.1037/0022-3514.69.6.1216.

Oyserman, D., & Lewis, N. A., Jr. (2017). Seeing the destination AND the path: Using identity-based motivation to understand and reduce racial disparities in academic achievement. *Social Issues and Policy Review, 11*(1), 159–194.

Pinedo, A., Vossoughi, N., & Lewis, N. A. (2021). Critical pedagogy and children's beneficial development. *Policy Insights from the Behavioral and Brain Sciences, 8*(2), 183–191.

Rapa, L. J., Diemer, M. A., & Bañales, J. (2018). Critical action as a pathway to social mobility among marginalized youth. *Developmental Psychology, 54*, 127–137. https://doi.org/10.1037/dev0000414.

Ray, V. E. (2019). A theory of racialized organizations. *American Sociological Review, 84*, 26–53.

Robinson, C. J. (1983). *Black Marxism the making of the Black radical tradition, 2000 ed.* Chapel Hill.

Rogers, L. O., & Way, N. (2016). "I have goals to prove all those people wrong and not fit into any one of those boxes": Paths of resistance to stereotypes among Black adolescent males. *Journal of Adolescent Research, 31*, 263–298. https://doi.org/10.1177/0743558415600071.

Rogers, L. O., & Way, N. (2021). Child development in an ideological context: Through the lens of resistance and accommodation. *Child Development Perspectives, 15*, 242–248. https://doi.org/10.1111/cdep.12433.

Ross, L., & Nisbett, R. E. (2011). *The person and the situation: Perspectives of social psychology.* Pinter & Martin Publishers.

Rothstein, R. (2017). *The color of law: A forgotten history of how our government segregated America.* Liveright Publishing.

Salter, P. S., Adams, G., & Perez, M. J. (2018). Racism in the structure of everyday worlds: A cultural-psychological perspective. *Current Directions in Psychological Science, 27*(3), 150–155. https://doi.org/10.1177/0963721417724239.

Santiago-Rivera, A. L., Adames, H. Y., Chavez-Dueñas, N. Y., & Benson-Flórez, G. (2016). The impact of racism on communities of color: Historical contexts and contemporary issues. In A. N. Alvarez, C. T. H. Liang, & H. A. Neville (Eds.), *Cultural, racial, and ethnic psychology book series. The cost of racism for people of color: Contextualizing experiences of discrimination* (p. 229–245). American Psychological Association. https://doi.org/10.1037/14852-011.

Seider, S., Clark, S., & Graves, D. (2020). The development of critical consciousness and its relation to academic achievement in adolescents of color. *Child Development, 91*(2), e451–e474. https://doi.org/10.1111/cdev.13262.

Seider, S., & Graves, D. (2020). *Schooling for critical consciousness: Teaching black and Latinx youth to analyze, navigate, and challenge racial injustice.* Harvard Education Press.

Sleeter C. E., & Zavala, M. (2020). *Transformative ethnic studies in schools: Curriculum pedagogy & research.* New York: Teachers College Press.

Smith, K. B., & Stone, L. H. (1989). Rags, riches, and bootstraps: Beliefs about the causes of wealth and poverty. *Sociological Quarterly, 30*(1), 93–107.

Steele, C. M. (1997). A threat in the air: How stereotypes shape intellectual identity and performance. *American Psychologist, 52*, 613–629.

Suárez-Orozco, C. (2004). Formulating identity in a globalized world. In M. M. Suárez-Orozco & D. B. Qin-Hilliard (Eds.), *Globalization: Culture and education in the new millennium* (pp. 173–202). University of California Press.

Treskon. (2017, March 28). Less segregated communities aren't only more inclusive. They're more prosperous. Urban Institute. www.urban.org/urban-wire/less-segregated-communities-arent-only-more-inclusive-theyre-more-prosperous.

Tuck, E. (2009). Suspending damage: A Letter to communities. *Harvard Educational Review, 79*(3), 409–428.

Tuck, E., & Yang, K. W. (2014). Decolonization is not a metaphor. *Decolonization, Indigeneity, Education, and Society, 1*, 1–40.

Turner, C. (2016, April 18). *Why America's schools have a money problem.* Morning Edition. www.npr.org/2016/04/18/474256366/why-americas-schools-have-a-money-problem.

Uriostegui, M., Roy, A. L., & Li-Grining, C. P. (2021). What drives you? Black and Latinx youth's critical consciousness, motivations, and academic and career activities. *Journal of Youth and Adolescence, 50*, 58–74. https://doi.org/10.1007/s10964-020-01343-6.

Wang, M.-T., Henry, D. A., Smith, L. V., Huguley, J. P., & Guo, J. (2020). Parental ethnic-racial socialization practices and children of color's psychosocial and behavioral adjustment: A systematic review and meta-analysis. *American Psychologist, 75*(1), 1–22. https://doi.org/10.1037/amp0000464.

Watts, R. J., Diemer, M. A., & Voight, A. M. (2011). Critical consciousness: Current status and future directions. In B. Christens & C. Flanagan (Eds.), *Youth Civic Development: Work at the Cutting Edge* (Vol. 134, pp. 43–57). John Wiley & Sons. https://doi.org/10.1002/cd.310.

Watts, R. J., & Flanagan, C. (2007). Pushing the envelope on youth civic engagement: A developmental and liberation psychology perspective. *Journal of Community Psychology, 35*(6), 779–792.

Watts, R. J., & Hipolito-Delgado, C. (2015). Thinking ourselves to liberation: Advancing sociopolitical action in critical consciousness. *The Urban Review, 47*, 847–867. https://doi.org/10.1007/s11256-015-0341.

Watts, R. J., Williams, N. C., & Jagers, R. J. (2003). Sociopolitical development. *American Journal of Community Psychology, 31*, 185–194. http://dx.doi.org/10.1023/A:1023091024140.

Weiner, B. (1972). Attribution theory, achievement motivation, and the educational process. *Review of Educational Research, 42*(2), 203–215. https://doi.org/10.2307/1170017.

2

# Situating Critical Consciousness Within the Developmental System

## *Insights from the Phenomenological Variant of Ecological Systems Theory*

SARA SUZUKI, SARA K. JOHNSON, AND KEVIN A. FERREIRA VAN LEER

The framework of critical consciousness (CC) has contributed to theoretical and practical progress in understanding how young people resist and undo oppression – experiences of marginalization from social institutions (e.g., health, education) that affect all aspects of life (Diemer et al., 2016; Heberle et al., 2020). CC draws largely from the works of Paulo Freire (1972, 1998, 2014, 2016). Freire, working within the context of South American class struggles (Holst, 2006), wrote about CC as a way that individuals can be empowered to transform reality by engaging in "reading the world" (Freire & Macedo, 1987). It was important to Freire that individuals understood the historical, sociocultural, and political contours of the settings they were in so they could discern how systems of oppression influenced their daily realities. More recently, scholars have applied the concept of CC by reflecting on the struggles of young people of color against oppression in the US context. To "read the world" in the context of a nation-state founded on white supremacy and settler colonialism (Saito, 2020; Tuck & Yang, 2012) is to perceive the dominant narratives around individualism, meritocracy, and color-evasiveness that permeate the fabric of society.

In the CC framework, oppression is not insurmountable (Diemer et al., 2016; Watts et al., 2011); individuals can use their power to interrogate oppression (critical reflection) and take part in actions to dismantle it (critical action). These two components form the praxis of CC, wherein thinking and doing reciprocally and iteratively interact to pave the way for liberation. The proliferation of research on CC has expanded our understanding of how youth engage in CC, its implications for other developmental domains (e.g., educational achievement; Cadenas et al., 2018; Seider et al., 2019), and how CC can be supported (e.g., in community-based organizations; Ginwright & Cammarota, 2007).

The widespread adoption of the CC framework within fields of study that focus on young people (Heberle et al., 2020) suggests that researchers – either explicitly or implicitly – believe that young people who experience oppression can enact resilience, resistance, and, ultimately, liberation as outcomes that are important to development (both individual and collective). Yet, the CC framework itself does not focus on development, so it could be expanded and enriched through integration with other theories that emphasize individuals as existing within developmental systems.

In this chapter, we examine CC through the lens of the phenomenological variant of ecological systems theory (PVEST; Spencer, 2006; Spencer et al., 2015), a theoretical framework rooted in developmental systems. PVEST shares several underlying assumptions and emphases with the CC framework, including explicitly centering oppression and privilege as features of young people's contexts, acknowledging the inequities in developmental contexts as factors that influence – but do not determine – young peoples' lives, and emphasizing the agency that they have to cope with and change their contexts. At the same time, PVEST contains other foci that can help enrich CC theory and research, including an emphasis on the multiple layers of youth's contexts and the meaning that they make of those contexts.

Given these features, linking PVEST with CC draws attention to the ways CC theory – and, by extension, research – may be expanded to align with a contextualized, developmental, and dynamic lens on young people's lives. Other developmental theories could productively be used in combination with the CC framework, and we hope other scholars will use the ideas we present here as a starting point to pursue that work.

The outline of the chapter is as follows. First, we give a brief overview of PVEST. Then, we describe four recommendations for how PVEST might be used to expand our thinking about and use of the CC framework: (1) considering the larger developmental context of CC; (2) addressing meaning-making as a primary process within contexts; (3) considering changes in CC; and (4) focusing on the dynamic nature of CC, including emphasizing praxis and considering CC processes as collective. Within each of these four sections, we highlight research that sheds light on these recommendations and provide actionable suggestions for how these recommendations can be used in future research.

## OVERVIEW OF THE PHENOMENOLOGICAL VARIANT OF ECOLOGICAL SYSTEMS THEORY (PVEST)

PVEST (Spencer, 2006; Spencer et al., 2015) extends other ecological theories of human development – such as Bronfenbrenner's ecological model (Bronfenbrenner & Morris, 2007) and García Coll's integrative model for the study of developmental competencies in minority children (García Coll et al., 1996) – by incorporating how intersubjective experience influences the impact contexts have on development. According to PVEST, the multiple interacting levels of context that the person is embedded in (e.g., microsystem, macrosystem; Bronfenbrenner & Morris, 2007) and the social positions that individuals occupy (e.g., race, gender; García Coll et al., 1996) are not deterministic of developmental outcomes. Instead, phenomenology – how individuals interpret and make meaning of self, others, experiences, and environment – plays a key role (Spencer, 2006; Spencer et al., 2015). The development of the person (e.g., increasing cognitive capacities) shapes phenomenological processes, and the individuals' meaning-making in turn impacts their development by influencing how they interact with their context. Accordingly, individuals with similar social locations can have notably different developmental trajectories (Spencer, 2006; Spencer et al., 2015). This nondeterministic view of development is important for countering deficit-based views of groups who experience oppression (e.g., youth of color) and for considering how young people's strengths may support them to transform their own and others' lives.

We describe PVEST in more detail by describing five different "angles" the theory presents with respect to the developmental process (Spencer, 2006; Spencer et al., 2015). In PVEST, each angle is a moment in the entire view of human development and therefore operates in concert with all other angles. Development does not begin with the first angle and end with the last in a linear fashion; adjacent angles influence each other bidirectionally, and the five parts form a cyclical model that is recursive. Nevertheless, the angles must be separated in order to describe each one. We begin our discussion with the first angle, which attends to the contextual features of the developing person.

1. **Net Vulnerability:** The first angle of PVEST, *net vulnerability*, captures the balance between risk and protective factors for development. Net vulnerability is defined as the sum of all the supports that individuals may have access to, minus the potential stressors within individuals and their environments. Accordingly, it captures the level of developmental challenges for each person. For people who experience marginalization, systems of oppression can contribute to a high presence of potential risk factors in their developmental context. For example, youth of color may be exposed to negative influences on their development due to racism, such as living in neighborhoods with high levels of poverty (Reardon et al., 2015), attending underfunded schools (Morgan, 2018), and experiencing discrimination within the justice system (Rovner, 2016). In contrast, they may also have access to individual, family, and community protective characteristics that can offset these elements of stress. For example, their neighborhoods may have strong social ties between members (Chung & Docherty, 2011), and teachers or other adults may be highly involved in their lives (Herrera et al., 2011; Suldo et al., 2009).

2. **Net Stress:** The second angle of PVEST is *net stress*, which builds on net vulnerability to incorporate the idea that how individuals make meaning of self and context affects their actual experience of the developmental system they are embedded in. Accordingly, the individual perceives the net level of vulnerability (i.e., the balance of potential risk factors versus potential protective factors) and interprets it; this interpretation is the actual level of stress that the person experiences. Due to differences in their phenomenological experiences, individuals with similar net vulnerabilities can have different experiences of net stress.

   Overall, the net vulnerability present within an individual's developmental system is not seen as a certain detriment to development; rather, the individual has experiences that can present potential challenges or facilitators (i.e., net stress) for their development. For example, because racism is a risk factor for youth of color, they may have specific experiences of racism in their everyday lives (e.g., having a derogatory remark directed at them) that act as stressors. Negative impacts of stressors can be mitigated by supports at the individual level (e.g., positive feelings about one's ethnic/racial membership, or private regard; Neblett et al., 2012) or within their surroundings (e.g., presence of cultural assets, such as familism; Romero et al., 2020). In addition, stressors do not always lead to negative outcomes and could actually facilitate development. For example, the "stress" of transitioning to a new school may prompt youth to learn new ways of interacting with peers. Thus, stress can generate meaningful challenges that spur growth.
3. **Reactive Coping Processes:** The third angle of PVEST is *reactive coping processes*. These refer to the strategies that young people engage in to counteract the stress that is perceived and interpreted from the net level of vulnerability in their developmental system. These coping processes are deployed to reduce states of dissonance for the individual and may be adaptive or maladaptive in various ways. Some strategies may be immediately helpful but have negative long-term consequences, and some strategies may be productive in one context but counterproductive in another. As an example, aggression may be the most logical mode of coping in an oppressive neighborhood context with high levels of poverty, crime, and police presence, but it can result in punitive actions in the classroom context (Harris et al., 2019). Because reactive coping processes are but one angle within PVEST, they should not be labeled as "pathological" or "problematic" without taking into account the larger context (i.e., net vulnerability) as well as how they made meaning of their situation (i.e., net level of stress).
4. **Emergent Identities:** The fourth angle of PVEST is *emergent identities*. Over time, youth may repeat the reactive coping strategies that were most successful, and these strategies may become stable responses that are a recurrent part of the way they interact with the world. In this way, coping

reactions can become internalized as part of young people's self-conceptualizations. For example, sustained civic engagement as a coping strategy can support the development of a sense of social responsibility and orientation toward activism (Hope & Spencer, 2017). Among young people of color, engagement in antiracist activism as a way to promote justice for themselves and their peers may also shape their sense of racial identity (Mathews et al., 2019), such as through strengthening the sense of private regard they feel about their group. In turn, these developing identities reciprocally influence their coping processes by changing how they make meaning of self, others, and context (Spencer, 2006; Spencer et al., 2015). For example, a strengthened sense of private regard for one's racial group can change the net stress felt by the young person in the face of racism they encounter in some situations.

5. **Stage-Specific Coping Outcomes:** The fifth angle is *stage-specific coping outcomes*. Emergent identities may stabilize how individuals cope with the net stress that they perceive in their developmental system and, accordingly, produce adverse and/or productive outcomes (Spencer, 2006; Spencer et al., 2015). These outcomes (and which aspects are considered adverse or productive) are specific to particular developmental periods. For adolescents, important outcomes are related to current and future educational and work plans, developing positive relationships, and engaging in health-promoting behaviors (among others). Research has shown that aspects of civic engagement and CC may promote these positive outcomes. For example, among youth of color in the US, commitment to helping others and fighting inequality were positively associated with vocational expectations (Diemer et al., 2010), and critical reflection about inequality positively predicted academic achievement (Seider et al., 2019). Some aspects of CC may also have adverse outcomes for youth: for example, activism has also been associated with health-risk behaviors (Ballard et al., 2019), and, among Black college students, high engagement in political activism may magnify experiences of microaggressions, with negative consequences for mental health (Hope et al., 2018). These outcomes feed back into young people's level of vulnerability: for example, higher levels of academic achievement may serve as a protective factor, whereas higher levels of symptoms of depression or anxiety may increase vulnerability.

## CC AND THE DEVELOPMENTAL SYSTEM: INSIGHTS FROM PVEST

In the rest of the chapter, we explore how the framework of CC may be extended to better integrate with the understanding of young people as embedded within developmental systems. Drawing on the implications of

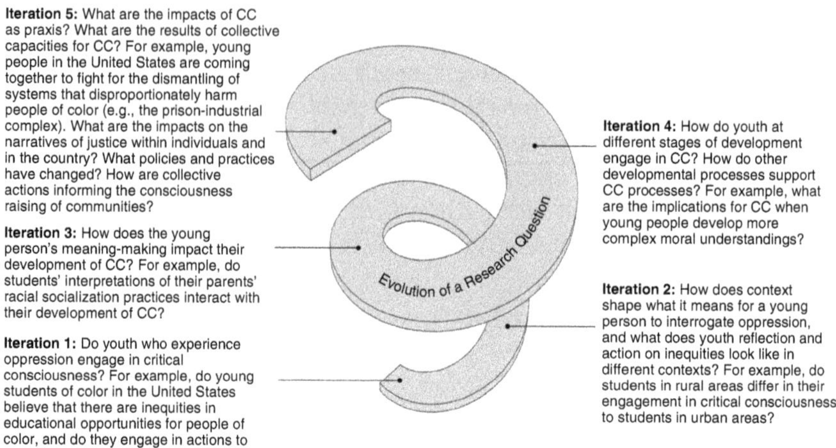


FIGURE 2.1 The evolution of a research question using the CC framework over multiple iterations. In each iteration, the research agenda reflects a CC framework that is more deeply integrated within developmental systems theory.

the five angles of PVEST described herein, we outline specific recommendations for how CC scholarship may be extended so that it accounts for how individuals exist within developmental systems. We also consider how each recommendation might influence research using the CC framework. In Figure 2.1, we present a helix depicting the possible evolution of a single CC-based research question over the course of five iterations. In the first iteration, we outline a research question that has been explored extensively within the existing CC research body (Heberle et al., 2020): Do youth who experience oppression engage in CC? In subsequent iterations (i.e., iterations 2 to 5), we propose additional research questions that build upon the recommendations in this chapter.

## ADDRESSING THE ROLE OF DEVELOPMENTAL CONTEXT IN CC

In the first recommendation, we consider how CC theory may address the role of context in ways that are more aligned with PVEST, a developmental systems theory. CC is fundamentally about the relationship between an individual and their context; more specifically, it is about how one analyzes and transforms the ways that systems of privilege and oppression embedded within contexts shape their opportunities and outcomes (Diemer et al., 2016; Freire, 2016; Watts et al., 2011). Indeed, a major strength of the CC perspective is the focus on the impact a critical understanding of context can have on one's life. Context is intimately entwined within the CC perspective, and the

CC framework would not exist (it would disintegrate, so to speak) without the idea of context. Nevertheless, we propose that an advanced integration of CC with ideas of development requires that the CC framework take into account how context has implications for all other processes within a developmental system, including CC processes themselves. Furthermore, we suggest that our understanding of CC can be enhanced by analyzing the role of context – either by examining through a grounded approach how CC unfolds in specific settings, or by analyzing how variation between contexts impact CC processes.

PVEST can help us expand our conceptualization of CC to include the role of context (as articulated in developmental systems theories) on the CC processes. As it is built upon ecological systems theory (Bronfenbrenner & Morris, 2007), PVEST considers all levels of a person's ecology, ranging from the microsystem to the chronosystem, as influencing individuals' development. For example, the first "angle" of PVEST of net vulnerability highlights that youth's contexts all have strengths and challenges. The angles in PVEST are a cyclical process that feed back onto each other, so that the net vulnerabilities in the context are "infused" throughout the rest of the developmental system. Therefore, according to PVEST, it is vitally important to consider the location within the developmental system at which CC is occurring. Looking at CC through PVEST, we are also encouraged to incorporate information about the specificity of the contexts into our conceptualization of CC. How a young person engages in CC is likely unique to the specific space and time within which the young person is located, and this both constrains and opens up possibilities as to what transformations the individual (or collective) can enact through CC.

An important direction for CC research is to consider how the specific context a young person is embedded in influences their CC. Many recent studies using a CC framework have been conducted in urban areas in the United States among youth who are racially and economically marginalized, mostly youth in school-based settings (Heberle et al., 2020). In these studies, acknowledging structural obstacles for some people toward gaining a good education is considered an important indicator of understanding how oppression operates in the US context. This analysis directly counters racist notions about people of color not having success because they are less intelligent and less hardworking, and it accordingly is considered an important indicator of CC (specifically, of critical reflection). Researchers' assessment of CC processes needs to be responsive to context, as CC likely manifests in different ways depending on the specific social location of the individual, as well as their geography, history, and culture. For example, in some settings, discerning the harmful ideologies that are held up to support caste systems; ethnic, religious, or linguistic systems of oppression; and/or ongoing territorial expansion may be crucial. In the beginning of the helix, where there is a shift from iteration 1 to iteration 2 (Figure 2.1), we explore the research questions that may arise from considering context more directly.

Although we do not discount the importance of research findings among US youth, we suggest that CC research has lacked attention to how multiple levels of youth's specific contexts have influenced their CC development. The PVEST framework, through its emphasis on multiple integrated levels of context, helps us to clarify how inequality and oppression are passed through developmental systems. For example, for many US youth who experience marginalization, their CC may need to respond to the legacy of white supremacy (macrosystem) embedded within institutions like the educational and legal systems (exosystem) in ways specific to the era post-*Brown* v. *Board of Education* (chronosystem). Further, their enactment of CC needs to be responsive to the proximal settings young people are in, such as the classroom (microsystem). Future research could investigate critical reflection of and critical action against different levels of the system: for example, what are the differences between critical reflection of how oppression is upheld within immediate settings we are in, such as schools and neighborhoods, versus how oppression is perpetuated in present-day geopolitical activities? It is important, moreover, to examine how engagement in CC may be recursively shaping the settings youth are embedded in, whether through policy changes, cultural shifts, or other social phenomena.

Much of the existing literature has been guided by an etic perspective, where the researcher bounds the measurement and analysis of CC with their (the researcher's) understanding of what it means to be critically reflective or critically active. This methodological enclosing is evident in quantitative research, where the constructs of CC are defined and operationalized by the researcher. It is less evident, but still present, in qualitative research when researchers code data using their own analysis of the world (i.e., their own CC) as a frame of reference. An example of CC research that has taken an emic perspective is the mixed methods study conducted by Baker and Brookins (2014), in which they used photovoice to discern how rural youth in El Salvador discuss the issues affecting them and their communities. The photovoice results informed the development of a scale that was then administered to youth in various settings in El Salvador. In this particular research setting, young people articulated a role for local government (and police) in solving issues such as pollution while criticizing the ways these power-holding institutions discriminate against the poor. This articulation of critical reflection is complex in that youth are holding local official structures accountable for improving their communities while, at the same time, pinpointing how these institutions perpetuate economic marginalization. In the quantitative portion of the study, we see that the effectiveness of local official structures is an important factor for CC within these communities and that critical action in such settings may appear as "changing public policy" or "making reforms within the current system." Both the emphasis on well-functioning government-related bodies as community-based sociopolitical efficacy and the emphasis on reforms and change within existing systems as critical action are unique to this setting.

Another way to account for context in CC research is to design multilevel studies that introduce and account for variation in context. This allows for analyses that capture how changes in context are related to CC, and can inform the relationship between CC processes and context. The explicit modeling of context through multilevel designs can occur at various levels of the ecological system. For example, Seider and colleagues (2018) examined how distinct pedagogical models as carried out by different schools related to youth CC development. In the current US context, for example, legislative action against teaching "critical race theory" in schools is deepening disparities in opportunities for civic education (Pollock et al., 2022). This may have implications for the development of CC for youth, as research has shown that civic education is critical for supporting growth in youth's self-efficacy about taking part in sociopolitical action (Dassonneville et al., 2012). Other microsystem settings, such as neighborhoods, may influence CC in profound ways that are yet unexamined. For example, in one study, African American youth perceived the amount of social support and cohesion in their neighborhoods to be higher when the neighborhood had higher concentrations of African American residents (Hurd et al., 2013). This was further related to having fewer internalizing symptoms, but it is possible that such neighborhood-level factors can influence CC-related processes as well, such as whether youth feel they can make changes in their community. As youth settings are comprised of multiple layered elements (families, schools, peer groups, neighborhoods, and so on), it will be important to examine variations within contexts that are of a similar kind (e.g., variation in peer groups) as well as to examine multiple systems at once in tiered, multilevel designs.

## VARIATION WITHIN CONTEXTS IN CC PROCESSES: THE ROLE OF MEANING-MAKING

A defining feature of PVEST as a developmental systems theory is its emphasis on how intersubjective experience influences the impact contexts have on development. As noted, PVEST supplements other theories of human development – such as Bronfenbrenner's ecological model (Bronfenbrenner & Morris, 2007) and García Coll's integrative model for the study of developmental competencies in minority children (García Coll et al., 1996) – with a phenomenological component. By positing the sense that individuals make of interactions with their environment as one way in which the developmental context plays a role in developmental trajectories, PVEST outlines how the context comes to be integrated within internal processes.

The phenomenology aspect enables PVEST to maintain a strengths-based view of youth who experience marginalization, even while having as a foundational assumption how oppressive structures pose vulnerabilities for development. PVEST maintains that youth experiencing similar contexts may differ in how they make meaning of that context, thereby creating variation within individuals or groups that otherwise share similar positions in society. The vulnerability inherent in a young person's developmental system due to exposure to multiple forces of oppression does not determine that they inevitably face crises and deprivation; instead, the meaning-making can alter the course of the individual's life. The CC framework, and research based on it, may be enhanced by addressing phenomenology as something that connects the external and the internal in lived experiences.

One way in which a focus on phenomenology can enrich CC research is through a re-examination of critical reflection. As a main component of CC, it is typically conceptualized as an assessment of the systemic roots of existing inequalities. Accordingly, it is distinct from PVEST-related phenomenology, which encompasses more generally the interpretations of one's interaction with the environment. Bringing these two ideas together could move us away from the typical conceptualization of critical reflection as a static fact or generalized assessment that one has about the world and toward a view of critical reflection as one form or type of meaning-making that allows individuals to imagine acting on their context in a way that tackles oppression. With that view, we can better envision how young people may become equipped to interpret a dynamic and ever-changing world with critical reflection.

Viewing critical reflection as a *form* or *type* of meaning-making also highlights the idea that it may be connected to other meaning-making processes. In other words, youth's views of the historical, sociocultural, and political roots of oppression are likely shaped by (and shape) how they interpret other aspects of their lives. For example, a young person's interrogation of how disparities in educational opportunities impact the lives of people of color may be influenced by how they interpret the parental socialization they receive around race and culture. In one study among Black adolescents, critical reflection about racial gaps in educational achievement was positively related to youth's perceptions of their parents' racial socialization (preparation for bias and racial pride socialization) and parents' own critical reflection (Bañales et al., 2020). However, parents' own reports of racial socialization were not associated with increases in youth's critical reflection; this pattern of results emphasizes the important role of youth's own interpretations of their parents' socialization efforts.

The phenomenological perspective of PVEST can also enrich CC work by highlighting how engagement in CC may become differentiated within groups of individuals who share social identities. Young people of color may begin their CC process with internalizations of racism that attribute the kind of person they are (e.g., a "high" or "low" achiever) to the limitations they face in their education. A subgroup that begins to understand the ways structural racism disproportionately constrains opportunities for racialized groups may engage in coping strategies (e.g., identifying collective strategies for fighting oppression) which are then solidified into different aspects of identity (e.g., an activist identity). As outlined in angle 4, according to PVEST, this new identity can impact the subgroups' subsequent experiences of racism in ways that can prompt further development of CC (for instance, they may become less likely to engage in victim blaming). Meanwhile, their peers who are less engaged in CC processes may set out on a different trajectory in terms of the coping strategies they utilize and the identities that they commit to. While CC processes outline how young people make sense of the world, phenomenology allows us to outline how the world, as viewed through CC, comes to be instilled in the person as developmental system.

A third way that phenomenology may play a part in CC is related to intermediary processes between reflection and action, such as sociopolitical self-efficacy (sometimes also called political efficacy or critical motivation; Watts et al., 2011). Sociopolitical self-efficacy refers to whether the individual feels they can enact successful actions in the sociopolitical domain (often measured using the Sociopolitical Control Scale; Diemer & Li, 2011; Zimmerman & Zahniser, 1991). The potential for sociopolitical self-efficacy to empower young people may depend on how they are making meaning of other parts of their developmental system. For example, Uriostegui and colleagues (2021) found that youth's sociopolitical self-efficacy was related to engagement in academic and career activities both through encouragement by important individuals (e.g., role models) and through perceived pressure from family. Encouragement was related to a higher frequency of activities important to academic and career success, but pressure was related to disengagement from such activities. These findings highlight how youth's perception of various supports and barriers in their contexts impact the ways in which sociopolitical self-efficacy may shape developmental outcomes.

## CONSIDERING CHANGES IN CC

Why do some people not like the Quiché? This was the question that Quintana and Segura-Herrera (2003) asked young children in Guatemala during the last years of the brutal 36-year civil war and closely following the signing of peace agreements in 1996. In their study, the researchers found that younger children (average grade 2.1) made ingroup-blaming statements such as "because they have dirty clothes" or "because we do not speak like they [the Ladinos, or European-descendant people] do" while older children (average grade 3.5) instead made statements such as "because the Ladinos have killed our ancestors, have mistreated, and humiliated them, now they [Quichés] do not appear very well to Ladinos."

We share this example to highlight the importance of attending to changes over time in CC research. The subgroup of younger children made statements about their own group that reflect a lack of understanding for how the historical context may explain the lower social class of the Quiché at present. However, the older children were able to both recount a history of ill-treatment of Quiché as well as speak to the fact that the Ladinos are the ones who are holding prejudicial views. In the study, the researchers also found that ethnic pride was high for the youngest Quiché children; it decreased considerably as children reached an average grade level of 2.8 and then increased again. Considering the axis of time within CC research means considering parallel developmental processes, such as changes in ethnic identity – processes that may have complex relations with CC. In the current example, both the children with low and high critical reflection manifested high ethnic pride, suggesting that identity processes occurring alongside CC are nonlinear, with distinct functions for elements like ethnic pride at different moments of CC.

Overall, there are at least two distinct ways that time as a component of the developmental system can be incorporated into CC theory. One important thing to consider in future work is how CC differs across multiple points in the developmental continuum (i.e., how CC varies by age) and how other developmental processes that are unfolding are interrelated with CC. Another way that CC research can attend to changes over time is by considering the variation in which parts of the CC process are more static and trait-like versus which parts are more fluid and state-like (and how these may interrelate; see Tyler et al., Chapter 9 [this volume]). Development also has implications for supporting the action component of CC due to the fact that roles within established political institutions are circumscribed by age (e.g., age limits on voting).

Looking at CC across the developmental continuum is important as how CC is enacted by younger children is likely different from what older adolescents do because a person's biophysical, social-emotional, and cognitive development shape and constrain CC enactment. As individuals develop, new capacities emerge that may support CC. For example, abstract thinking is likely crucial to CC, as one must hold up analyses of societal structures against concepts such as equity in order to practice critical reflection and critical action. However, abstract thinking usually does not emerge until around age eleven or twelve (Dumontheil, 2014). Ancillary developmental processes may also shape the consequences of CC over time. For example, Yu and colleagues (2019) found that among eight-year-olds, high critical reflection was related to poor outcomes. The young children in their study who perceived that their group may experience challenges because of their race had lower academic achievement as well as poor adjustment (high hyperactivity, emotional symptoms, and conduct problems). This finding of a negative relationship between CC and other developmental outcomes is different from findings among the literature with older adolescents. For example, Bowers et al. (2020) found that critical reflection among college students was related to positive outcomes, and more so for older students. For the young children in Yu et al. (2019), a dissonance between pride about their identity and their knowledge of how their group is treated in society may explain the poor outcomes. For older adolescents, a reconciliation between one's positive self-regard and critical reflection may be occurring (Spencer, 1999), and may explain why CC relates to positive outcomes. It will be important for future studies to examine the factors – such as specific racial socialization practices – that support youth to hold both a strong sense of self and a critical understanding of inequities and injustices their group faces within society.

Understanding the interrelationship between CC and other developmental processes is also important for the design of interventions to support growth in CC. Ilten-Gee and Manchanda (2021) explore in detail how young people's development as understood through the lens of social domain theory (Smetana et al., 2014) may interact with their CC, with implications for classroom practice. According to social domain theory, children coordinate concerns in three domains when making decisions and judgments that are social or moral in nature: the domain of conventions or rules; the personal domain, which includes the development of self-concept and identity; and the moral domain of considering the harmful versus helpful consequences of actions. Furthermore, as children grow older, they experience shifts in each of the three domains. Understanding these developmental shifts across social domains may inform the developmental appropriateness of interventions designed to support CC development. For example, it is only around grades 5–6 that children begin to understand that rules can have exceptions (shift in conventional domain) and that accommodations such as limitations on individual autonomy may need to be made in order to pursue fairness (a shift in the moral domain). This development could support dialogue in the classroom that fosters CC development. For example, an educator may highlight the convention of having single-sex bathrooms and ask students to bring up why this may create an unfair environment for some people. Students could then learn about more inclusive bathroom arrangements and how this may support belonging for transgender people, among others. In their paper, Ilten-Gee and Manchanda (2021) provide other ideas for lessons that highlight the contradictions and power dynamics of society and opportunities for students to resolve them that are appropriate for different developmental periods.

Freire and some early interpretations of his work proposed stage-like models of CC. However, Watts and colleagues (2003), in their interviews with young African American men, came to the conclusion that sociopolitical development, as a process where individuals become increasingly engaged in CC, may be a developmental process that is more dynamic than such a stage-like model can account for. Watts et al. (2003) saw sociopolitical development as consisting of "transactions ... a cumulative and recursive process where future transactions are guided and given meaning by previous ones, and future ones can alter the interpretation of past ones" (p. 192). Indeed, they highlight how an experience such as attending a workshop can lead to very distinct trajectories of CC depending on the person's "experience venue, aspects of the self, social influences, significant events, and functioning in an organizational role" (p. 192). It is possible that CC is a complex combination of an overall state with more fluid components that respond to specific situations. Future research could use modeling strategies based on latent state–trait theory (Steyer et al., 2012) to uncover these nuances.

## CAPTURING THE DYNAMIC NATURE OF CC: HIGHLIGHTING PRAXIS AND THE COLLECTIVE

Viewing CC from the lens of PVEST drives us to (re)consider the dynamic nature of CC. PVEST conceptualizes development as inherently nonstatic, because individuals make meaning of their environment and themselves in ways that shape how they interact with the environment. Their actions on their context are reflected in their subsequent meaning-making, in a recursive model of development. This understanding of development as a dynamic, continuously evolving process connects well to the concept of praxis within the CC framework: praxis is the interrelationship between critical reflection and critical action.

Freire's original conception of CC (or, more often in his writings, *conscientização* – i.e., conscientization) was founded on the notion of praxis, wherein new understandings of one's reality leads to engagement in interventions to transform the world, which necessitates further reflection. Freire's renderings of how social transformation occurs through praxis is rooted in philosophical foundations emphasizing dialectics (mainly Marxist dialectical materialism); thus, synergy between understanding and action is the path through which those experiencing oppression create liberation.

A phenomenological perspective facilitates a dynamic understanding of CC that emphasizes the notion of praxis. According to PVEST, as individuals interact with the world, their experiences are incorporated into their self-understandings and their interpretations of context, with implications for their identity formation and subsequent interactions with context. In other words, understanding is formed through actions, and actions are taken as a response to new understandings. Many young people are engaged in acts of resistance against oppression, or critical actions. For example, they may be engaged in youth organizing (Kirshner, 2015; Kirshner & Ginwright, 2012), building collective power and working to bring transformative change to issues affecting their communities. Engagement in such movements may mean that they experience successful negotiations of power within systems. As such, critical action can influence subsequent critical reflection – how they make meaning of the world in ways that reveal inequities and injustice. Thus, young people's realization of CC is a dynamic process at the nexus of meaning-making and interaction with context. It is not a unitary, stable process, and instead must focus on how critical actions prompt continuous reinterpretations of their experiences of oppression. As implied within the concept of praxis, individuals' critical reflection may change in an iterative manner in relation to their critical actions, and vice versa.

Despite some endorsement of the notion of praxis within CC at the theoretical level, studies of CC among young people in the United States have largely been conducted using measures that separate reflection and action (Diemer et al., 2015; Heberle et al., 2020). Questions about critical reflection do not ask about the associated action-taking (e.g., What do you think needs to be done about the high rates of unemployment in your neighborhood?), and questions about critical action do not probe the analyses guiding the action or gained through the action (e.g., "Why did you participate in this rally outside the state house?"; "What did you learn about educational justice issues affecting your community by organizing this social media campaign?"). A stronger integration of praxis within CC research may be advanced through developing measures of how young people develop new views of their reality through taking part in actions and how actions can support reframing their understanding of the world. Another way that praxis may be more deeply embedded into CC research endeavors is through a focus on dialogue (and other dialogic encounters) as a tool with which to analyze and understand CC. Freire and liberation psychologists viewed dialogue as a way to enact praxis in relationship with others (Freire, 2014; Montero, 2009). During dialogue, current understandings can be problematized to reveal asymmetries in power relations and create connections between current conditions and systems of oppression and privilege (Montero, 2009; Sánchez Carmen et al., 2015).

A phenomenological perspective may also provide a method in which researchers can better integrate collective understandings of liberation that have been central to CC theory and other work focusing on liberation (Sonn & Montero, 2009). Although this focus on the collective has not received much attention in recent CC scholarship, especially within psychology, the idea of collective liberation is important within both CC and developmental theory. The emphasis on identity within PVEST – and the ways that individuals construct their perceptions of self in interaction with their context – offers a venue in which to incorporate collective experiences of groups. CC research (Watts & Hipolito-Delgado, 2015) and many other bodies of scholarship (DiFulvio, 2011; Suyemoto et al., 2015; Terriquez, 2015) show that identifying with a common struggle of one's people helps individuals develop identities that incorporate a commitment to fighting oppression (Quintana & Segura-Herrera, 2003). For example, when young people have access to counterspaces (Case & Hunter, 2012), they may be able to engage in identity work in community with others such that their experiences of oppression are both affirmed and recrafted to bring about possibilities for resistance. Research on the relations between ethnic identity and empowerment also shows that individuals who have a strong sense of "peoplehood" within a group (Phinney & Ong, 2007) are more likely to have discussions about their context of social oppression, which may inspire collective actions (Flanagan et al., 2009; Gutiérrez, 1995). These examples help us conceptually integrate the importance of a focus on collective processes for adopting coping strategies to react to oppressive environments, developing an emergent identity centered around addressing injustice and making meaning of their experiences in new ways.

Nonetheless, we acknowledge that a shortcoming of our integration of PVEST with CC frameworks is how it continues to limit our understanding of collective processes for liberation. Communities experiencing oppression have, in various moments throughout history, joined together to resist and heal. The experience of oppression (Young, 2011) demands a collective response in many ways. However, PVEST focuses on *individual* experiences as shaping *individual* phenomenological understandings. We assert that solidarity forged across individuals is essential to liberation and therefore cannot be omitted from our theorizing about human development. One rationale for concentrating on the collective experience of groups under oppression is that a focus on individuals directly feeds into the projects of hegemony that we seek to dissemble (French et al., 2020). Many communities of color value interconnectedness and interdependence: for example, Asian cultures emphasize group harmony (Sue et al., 2019), Mexican-origin communities value familismo (Piña-Watson et al., 2019), and many Native American teachings center relationships (Absolon, 2010). Being able to orient toward such collectivist practices runs counter to the many individualistic narratives (e.g., "pull yourself up by your bootstraps") that erode the well-being and power of people. If developmental theories are to include an avenue through which groups will achieve liberation, a focus on the collective must be incorporated. As Freire (2016) observed, "domination is itself objectively divisive" (p. 173), whereas transformation of the world through CC is not an individual act but rather a collective process.

## CONCLUSION

The CC framework has formed the basis of important research on how young people contend with and dismantle oppression (Diemer et al., 2016; Heberle et al., 2020). In this chapter, we illustrated how a developmental systems theory, PVEST (Spencer, 2006; Spencer et al., 2015), can illuminate new directions for CC scholarship. We described four recommendations for combining the strengths of CC and PVEST, including: (1) considering the broader developmental context of CC (e.g., through multilevel models); (2) addressing meaning-making as a primary process (e.g., through connecting critical reflection to youth's perceptions of other aspects of their contexts); (3) considering changes in CC (e.g., through attending to age-related differences); and (4) focusing on the dynamic nature of CC (e.g., through longitudinal studies of the bidirectional relationships between reflection and action). We offer these recommendations as a starting point for how CC might be situated within a developmental systems theory, and we hope that CC scholars will not only expand on these recommendations but also pursue linkages with other developmentally oriented theories. These theoretical interchanges can help us move CC scholarship forward to capture the contextualized and dynamic ways that young people recognize, grapple with, and dismantle systems of oppression across development.

## REFERENCES

Absolon, K. (2010). Indigenous wholistic theory: A knowledge set for practice. *First Peoples Child & Family Review*, *5*(2), 74–87. www.erudit.org/en/journals/fpcfr/1900-v1-n1-fpcfr05254/1068933ar.pdf.

Baker, A. M., & Brookins, C. C. (2014). Toward the development of a measure of sociopolitical consciousness: Listening to the voices of Salvadoran youth. *Journal of Community Psychology*, *42*(8), 1015–1032. https://doi.org/10.1002/jcop.21668.

Ballard, P. J., Hoyt, L. T., & Pachucki, M. C. (2019). Impacts of adolescent and young adult civic engagement on health and socioeconomic status in adulthood. *Child Development*, *90*(4), 1138–1154. https://doi.org/10.1111/cdev.12998.

Bañales, J., Marchand, A. D., Skinner, O. D. et al. (2020). Black adolescents' critical reflection development: Parents' racial socialization and attributions about race achievement gaps. *Journal of Research on Adolescence: The Official Journal of the Society for Research on Adolescence*, *30* Suppl 2, 403–417. https://doi.org/10.1111/jora.12485.

Bowers, E. P., Winburn, E. N., Sandoval, A. M., & Clanton, T. (2020). Culturally relevant strengths and positive development in high achieving youth of color. *Journal of Applied Developmental Psychology*, *70*, 101182. https://doi.org/10.1016/j.appdev.2020.101182.

Bronfenbrenner, U., & Morris, P. A. (2007). The bioecological model of human development. In W. Damon & R. M. Lerner (Eds.), *Handbook of Child Psychology* (Vol. 3, p. 266). John Wiley & Sons, Inc. https://doi.org/10.1002/9780470147658.chpsy0114.

Cadenas, G. A., Bernstein, B. L., & Tracey, T. J. G. (2018). Critical consciousness and intent to persist through college in DACA and US citizen students: The role of immigration status, race, and ethnicity. *Cultural Diversity & Ethnic Minority Psychology*, *24*(4), 564–575. https://doi.org/10.1037/cdp0000200.

Case, A. D., & Hunter, C. D. (2012). Counterspaces: A unit of analysis for understanding the role of settings in marginalized individuals' adaptive responses to oppression. *American Journal of Community Psychology, 50*(1–2), 257–270. https://doi.org/10.1007/s10464-012-9497-7.

Chung, H. L., & Docherty, M. (2011). The protective function of neighborhood social ties on psychological health. *American Journal of Health Behavior, 35*(6), 785–796. https://doi.org/10.5993/ajhb.35.6.14.

Dassonneville, R., Quintelier, E., Hooghe, M., & Claes, E. (2012). The relation between civic education and political attitudes and behavior: A two-year panel study among Belgian late adolescents. *Applied Developmental Science, 16*(3), 140–150. https://doi.org/10.1080/10888691.2012.695265.

Diemer, M. A., & Li, C. (2011). Critical consciousness development and political participation among marginalized youth. *Child Development, 82*(6), 1815–1833. https://doi.org/10.1111/j.1467-8624.2011.01650.x.

Diemer, M. A., McWhirter, E. H., Ozer, E. J., & Rapa, L. J. (2015). Advances in the conceptualization and measurement of critical consciousness. *The Urban Review, 47*(5), 809–823. https://doi.org/10.1007/s11256-015-0336-7.

Diemer, M. A., Rapa, L. J., Voight, A. M., & McWhirter, E. H. (2016). Critical consciousness: A developmental approach to addressing marginalization and oppression. *Child Development Perspectives, 10*(4), 216–221. https://doi.org/10.1111/cdep.12193.

Diemer, M. A., Wang, Q., Moore, T. et al. (2010). Sociopolitical development, work salience, and vocational expectations among low socioeconomic status African American, Latin American, and Asian American youth. *Developmental Psychology, 46*(3), 619–635. https://doi.org/10.1037/a0017049.

DiFulvio, G. T. (2011). Sexual minority youth, social connection and resilience: From personal struggle to collective identity. *Social Science & Medicine, 72*(10), 1611–1617. https://doi.org/10.1016/j.socscimed.2011.02.045.

Dumontheil, I. (2014). Development of abstract thinking during childhood and adolescence: The role of rostrolateral prefrontal cortex. *Developmental Cognitive Neuroscience, 10*, 57–76. https://doi.org/10.1016/j.dcn.2014.07.009.

Flanagan, C. A., Syvertsen, A. K., Gill, S., Gallay, L. S., & Cumsille, P. (2009). Ethnic awareness, prejudice, and civic commitments in four ethnic groups of American adolescents. *Journal of Youth and Adolescence, 38*(4), 500–518. https://doi.org/10.1007/s10964-009-9394-z.

Freire, P. (1972). Education: Domestication or liberation? *Prospects, 11*(2), 173–181.

Freire, P. (1998). Cultural action for freedom. *Harvard Educational Review, 68*(4), 476–521. https://doi.org/10.17763/haer.68.4.656ku47213445042.

Freire, P. (2014). *Education for critical consciousness.* Continuum. (Original work published 1974).

Freire, P. (2016). *Pedagogy of the oppressed* (M. B. Ramos, trans.). Bloomsbury Academic. (Original work published 1970).

Freire, P., & Macedo, D. P. (1987). *Literacy: Reading the word and the world.* Bergin & Garvey Publishers.

French, B. H., Lewis, J. A., Mosley, D. V. et al. (2020). Toward a psychological framework of radical healing in communities of color. *The Counseling Psychologist*, *48*(1), 14–46. https://doi.org/10.1177/0011000019843506.

García Coll, C., Lamberty, G., Jenkins, R. et al. (1996). An integrative model for the study of developmental competencies in minority children. *Child Development*, *67*(5), 1891–1914. https://doi.org/10.1111/j.1467-8624.1996.tb01834.x.

Ginwright, S., & Cammarota, J. (2007). Youth activism in the urban community: Learning critical civic praxis within community organizations. *International Journal of Qualitative Studies in Education: QSE*, *20*(6), 693–710. https://doi.org/10.1080/09518390701630833.

Gutiérrez, L. M. (1995). Understanding the empowerment process: Does consciousness make a difference? *Social Work Research*, *19*(4), 229–237. https://doi.org/10.1093/swr/19.4.229.

Harris, J. A., Beale Spencer, M., Kruger, A. C., & Irving, M. A. (2019). An examination and interrogation of African American males' racial identity, prosocial behaviors and aggression. *Research in Human Development*, *16*(1), 76–91. https://doi.org/10.1080/15427609.2018.1556068.

Heberle, A. E., Rapa, L. J., & Faragó, F. (2020). Critical consciousness in children and adolescents: A systematic review, critical assessment, and recommendations for future research. *Psychological Bulletin*, *146*(6), 525–551. https://doi.org/10.1037/bul0000230.

Herrera, C., Grossman, J. B., Kauh, T. J., & McMaken, J. (2011). Mentoring in schools: An impact study of big brothers big sisters school-based mentoring. *Child Development*, *82*(1), 346–361. https://doi.org/10.1111/j.1467-8624.2010.01559.x.

Holst, J. D. (2006). Paulo Freire in Chile, 1964–1969: Pedagogy of the Oppressed in its sociopolitical economic context. *Harvard Educational Review*, *76*(2), 243–270. https://doi.org/10.17763/haer.76.2.bm6532lgln2744t3.

Hope, E. C., & Spencer, M. B. (2017). Civic engagement as an adaptive coping response to conditions of inequality: An application of Phenomenological Variant of Ecological Systems Theory (PVEST). In N. Cabrera & B. Leyendecker (Eds.), *Handbook on Positive Development of Minority Children and Youth* (pp. 421–435), Springer. https://doi.org/10.1007/978-3-319-43645-6_25.

Hope, E. C., Velez, G., Offidani-Bertrand, C., Keels, M., & Durkee, M. I. (2018). Political activism and mental health among Black and Latinx college students. *Cultural Diversity & Ethnic Minority Psychology*, *24*(1), 26–39. https://doi.org/10.1037/cdp0000144.

Hurd, N. M., Stoddard, S. A., & Zimmerman, M. A. (2013). Neighborhoods, social support, and African American adolescents' mental health outcomes: A multilevel path analysis. *Child Development*, *84*(3), 858–874. https://doi.org/10.1111/cdev.12018.

Ilten-Gee, R., & Manchanda, S. (2021). Using social domain theory to seek critical consciousness with young children. *Educational Research and Evaluation: An International Journal on Theory and Practice*, *19*(3), 235–260. https://doi.org/10.1177/14778785211057485.

Kirshner, B. (2015). *Youth activism in an era of education inequality*. New York University Press. www.degruyter.com/document/doi/10.18574/9781479805563/html.

Kirshner, B., & Ginwright, S. (2012). Youth organizing as a developmental context for African American and Latino adolescents. *Child Development Perspectives, 6*(3), 288–294. https://doi.org/10.1111/j.1750-8606.2012.00243.x.

Mathews, C. J., Medina, M. A., Bañales, J. et al. (2019). Mapping the intersections of adolescents' ethnic-racial identity and critical consciousness. *Adolescent Research Review, 5*, 363–379. https://doi.org/10.1007/s40894-019-00122-0.

Montero, M. (2009). Methods for liberation: Critical consciousness in action. In M. Montero & C. C. Sonn (Eds.), *Psychology of Liberation: Theory and Applications* (pp. 73–91). Springer Science+Business Media, LLC. https://doi.org/10.1007/978-0-387-85784-8_4.

Morgan, I. (2018, February 26). Students of color face steep school funding gaps. The Education Trust. https://edtrust.org/the-equity-line/students-color-face-steep-school-funding-gaps/.

Neblett, E. W., Jr, Rivas-Drake, D., & Umaña-Taylor, A. J. (2012). The promise of racial and ethnic protective factors in promoting ethnic minority youth development. *Child Development Perspectives, 6*(3), 295–303. https://doi.org/10.1111/j.1750-8606.2012.00239.x.

Phinney, J. S., & Ong, A. D. (2007). Conceptualization and measurement of ethnic identity: Current status and future directions. *Journal of Counseling Psychology, 54*(3), 271–281. https://doi.org/10.1037/0022-0167.54.3.271.

Piña-Watson, B., Gonzalez, I. M., & Manzo, G. (2019). Mexican-descent adolescent resilience through familismo in the context of intergeneration acculturation conflict on depressive symptoms. *Translational Issues in Psychological Science, 5*(4), 326–334. https://doi.org/10.1037/tps0000210.

Pollock, M., Kendall, R., Bingener, C. et al. (2022). *The conflict campaign: Exploring local experiences of the campaign to ban "critical race theory" in public K-12 education in the US, 2020–2021*. UCLA's Institute for Democracy, Education, and Access.

Quintana, S. M., & Segura-Herrera, T. A. (2003). Developmental transformations of self and identity in the context of oppression. *Self and Identity: The Journal of the International Society for Self and Identity, 2*(4), 269–285. https://doi.org/10.1080/714050248.

Reardon, S. F., Fox, L., & Townsend, J. (2015). Neighborhood income composition by household race and income, 1990–2009. *The Annals of the American Academy of Political and Social Science, 660*(1), 78–97. https://doi.org/10.1177/0002716215576104.

Romero, A. J., White, R. M. B., Anguas, M. M., Curlee, A., & Rodas, J. M. (2020). Resilience of Mexican descent youth in a low-income neighborhood: Examining family and neighborhood factors. *Journal of Latinx Psychology, 8*(4), 265–279. https://doi.org/10.1037/lat0000149.

Rovner, J. (2016, April 1). Racial disparities in youth commitments and arrests. www.sentencingproject.org/publications/racial-disparities-in-youth-commitments-and-arrests/.

Saito, N. T. (2020). *Settler Colonialism, Race, and the Law: Why Structural Racism Persists.* New York University Press.

Sánchez Carmen, S. A., Domínguez, M., Greene, A. C. et al. (2015). Revisiting the collective in critical consciousness: Diverse sociopolitical wisdoms and ontological healing in sociopolitical development. *The Urban Review, 47*(5), 824–846. https://doi.org/10.1007/s11256-015-0338-5.

Seider, S., Clark, S., & Graves, D. (2019). The development of critical consciousness and its relation to academic achievement in adolescents of color. *Child Development, 91*(2), e451–e474. https://doi.org/10.1111/cdev.13262.

Seider, S., Graves, D., El-Amin, A. et al. (2018). Developing sociopolitical consciousness of race and social class inequality in adolescents attending progressive and no excuses urban secondary schools. *Applied Developmental Science, 22*(3), 169–187. https://doi.org/10.1080/10888691.2016.1254557.

Smetana, J. G., Jambon, M., & Ball, C. (2014). The social domain approach to children's moral and social judgments. In J. G. Smetana & M. Killen (Eds.), *Handbook of Moral Development* (2nd ed., pp. 23–45). Psychology Press.

Sonn, C. C., & Montero, M. (Eds.). (2009). *Psychology of liberation: Theory and applications.* New York: Springer. https://doi.org/10.1007/978-0-387-85784-8.

Spencer, M. B. (1999). Social and cultural influences on school adjustment: The application of an identity-focused. *Educational Psychologist, 34*(1), 43–57. https://doi.org/10.1207/s15326985ep3401_4.

Spencer, M. B. (2006). Phenomenology and ecological systems theory: Development of diverse groups. In R. M. Lerner (Ed.), *Handbook of child psychology: Theoretical models of human development.* John Wiley & Sons, Inc. (6th ed., Vol. 1, pp. 829–893). https://doi.org/10.1002/9780470147658.chpsy0115.

Spencer, M. B., Harpalani, V., Cassidy, E. et al. (2015). Understanding vulnerability and resilience from a normative developmental perspective: Implications for racially and ethnically diverse youth. In D. Cicchetti & D. J. Cohen (Eds.), *Developmental Psychopathology* (2nd ed., Vol. 1, pp. 627–672). John Wiley & Sons, Inc. https://doi.org/10.1002/9780470939383.ch16.

Steyer, R., Geiser, C., & Fiege, C. (2012). Latent state-trait models. In *APA handbook of research methods in psychology, Vol 3: Data analysis and research publication* (pp. 291–308). American Psychological Association. https://doi.org/10.1037/13621-014.

Sue, D. W., Sue, D., Neville, H. A., & Smith, L. (2019). *Counseling the culturally diverse: Theory and practice.* John Wiley & Sons.

Suldo, S. M., Friedrich, A. A., White, T. et al. (2009). Teacher support and adolescents' subjective well-being: A mixed-methods investigation. *School Psychology Review, 38*(1), 67–85. https://doi.org/10.1080/02796015.2009.12087850.

Suyemoto, K. L., Day, S. C., & Schwartz, S. (2015). Exploring effects of social justice youth programming on racial and ethnic identities and activism for Asian American youth. *Asian American Journal of Psychology, 6*(2), 125–135. https://doi.org/10.1037/a0037789.

Terriquez, V. (2015). Intersectional mobilization, social movement spillover, and queer youth leadership in the immigrant rights movement. *Social Problems, 62*(3), 343–362. https://doi.org/10.1093/socpro/spv010.

Tuck, E., & Yang, K. W. (2012). Decolonization is not a metaphor. *Decolonization: Indigeneity, Education & Society*, *1*(1), 1–40.

Uriostegui, M., Roy, A. L., & Li-Grining, C. P. (2021). What drives you? Black and Latinx youth's critical consciousness, motivations, and academic and career activities. *Journal of Youth and Adolescence*, *50*(1), 58–74. https://doi.org/10.1007/s10964-020-01343-6.

Watts, R. J., Diemer, M. A., & Voight, A. M. (2011). Critical consciousness: Current status and future directions. *New Directions for Child and Adolescent Development*, 2011(134), 43–57. https://doi.org/10.1002/cd.310.

Watts, R. J., & Hipolito-Delgado, C. P. (2015). Thinking ourselves to liberation? Advancing sociopolitical action in critical consciousness. *The Urban Review*, *47*(5), 847–867. https://doi.org/10.1007/s11256-015-0341-x.

Watts, R. J., Williams, N. C., & Jagers, R. J. (2003). Sociopolitical development. *American Journal of Community Psychology*, *31*(1/2), 185–194. https://doi.org/10.1023/a:1023091024140.

Young, I. M. (2011). Five faces of oppression. In *Justice and the politics of difference* (pp. 39–65). Princeton University Press. (Original work published 1990).

Yu, D., Smith, E. P., & Oshri, A. (2019). Exploring racial–ethnic pride and perceived barriers in positive youth development: A latent profile analysis. *Applied Developmental Science*, *25*(4), 332–350. https://doi.org/10.1080/10888691.2019.1640607.

Zimmerman, M. A., & Zahniser, J. H. (1991). Refinements of sphere-specific measures of perceived control: Development of a sociopolitical control scale. *Journal of Community Psychology*, *19*(2), 189–204. https://doi.org/10.1002/1520-6629(199104)19:2<189::AID-JCOP2290190210>3.0.CO;2-6.

3

# Integrating Critical Consciousness and Social Empathy

## *A New Framework to Enhance Conscientization*

LUKE J. RAPA, CANDICE W. BOLDING, AND CARI ALLYN BROOKS

Inequitable social conditions shape individuals' development and have effects across all developmental domains (Brown et al., 2019; Ruck et al., 2019). However, experiences are not uniform, and the extent to which individuals experience marginalization and privilege varies due to interacting sociocontextual factors, including economic conditions, social class, ethnic/racial identification, gender identification, sexual orientation, citizenship and/or immigration status, religion, and dis/ability status, among others. Given how social identity/ies shape experiences and perceptions of inequity (Diemer et al., 2016), individuals may be subject to relatively more or less marginalization, depending on the contexts in which they are embedded, their relative positionality within those contexts, and the various intersectional and interlocking forms of oppression with which they contend (Causadias & Umaña-Taylor, 2018; Collins, 1993; Crenshaw, 1989; Godfrey & Burson, 2018).

In recent decades, applied psychologists and educators have drawn on critical consciousness theory (Freire, 1968/2000; Watts et al., 2011) to inform research and practice to address marginalization and oppression. There has been a surge in scholarship examining how marginalizing systems shape individuals' development, adaptive functioning, and general well-being, as well as on explaining how people navigate and actively work to change such marginalizing systems (Heberle et al., 2020). In short, critical consciousness has proven to be a useful framework for understanding and contending with inequitable societal conditions (Diemer et al., 2016). Critical consciousness is most often conceptualized as comprising three distinct dimensions – reflection, motivation, and action – that operate reciprocally to equip individuals to understand and transform oppressive elements of their sociocultural and sociopolitical realities (Freire, 1968/2000; Watts et al., 2011). Critical consciousness was initially theorized to be relevant to relatively more marginalized individuals (Diemer et al., 2016; Heberle et al., 2020). However, a number of scholars have recently suggested – and demonstrated empirically – that it applies more broadly, including to those who hold positions of relatively greater power and privilege.

A framework complementary to critical consciousness, developed within the field of social work, has loosely drawn on Freire's theory to advance something called "social empathy" as one specific means by which those holding relative privilege (e.g., social workers, clinicians, teachers, and others) might address societal inequities and promote social justice (Segal, 2007). As we will argue more fully, social empathy – defined as "the ability to understand people by perceiving or experiencing their life situations and as a result gain insight into structural inequalities or disparities" (Segal, 2011, pp. 266–267) – may be particularly useful for heightening critical consciousness, especially among those with relative privilege. That is, when social empathy is paired with critical consciousness, it may enable individuals to be "conscious allies" (Watts et al., 2003) to those experiencing relatively greater levels of marginalization, equipping them to collaborate with the oppressed in their efforts to dismantle systems of oppression. When oppressors "join the oppressed in their struggle for liberation," as Freire (1968/2000) himself noted, they become "converts" who "truly desire to transform the unjust order" through their work (p. 60).

Scholars have noted that empathy, along with its subcomponents (e.g., perspective taking), can be viewed as an attribute or skill that acts as a precursor to or facilitator of critical consciousness (Ibrahim et al., in press; Keefe, 1980; see also Clark & Seider, 2017; Diemer & Blustein, 2006). In the same way, social empathy may also interact with critical consciousness to shape or enhance individuals' critical reflection–motivation–action praxis, or the process of conscientization (Freire, 1968/2000). In this chapter, we briefly describe both the critical consciousness and social empathy frameworks, and then present an integrated framework that brings the two together. After introducing the integrated critical consciousness–social empathy framework, we present results from an exploratory study testing the framework with data drawn from a US national sample of adults. We conclude by considering some implications of this new framework for future research and practice.

## CRITICAL CONSCIOUSNESS AND SOCIAL EMPATHY: A BRIEF OVERVIEW

### Critical Consciousness

Critical consciousness is grounded in the work of Brazilian activist and educator Paulo Freire (1921–1997). Critical consciousness reflects one's ability to analyze societal inequities and their sociopolitical and sociohistorical roots, the motivation and perceived capacity to rectify such inequities, and the action taken, individually or collectively, to promote positive societal change and advance justice (Freire, 1973). As noted previously, building on Freire's work, most contemporary scholars (e.g., Watts et al., 2011) view critical consciousness as comprising three distinct dimensions or components: (1) critical reflection, defined as the critical analysis of marginalizing and oppressive social structures, systems, and conditions; (2) critical motivation, sometimes referred to as sociopolitical efficacy, which reflects the interest and agency one has to correct systemic inequities and oppression; and (3) critical action, or the action taken to facilitate and/or participate in activities that prompt societal change (Freire, 1968/2000, 1973; Heberle et al., 2020; Watts et al., 2011). The relation between critical reflection and critical action is often considered to be reciprocal, with reflection leading to action and action leading to further reflection (Watts et al., 2011). Moreover, the reflection–action association is theorized to be moderated and/or mediated by critical motivation (Heberle et al., 2020; Watts et al., 2011).

Empirical research conducted over the past few decades has linked critical consciousness to a number of adaptive outcomes, such as enhanced mental health and well-being (e.g., Godfrey et al., 2019), higher levels of civic development and engagement (e.g., Bañales et al., 2020; Diemer & Rapa, 2016), heightened political participation (e.g., Tyler et al., 2020), increased academic performance (e.g., Seider et al., 2020), and bolstered occupational aspirations and attainment (e.g., Rapa et al., 2018).[1] Indeed, a burgeoning literature investigates the antecedents and consequences of critical consciousness, as well as the interrelations among critical consciousness's component parts; this growing body of evidence suggests critical consciousness is a meaningful developmental asset that often promotes positive outcomes and downstream effects (Diemer et al., 2015, 2016; Heberle et al., 2020). Despite scholarship demonstrating the importance of critical consciousness in promoting adaptive outcomes, however, more research is needed to examine the interrelations among critical consciousness dimensions and to examine mechanisms that may support (or constrain) reflection–motivation–action praxis (Heberle et al., 2020; Rapa & Geldhof, 2020; see also Diemer et al., 2022; Rapa, Bolding, et al., 2020a).

## Social Empathy

Empathy benefits individuals and society at large (Silke et al., 2018). Allemand et al. (2015) have noted that "adolescents who report higher empathy also report more prosocial goals, are more socially competent, are less aggressive, have more supportive peer relationships, are well liked by their peers, and are more likely to help others" (p. 229). These benefits persist into adulthood,

[1] For recent systematic, comprehensive reviews, we direct the reader to Heberle et al. (2020) and Maker Castro et al. (2022).

leading to better relationships, less loneliness, less aggression, and more prosocial activity (Allemand et al., 2015; Maxwell & DesRoches, 2010; Shiner & Masten, 2012; Silke et al., 2018; Szanto & Krueger, 2019).

Empathy, also referred to as interpersonal empathy, is one's ability to feel with and for another person as an individual. Building on interpersonal empathy, social empathy is "the ability to understand people from different socioeconomic classes, racial/ethnic backgrounds, and other diversities and to have insight into the context of institutionalized inequalities and disparities" that affect those whose experiences and positionalities differ from one's own (Segal et al., 2017, p. 119). Social empathy entails processing the contexts, feelings, and experiences of groups and group members, particularly outgroups, and engaging in empathic connection with them (Gerdes & Segal, 2009).

Interpersonal empathy comprises four dimensions: (1) affective mentalizing (assessing another's emotional state); (2) self–other awareness (retaining a distinction between one's self and another(s)); (3) emotion regulation (avoiding taking on another's emotions as one's own); and (4) perspective-taking (viewing a situation or experience through another's eyes). Social empathy incorporates these four dimensions of interpersonal empathy, but includes two additional dimensions as well: (1) contextual understanding of systemic barriers (having a knowledge of the history, social systems, power structures, and patterns of marginalization, oppression, and injustice that shape the experiences of certain social groups and their membership); and (2) macro self–other awareness and perspective taking (comprehending the situations and experiences of groups of people, beyond the individual, who are different from one's self and/or who are members of a different population or social group) (Segal et al., 2017).

Social empathy leads to a greater understanding of and appreciation for the lives and experiences of others, particularly those of outgroup members (cf. Burson & Godfrey, 2020). People with high levels of social empathy have the capacity to look beyond their own lived experiences and social contexts to consider the lived experiences and social contexts of others, and to see, care for, and appreciate them as human beings as opposed to seeing them as distant abstractions (cf. Freire, 1968/2000). Social empathy also helps people recognize unjust situations, enhances sensitivity to such injustice, and fosters motivation, agency, and empowerment to act (Junker & Jacquemin, 2017; Rios et al., 2003; Segal et al., 2017; Wagaman, 2011). Thus, integrating social empathy and its six dimensions with critical consciousness – dimensions that either clearly complement critical consciousness (e.g., contextual understanding of systemic barriers clearly aligns with critical reflection) or that have been shown to be facilitative of its development (e.g., perspective taking) – may provide new insights for understanding how critical consciousness develops and operates and may foster new avenues for enhancing conscientization.

## INTEGRATING CRITICAL CONSCIOUSNESS AND SOCIAL EMPATHY

A number of scholars have recently raised questions about the broad applicability of critical consciousness, particularly for those who hold positions of relative power and privilege compared to their counterparts who are subject to more marginalizing conditions (Diemer et al., 2016, Godfrey & Burson, 2018; Heberle et al., 2020, Rapa & Geldhof, 2020). Since critical consciousness was initially articulated as something emanating from the experiences of the oppressed and envisioned as something leading to their liberation (Freire, 1968/2000; 1973), it is conceivably less relevant to those who do not contend as much with marginalizing forces like racism, classism, sexism, or other oppressive "-isms" (e.g., ableism, colorism, oppression due to immigrant status or religious beliefs, among others).

This view is complicated, however, by the fact that marginalization and privilege operate on manifold axes (Godfrey & Burson, 2018) and are not merely statuses possessed or uniformly experienced (Kimmel & Ferber, 2018). Instead, marginalization and privilege manifest based on various aspects of the social identity/ies individuals hold, and there is variation in how such identities interact with(in) the context and the broader social structures that marginalize or confer power and privilege (Collins, 1993; Combahee River Collective, 1977/2014; Coston & Kimmel, 2012; Crenshaw, 1989).

Scholarship focused on integrating an intersectional perspective with critical consciousness has brought this issue into sharp relief. Building on the foundational theory of intersectionality (Crenshaw, 1989), Godfrey and Burson (2018) argued that "marginalization and opportunity" are "a set of interlocking systems or forces of oppression and privilege" (p. 6) and suggested that individuals "are subject to varying systems of oppression *and* privilege in their lives, making it more difficult to draw distinctions between those who are wholly marginalized and those who are wholly privileged" (p. 8). Additionally, there is broad recognition that systems of white supremacy, (racial) capitalism, and cis-heteropatriarchy exert their influence on all individuals and groups within contemporary American society (Lee et al., 2015; see also Pinedo et al., Chapter 1 [this volume]; Shin et al., Chapter 11 [this volume]; Wray-Lake et al., Chapter 5 [this volume]), meaning everyone is subject to their effects. While Freire's theorization (1968/2000) predates more contemporary writings about the particular systems of oppression that order our societal structures, critical consciousness – *conscientização*, in Freire's terms, defined explicitly as "learning to perceive social, political, and economic contradictions, and to take action against the oppressive elements of reality" (p. 35) – is indeed a process relevant to everyone, regardless of relative privilege or marginalization (Jemal, 2017).

While consonant with the type of social analysis that characterizes critical reflection (Watts et al., 2011), and the broader framework of sociopolitical development (Watts et al., 1999, 2003; Watts & Flanagan, 2007), the specific focus within social empathy on knowledge of institutionalized and systemic sociopolitical and sociohistorical realities that contribute to current-day marginalization and oppression has been relatively underemphasized in existing measures of critical consciousness (for more extensive discussion, see Burson et al., Chapter 6 [this volume]; Rapa et al., Chapter 7 [this volume]). Taking all this into account – perhaps at least until critical consciousness measures are further adapted to more holistically attend to sociohistorical and sociopolitical origins of contemporary forms of marginalization and oppression – a new framework integrating critical consciousness and social empathy may be useful in providing greater depth of understanding and in generating novel insights about how to enhance critical reflection–motivation–action praxis. This may be especially the case given social empathy's utility in engendering empathic responses to outgroup members, for those who experience relatively less marginalization or oppression themselves.

Figure 3.1 depicts our framework integrating critical consciousness and social empathy. The shaded box at the top of the figure represents the process of critical reflection–motivation–action praxis (Freire 1968/2000; Watts et al., 2011; Watts & Flanagan, 2007). Critical reflection and critical action are linked by a double-headed arrow, indicating the reciprocal relation between the two critical consciousness dimensions. While critical reflection is often thought of as a precursor to critical action, both theory and empirical research have suggested that action can indeed serve as a precursor of reflection (Heberle et al.,

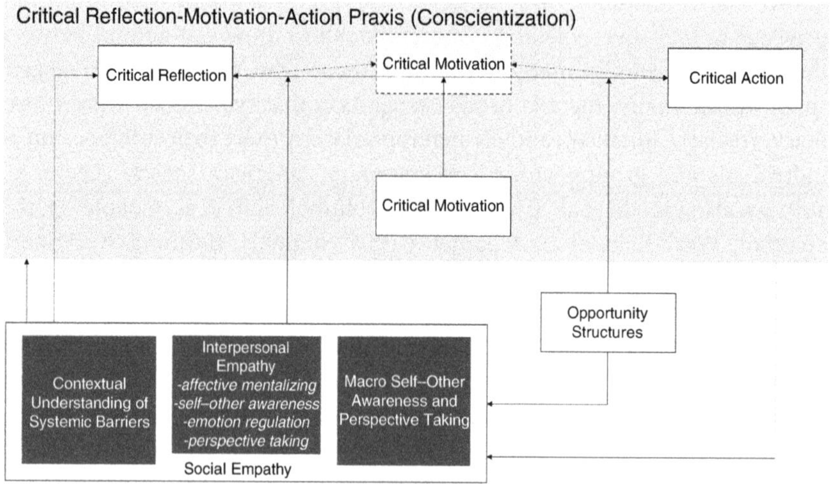


FIGURE 3.1 Framework integrating critical consciousness and social empathy.

2020; see also Diemer et al., 2021; Watts & Hipolito-Delgado, 2015). We have depicted critical motivation as both a moderator and a mediator of the association between critical reflection and critical action, again because both theory and empirical work have demonstrated these relations in critical consciousness scholarship (Diemer et al., 2016; Diemer & Rapa, 2016; Watts et al., 2011), though with somewhat mixed results (Heberle et al., 2020).[2] Opportunity structures are also depicted (cf. Watts & Flanagan, 2007) which, in our view, entail both marginalizing systems (Godfrey & Burson, 2018) and consciousness-raising systems (Heberle et al., 2020) that provide access or opportunity for individuals to engage in critical reflection–motivation–action praxis. These systems are envisioned to support (or constrain) the development of social empathy as well, and they also interact with the associations between critical reflection, critical motivation, and critical action. Finally, social empathy itself is envisioned to interact with the process of conscientization, along with the associations between critical reflection, critical motivation, and critical action individually.

This framework gives rise to numerous testable hypotheses that may be worth exploring in empirical research. For example, as noted, we postulate that social empathy moderates critical reflection–motivation–action associations. We suspect this may be the case primarily because aspects of social empathy (e.g., contextual understanding of systemic barriers) complement, align with, or seem likely to augment the functioning of the canonical critical consciousness dimension of critical reflection. This is why our initial inquiry to test the framework, as presented in the section that follows, was focused on the pathway between critical reflection and critical action. We illustrate how the framework might guide inquiry, more generally, with a few examples. Using the framework, researchers might hypothesize and test the following, though numerous other possibilities exist:

- Social empathy is *less important* (or may play less of a moderating role) when marginalizing conditions are *more salient* to the individual;
- In contrast, social empathy is *more important* (or may play more of a moderating role) when marginalizing conditions are *less salient* to the individual;
- Social empathy is *less important* (or may play less of a moderating role) when critical reflection–motivation–action praxis is directed toward one's *ingroup*;
- In contrast, social empathy is *more important* (or may play more of a moderating role) when reflection–motivation–action praxis is directed toward one's *outgroup*.

In order to establish preliminary evidence for the viability of the integrated critical consciousness–social empathy framework, and to lay the groundwork

[2] We acknowledge that any single study would be likely to emphasize either the moderating or the meditating effects of critical motivation as opposed to both. Even so, some research does interrogate both (e.g., Diemer & Rapa, 2016).

for future empirical work in this area, in the next section of this chapter we present results from an exploratory study. In this exploratory study, we first examined associations among critical consciousness dimensions and then assessed the moderating effects of social empathy, as a whole, on the pathway between critical reflection: perceived inequality and critical motivation. We focused on this pathway, in particular, because we expected social empathy to shape this association due to the focus it shares with critical consciousness on the critical analysis of systemic and structural inequities that contribute to marginalization and oppression. We expected that higher critical reflection would be associated with higher critical motivation. However, because this integrated framework is new and our analyses were exploratory, we were uncertain how the relation between critical reflection and critical motivation might change in the face of social empathy. Other pathways, such as the one between critical motivation and critical action, could be similarly examined for moderating effects; we save such analysis for future inquiry.

## Testing the Integrated Critical Consciousness–Social Empathy Framework: An Exploratory Study

Building on our recent work (e.g., Bolding et al., 2021; Rapa, Bolding, et al., 2020a; Rapa, Bolding, et al., 2020b), in this exploratory study we tested the integrated critical consciousness–social empathy framework by examining, among a national sample of US adults: (1) the associations among critical consciousness dimensions (Figure 3.2, Panel A); and (2) the moderating effects of social empathy on the pathway between critical reflection: perceived

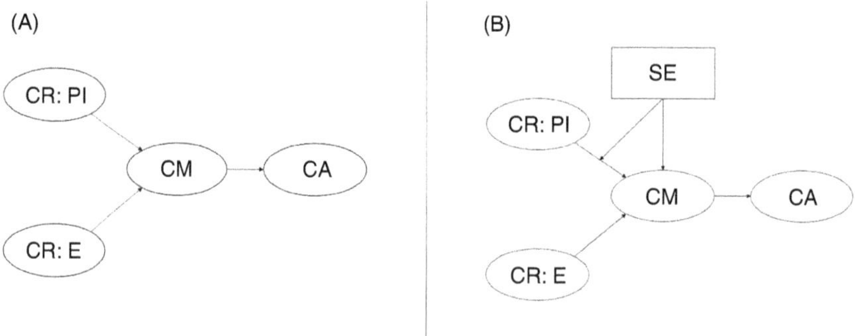


FIGURE 3.2 A model for testing the integrated critical consciousness–social empathy framework. Panel A depicts the associations among critical consciousness dimensions, including critical reflection: perceived inequality (CR: PI), critical reflection: egalitarianism (CR: E), critical motivation (CM), and critical action (CA). Panel B depicts the moderating effect of social empathy (SE) on the pathway between critical reflection: perceived inequality (CR: PI) and critical motivation.

inequality and critical motivation (Figure 3.2, Panel B). We considered our analyses to be exploratory for three primary reasons: (1) research has only recently begun using validated critical consciousness instruments with adults (e.g., Maker Castro et al., 2021; Shin et al., 2016, 2018) and we do not understand fully how critical consciousness manifests within adults (Diemer, 2020; Rapa & Geldhof, 2020); (2) more research is needed to examine associations among critical consciousness dimensions using measures that capture all of its dimensions (Heberle et al., 2020; Rapa & Geldhof, 2020); and (3) research has not yet examined critical consciousness and social empathy together.

## METHOD

### Sample and Procedures

This study used a national sample of US adults recruited using the research service Prolific (www.prolific.co/). Participants were drawn from Prolific's representative US adult sample, established based on age, sex, and ethnic group identification proportions for the US, calculated using the 2015 US Census Bureau population group estimates. Eligible participants were provided with an overview of the study and an external link to the online survey platform Qualtrics. Prospective participants were presented with a consent form and additional information about the study, and then they had the choice to opt into the study. Each participant was guaranteed compensation of $3.01 for their participation, paid upon their return of a completed questionnaire. The time commitment for participating in the study was estimated to be approximately 20 minutes, resulting in an hourly rate of pay of about $9.50/hour. Budget capacity for the project was established based on the maximum respondents supported by Prolific for a representative sample of US adults, which was a maximum of $N$ = 1,000 at the time of the data collection. Consented participants completed the survey in November 2021. Survey completions were received until the representative sample was indicated as complete by Prolific. After validity checks, the analytic sample for the study was $n$ = 973. All study procedures were approved by Clemson University's Institutional Review Board (IRB# 2021–0665).

The analytic sample of 973 included adults between the ages of 18–83 ($M_{age}$ = 44.91, $SD$ = 16.01). A slight majority of the sample identified as women (50.3%), while a large portion of the remainder of the sample identified as men (48.5%). A very small percentage of the sample (1.2%) identified with another gender categorization (e.g., nonbinary, genderqueer). A similar percentage of the sample identified as transgender (1.5%).

Most of the sample identified as white (75.4%), followed by Black or African American (11.6%), Asian or Asian American (5.7%), and a combination of two or more races (4.8%). Those identifying as Latinx (1.8%), Middle

Eastern or North African (0.3%), American Indian or Native American (0.1%), or another ethnic/racial identification categorization (0.2%) comprised a very small proportion of the sample.

Most of the sample (88.5%) indicated they were not currently students, though some denoted status as either a full-time or part-time undergraduate (8.3%) or graduate student (3.2%). A fair proportion of the sample indicated their employment status to be either full-time (39.9%), part-time (12.4%), or self-employed (13.6%), and some reported they were voluntarily unemployed (17.8%). Just over one in ten (11%) were unemployed involuntarily. The remainder reported being on disability benefits and/or being unable to work (5.4%). Less than half of the sample (40.4%) described their social class as lower class or working class, while the balance (59.6%) described their social class as middle class or above. Demographic information is summarized in Table 3.1.

TABLE 3.1 Sample demographic profile (n = 973)

| | n | % |
|---|---|---|
| Gender Identification | | |
| Men | 472 | 48.5 |
| Women | 489 | 50.3 |
| Nonbinary or another gender identification | 12 | 1.2 |
| Transgender | 15 | 1.5 |
| Ethnic/Racial Identification | | |
| Asian or Asian American | 55 | 5.7 |
| American Indian/Native American/First Nation/Alaska Native | 1 | 0.1 |
| Black or African American | 113 | 11.6 |
| Latina/o/x | 18 | 1.8 |
| Middle Eastern or North African | 3 | 0.3 |
| White | 734 | 75.4 |
| Two or more races | 47 | 4.8 |
| Other | 2 | 0.2 |
| Social Class | | |
| Lower class | 69 | 7.1 |
| Working class | 324 | 33.3 |
| Middle class | 429 | 44.1 |
| Upper middle class | 145 | 14.9 |
| Upper class | 6 | 0.6 |

TABLE 3.1 *(cont.)*

| | n | % |
|---|---|---|
| Education Level | | |
| Less than high school | 7 | 0.7 |
| Some high school | 9 | 0.9 |
| High school graduate | 93 | 9.6 |
| Trade or vocational school | 31 | 3.2 |
| Some college | 237 | 24.4 |
| 2-year college graduate | 75 | 7.7 |
| 4-year college graduate | 334 | 34.3 |
| Master's or professional degree graduate | 144 | 14.8 |
| Doctoral degree graduate | 43 | 4.4 |

## MEASURES

### Critical Consciousness

Critical consciousness was measured using the Short Critical Consciousness Scale (CCS-S), a validated 14-item instrument assessing the three dimensions of critical consciousness (Rapa, Bolding, et al., 2020a). Like the original CCS (Diemer et al., 2017), the CCS-S measures critical reflection's two subcomponents: (1) perceived inequality and (2) egalitarianism; it also measures critical motivation (Rapa, Diemer, et al., 2020) and critical action. The initial validation of the CCS-S was carried out with a youth sample, so we were especially interested to see how the instrument would assess critical consciousness among adults. We expected the scale to function well based on recent research with college-aged adults that measured critical consciousness using a similar instrument (Maker Castro et al., 2021).

**Critical Reflection: Perceived Inequality.** The CCS-S scale measuring critical reflection: perceived inequality consisted of three items that assess awareness of inequity across ethnic/racial, class, and gender lines. Items were answered on a 6-point Likert-type scale (1 = *Strongly Disagree*, 6 = *Strongly Agree*). A sample item for the critical reflection: perceived inequality scale is "Certain racial or ethnic groups have fewer chances to get ahead." Internal consistency for the scale was high, with a Cronbach's alpha of 0.90 and a mean inter-item correlation of 0.76. Across items, average critical reflection: perceived inequality reflected high endorsement ($M$ = 4.56, $SD$ = 0.33).

**Critical Reflection: Egalitarianism.** The scale for critical reflection: egalitarianism consisted of three items measuring beliefs about group equality. Items were answered on a 6-point Likert-type scale (1 = *Strongly Disagree*, 6 = *Strongly Agree*). A sample item for critical reflection: egalitarianism is "It would be good if groups could be equal." Internal consistency for the scale was high, with a Cronbach's alpha of 0.82 and a mean inter-item correlation of 0.62. Across items, average critical reflection: egalitarianism reflected very high endorsement ($M$ = 5.21, $SD$ = 0.22).

**Critical Motivation.** The scale for critical motivation consisted of four items assessing commitment to and interest in bringing about change to society, in order to correct systems of marginalization and oppression. Items were answered on a 6-point Likert-type scale (1 = *Strongly Disagree*, 6 = *Strongly Agree*). A sample item for critical motivation is "It is important to correct social and economic inequality." Internal consistency for the scale was high, with a Cronbach's alpha of 0.81 and a mean inter-item correlation of 0.52. Across items, average critical motivation reflected high endorsement ($M$ = 4.72, $SD$ = 0.23).

**Critical Action.** The scale for critical action consisted of four items assessing the frequency of participation during the last year in activities centered on promoting social change and correcting inequities across ethnic/racial, gender, and social class lines. Items were answered on a 5-point Likert-type scale (1 = *Never Did This*, 5 = *At Least Once a Week*). A sample item for critical action is "In the last year, how often have you participated in a civil rights group or organization." Internal consistency for the scale was high, with a Cronbach's alpha of 0.82 and a mean inter-item correlation of 0.55. Across items, average critical action was relatively infrequent ($M$ = 1.53, $SD$ = 0.16).

## Social Empathy

Social empathy was assessed as a composite variable using the 40-item Social Empathy Index (Segal et al., 2017; see also Segal et al., 2012). The Social Empathy Index is composed of 22 items that measure interpersonal empathy vis-à-vis each of its component parts – affective mentalizing, self–other awareness, emotion regulation, and perspective-taking – and 18 items that measure the two other components of social empathy: contextual understanding of systemic barriers and macro self–other awareness and perspective-taking. All items were answered on a 6-point Likert-type scale (1 = *Never*, 6 = *Always*). While upwardly biased due to the number of items in the scale (Streiner, 2003), the internal consistency was high, with a Cronbach's alpha of 0.92. The mean inter-item correlation was 0.23. Across items, average social empathy, as measured by the complete Social Empathy Index, reflected high endorsement ($M$ = 4.50, $SD$ = 0.45).

### Covariates

Given the potential association between a respondent's gender, ethnic/racial identification, social class, and age and critical consciousness, these sociodemographic characteristics were used as covariates in all applicable analyses.

## ANALYTIC STRATEGY

Analyses were conducted in either SPSS 24 (IBM Corp., 2016) or M*plus* 8.6 (Muthén & Muthén, 1998–2021). After using SPSS to perform descriptive analyses, we used M*plus* to carry out structural equation modeling. Confirmatory factor analyses were conducted to verify that critical consciousness and social empathy were adequately measured in the study sample. Then, structural equation modeling was utilized to examine associations among critical consciousness dimensions and to test the moderating effects of social empathy on the relation between critical reflection: perceived inequality and critical motivation.

We identified structural equation modelling (SEM) as our preferred analytic approach because of its affordances in testing relations among constructs simultaneously, while adjusting for measurement error, and also because of its utility in assessing how complex models fit sample data (Kline, 2016). As we have done elsewhere (Rapa, Bolding, et al., 2020a, 2020b), we used the MLR estimator in order to provide maximum likelihood parameter estimates robust to non-normality. Across sociodemographic and measure indicators, missing data were minimal due to the predominant use of forced choice methodology within Qualtrics (cf. Maker Castro et al., 2021). Notwithstanding, analyses relied on full information maximum likelihood (FIML) methods and used all existing data, as opposed to excluding cases listwise or pairwise, thus avoiding loss of statistical power (Enders, 2010).

## RESULTS

Given that the CCS-S had not previously been utilized with a large-scale sample of adults, we used confirmatory factor analysis (CFA) to verify that a measurement model including critical reflection: perceived inequality, critical reflection: egalitarianism, critical motivation, and critical action well fit the sample data. We used a combination of fit indices to assess model fit, including root mean square error of approximation (RMSEA), comparative fit index (CFI), Tucker-Lewis Index (TLI), and standardized root mean square residual (SRMR). RMSEA values less than or equal to 0.05 reflect very good fit, while those less than 0.08 are good (Hu & Bentler, 1998; Kline, 2016). CFI and TLI at or above 0.95 are preferred, while those above 0.90 are good (Hu & Bentler, 1998; Kline, 2016). SRMR values less than 0.08 are also reflective of good fit (Hu & Bentler, 1999).

CFA results showed the measurement model was a decent fit, though fit indices did not meet preferred thresholds: RMSEA = 0.086 (90% CI = 0.080, 0.092), CFI = 0.901, TLI = 0.873, and SRMR = 0.062. Modification indices indicated that a few items within the critical motivation measure may have some shared error covariance, so the model was respecified to account for this. The respecified CFA results revealed improved model fit across all fit indices: RMSEA = 0.054 (90% CI = 0.047, 0.061), CFI = 0.963, TLI = 0.950, SRMR= 0.059. All indicators loaded significantly as expected onto their respective specified latent constructs.

After verifying adequate measurement model fit for the respecified measurement model, we then carried out analyses to test the structural model, assessing relations among the dimensions of critical consciousness (Model 1). In this analysis, we simultaneously regressed critical action onto critical motivation and critical motivation onto both critical reflection: perceived inequality and critical reflection: egalitarianism, controlling for all sociodemographic covariates (Figure 3.2, Panel A).[3] The correlation between the critical reflection dimensions of perceived inequality and egalitarianism was also estimated.

The structural model demonstrated good fit, as had the respecified measurement model: RMSEA = 0.059 (90% CI = 0.054, 0.065), TLI = 0.938, CFI = 0.918, SRMR = 0.056. Critical reflection: perceived inequality and critical reflection: egalitarianism were correlated ($r$ = 0.628, $p$ < 0.001). Critical reflection: perceived inequality was significantly associated with critical motivation ($\beta$ = 0.254, $p$ < 0.001), as was critical reflection: egalitarianism ($\beta$ = 0.770, $p$ < 0.001). Critical motivation was significantly associated with critical action ($\beta$ = 0.272, $p$ < 0.001).

Next, we tested the moderating effect of social empathy (Figure 3.2, Panel B) on the pathway between critical reflection: perceived inequality and critical motivation. Given the use of the Social Empathy Index as a composite, reflecting the broad construct of social empathy (Segal et al., 2017), social empathy was modeled as a single observed variable.[4] Building on Model 1, we added a pathway regressing critical motivation onto social empathy, along with the interaction of critical reflection: perceived inequality and social empathy, a variable created using the XWITH command in *Mplus*. All

3 We acknowledge this is not the only way we might have modeled relations among critical consciousness dimensions. For example, reciprocal relations could have been modeled, as could direct associations between critical reflection and critical action. We began with this configuration as it corresponds with one of the more commonly theorized sets of associations among dimensions of critical consciousness (e.g., Diemer & Rapa, 2016), yet empirical research including all three dimensions is sparse – in large part because explicit measures including all three dimensions of critical consciousness are just emerging. Future work in this area should surely explore competing models or alternate configurations.

4 As a sensitivity check, we also attempted to model social empathy as a single latent construct, loading all items from the Social Empathy Index onto it. That model failed to converge.

TABLE 3.2 AIC and BIC for Model 1 and Model 2

| | Model 1 | Model 2 |
|---|---|---|
| AIC | 34143.607 | 34043.243 |
| BIC | 34460.832 | 34370.229 |
| Sample-Size Adjusted BIC | 34254.392 | 34157.436 |

*Note.* Akaike Information Criteria = AIC; Bayesian Information Criteria = BIC.

other aspects of the analysis for this moderation model were identical to Model 1.

Fit indices are not provided within M*plus* for interaction models (i.e., moderation models) of this type, so an assessment of model fit for Model 2 could not be made using RMSEA, TLI, CFI, and SRMR. However, because the dependent variables in both Model 1 and Model 2 were identical, we could assess model fit for Model 2 using Akaike Information Criteria (AIC) and Bayesian Information Criteria (BIC). Decrements in AIC and BIC were not observed (Table 3.2), suggesting the model fit of Model 2 was more than adequate to proceed with an assessment of model estimates and subsequent interpretation.

In Model 2, critical reflection: perceived inequality and critical reflection: egalitarianism were correlated ($r = 0.627$, $p < 0.001$). Critical reflection: perceived inequality was significantly associated with critical motivation ($\beta = 1.240$, $p < 0.001$), as was critical reflection: egalitarianism ($\beta = 0.723$, $p < 0.001$) and social empathy ($\beta = 0.222$, $p < 0.001$). Critical motivation was significantly associated with critical action ($\beta = 0.248$, $p < 0.001$). The interaction between critical reflection: perceived inequality and social empathy was also significant, but it was negatively associated with critical motivation ($\beta = -0.124$, $p < 0.001$). That is, while the effect of critical reflection: perceived inequality on critical motivation itself was significant and positive (i.e., a 1-unit change in critical reflection: perceived inequality was associated with a 1.24-unit change in critical motivation), the magnitude of that effect was lessened in the face of increasing social empathy (see Table 3.3).

## DISCUSSION

In this chapter, we set out to present a framework integrating critical consciousness and social empathy and to present results from an exploratory study testing the integrated framework with data drawn from a US national adult sample, a relatively understudied group in contemporary critical consciousness scholarship and, arguably – considering the sociodemographic characteristics of study participants (Table 3.1) – a group holding relatively

TABLE 3.3 Overview of structural model paths

| | Model 1 | Model 2 |
|---|---|---|
| CR: PI → CM | $\beta = 0.254^{*}$ (.05) | $\beta = 1.240^{*}$ (.26) |
| CR: E → CM | $\beta = 0.770^{*}$ (.04) | $\beta = 0.723^{*}$ (.05) |
| CM → CA | $\beta = 0.272^{*}$ (.03) | $\beta = 0.248^{*}$ (.03) |
| SE → CM | - | $\beta = 0.222^{*}$ (.04) |
| CR: PI x SE → CM | - | $\beta = -0.124^{*}$ (.03) |

Note. Critical reflection: perceived inequality = CR: PI; critical reflection: egalitarianism = CR: E; critical motivation = CM; critical action = CA; social empathy (observed composite) = SE. Beta is the standardized estimate; the standard error of the estimate is reported in parentheses.
$^{*}p < 0.001$.

more privilege compared to samples typically examined in critical consciousness scholarship. That is, in our study, participants were predominantly white, predominantly middle or upper class, and mostly well educated. We wanted to determine if critical consciousness could be assessed among this population using the CCS-S (Rapa, Bolding, et al., 2020a) and, if so, to explore associations among critical consciousness dimensions. As a first step in testing our integrated framework, we also wanted to examine the extent to which social empathy might moderate the effects of critical reflection: perceived inequality on critical motivation, focusing on this pathway in particular because of the shared focus between critical consciousness and social empathy on the critical analysis of systemic and structural inequities contributing to marginalization and oppression – that is, because of the presumed correspondence between critical reflection and certain aspects of social empathy.

While critical consciousness research has been rapidly expanding in recent years (Heberle et al., 2020), instrumentation that incorporates all three dimensions of critical consciousness is just emerging (Diemer et al., 2022; Rapa, Bolding, et al., 2020a) and research that examines critical consciousness among adults – including relatively more privileged adults – is fairly scant (Heberle et al., 2020; Rapa & Geldhof, 2020). Results suggested that critical consciousness can be well measured in adults, including adults with relatively more privilege (or, at least, among adults exhibiting certain kinds of privilege, e.g., in terms of ethnic/racial, educational, and social class positioning). The results of this exploratory study suggested that critical consciousness manifested predictably within this group of adults, based on extant empirical evidence and in line with contemporary critical consciousness theory (Watts et al., 2011). In particular, critical reflection – in terms of both its perceived inequality and egalitarianism subdimensions – was significantly associated with critical motivation, and critical motivation was in turn significantly associated with critical action. These results correspond with what we would expect about associations between critical consciousness dimensions, and they provide evidence in support of the hypothesized linkages that comprise critical reflection–motivation–action praxis (i.e., reflection predicts motivation and motivation predicts action).[5] In our exploratory study, we modeled critical consciousness among adults using the CCS-S (Rapa, Bolding, et al., 2020a), and we found predicable associations among critical consciousness's reflection, motivation, and action dimensions. In this way, this study adds to the evidence base demonstrating that these dimensions of critical consciousness are linked. Future research should examine these associations longitudinally, over time, in order to assess temporal ordering among dimensions and/or establish more clear evidence about causal associations – though we would expect reciprocal relations to emerge among adults as well, just as they have among youth (Heberle et al., 2020). Future research should also examine these associations with other populations, including youth and individuals who may experience relatively more marginalization.

The results of our exploratory work also suggested that associations among dimensions of critical consciousness may be augmented by social empathy – or at least the critical reflection: perceived inequality and critical motivation link, as examined here. As seen in Model 2, when accounting for social empathy as a composite variable, social empathy was significantly and positively associated with critical motivation ($\beta = 0.222$, $p < 0.001$), even as the association between critical reflection: perceived inequality and critical motivation was tempered by it. Higher levels of social empathy predicted higher levels of critical motivation, suggesting that if one's capacity for social empathy is high (or is perhaps developing), then one's motivation to address societal inequities may also be enhanced.

Additionally, the interaction between critical reflection: perceived inequality and social empathy was significant, and that interaction was negatively associated with critical motivation. In effect, social empathy moderated the effect of critical reflection: perceived inequality on critical motivation, attenuating its effect ($\beta = -0.124$, $p < 0.001$). Said differently, the magnitude of the effect of critical reflection: perceived inequality was lessened when levels of social empathy were greater. We suspect this may be the case due to the complementary but distinct nature of certain aspects of social empathy, as measured by the Social Empathy Index – specifically, how the index probes contextual understanding of systemic barriers faced by marginalized and oppressed groups. Future scholarship in this area should consider assessment

[5] Of course, the data analyzed in our exploratory study were cross-sectional in nature, so we do not intend to make definitive claims about the temporal ordering of constructs and/or imply sure causality here. Even so, because instruments that include all three dimensions of critical consciousness are just emerging, this finding is noteworthy.

and further analysis of this aspect of social empathy more particularly, in order to consider how it converges and diverges from critical reflection as measured by the CCS-S. This may help elucidate further the attenuating effects observed here.

Nevertheless, social empathy appears to shape at least some critical reflection–motivation–action associations. As noted, the emphasis within social empathy instrumentation on assessing institutionalized and systemic sociopolitical and sociohistorical realities contributing to marginalization and oppression – while aligned with critical reflection and reflective of the kind of social analysis that critical consciousness entails – has not been realized in measures of critical consciousness (e.g., Diemer et al., 2017, 2022; McWhirter & McWhirter, 2016; Rapa, Bolding, et al., 2020a). Until further research addresses how this dimension of social empathy converges or diverges from critical reflection, because of the additional nuance the Social Empathy Index provides about individuals' thinking about contextual barriers, measuring social empathy alongside critical consciousness may help to generate new insights into how critical reflection–motivation–action dimensions interrelate and function together – both within a given developmental context, at a particular point in time, and longitudinally over time. Such links may be especially relevant for those experiencing relative privilege, like those within our sample. Future work should consider assessing the moderating role of social empathy on the critical reflection: perceived inequality to critical motivation pathway for other populations, including youth and those presumably experiencing relatively more marginalization. Doing so would perhaps provide even more insight into how social empathy may attenuate (or enhance) relations between critical consciousness dimensions, for whom, and under what conditions.

Due to space constraints, in this chapter we could not explore all the potential effects of social empathy (or its component parts) on critical consciousness that our integrated framework suggests as plausible (Figure 3.1). Instead, we carried out just one set of preliminary analyses regarding just one aspect of the role social empathy may play in shaping conscientization among a sample of US adults. We did this both to establish preliminary evidence for the viability of our integrated critical consciousness–social empathy framework and to lay the groundwork for future empirical work in this area. As introduced earlier, we also focused our work in this way because: (1) there has been limited research using validated critical consciousness instruments with adults and we do not understand fully how critical consciousness manifests in adulthood; (2) more research is needed to examine associations among critical consciousness dimensions using measures that capture all of its dimensions; and (3) research has not yet examined critical consciousness and social empathy together.

Future work should consider exploring other aspects of the integrated critical consciousness–social empathy framework that we have advanced here. For example, researchers might consider examining how ingroup/outgroup status shapes associations between or among critical consciousness, social empathy, and their respective dimensions. Researchers might also consider, in more particular terms, examining the extent to which one's status as relatively more marginalized versus relatively less marginalized (within a given context) shapes these associations. Indeed, as discussed earlier, based on the extent to which social empathy explicitly implies empathic responses to outgroups and outgroup members, it may be an especially poignant mechanism in support of the development and deployment of critical consciousness among those experiencing relative privilege.

Researchers might also consider how specific opportunity structures shape the development and operation of critical consciousness and social empathy, among both youth and adults. Additionally, future work might interrogate more specifically the moderating role of social empathy subdimensions – including contextual understanding of systemic barriers, as that aspect of social empathy is particularly well aligned with critical reflection: perceived inequality – on the associations between critical consciousness dimensions. Other directions are worthy of pursuit as well, and we invite others to consider how this framework may be taken up, adapted, or extended through additional inquiry.

In terms of practice, those working in applied settings (e.g., P-12 schools, postsecondary institutions, youth development programs, or clinical social work or clinical mental health settings) could benefit from considering how social empathy might develop alongside critical consciousness. Pedagogical models for teaching social empathy have been proposed, and these could be adapted or extended to support more explicitly the development of critical consciousness along with social empathy (see Gerdes et al., 2011; Segal et al., 2011). For example, Segal (2011) describes the development of social empathy via a three-stage model that includes exposure, explanation, and experience; this approach could be applied to and tested for efficacy with programming or interventions explicitly designed to develop critical consciousness along with social empathy (cf. Segal & Wagaman, 2017).

## LIMITATIONS

As with any empirical research, our exploratory study was not without limitations. We have already noted the constraints of our data as cross-sectional and we have encouraged researchers working in this area in the future to consider collecting critical consciousness and social empathy data longitudinally in order to be able to account better for the temporal ordering of construct relations and associations over time. This might help elucidate more clearly whether and how social empathy and critical consciousness codevelop, and for whom, and the extent to which social empathy or its component parts may operate in tandem with critical consciousness and critical reflection–motivation–action praxis processes.

Our study was also limited due to the sample and sampling procedures utilized for this work. While we recruited a US adult sample for this study, using Prolific for sample recruitment – even though drawing on their national sample as a way to maximize the credibility of results – means that findings from this study may not generalize to the US adult population as a whole, or to other populations such as youth. Future research should be carried out to determine the extent to which study results manifesting here replicate to other samples or using data collected by other means.

It is also likely that our findings were shaped by the sociocultural, sociopolitical, and sociohistorical context or the moment in which these data were collected. Study data were collected from US residents in November 2021, against the backdrop of the "dual pandemics" of COVID-19 and systemic racism (e.g., Jones, 2021; Yeh et al., 2022). It is conceivable that data collected on critical consciousness and social empathy in November 2021 reflected heightened sensitivity to and awareness of racial (and other forms of societal) injustice, given what was happening across the nation and throughout the world at that time. It may be useful to collect data from a comparable sample, at a different point in time, in order to ascertain if associations between critical consciousness and social empathy manifest similarly under different sociocultural, sociopolitical, and sociohistorical contexts than those present when the data for this study were initially collected.

## CONCLUSION

In this chapter, we briefly introduced critical consciousness and social empathy frameworks, both of which focus on understanding and addressing inequitable societal conditions, structural disparities, marginalization, and oppression. We then presented an integrated framework that brings critical consciousness and social empathy together. After introducing the integrated critical consciousness–social empathy framework, we presented results from an exploratory study testing the framework with data drawn from a US national adult sample.

Study results revealed that social empathy moderated associations between critical reflection: perceived inequality and critical motivation, providing preliminary evidence that it may be useful to consider social empathy alongside critical consciousness. We also considered some implications of our work for research and practice, viewing the integrated critical consciousness–social empathy framework as useful to guide further research in this area and support additional inquiry into whether and how critical consciousness and social empathy may develop and operate to help individuals understand, contend with, and redress inequitable societal conditions. We hope this framework is useful in suggesting new lines of inquiry and providing new avenues for researchers and practitioners to promote more just and equitable conditions that lead to liberation for all.

## REFERENCES

Allemand, M., Steiger, A. E., & Fend, H. A. (2015). Empathy development in adolescence predicts social competencies in adulthood. *Journal of Personality*, *83*(2), 229–241. https://doi.org/10.1111/jopy.12098.

Bañales, J., Mathews, C., Hayat, N., Anyiwo, N., & Diemer, M. A. (2020). Latinx and Black young adults' pathways to civic/political engagement. *Cultural Diversity and Ethnic Minority Psychology*, *26*(2), 176–188. http://doi.org/10.1037/cdp0000271.

Bolding, C. W., & Ogle, J. H., & Rapa, L. J. (2021, July). Exploring undergraduate civil engineering students' perceptions of infrastructure inequities: A pilot study. Paper presented at 2021 ASEE Virtual Annual Conference Content Access, Virtual Conference. https://peer.asee.org/37166.

Brown, C. S., Mistry, R. S., & Yip, T. (2019). Moving from the margins to the mainstream: Equity and justice as key considerations for developmental science. *Child Development Perspectives*, *13*(4), 235–240. https://doi.org/10.1111/cdep.12340.

Burson, E., & Godfrey, E. B. (2020). Intraminority solidarity: The role of critical consciousness. *European Journal of Social Psychology*, *50*, 1362–1377. https://doi.org/10.1002/ejsp.2679.

Causadias, J. M., & Umaña-Taylor, A. J. (2018). Reframing marginalization and youth development: Introduction to the special issue. *American Psychologist*, *73*(6), 707–712. https://doi.org/10.1037/amp0000336.

Clark, S., & Seider, S. (2017). Developing critical curiosity in adolescents. *Equity & Excellence in Education*, *50*(2), 125–141.

Collins, P. H. (1993). Toward a new vision: Race, class, and gender as categories of analysis and connection. *Race, Sex, & Class*, *1*(1), 25–45.

Combahee River Collective. (1977/2014). A Black feminist statement. *Women's Studies Quarterly*, *42*, 271–280.

Coston, B. M., & Kimmel, M. S. (2012). Seeing privilege where it isn't: Marginalized masculinities and the intersectionality of privilege. *Journal of Social Issues*, *68*(1), 97–111. https://doi.org/10.1111/j.1540-4560.2011.01738.x.

Crenshaw, K. (1989). Demarginalizing the intersection of race and sex: A Black feminist critique of antidiscrimination doctrine, feminist theory and antiracist politics. *University of Chicago Legal Forum*, *140*(1), 139–167. http://chicagounbound.uchicago.edu/uclf/vol1989/iss1/8.

Diemer, M. A. (2020). Pushing the envelope: The who, what, when, and why of critical consciousness. *Journal of Applied Developmental Psychology*, *70*, 101192. https://doi.org/10.1016/j.appdev.2020.101192.

Diemer, M. A., & Blustein, D. L. (2006). Critical consciousness and career development among urban youth. *Journal of Vocational Behavior*, *68*(2), 220–232.

Diemer, M. A., Frisby, M. B., Pinedo, A. et al. (2022). Development of the Short Critical Consciousness Scale (ShoCCS). *Applied Developmental Science, 26*(3), 409–425. https://doi.org/10.1080/10888691.2020.1834394.

Diemer, M. A., McWhirter, E., Ozer, E., & Rapa, L. J. (2015). Advances in the conceptualization and measurement of critical consciousness. *The Urban Review, 47*, 809–823. https://doi.org/10.1007/s11256-015-0336-7.

Diemer, M. A., Pinedo, A., Bañales, J. et al. (2021). Recentering action in critical consciousness. *Child Development Perspectives, 15*(1), 12–17. https://doi.org/10.1111/cdep.12393.

Diemer, M. A., & Rapa, L. J. (2016). Unraveling the complexity of critical consciousness, political efficacy, and political action among marginalized adolescents. *Child Development, 87*, 221–238. https://doi.org/10.1111/cdev.12446.

Diemer, M. A., Rapa, L. J., Park, C. J., & Perry, J. C. (2017). Development and validation of the Critical Consciousness Scale. *Youth & Society, 49*(4), 461–483. https://doi.org/10.1177/0044118X14538289.

Diemer, M. A., Rapa, L. J., Voight, A. M., & McWhirter, E. H. (2016). Critical consciousness: A developmental approach to addressing marginalization and oppression. *Child Development Perspectives, 10*(4), 216–221. https://doi.org/10.1111/cdep.12193.

Enders, C. (2010). *Applied missing data analysis*. Guilford Press.

Freire, P. (1973). *Education for critical consciousness*. Continuum.

Freire, P. (1968/2000). *Pedagogy of the oppressed*. Continuum.

Gerdes, K. E., & Segal, E. A. (2009). A social work model of empathy. *Advances in Social Work, 10*(2), 114–127.

Gerdes, K. E., Segal, E. A., Jackson, K. F., & Mullins, J. L. (2011). Teaching empathy: A framework rooted in social cognitive neuroscience and social justice. *Journal of Social Work Education, 47*(1), 109–131. https://doi.org/10.5175/JSWE.2011.200900085.

Godfrey, E. B., & Burson, E. (2018). Interrogating the intersections: How intersectional perspectives can inform developmental scholarship on critical consciousness. In C. E. Santos & R. B. Toomey (Eds.), *Envisioning the Integration of an Intersectional Lens in Developmental Science. New Directions for Child and Adolescent Development, 161*, 17–38. https://doi.org/10.1002/cad.20246.

Godfrey, E. B., Burson, E. L., Yanisch, T. M., Hughes, D., & Way, N. (2019). A bitter pill to swallow? Patterns of critical consciousness and socioemotional and academic well-being in early adolescence. *Developmental Psychology, 55*(3), 525–537. https://doi.org/10.1037/dev0000558.

Heberle, A. E., Rapa, L. J., & Faragó, F. (2020). Critical consciousness in children and adolescents: A systematic review, critical assessment, and recommendations for future research. *Psychological Bulletin, 146*(6), 525–551. https://doi.org/10.1037/bul0000230.

Hu, L., & Bentler, P. M. (1998). Fit indices in covariance structure modeling: Sensitivity to underparameterized model misspecification. *Psychological Methods, 3*, 424–453.

Hu, L., & Bentler, P. M. (1999). Cutoff criteria for fit indexes in covariance structure analysis: Conventional criteria versus new alternatives. *Structural Equation Modeling, 6*, 1–55.

IBM Corp. (2016). *IBM SPSS Statistics for Windows, Version 24.0*. Armonk, NY: IBM Corp.

Ibrahim, D., Nalani, A., & Godfrey, E. B. (in press). Breaking down the arts: A novel exploration of how varying kinds of arts participation relate to critical consciousness among youth of color. In E. B. Godfrey & L. J. Rapa (Eds.), *Developing Critical Consciousness in Youth: Contexts and Settings*. Cambridge University Press.

Jemal, A. (2017). Critical consciousness: A critique and critical analysis of the literature. *The Urban Review*, *49*, 602–626. https://doi.org/10.1007/s11256-017-0411-3.

Jones, J. M. (2021). The dual pandemics of COVID-19 and systemic racism: Navigating our path forward. *School Psychology*, *36*(5), 427–431. https://doi.org/10.1037/spq0000472.

Junker, R. J., and Jacquemin, S. J. (2017). How does literature affect empathy in students? *College Teaching*, *65*(2), 79–87. https://doi.org/10.1080/87567555.2016.1255583.

Keefe, T. (1980). Empathy skill and critical consciousness. *Social Casework: The Journal of Contemporary Social Work*, *61*(7), 387–393.

Kimmel, M. S., & Ferber, A. L. (2018). *Privilege: A reader* (4th ed.) New York: Routledge.

Kline, R. B. (2016). *Principles and practice of structural equation modeling: Methodology in the social sciences* (4th ed.). New York: Guilford Press.

Lee, Y., Muennig, P., Kawachi, I., & Hatzenbuehler, M. L. (2015). Effects of racial prejudice on the health of communities: A multilevel survival analysis. *American Journal of Public Health*, *105*(11), 2349–2355. https://doi.org/10.2105/AJPH.2015.302776.

Maker Castro, E., Dull, B., Hoyt, L. T., & Cohen, A. K. (2021). Associations between critical consciousness and well-being in a national sample of college students during the COVID-19 pandemic. *Journal of Community Psychology*. Advanced online publication. https://doi.org/10.1002/jcop.22678.

Maker Castro, E., Wray-Lake, L., & Cohen, A. K. (2022). Critical consciousness and wellbeing in adolescents and young adults: A systematic review. *Adolescent Research Review*. Advanced online publication. https://doi.org/10.1007/s40894-022-00188-3.

Maxwell, B., & DesRoches, S. (2010). Empathy and social-emotional learning: Pitfalls and touchstones for school-based programs. *New Directions for Child and Adolescent Development*, 2010(129), 33–53. https://doi.org/10.1002/cd.274.

McWhirter, E. H., & McWhirter, B. T. (2016). Critical consciousness and vocational development among Latina/o high school youth: Initial development and testing of a measure. *Journal of Career Assessment*, *24*(3), 543–558. https://doi.org/10.1177/1069072715599535.

Muthén, L. K., & Muthén, B. O. (1998–2021). *Mplus user's guide*. (8th ed.). [published by author].

Rapa, L. J., Bolding, C. W., & Jamil, F. M. (2020a). Development and initial validation of the Short Critical Consciousness Scale (CCS-S). *Journal of Applied Developmental Psychology*, *70*, 101164. https://doi.org/10.1016/j.appdev.2020.101164.

Rapa, L. J., Bolding, C. W., & Jamil, F. M. (2020b). (Re)Examining the effects of open classroom climate on the critical consciousness of preadolescent and adolescent youth. *Applied Developmental Science, 26*(3), 471–487. https://doi.org/10.1080/10888691.2020.1861946.

Rapa, L. J., Diemer, M. A., & Bañales, J. (2018). Critical action as a pathway to social mobility among marginalized youth. *Developmental Psychology, 54*(1), 127–137. https://doi.org/10.1037/dev0000414.

Rapa, L. J., Diemer, M. A., & Roseth, C. J. (2020). Can a values-affirmation intervention bolster academic achievement and raise critical consciousness? Results from a small-scale field experiment. *Social Psychology of Education, 23*(2), 537–557. https://doi/org/10.1007/s11218-020-09546-2.

Rapa, L. J., & Geldhof, G. J. (2020). Critical consciousness: New directions for understanding its development during adolescence. *Journal of Applied Developmental Psychology, 70*, 101187. https://doi.org/10.1016/j.appdev.2020.101187.

Rios, F., Trent, A., & Castañeda, L. V. (2003). Social perspective taking: Advancing empathy and advocating justice. *Equity & Excellence in Education, 36*(1), 5–14. https://doi.org/10.1080/10665680303506.

Ruck, M. D., Mistry, R. S., & Flanagan, C. A. (2019). Children's and adolescents' understanding and experiences of economic inequality: An introduction to the special section. *Developmental Psychology, 55*, 449–456. https://doi.org/10.1037/dev0000694.

Segal, E. A. (2007). Social empathy: A new paradigm to address poverty. *Journal of Poverty, 11*(3), 65–81. https://doi.org/10.1300/J134v11n03_06.

Segal, E. A. (2011). Social empathy: A model built on empathy, contextual understanding, and social responsibility that promotes social justice. *Journal of Social Service Research, 37*(3), 266–277. https://doi.org/10.1080/01488376.2011.564040

Segal, E. A., Gerdes, K. E., Lietz, C. A., Wagaman, M. A., & Geiger, J. M. (2017). *Assessing empathy*. New York: Columbia University Press.

Segal, E. A., & Wagaman, M. A. (2017). Social empathy as a framework for teaching social justice. *Journal of Social Work Education, 53*(2), 201–211. https://doi.org/10.1080/10437797.2016.1266980.

Segal, E. A., Wagaman, M. A., & Gerdes, K. E. (2012). Developing the Social Empathy Index: An exploratory factor analysis. *Advances in Social Work, 13*(3), 541–560. https://doi.org/10.18060/2042.

Seider, S., Clark, S., & Graves, D. (2020). The development of critical consciousness and its relation to academic achievement in adolescents of color. *Child Development, 91*(2), e451–e474. https://doi.org/10.1111/cdev.13262.

Shin, R. Q., Ezeofor, I., Smith, L. C., Welch, J. C., & Goodrich, K. M. (2016). The development and validation of the contemporary critical consciousness measure. *Journal of Counseling Psychology, 63*, 210–223. https://doi.org/10.1037/cou0000137.

Shin, R. Q., Smith, L. C., Lu, Y. et al. (2018). The development and validation of the contemporary critical consciousness measure II. *Journal of Counseling Psychology, 65*, 539–555. https://doi.org/10.1037/cou0000302.

Shiner, R. L., & Masten, A. S. (2012). Childhood personality as a harbinger of competence and resilience in adulthood. *Development and Psychopathology*, 24(2), 507–528. https://doi.org/10.1017/S0954579412000120.

Silke, C., Brady, B., Boylan, C., & Dolan, P. (2018). Factors influencing the development of empathy and pro-social behaviour among adolescents: A systematic review. *Children and Youth Services Review*, *94*, 421–436. https://doi.org/10.1016/j.childyouth.2018.07.027.

Streiner, D. L. (2003). Starting at the beginning: An introduction to coefficient alpha and internal consistency. *Journal of Personality Assessment*, *80*, 99–103.

Szanto, T., & Krueger, J. (2019). Introduction: Empathy, shared emotions, and social identity. *Topoi*, *38*(1), 153–162. https://doi.org/10.1007/s11245-019-09641-w.

Tyler, C. P., Olsen, S. G., Geldhof, G. J., & Bowers, E. P. (2020). Critical consciousness in late adolescence: Understanding if, how, and why youth act. *Journal of Applied Developmental Psychology*, *70*, 101165. https://doi.org/10.1016/j.appdev.2020.101165.

Wagaman, M. A. (2011). Social empathy as a framework for adolescent empowerment. *Journal of Social Service Research*, *37*(3), 278–293. https://doi.org/10.1080/01488376.2011.564045.

Watts, R. J., Diemer, M. A., & Voight, A. M. (2011). Critical consciousness: Current status and future directions. In C. A. Flanagan & B. D. Christens (Eds.), *Youth civic development: Work at the cutting edge. New Directions for Child and Adolescent Development*, *134*, 43–57. https://doi.org/10.1002/cd.310.

Watts, R. J., & Flanagan, C. (2007). Pushing the envelope on youth civic engagement: A developmental and liberation psychology perspective. *Journal of Community Psychology*, *35*(6), 779–792. https://doi.org/10.1002/jcop.20178.

Watts, R. J., Griffith, D. M., & Abdul-Adil, J. (1999). Sociopolitical development as an antidote for oppression – theory and action. *American Journal of Community Psychology*, *27*, 255–271. https://doi.org/10.1023/A:1022839818873.

Watts, R. J., & Hipolito-Delgado, C. (2015). Thinking ourselves to liberation? Advancing sociopolitical action in critical consciousness. *The Urban Review*, *47*, 847–867. https://doi.org/10.1007/s11256-015-0341-x.

Watts, R. J., Williams, N. C., & Jagers, R. J. (2003). Sociopolitical development. *American Journal of Community Psychology*, *31*, 185–194. https://doi.org/10.1023/A:1023091024140.

Yeh, C. J., Stanley, S., Ramirez, C. A., & Borrero, N. E. (2022). Navigating the "dual pandemics": The cumulative impact of the COVID-19 pandemic and rise in awareness of racial injustices among high school students of color in urban schools. *Urban Education*. Advanced online publication. https://doi.org/10.1177/00420859221097884.

# 4

# Critical Consciousness in Early to Middle Childhood

AMY E. HEBERLE, FLÓRA FARAGÓ, AND NOAH HOCH

In recent years, developmental scholars have shown an increasing interest in the impacts of structural oppression, including racism, capitalistic oppression, and patriarchy, on the psychological functioning of children and families. Increased attention is being paid to how children, families, and communities resist oppressive systems, pursue personal and collective thriving, and, in some cases, make systems more just. In this vein, researchers have begun to attend to the role children play as agents of change for social justice and the impacts that social justice knowledge and action have on children's development. In the current chapter, we focus on critical consciousness (CC) in an understudied population: children in early to middle childhood, or those between the ages of three and eleven. Throughout the chapter, we refer to this population as "preadolescents," and we give particular attention to children in the younger two-thirds of our age distribution – those we consider to be "young children" or in "early childhood" (approximately ages 3–8), which can be broken down further into "preschool-aged" (approximately ages 3–5) and "early-school-aged" (approximately ages 6–8) – as we consider this group to be especially underrepresented in the larger literature. We also give attention to middle childhood (approximately ages 9–11). We emphasize how CC – defined as seeing and understanding oppressive systems (critical reflection), feeling motivated and efficacious in resisting oppressive systems (critical motivation), and engaging in individual or collective action against oppressive systems (critical action) – may contribute to individual and family thriving prior to adolescence and how systems change could occur through fostering CC in young children.

One hallmark of oppressive systems is their replication from one generation to the next, including through family socialization, educational experiences, cultural socialization, and other societal and structural forces. A robust literature documents how residential and educational segregation; power hierarchies based on class, race, and gender; cultural norms of silence regarding racial and class disparities; and other structural forces create the conditions in which oppressive systems are sustained and taught to children (Kendi, 2019; Roberts & Rizzo, 2020; Shedd, 2015). Importantly, this is not an exhaustive list of the oppressive and privileging forces that shape children's experiences; xenophobia, cis-sexism, transphobia and homophobia, hetero-sexism, and other systems are also relevant though are not discussed in-depth in this chapter. Further, scholarship on children's awareness of race, gender, and social class; ingroup and outgroup biases; and stereotyping provide evidence of how effectively the ideologies that uphold oppressive systems are socialized at early ages (e.g., Heberle & Carter, 2015; Martin & Ruble, 2010; Quintana, 1998, 2008). Thus, the premise of this chapter is that developing CC in early to middle childhood is *necessary* for building a more just society, dismantling oppressive systems, and supporting thriving for all children. We argue that preadolescence is a uniquely important time to study CC given the degree to which preadolescent children's lives are controlled and constrained by adults and formal institutions (see Heberle et al., 2020a for further discussion of this topic) and the extent to which foundational ontological, epistemological, and moral beliefs are socialized in early to middle childhood.

Oppressive socialization does not wait for the moment when children reach adolescence, therefore *anti*oppressive socialization cannot wait either. Our goal is to outline the forms that CC may take in childhood to guide future research on CC in the preadolescent period and to provide evidence for our assertion that young children have the competencies to begin seeing social systems, recognizing the inequalities within them, and taking on a role in building more just systems. We contend that the sociopolitical and civic dimensions of early to middle childhood development – for example, the ways in which children develop their beliefs and practices related to politics, engagement in community and institutional spaces, justice, and participation in society – have been understudied and that the near-exclusive focus on adolescence in the sociopolitical development literature overlooks that adolescent beliefs and actions rest on foundations formed as early as preschool. We understand CC as an element of sociopolitical and civic development that centers understanding and resistance of oppressive systems. In addition, we show that the structural emphasis of the CC literature and other literatures that inform CC scholarship (e.g., work on critical race theory and intersectionality) adds much-needed context to the study of bias and stereotyping in early childhood.

We begin with a statement regarding the theories that inform our thinking in this chapter. Next, we review the literatures on young children's awareness and understanding of social groups and social systems, including evidence for the early socialization of children into systems of racism, classism, and patriarchy, among other oppressive systems. Then, we review the small literature that has examined CC in children, highlight key findings from work with older youth, and review models of CC development that may transfer to young children. The final section of the chapter offers a road map for CC research and CC-promotive praxis with young children.

## STATEMENT OF THEORY

Several major theories shape the work of this chapter; these include ecological systems theory, critical race theory (CRT), critical whiteness studies (CWS), and intersectionality. We utilize these frameworks to guide and deepen our thinking about the form and function of CC in preadolescents.

The central assumption of ecological systems theory (Bronfenbrenner, 1979) is that individuals are shaped by forces that exist at multiple levels of the social environment, including family and personal relationships, neighborhoods and communities, local institutions, and broad cultural and political influences. Thus, children are shaped by interactions with their parents, peers, neighbors, and schools, as well as by government policies and practices and cultural values. These various individuals and institutions also shape one another, and children impact the people and institutions with whom they interact. The core assumptions of ecological systems theory shape our thinking about the contexts in which CC might be learned (or not), the impacts CC might have for the child and others, and the long-term implications of early CC for the institutions in which children participate.

In addition, CRT and CWS provide a lens through which we view this work (Coleman et al., 2020; Delgado & Stefancic, 2017). Critical race theorists assert that racism is foundational and normative across US institutions and US culture. Thus, racism shapes and is replicated through the various elements of the ecological system and shapes socialization across the lifespan. CWS adds an emphasis on whiteness as the system that underlies racism, enforcing a narrative in which white identities are seen as neutral and ahistorical and the impacts of whiteness and racism are therefore invisible, especially to white people (Feagin, 2013; Kendi, 2019). We, as authors of this chapter, all identify as white and are therefore susceptible to the influence of whiteness in cloaking the reality of racism from our awareness. Throughout our work on the chapter, we have attempted to counter the influence of whiteness on our thinking by educating ourselves on whiteness and racism and by challenging our assumptions about the systems we live in by exposing ourselves to counterstories. In addition, our argument in this chapter rests on several foundational assumptions of CRT, most importantly the assumption that racism shapes all aspects of life in the US and is therefore an unavoidable influence on early childhood development and socialization.

Finally, scholarship on intersectionality (Beal, 1970; Combahee River Collective, 1977/2014; hooks, 1981) guides how we think in this chapter about the influence of power operating across different systems (e.g., racism, classism, and capitalism) and institutions (e.g., schools, social services) on children's development, their socialization experiences, and their relationship to CC. Understanding CC through the lens of intersectionality draws our attention to power and privilege as forces shaping early childhood and draws us away from unidimensional analyses of identity and experience. We view CC as fundamentally about understanding power and acting to reshape power hierarchies. Throughout the chapter, we emphasize how children might learn to recognize systems of power and oppression and resist them. We focus particularly on racism, which is consistent with much of the CC literature and the assertion of CRT that racism is a foundational force shaping US society. However, we contend that CC is fundamentally domain general and can be applied to any system within which power is inequitably distributed.

In addition to these framing theories, we utilize Byrd's (2021) model of CC development to inform our hypotheses regarding preadolescent CC. We describe this model later in the chapter.

## MAJOR DEVELOPMENTAL CONSIDERATIONS ACROSS EARLY TO MIDDLE CHILDHOOD

Dramatic shifts in children's cognitive and social-emotional functioning occur between early and middle childhood, and these shifts may shape the nature of children's CC as well as the degree to which children have access to different aspects of CC. In the preschool period, for example, children make substantial leaps toward independence and often have a greater interest than infants and toddlers in other children and people outside their families. This curiosity and tendency toward exploration may combine with new cognitive skills, such as the ability to call to mind things that they cannot see, to allow children in this period to grapple with social realities that they did not previously comprehend, including realities regarding oppression. Because very young children are highly egocentric, they may connect with ideas that clearly relate to them and their present-day experiences. That being said, memory, language, and executive functioning – including the ability to organize thoughts – are often limited in this period. Thus, relatively persistent, logically organized, and nuanced knowledge of systems of oppression may come later in childhood. Critical motivation in this period may be experienced in a relatively concrete way, particularly if critical motivation is socialized as a family or classroom value. Similarly, children in this period may follow adult guidance regarding critical action in support of peers or others, or may engage in action that adults mediate. However, they are unlikely to experience critical motivation or action that they link to their own knowledge of oppressive systems or that they generate independently.

As children move into the school-age period, they typically have more contact with the outside world unmediated by caretakers, a greater capacity to reflect on themselves-in-context, greater verbal abilities, and an enhanced ability to imagine others' thoughts that may be different from their own. These capacities mean that children may be capable both of greater engagement in critical reflection and that they may have a greater capacity to link their knowledge with motivation and action. Moving into middle childhood, along with continued cognitive development, children's peer relationships begin to shift, becoming even more central to their lives even as the dynamics of these relationships become increasingly complex. The importance of peer relationships in middle childhood may mean that children have increased opportunities to experience critical motivation and to engage in critical action in relation to their peers within their school and community contexts. Their increased cognitive capacities may mean that children in middle childhood are able to link their knowledge of history to their own and others' present-day experiences of privilege and oppression. Throughout the remainder of the chapter, we highlight ways in which children's developmental competencies may relate to their CC.

## AWARENESS AND UNDERSTANDING OF SOCIAL GROUPS AND SOCIAL SYSTEMS IN PREADOLESCENT CHILDREN

In this section, we summarize the robust literature on preadolescent children's awareness and understanding of race, gender, and social class, as well as their alignment with racism, sexism, and classism. While a systematic review of these literatures is beyond the scope of the current manuscript, we highlight key findings from these literatures. This section of the chapter has two goals: (1) to challenge the notion that preadolescent children are too young to demonstrate CC by showing that they understand racialized, gendered, and classed social groups and related inequalities; and (2) to provide an empirical foundation on which to base preliminary hypotheses regarding children's CC. Importantly, as with much of the developmental literature, many of the studies reviewed draw on predominantly white, middle-class samples of children, which limits the generalizability of findings. Our use of CRT, CWS, and intersectionality to frame our own theorizing regarding preadolescent CC is an effort to redress this limitation in the literature. With these limitations in mind, two major questions guide this section:

(1) What is the evidence that preadolescent children recognize racialized, gendered, and classed social groups and inequalities?
(2) What is the evidence that preadolescent children are aware of social and community systems (e.g., the justice system, social service systems, and education systems) or political systems?

We selected these questions for their relevance to CC, which focuses on individuals' understanding of, motivation to act against, and actual action taken to redress societal inequities. Throughout this section, we use the terms of the original authors to refer to racial groups (e.g., Black versus African American). Our guiding questions for this section relate most directly to children's capacity for critical reflection, and indirectly to their capacity for critical motivation and critical action. The reasons for this are two-fold: (1) skepticism regarding preadolescent CC often focuses on children's capacity for critical reflection and less on their capacity for motivation or action; and (2) robust interest in children's social and cognitive development means that there is a great deal of literature to draw on to understand children's capacity for critical reflection, which many (though not all) scholars have argued is foundational for critical motivation or action to develop.

## EVIDENCE THAT PREADOLESCENT CHILDREN RECOGNIZE RACIALIZED, GENDERED, AND CLASSED SOCIAL GROUPS

There is a plethora of evidence that young children recognize race, gender, and other social categories and that children's perceptions of these social markers guide their preferences and attitudes about others (see Pauker et al., 2019; Quintana, 1998, 2008; Shutts, 2015). Research suggests that by age 2 children are aware of gender as a category into which people can be grouped (e.g., Martin & Ruble, 2010), and awareness of race and social class becomes apparent only slightly later (Elenbaas & Killen, 2016; Shutts et al., 2013). By 3–5 years of age, children hold rudimentary stereotypes and prejudice about race, class, and gender groups (see Cristol & Gimbert, 2008; Raabe & Beelmann, 2011; Rutland et al., 2010), and these stereotypes persist into later childhood (e.g., Heberle & Carter, 2020; Mistry et al., 2015).

Children's group-based stereotypes and prejudices have a real impact on their social lives, emotional development, and play. For example, children's peer selections reveal intergroup biases (for a review, see Skinner & Meltzoff, 2019), with children at times preferring their own gender and own race peers. Studies find that preschool-age children prefer higher socioeconomic groups and higher wealth targets compared to lower socioeconomic groups and lower wealth targets (Horowitz et al., 2014; Shutts et al., 2016). The particular nature of children's intergroup biases appears to depend on their own positionalities; for instance, 3–5-year-old Black girls are more likely to show preference based on gender than on race, while white girls of the same age are equally likely to show preference based on gender or race (Kurtz-Costes et al., 2011). In another study, though, 3–4-year-old predominantly white children relied on gender, more so than race, in deciding who to be friends with (Shutts et al., 2013). These contradictory results suggest that additional factors other than race are at play in determining young children's intergroup biases. As an example of the impact of intergroup bias on emotional development, studies have found that racial bias manifests in young white children who assume that Black people feel less pain than white people (Dore et al., 2014, 2018). Thus, racial bias may impact white children's capacity for empathy for and connection with Black children and may render relationships with white children harmful for Black children.

According to developmental intergroup theory (DIT; Arthur et al., 2008; Bigler & Liben, 2006, 2007), explicit and implicit messages about social categories such as race, in combination with environmental factors such as segregation, group labeling, numerical representation of groups, and the child's cognitive developmental level, contribute to the identification of certain social groups as salient (e.g., gender, class, and racial groups) while other groups are identified as meaningless (e.g., eye-color groups). Having identified the social groups that are meaningful in their environments, children then develop stereotypes and prejudice based on their observations of inequities between groups. DIT posits that the explicit and implicit use of visually perceptible social categories contribute to prejudice development. DIT further suggests that, in the absence of explanations, children may construct their own stereotyped beliefs to explain group segregation or other group differences (Bigler & Liben, 2006, 2007). For instance, when children observe that neighborhoods are segregated by race, they may infer that these social divisions are based on meaningful and inherent differences between groups. Therefore, *not* discussing race and racism with young children likely does more harm than explicitly addressing these topics (see Boutte et al., 2011).

## EVIDENCE THAT PREADOLESCENT CHILDREN RECOGNIZE INEQUALITIES ACROSS GROUPS

Research on children's stereotypes about groups provides indirect evidence that children are aware of group inequalities. However, research looking directly at how young children understand and explain inequalities within systems of racism, classism, and patriarchy is limited (Brown, 2017; Brown & Anderson, 2019). Some studies indicate that children as young as age 3 are attuned to material resource inequalities across groups (Baumard et al., 2012; Fehr et al., 2008). By age 3.5, children attempt to justify resource differences across novel groups by attributing them to merit (Olson et al., 2011); children then favor groups that have previously been shown to have more resources (Horwitz et al., 2014). A similar study found that when preschoolers were presented with resource inequalities between two groups, they demonstrated a preference for the more advantaged group (Li et al., 2014). Another study with low-income 6–9-year-olds found that children were aware of the hardships faced by people in poverty, such as lacking material resources (e.g., school supplies, food, money, medicine, and housing) and the challenges these hardships can lead to across many areas of life, such as academics (Heberle et al., 2018). However, a large number of children simultaneously believed that children in poverty are less competent than nonpoor children and that children in poverty have behavioral issues and a poor work ethic (Heberle et al., 2018).

Interestingly, young children appear to recognize that race and gender intersect with social class and wealth. For example, 3–10-year-old children consider wealth and possessions when making judgments about the status of racial groups (e.g., Olson et al., 2012). Studies also find that children as young as 3 associate being Black with being poor and being white with being rich (Dore et al., 2018; Elenbaas & Killen, 2016; Mandalaywala et al., 2020; Olson et al., 2012; Shutts et al., 2016). Mandalaywala and colleagues (2020) found that 3–7-year-old children use gender *and* race as status cues. Children expected boys to have more decision power and more access to resources than girls, and children expected white people to be wealthier than Black people (Mandalaywala et al., 2020). Overall, findings suggest that children are aware of group-based inequalities in material resources and access to power, and, where real inequalities exist among groups (e.g., gender, class, and racial groups), children's preference for high-resource individuals may drive stereotyping and bias.

Extant scholarship also suggests that children not only recognize inequalities based on group status, but also utilize their understanding of group differences to reason about new information, which may lead them to perpetuate inequality. For example, children reproduce existing social hierarchies when making judgments about occupational status (Bigler et al., 2003; Liben et al., 2001). In one study, 6–8-year-old African American children accorded higher status to novel jobs that had high concentrations of white people and low concentrations of Black people than to novel jobs with low concentrations of white people and high concentrations of Black people (Bigler et al., 2003). In another study, 6–11-year-old children rated traditionally masculine jobs as higher in status than traditionally feminine jobs and also rated novel, unfamiliar jobs as higher in status when portrayed with male workers than when portrayed with female workers (Liben et al., 2001). As a whole, the literature is consistent in showing that status is relevant to young children and that children observe group differences based on status.

Other research indicates that children understand the causes of social inequality (Short, 1991) and may have the motivation and capacity to understand and reduce inequality, highlighting how critical reflection and critical motivation may be linked for children. For instance, Elenbaas (2019) found that when 8–14-year-olds perceived higher levels of economic inequality, they were more critical of educational opportunities given solely to wealthy peers. Also, children were more supportive of admitting low-wealth peers into an educational summer camp when low-wealth peers had been excluded from this opportunity in the past. In another study, 10–11-year-old children were aware that discriminatory treatment underlies socioeconomic inequalities among whites and Blacks and that socioeconomic inequalities are linked to unequal resources allocated to various institutions such as schools (Elenbaas & Killen, 2017). Rogers and colleagues (2021) found that some elementary school children are aware of structural forces shaping racial identity and race relations. Further, Rizzo and Killen (2020) found that a group of predominantly white 3–8-year-old children evaluated structurally based inequalities to be more unfair and worthy of rectification than individually based inequalities. Overall, young children, much like adults, have the capacity to understand structural forces behind inequality and to align with policies and practices to reduce structural oppression. With support and interventions, such as fostering CC in young children, it is possible to build young children's capacity to recognize, name, and act against structural inequities.

## EVIDENCE THAT GROUP-BASED BELIEFS ARE CHANGEABLE

Evidence from intervention and pedagogical research suggests that stereotyped beliefs and intergroup biases are malleable. As one example, *race-* or *color-conscious* practices have been used to foster antiracist beliefs and actions (see Bell, 2016 for a review). Race consciousness entails being informed and transparent about the existence and causes of racial inequality as well as strategies to intentionally redress it. Some benefits of race-conscious discourses are theorized to be a reduction of prejudice, improved intergroup relations, and a greater sense of empathy and perspective taking. In one study, 6–11-year-old white and Black children received history lessons that included information about racism experienced by African Americans (*racism condition*) or identical lessons that omitted this information (*control condition*) (Hughes et al., 2007). Among white children, participants showed less prejudiced attitudes toward African Americans in the racism condition than in the control condition. This work demonstrates the benefits of learning about historical discrimination for white children's racial attitudes. Interestingly, Black children's racial attitudes were not affected by the intervention, perhaps because of previous life experiences and familiarity with racial discrimination. Some scholars have been calling for the integration of antiracist pedagogies and approaches into curricula used with young children to promote racial justice and healing among children, families, and communities (e.g., Escayg, 2018, 2020; Husband, 2012, 2016). Antiracist early childhood approaches call for the interrogation of white privilege, white power, and white supremacy in early childhood spaces and advocate for focusing on systemic injustices alongside stereotypes, biases, and prejudices (Escayg 2018, 2020).

Promising practices for shifting social class and gender beliefs have also been identified. For example, in one study with eighth graders, Mistry and colleagues (2012) found that a social studies curricular intervention helped children expand their notions about poverty and helped children blame structural, rather than individual, causes for poverty. Vilkin and colleagues (2020) found that an arts-based curriculum for grades K–5 that embraced expansive understandings of gender improved children's gender attitudes. After the curriculum, more students reported their gender in expansive terms and children's attitudes became more positive toward gender nonconformity. Unfortunately, empirical work on promising antibias interventions in the preschool period has been limited. Further, most interventions have focused on children's intergroup attitudes and peer relationships without an explicit focus on larger structural issues such as racism and sexism.

## EVIDENCE THAT PARENTS SHAPE CHILDREN'S UNDERSTANDING OF AND RESISTANCE TO RACISM: ETHNIC/RACIAL SOCIALIZATION

The research on how families intentionally socialize their children in relation to race and racism offers important insights to the study of young children's CC. It is clear that some children learn about race and racism from direct, careful teaching by their parents. For example, some Black families report engaging in ethnic/racial socialization, speaking intentionally with their young children about race, racism, and racial identity to prepare children for encountering racism, protect children from harm, and foster children's resilience (e.g., Barbarin & Jean-Baptiste, 2013; Blanchard et al., 2019; Caughy et al., 2011; Lesane-Brown et al., 2010; Doucet et al., 2018; Osborne et al., 2021). Such efforts may foster the development of CC of racism. White parents of young white children, in contrast, often avoid the topic of race and often adopt a "color-blind" approach to ethnic/racial socialization (e.g., Loyd & Gaither, 2018; Pahlke et al., 2014; Vittrup, 2018; Zucker & Patterson, 2018). Thus, white children are less likely than children of color to learn about race through explicit discussions with their parents or to engage in active and informed resistance to racism; this racial ignorance means that white children are less likely than Black children and other children of color to demonstrate CC of racism. While a full review of the substantial ethnic/racial socialization literature is beyond the scope of this chapter, we note that this literature is highly relevant to the study of CC in young children, and particularly to the study of CC as it relates to racism.

## EVIDENCE THAT PREADOLESCENT CHILDREN ARE AWARE OF SOCIAL, COMMUNITY, OR POLITICAL SYSTEMS

Generally, the literature on preadolescent children's awareness of social, community, and political systems is less developed than the literature on children's group-based beliefs and attitudes. However, one study of African American children's attitudes and beliefs regarding the response to Hurricane

Katrina found that some children in second, fourth, sixth, and eighth grades attributed the delayed government-funded relief efforts to class or race discrimination. While these were not the most commonly endorsed attributions, both were present across all grade levels (Brown et al., 2007). In another study, older elementary-school-aged children showed knowledge of the structural aspects of racism and of the Black Lives Matter movement (Rogers et al., 2021). Qualitative evidence from interviews with young children (ages 6–9) living in poverty found that some attributed the link between poverty and academic failure to systemic factors – including poor-quality schools and poor-quality teachers (Heberle et al., 2018). Children have also demonstrated differential responses to inequities that were structural (e.g., based on gender) versus inequities that were individual (e.g., based on merit), suggesting that children do perceive social structures (Rizzo & Killen, 2020).

While understudied, there is also evidence that children in the early years of elementary school already demonstrate consistent, structured political orientations (van Deth et al., 2011) and that elementary-school-aged children can learn and retain information regarding the structure of government, legal systems, and relations between school employees and the government (Berti & Andriolo, 2001). Elementary-school-aged children in the United States (6–10-year-olds) also express preferences for particular political candidates (Patterson et al., 2013). Research involving children in areas experiencing intractable conflict has shown that children develop political beliefs and knowledge as early as preschool (Bar-Tal et al., 2017). Further, research by Bigler et al. (2008) found that US 5–10-year-olds attributed the lack of female, African American, and Latinx presidents to discrimination, indicating awareness of the links between political power structures and group-based prejudice.

Children may be actively discouraged from learning about and participating in political and other systems – and, certainly, from acting to change those systems. As argued by critical whiteness scholars, US society is structured to foster ignorance of how racism shapes access to power across systems and institutions, particularly among white people (Coleman et al., 2020); we argue that this ignorance is sustained through the perspective that children are too naïve and unsophisticated to understand social and political systems. As noted by Patterson et al. (2019), there are historical as well as cross-cultural examples of societies in which children's involvement in politics has been clear and children's views on political and social systems have been sought by policy makers; however, in other contexts, children have been viewed as lacking the maturity to participate in political activity. Patterson et al. (2019) further note that in the US context, children are encouraged into assimilating to US nationalism (e.g., saying the Pledge of Allegiance at school) while being excluded from formal political participation and, in many cases, from informal political exposure. It is important to note, however, that limitations in awareness of political (and other) systems are not exclusive to children; one study, for example, found that only 34% of US adults can name the three branches of the US government (Annenberg Public Policy Center, 2014). Thus, gaps in knowledge of the formal structures through which oppressive systems are maintained are not limited to children.

## CC IN YOUNG PEOPLE: WHAT WE KNOW

A recent systematic review of the literature on child and adolescent CC highlights several aspects of the literature that are particularly relevant to young children (Heberle et al., 2020b). First, Heberle et al. (2020b) found ample evidence for the effectiveness of social-justice-oriented teaching and curricular practices to promote CC, particularly when material is connected to youth's lived experiences and opportunities for open dialogue are provided. The review found that interventions with youth often emphasize critical reflection as a lever for movement toward greater CC overall; however, some interventions begin with critical action and build critical reflection through engagement in meaningful collective and individual action. The literature also highlights the importance of context and relationships in shaping the expression of CC. Across studies, youth whose parents, teachers, and peers were supportive of discussions of social justice and youth who attended schools that centered critical pedagogical approaches showed the highest levels of CC.

With respect to development, Heberle et al. (2020b) noted that the few studies that have examined CC over time have generally found that CC (particularly critical reflection) increases with age, specifically among youth of color. Importantly, however, measures of CC have generally not accounted for developmental changes in the form of the construct; that is, the items used to assess CC do not change with age despite changes in children's cognitive abilities, level of independence, social relationships, and other relevant factors.

Also, Heberle et al. (2020b) found that there is a dearth of CC research on children prior to adolescence. We summarize the scant literature on CC in children prior to adolescence, including studies that were covered by Heberle et al. (2020b) and the small number of studies that have been published since that review. We then go beyond the work of Heberle et al. (2020b) to describe next steps, predictions, and guidelines for research on CC with young children based on this small literature and the other relevant literatures that we have discussed in this chapter.

We only found nine studies (Abma & Schrijver, 2020; Fegley et al., 2006; Hawkins, 2014; Luguetti et al., 2019; Ngai & Koehn, 2011; Osorio, 2018; Pinetta et al., 2020; Silva, 2012; Tintiangco-Cubale et al., 2016) that have included preadolescent children; all but one of these studies primarily utilized qualitative methods and thus provide rich information on the experiences of participants. For instance, Fegley et al. (2006) found in focus group research that 6–13-year-old children showed an enhanced ability to engage in critical reasoning about social issues after participating in community-based programming, such as community service. Hawkins (2014) and Osorio (2018) used qualitative methods to examine critical engagement with texts that raised social justice issues, focusing on preschool children and second graders, respectively, with both studies finding that these young children were able to critically engage and connect texts to their own experiences. Similarly, Ngai and Koehn (2011) used mixed-methods to show that instruction focused on Indigenous education and critical democracy learning increased critical awareness in first–fifth grade students. Silva (2012) found that first graders prompted to discuss artists who had experienced various forms of bias initially reinforced stereotyping, showing the potential risks of classroom engagement with social justice topics. However, when teachers encouraged children to connect material to their own experiences, children began to engage in more critical dialogue regarding power, privilege, and oppression.

Three of the studies that we identified used participatory action methods. Tintiangco-Cubales et al. (2016) used YPAR to show that an ethnic studies curricular intervention increased children's ability to critically reflect on and confront injustice. Examining a case study of a Dutch participatory health research project with 8–11-year-olds, Abma and Schrijver (2020) found that photovoice – a method in which participants are given cameras to capture their perspectives on salient issues in their lives – can promote the CC of young children. Luguetti et al. (2019) completed a case study of a participatory action project that aimed to raise 7–13-year-olds' CC through an activist sport pedagogy: findings highlighted the importance of teachers attending to how an authoritarian relationship to students can fundamentally undermine the aims of a CC-raising curriculum. Finally, Pinetta et al. (2020) used quantitative methods, surveying fifth to eighth-grade Latinx children. They found that those whose parents more frequently discussed their ethnic/racial identity and the discrimination they might face were more likely to endorse a sense of responsibility to resist oppression through civic and community engagement.

Of note, these studies primarily or solely emphasized critical reflection, not motivation or action. Most focused on educational practices in a school-based setting, and none examined the development of CC over time, other aspects of functioning associated with CC, generalizability of CC skills outside of the study setting, or other key research questions related to child CC.

Acknowledging that children are in a process of intensive linguistic, social, and cognitive development, we argue that the degree to which children are able to see, communicate about, and act against injustice is largely a function of how the world is constructed around them, as opposed to some intrinsic limitation situated within children. That is to say, barriers to

CC development in children may be less about their developmental capabilities and more about the ways in which their environments are constructed to facilitate or neglect their CC, and to nurture or ignore their sociopolitical development. Though the literature is small, we see from these studies that when social arrangements are made for children to communicate and act on their experiences and perspectives in modalities fit to their skills, they have much to communicate and can exert real influence over the conditions and circumstances of the world around them.

## MODELS OF CC DEVELOPMENT

Although models of CC development for preadolescent children are lacking, models of CC development in older populations may nevertheless inform theorizing about younger children's CC. Byrd (2021) integrates theories of CC and cultural competence and proposes that individuals move from awareness (in stage 1) into knowledge (in stage 2). Knowledge then has reciprocal impacts on the reflection, agency, and action cycle. Other writings suggest that reflection precedes agency, which precedes action, at least in the initial development of CC, after which these competencies have reciprocal impacts (Diemer et al., 2016; Heberle et al., 2020b; Watts et al., 2011). Byrd's model, however, diverges from others in considering awareness and knowledge as competencies and practices distinct from reflection.

In Byrd's model, stage 1 includes awareness of social identities, awareness of structural inequality, and knowledge of identity-general characteristics of inequality. Stage 2 includes knowledge of group characteristics, knowledge of identity-specific mechanisms, and knowledge of history. Byrd further argues that movement through stage 1 into stage 2 is driven by motivation. Stage 2 processes are identity specific, such that a person would generally focus on a particular aspect of identity (e.g., race) rather than on general inequality while building knowledge in this stage. Byrd argues that individuals cannot move into the reflection, agency, action cycle that occurs in tandem with knowledge-building in stage 2 until they have mastered stage 1. As we explore possibilities for research on CC in preadolescent children in the next section of this chapter, we return to Byrd's model to consider its relevance for this young population (see Table 4.1).

## A RESEARCH AGENDA FOCUSED ON CHILDREN'S CRITICAL CONSCIOUSNESS

Our goal in focusing on CC in the preadolescent period is to understand the potential of CC as a protective factor against multiple, early-occurring, and lasting experiences and impacts of oppression. We are interested in the potential of CC to serve as a protective factor for children experiencing

TABLE 4.1 Possible influences on critical consciousness competencies from Byrd's 2021 model across preadolescence

| Age | Stage 1 | | | Stage 2 | | |
|---|---|---|---|---|---|---|
| | **Awareness of social identities** | **Awareness of structural inequality** | **Knowledge of identity-general characteristics of inequality** | **Knowledge of group characteristics** | **Knowledge of identity-specific mechanisms** | **Knowledge of history** |
| Preschool (3 to 5) | Adult and peer labeling of social groups<br>Sorting by social groups (e.g., gender groups) | Observation of inequitable experiences (e.g., housing, treatment by others, and segregation) | Texts dealing with privilege and oppression; simple adult explanations of these forces | Adult and peer discussions of groups<br>Observations of groups | Adult and peer discussion of group-specific experiences; could include discussions of current events | Woven into texts and other media |
| Early school age (6 to 8) | Classroom, home, and peer group discussions of personal and social identities and their interactions | Adult, peer, and media messaging about inequality<br>Adult responses to questions about the structure of society | Texts and conversations engaging history and politics; where these name violence, privilege, and oppression, children may come to understand these drivers of inequality | Discussions of own cultural experiences and values; identity-related experiences<br>Adult and peer discussions of other groups | Continued adult and peer discussion; engagement with identity-specific mechanisms as they relate to history, civics, and other topics | Critical curricula at school; home discussions that challenge acritical school curricula |
| Middle childhood (9 to 11) | Increasingly independent, sophisticated engagement with academic content, dialogues, media materials, and other sources, utilizing competencies attained in previous developmental stages and supported by adult and peer influences. | | | | | |

marginalization and as a promotive factor for allyship and antiracist attitudes in children experiencing privilege. In this final section of the chapter, we make suggestions for research focused on preadolescent CC.

First, we argue that the literature on children's awareness of social groups, group-based inequalities, stereotypes, and social and political structures suggests that somewhere between preschool and elementary school most children have the cognitive and social capacity to master stage 1 of Byrd's model (2021). The literature suggests that children will acquire beliefs relevant to stage 1 – that is, awareness of social identities, awareness of inequality, and knowledge of identity-general characteristics of inequality – whether or not adults intentionally and consciously shape those beliefs. What CC offers is a structural lens for stage 1 beliefs and a general frame for interrogating observed inequalities with questions about the historical and current systemic and institutional forces that have led to those inequalities. We suggest that research on preadolescent CC begin with the assumption that children can develop the competency to see inequality and to understand how that inequality is linked to structural rather than individual forces. We suggest that researchers move beyond questions about the existence of these competencies and rather explore how these competencies develop and manifest across preadolescent development. Children who have mastered stage 1 competencies can move into developing stage 2 knowledge, similar to the race knowledge that some children of color develop via ethnic/racial socialization (Barbarin & Jean-Baptiste, 2013; Lesane-Brown et al., 2010). As children build knowledge, in conjunction with adult support, children could reasonably be expected to engage in reflection, agency, and action cycles that build their CC. A critical area for future research will be to interrogate what agency/motivation and action look like in different developmental periods. For example, children may stand up for peers who experience social exclusion and discrimination, or they may push adults in their lives to interrogate the ways in which their own choices uphold oppressive systems. Future research can clarify the conditions under which behaviors reflect informed and intentional critical action and other means by which young children engage in critical action. Similarly, researchers should consider the ways in which critical motivation may manifest as motivation to work for local change or to contribute to a more just classroom, family life, or school – contexts and systems directly salient to young children.

CC in young children will likely look different than CC in adolescents and adults – and may be less independent, individual, and cross-contextual, and more interdependent, relational, and contextually specific. Children's ability to demonstrate CC can be expected in part to depend on whether adults in their lives foster critical reflection, provide education on systems of oppression, support children's sense of efficacy to resist oppression, and support engagement in critical action. Children who demonstrate CC in one setting may not in another, as children's lives are highly constrained and structured by adults and as children's own identities and personalities may shape how and when they demonstrate CC. Insights from research with children may push forward research on the contextual and relational dimensions of CC across the lifespan.

Schools have been identified as a key context for the development of CC in adolescents (Heberle et al., 2020b), and we hypothesize that findings regarding the impact of school climate would extend down to the preadolescent period. We hypothesize that children in preschool and elementary school settings in which teachers are committed to engaging students in critical inquiry and conversations about social justice issues would exhibit higher levels of personal CC than children in other settings. This hypothesis is consistent with theorizing on prejudice development and enactment of social exclusion, which argues that the process of integrating moral and group identity considerations begins in preschool (Rutland et al., 2010). The climate of the school or classroom transmits implicit messages about group norms and values to children; thus, a classroom climate in which social justice and systemic oppression are open topics of discussion might enhance the degree to which children view antioppressive thinking and action as norms. Such a classroom climate might therefore steer children toward the use of moral reasoning rather than social conventional reasoning (Rutland et al., 2010), consistent with a CC perspective. This might reduce prejudice and exclusion as well as provide children with a framework in which to resist their own exclusion on moral grounds. Relatedly, another aspect of CC where teacher and parental involvement could be emphasized is critical action. The degree to which young children can engage in critical action likely depends on whether the adults in children's lives allow space and provide practical support for this. An important distinction that researchers will need to make when working on questions about social support for critical action will be between action that is authentically critical and focused on dismantling oppressive systems and action that serves to benefit the oppressor by creating the illusion of justice or fairness while maintaining the oppressor's power and privilege.

These insights regarding educational contexts are consistent with findings on interventions designed to enhance CC, which generally aimed to engage youth in discussion of social justice issues, racism, classism, and related topics; to engage youth in action for social justice; and to subvert the conventional power dynamics typically at play in conversations between adults and children (Heberle et al., 2020b). These approaches could be adapted to the preadolescent population. In fact, the strategies identified in the literature on CC interventions for adolescents (Heberle et al., 2020b) share many parallels with antibias strategies already in use in some early education programs, such as those described by Derman-Sparks and Edwards (2010), who advise early educators to emphasize (a) developing children's self-awareness and confidence, (b) developing children's comfort and joy with human diversity and accurate language for human differences and authentic connections with others, (c) developing children's increasing recognition of unfairness and language with which to speak about unfairness, and (d) developing children's empowerment and skills to act against prejudice and discrimination. While Derman-Sparks and Edwards (2010) do not frame their model as one aimed at building CC, it is well aligned with the CC intervention literature and suggests a promising opportunity to study changes in CC associated with existing early education models. Researchers could also study existing models modified with adaptations that might further enhance CC (e.g., intentional engagement in teacher-supported critical action and greater support for children to make visible the institutions and systems that shape their own lives). Some research indicates that a small minority of early childhood teachers already engage in antioppressive and antiracist practices; however, many struggle with engaging children in difficult conversations around race and gender (e.g., Faragó, 2017; Husband, 2018; Vittrup, 2016) and, to our knowledge, no studies to date have examined how antibias practices directly impact children in the short and the long term.

Preadolescent children are particularly susceptible to parental influence, and we therefore consider this area of literature to be of particular importance to our topic of interest. There is evidence that young children in particular look to their parents for cues on how to respond to people who are racially different from themselves (Castelli et al., 2008; 2009) and on how to cope with racism (Barbarin & Jean-Baptiste, 2013; Lesane-Brown et al., 2010; Thornton et al., 1990). In addition, there is evidence that elementary-school-age children are able to learn and retain complex information about political systems and events, and that even preschool-age children show knowledge of this information when it is particularly salient in their contexts (e.g., in contexts of intractable conflict) (Bar-Tal et al., 2017). Research suggests that children's political beliefs in adulthood are highly correlated with their parents' political beliefs, suggesting a lasting influence of parents on political beliefs and, likely, related beliefs (Patterson et al., 2019). Thus, we hypothesize that children who experience discussions of racism, classism, and other forms of oppression; who discuss the existence of and nature of institutions and systems in their lives; and who discuss political and current events in their families would demonstrate higher levels of CC than children who do not experience these discussions. Similarly, children whose parents model critical motivation and action may themselves develop these skills and practices more readily than those whose parents do not.

The field of CC scholarship has not reached a consensus regarding the degree to which CC is an appropriate or meaningful construct to apply to individuals in positions of privilege, and research on young children's CC will need to attend to this question. Some scholars have argued that CC is relevant specifically for youth experiencing oppression (Watts et al., 2011), while others have argued that the field should consider and attend to questions about CC in people holding privilege (Diemer et al., 2021; Rapa & Geldhof, 2020). Others have emphasized the complexity of privilege and oppression, highlighting that most individuals experience both privilege and oppression within the interlocking systems that shape their lives and communities (Godfrey & Burson, 2018); the implication is that classifying individuals or groups as privileged or oppressed misrepresents the reality of their experiences. It is clear that children's relative privilege shapes their experience within oppressive and privileging systems. As one concrete example, Sullivan et al. (2021) found that Black parents had more discussions about race and racism with their children following the murder of George Floyd while white parents, on average, showed no change in their discussions of race and racism. This finding highlights how white privilege distances white families from the realities of racism, allowing them to choose racial ignorance even as they experience racial privilege. At the same time, scholarship on allyship and accompliceship shows that some people in positions of privilege do engage in authentic and meaningful work to dismantle the systems that privilege them (Suyemoto & Hochman, 2021). We argue that scholarship on young children's CC should attend carefully to the question of how children's relative privilege shapes their experience of the system(s) of oppression as well as to the question of whether beliefs and actions coded as indicating CC reflect an actual, authentic commitment or act to disrupt oppressive systems and shift power.

## STUDYING CC IN PREADOLESCENT CHILDREN: METHODS AND POSSIBILITIES

We contend that methodological diversity and flexibility will be essential to moving forward the study of CC in preadolescents. Some of the most promising methods, in our view, are those that are not routinely used in psychology. For example, critical ethnographic approaches could be used to observe and make sense of the ways in which CC manifests, fails to manifest, is supported, or is neglected in early childhood and school-age communities of children. For example, Stockstill (2021) used ethnographic methods to examine the reproduction of class inequality via property rules in economically segregated early childhood settings, demonstrating how ethnographic work can be used to unpack the reproduction of oppressive systems – and, presumably, resistance to them. Other scholars have utilized ethnographic methods to study their own children's socialization into racism (e.g., Miller, 2015); this approach, too, may hold promise for scholars seeking to understand the complex, nuanced, contextualized process through which children develop or do not develop CC. Grounded theory and phenomenological work with parents or teachers may be useful in developing theory regarding the processes involved in young children's development of CC; in addition, such work could leverage critical social scholarship to interrogate adults' perspectives and examine the ways in which they may reinforce oppressive systems. Interview-based work can be conducted directly with children as young as 4–5 years of age, particularly if interviewers are patient and skilled in developing rapport; such work could be utilized to examine children's perspectives on topics that are salient to them and relevant to understanding their CC. Parent–child dialogues, play-based interactions centering on relevant themes, and discussions of literary or media stimuli may also be useful sources of data for qualitative or quantitative analysis.

**Next steps for the measurement of preadolescent CC.** In prior research, children's group-based beliefs have been measured using interviews (Chafel & Neitzel, 2005), focus groups (Fortier, 2006), and questionnaires (Woods et al., 2005). More recently, Sabol et al. (2021) used a tablet-based assessment paradigm for examining children's (4–8-year-olds) meaning-making about policy issues relevant to them. Next steps for developing measures of CC aimed at preadolescents could begin with children in middle childhood; the research illustrates that children in this age range are capable of completing questionnaire measures related to their experiences, and some early measurement work has been done in this area (Rapa et al., 2020). With modification of items from existing scales – or new items derived from theory and qualitative research – children in this age group may be reasonably expected to complete questionnaire measures of CC. Modifications may include adjusting the vocabulary level of existing items to suit children's literacy level. More complex modifications are also likely to be necessary, however. For example, children may benefit from items that are highly concrete and relatively specific: we would expect, for example, that children might be more comfortable responding to an item about differences in how teachers treat boys and girls than responding to an item about gender-based inequality in educational opportunities. In some studies, there may be benefit to prescreening children for basic knowledge needed to answer CC questions. For example, young children whose parents or educators talk about race and racism are likely to be able to answer questions about these topics, whereas children who have not had such exposure may not. Because of the advantages of concreteness and specificity in measures aimed at children, researchers may find the greatest benefit in developing measures of specific CC competencies within specific domains (e.g., a measure that assesses knowledge of the basic nature of oppressive systems or a measure that assesses engagement in action against racism) rather than trying to develop broadband CC measures for younger populations.

For younger children, existing measures that utilize props and allow for nonverbal responding could be adapted to address CC content. For example, the Berkeley Puppet Interview method (Ablow & Measelle, 1993) has been successfully adapted to assess social-class-related stereotyping in children ages 4–8 (Heberle & Carter, 2020). Others have utilized visual scales (e.g., a line along which children mark how well they think children from various social groups perform in an activity) to create Likert-type scores (Woods et al., 2005) to assess stereotypes; a similar approach could be used with CC items. Visual approaches combined with read-aloud technology (i.e., mediated through a computer or tablet) could make large-scale CC data collection with early school-age children feasible. Some studies have used vignettes (McGlothlin & Killen, 2006) to assess intergroup bias in children; pictorial vignettes or short stories may allow for the assessment of critical reflection, motivation, and action in young children. In Table 4.2, we provide examples of CC-related indicators that might be measurable in the preadolescent period.

**A note on intersectionality.** As a relatively new area of research, research on preadolescent CC is well positioned to address weaknesses and areas that have been ignored in the broader research on CC; as one example, we encourage researchers with an interest in this area to center intersectionality in their work. For instance, researchers interested in CC of racism could ask how children's awareness, action, and efficacy related to racism and antiracism are shaped by their own gendered, classed, and racialized experiences; power differentials linked to those experiences; and CC of other systems of oppression. Such questions extend to the larger family system as well. For instance, for children whose mothers demonstrate CC of patriarchy, how does this maternal CC impact children's own CC of patriarchy, children's understanding of their own gender identity, and children's attitudes about mothering? Bringing in institutional dynamics, researchers could ask how families with high CC experience interactions with schools where administrators have low CC and/or hierarchical banking models of education have been embraced, and how those experiences may differ depending on the racialized, classed, and gendered identities of family members and of school officials. All of these questions hold the potential for learning about how individual children's CC is shaped, is enacted, and functions for the child.

Further, intersectionality teaches us to center power in analyzing social issues (Overstreet et al., 2020), and we argue that CC's domain-generality is well suited to addressing questions regarding how individuals and institutions center or do not center power in their analyses and actions relating to social injustice. Intersectional CC scholarship with young children might ask questions such as: How do preadolescent children understand the concept of power, and what are the experiences that help children to see how power is

TABLE 4.2 Critical consciousness-related indicators measurable in the preadolescent period

| Age period | Relevant competencies | Critical reflection | Motivation/Efficacy | Critical action |
|---|---|---|---|---|
| Preschool (3 to 5) | Understanding of equality/inequality; ability to label others' race/gender; understanding that wealth differences exist | • Questioning stereotypes<br>• Questioning group differences in social status<br>• Expressing distress or discomfort regarding inequality | • Global self-efficacy and domain-specific self-efficacy<br>• Expressed desire to rectify inequalities | • Adult-mediated participation in conventional or unconventional political activity (protest, voting, community organizing)<br>• Interpersonal resistance to discrimination |
| Early school age (6 to 8) | Increased development of self-efficacy beliefs; increased development of stereotypes; increased verbal skills | • Lower endorsement of stereotypes or greater endorsement of system-level attributions for stereotypes than age peers<br>• Intolerance of inequality<br>• Seeking inclusion of marginalized outgroup members<br>• Questioning impact of power, institutions, history | • Global self-efficacy and domain-specific self-efficacy, with increasing sense of collective efficacy (in family or peer group)<br>• Expressed interest in activities to promote equity and inclusion | • Adult-mediated participation in conventional or unconventional political activity (protest, voting, community organizing), potentially initiated at the child's request<br>• Interpersonal action, including standing up for peers, challenging adults, pointing out injustice |

TABLE 4.2 *(cont.)*

| Age period | Relevant competencies | Critical reflection | Motivation/Efficacy | Critical action |
|---|---|---|---|---|
| Middle childhood (9 to 11) | Increasing interest and capacity for social comparison; increased verbal skills; increased importance of peer relationships; increased attunement to others' stereotypes | • Emerging ability to articulate understanding of social injustice<br>• Emerging ability to discuss own and others' identity, privilege, marginalization, power<br>• Emerging ability to identify systems-level inequalities and question them | • Emerging ability to articulate self- and collective efficacy specific to resisting oppression<br>• Expressed motivation to engage in activities aimed at resisting social injustice | • Adult-mediated participation in conventional or unconventional political activity (protest, voting, community organizing), potentially initiated at the child's request and with specific activities carried out independently by the child (writing letters, making signs)<br>• Interpersonal action as described above; organized collective action with peers |

operating in their own social environments? What are the experiences that lead children to question the role of power and systems that sustain power differentials when they are confronted with novel instances of intergroup inequality? How do children understand their own access to power? How and when do children use individual and collective action to shine light on or shift unequal systems? And, how can adults – who have been socialized in racist, classist, sexist systems and who work in institutions designed to uphold those systems – be supported in helping their children to develop a CC lens and do CC work?

## CONCLUSION

In this chapter, we have argued for the need to study CC in preadolescent children. The space of possibility for work on this area is rich. Very little attention has been paid in the literature to the topic of preadolescent CC, and some have assumed that CC requires a level of cognitive sophistication that young children do not have. However, we find the evidence from related literatures to be compelling with regard to children's ability to see, understand, and act on social inequalities. It will be imperative that research in this area begins with the question of whether children involved in such research have been given the opportunity to develop CC and have been supported in enacting CC in the context in which the research is taking place. It will also be important to consider a broader understanding of CC than the traditional individualistic framing of the construct: that is, we encourage researchers to attend to the ways in which CC may manifest within close relationships and collectives rather than simply considering CC to be an individual construct.

As a final note, we consider it important to make clear that we consider preadolescent CC to be important in its own right, and we consider questions about how children experience CC early in their lives to be of great value to understanding this construct and its implications for individuals. It is common in the child development literature to frame children as people who are in progress and to emphasize research questions about how early functioning and early characteristics impact later functioning. This framing ultimately emphasizes a person's ability to be a contributing member of society – where the definition of a contributing member of society is framed from a capitalistic perspective that centers a person's ability to work and to participate non-disruptively in the institutions that they are part of (goals that may be expected to conflict with CC-aligned goals in many instances). When child development scholars take up longitudinal questions regarding the long-term implications of child CC, we encourage them to question whether traditional developmental "goals" are aligned with the foundational tenets of CC. Further, though, we urge scholars not to frame preadolescent CC as important only if it proves to have impacts on adolescent or adult functioning. We hypothesize that it will – that, for example, children who are nurtured in their CC development early in life will have less unlearning to accomplish as they grow into mature resisters than other children and will therefore be quicker to develop CC-aligned knowledge and skills than their developmental peers. However, if this hypothesis proves false it will still be important to continue studying preadolescent CC to understand how children develop and exhibit resistance to oppressive systems that shape their childhoods.

## REFERENCES

Ablow, J. C., & Measelle, J. R. (1993). *The Berkeley puppet interview.* University of California.

Abma, T. A., & Schrijver, J. (2020). "Are we famous or something?" Participatory health research with children using photovoice. *Educational Action Research, 28*(3), 405–426. https://doi.org/10.1080/09650792.2019.1627229.

Annenberg Public Policy Center. (2014). Americans know surprisingly little about their government, survey finds. Retrieved from www.annenbergpublicpolicycenter.org/americans-know-surprisingly-little-about-their-government-survey-finds/.

Arthur, A. E., Bigler, R. S., Liben, L. S., Gelman, S. A., & Ruble, D. N. (2008). Gender stereotyping and prejudice in young children. In S. Levy & M. Killen (Eds.). *Intergroup attitudes and relations in childhood through adulthood.* Oxford University Press; 2008. pp. 66–85.

Barbarin, O., & Jean-Baptiste, E. (2013). The relation of dialogic, control, and racial socialization practices to early academic and social competence: Effects of gender, ethnicity, and family socioeconomic status. *American Journal of Orthopsychiatry, 83*(2–3), 207. https://doi.org/10.1111/ajop.12025.

Bar-Tal, D., Diamond, A. H., & Nasie, M. (2017). Political socialization of young children in intractable conflicts: Conception and evidence. *International Journal of Behavioral Development, 41*(3), 415–425. https://doi.org/10.1177/0165025416652508.

Baumard, N., Mascaro, O., & Chevallier, C. (2012). Preschoolers are able to take merit into account when distributing goods. *Developmental Psychology, 48*(2), 492. https://doi.org/10.1037/a0026598.

Beal, F. M. (1970). Double jeopardy: To be Black and female. In T. Cade (Ed.), *The Black woman: An anthology.* New York: Signet, pp. 90–100. www.jstor.org/stable/40338758.

Bell, L. A. (2016). Telling on racism: Developing a race-conscious agenda. In H. A. Neville, M. E. Gallardo, D. W. E. Sue (Eds.), *The myth of racial color blindness: Manifestations, dynamics, and impact.* American Psychological Association, pp. 105–122. https://doi.org/10.1037/14754-007.

Berti, A. E., & Andriolo, A. (2001). Third graders' understanding of core political concepts (law, nation-state, government) before and after teaching. *Genetic, Social, and General Psychology Monographs, 127*(4), 346–378.

Bigler, R. S., Averhart, C. J. , & Liben, L. S. (2003). Race and the work force: Occupational status, aspirations, and stereotyping among African American children. *Developmental Psychology,* 39, 572–580.

Bigler, R. S., Arthur, A. E., Hughes, J. M., & Patterson, M. M. (2008). The politics of race and gender: Children's perceptions of discrimination and the US presidency. *Analyses of Social Issues and Public Policy*, *8*(1), 83–112. https://doi.org/10.1111/j.1530-2415.2008.00161.x.

Bigler, R. S., & Liben, L. S. (2006). A developmental intergroup theory of social stereotypes and prejudice. *Advances in Child Development and Behavior*, *34*, 39. https://doi.org/10.1016/S0065-2407(06)80004-2.

Bigler, R. S., & Liben, L. S. (2007). Developmental intergroup theory: Explaining and reducing children's social stereotyping and prejudice. *Current Directions in Psychological Science*, *16*(3), 162–166. https://doi.org/10.1111/j.1467-8721.2007.00496.x.

Blanchard, S. B., Coard, S. I., Hardin, B. J., & Mereoiu, M. (2019). Use of parental racial socialization with African American toddler boys. *Journal of Child and Family Studies*, *28*(2), 387–400. https://doi.org/10.1007/s10826-018-1274-2.

Boutte, G. S., Lopez-Robertson, J., & Powers-Costello, E. (2011). Moving beyond colorblindness in early childhood classrooms. *Early Childhood Education Journal*, *39*(5), 335. https://doi.org/10.1007/s10643-011-0457-x.

Bronfenbrenner, U. (1979). *The ecology of human development*. Harvard University Press.

Brown, C. S. (2017). *Discrimination in childhood and adolescence: A developmental intergroup approach*. London: Routledge. https://doi.org/10.4324/9781315208381.

Brown, C. S., & Anderson, R. E. (2019). It's never too young to talk about race and gender. *Human Development*, *63*(1), 1–3. https://doi.org/10.1159/000501242.

Brown, C. S., Mistry, R. S., & Bigler, R. S. (2007). Hurricane Katrina: African American children's perceptions of race, class, and government involvement amid a national crisis. *Analyses of Social Issues & Public Policy*, *7*(1), 191–208. https://doi.org/10.1111/j.1530-2415.2007.00139.x.

Byrd, C. M. (2021). Cycles of development in learning about identities, diversity, and equity. *Cultural Diversity and Ethnic Minority Psychology*. Advance online publication. https://doi.org/10.1037/cdp0000389.

Castelli, L., De Dea, C., & Nesdale, D. (2008). Learning social attitudes: Children's sensitivity to the nonverbal behaviors of adult models during interracial interactions. *Personality and Social Psychology Bulletin*, *34*(11), 1504–1513. https://doi.org/10.1177/0146167208322769.

Castelli, L., Zogmaister, C., & Tomelleri, S. (2009). The transmission of racial attitudes within the family. *Developmental Psychology*, *45*(2), 586–591. https://doi.org/10.1037/a0014619.

Caughy, M. O., Nettles, S. M., & Lima, J. (2011). Profiles of racial socialization among African American parents: Correlates, context, and outcome. *Journal of Child and Family Studies*, *20*, 491–502. https://doi.org/10.1007/s10826-010-9416-1.

Chafel, J. A., & Neitzel, C. (2005). Young children's ideas about the nature, causes, justification, and alleviation of poverty. *Early Childhood Research Quarterly*, *20*(4), 433–450. https://doi.org/10.1016/j.ecresq.2005.10.004.

Coleman, B. R., Collins, C. R., & Bonam, C. M. (2020). Interrogating whiteness in community research and action. *American Journal of Community Psychology* *67*(3–4), 486–504. https://doi.org/10.1002/ajcp.12473.

Combahee River Collective. (2014). A Black feminist statement. *Women's Studies Quarterly*, 42 (3/4), 271–280. (Original work published 1977.) https://doi.org/10.1353/wsq.2014.0052.

Cristol, D., & Gimbert, B. (2008). Racial perceptions of young children: A review of literature post-1999. *Early Childhood Education Journal*, *36*(2), 201–207. https://doi.org/10.1007/s10643-008-0251-6.

Delgado, R., & Stefancic, J. (2017). *Critical race theory: An introduction, vol.20*. New York University Press.

Derman-Sparks, L., & Edwards, J. O. (2010). What is anti-bias education? In *Anti-bias education for young children and ourselves* (pp. 1–9). Washington, DC: National Association for the Education of Young Children.

Diemer, M. A., Pinedo, A., Bañales, J. et al. (2021). Recentering action in critical consciousness. *Child Development Perspectives*, *15*(1), 1217. https://doi.org/10.1111/cdep.12393.

Diemer, M. A., Rapa, L. J., Voight, A. M., & McWhirter, E. H. (2016). Critical consciousness: A developmental approach to addressing marginalization and oppression. *Child Development Perspectives*, *10*, 216–221. http://doi.org/10.1111/cdep.12193.

Dore, R. A., Hoffman, K. M., Lillard, A. S., & Trawalter, S. (2014). Children's racial bias in perceptions of others' pain. *The British Journal of Developmental Psychology*, *32*(2), 218–231. https://doi.org/10.1111/bjdp.12038.

Dore, R. A., Hoffman, K. M., Lillard, A. S., & Trawalter, S. (2018). Developing cognitions about race: White 5-to 10-year-olds' perceptions of hardship and pain. *European Journal of Social Psychology*, *48*(2), O121–O132. https://doi.org/10.1002/ejsp.2323.

Doucet, F., Banerjee, M., & Parade, S. (2018). What should young Black children know about race? Parents of preschoolers, preparation for bias, and promoting egalitarianism. *Journal of Early Childhood Research*, *16*(1), 65–79. https://doi.org/10.1177/1476718X16630763.

Elenbaas, L. (2019). Perceptions of economic inequality are related to children's judgments about access to opportunities. *Developmental Psychology*, *55*(3), 471–481. https://doi.org/10.1037/dev0000550.

Elenbaas, L., & Killen, M. (2016). Age-related changes in children's associations of economic resources and race. *Frontiers in Psychology*, *7*, 884. https://doi.org/10.3389/fpsyg.2016.00884.

Elenbaas, L., & Killen, M. (2017). Children's perceptions of social resource inequality. *Journal of Applied Developmental Psychology*, *48*, 49–58. https://doi.org/10.1016/j.appdev.2016.11.006.

Escayg, K. A. (2018). The missing links: Enhancing anti-bias education with anti-racist education. *Journal of Curriculum, Teaching, Learning and Leadership in Education*, *3*(1), 15. https://digitalcommons.unomaha.edu/ctlle/vol3/iss1/4.

Escayg, K. A. (2020). Anti-racism in US early childhood education: Foundational principles. *Sociology Compass*, *14*(4), e12764. https://doi.org/10.1111/soc4.12764.

Faragó, F. (2017). Anti-bias or not: A case study of two early childhood educators. *International Critical Childhood Policy Studies Journal*, *6*(1), 7–21. https://scholarworks.sfasu.edu/humansci_facultypubs/27.

Feagin, J. R. (2013).*The white racial frame: Centuries of racial framing and counter-framing*. Routledge.

Fegley, C. S., Angelique, H., & Cunningham, K. (2006). Fostering critical consciousness in young people: Encouraging the "doves" to find their voices. *Journal of Applied Sociology/Sociological Practice*, *23*(1), 7–27. https://doi.org/10.1177%2F19367244062300102.

Fehr, E., Bernhard, H., & Rockenbach, B. (2008). Egalitarianism in young children. *Nature*, *454*(7208), 1079–1083. https://doi.org/10.1038/nature07155.

Fortier, S. M. (2006). On being a poor child in America: Views of poverty from 7–12-year olds. *Journal of Children and Poverty*, *12*(2), 113–128. https://doi.org/10.1080/10796120500502086.

Godfrey, E. B., & Burson, E. (2018). Interrogating the intersections: How intersectional perspectives can inform developmental scholarship on critical consciousness. In C. E. Santos & R. B. Toomey (Eds.), *Envisioning the Integration of an Intersectional Lens in Developmental Science. New Directions for Child and Adolescent Development*, *2018*(161), 17–38. https://doi.org/10.1002/cad.20246.

Hawkins, K. (2014). Teaching for social justice, social responsibility, and social inclusion: A respectful pedagogy for twenty-first century early childhood education. *European Early Childhood Education Research Journal*, *22*(5), 723–738. https://doi.org/10.1080/1350293X.2014.969085.

Heberle, A. E., & Carter, A. S. (2015). Cognitive aspects of young children's experience of economic disadvantage. *Psychological Bulletin*, *141*(4), 723. https://doi.org/10.1037/bul0000010.

Heberle, A. E., & Carter, A. S. (2020). Young children's stereotype endorsement about people in poverty: Age and economic status effects. *Children and Youth Services Review*, *108*, 104605. https://doi.org/10.1016/j.childyouth.2019.104605.

Heberle, A. E., Kaplan-Levy, S. A., Neuspiel, J. M., & Carter, A. S. (2018). Young children's reasoning about the effects of poverty on people experiencing it: A qualitative thematic analysis. *Children and Youth Services Review*, *86*, 188–199. https://doi.org/10.1016/j.childyouth.2018.01.036.

Heberle, A. E., Obus, E., Gray, S. A. O. (2020a). An intersectional perspective on the intergenerational transmission of trauma and state-perpetrated violence. *Journal of Social Issues*, *76*(4), 814–834. https://doi.org/10.1111/josi.12404.

Heberle, A. E., Rapa, L. J., & Faragó, F. (2020b). Critical consciousness in children and adolescents: A systematic review, critical assessment, and recommendations for future research. *Psychological Bulletin*, *146*(6), 525–551. https://doi.org/10.1037/bul0000230

hooks, b. (1981). *Ain't I a woman: Black women and feminism*. South End Press. https://doi.org/10.4324/9781315743264.

Horwitz, S. R., Shutts, K., & Olson, K. R. (2014). Social class differences produce social group preferences. *Developmental Science*, *17*(6), 991–1002. https://doi.org/10.1111/desc.12181.

Hughes, J. M., Bigler, R. S., & Levy, S. R. (2007). Consequences of learning about historical racism among European American and African American children. *Child Development*, *78*(6), 1689–1705. https://doi.org/10.1111/j.1467-8624.2007.01096.x.

Husband, T. (2012). "I don't see color": Challenging assumptions about discussing race with young children. *Early Childhood Education Journal, 39*(6), 365–371. https://doi.org/10.1007/s10643-011-0458-9.

Husband, T. (2018). Using multicultural picture books to promote racial justice in urban early childhood literacy classrooms. *Urban Education, 54*(8), 1058–1084. https://doi.org/10.1177/0042085918805145.

Husband, T. (Ed.). (2016). *But I don't see color: The perils, practices, and possibilities of antiracist education.* Springer.

Kendi, I. X. (2019). *How to be an antiracist.* OneWorld.

Kurtz-Costes, B., DeFreitas, S. C., Halle, T. G., & Kinlaw, C. R. (2011). Gender and racial favouritism in black and white preschool girls. *British Journal of Developmental Psychology, 29*, 270–287. http://doi.org/10.1111/j.2044-835X.2010.02018.x.

Lesane-Brown, C. L., Brown, T. N., Tanner-Smith, E. E., & Bruce, M. A. (2010). Negotiating boundaries and bonds: Frequency of young children's socialization to their ethnic/racial heritage. *Journal of Cross-Cultural Psychology, 41*(3), 457–464. https://doi.org/10.1177/0022022109359688.

Li, V., Spitzer, B., & Olson, K. R. (2014). Preschoolers reduce inequality while favoring individuals with more. *Child Development, 85*(3), 1123–1133. https://doi.org/10.1111/cdev.12198.

Liben, L. S., Bigler, R. S., & Krogh, H. R. (2001). Pink and blue collar jobs: Children's judgments of job status and job aspirations in relation to sex of worker. *Journal of Experimental Child Psychology, 79*(4), 346. https://doi.org/10.1006/jecp.2000.2611.

Loyd, A. B., & Gaither, S. E. (2018). Racial/ethnic socialization for White youth: What we know and future directions. *Journal of Applied Developmental Psychology, 59*, 54–64. https://doi.org/10.1016/j.appdev.2018.05.004.

Luguetti, C., Kirk, D., & Oliver, K. L. (2019). Towards a pedagogy of love: Exploring pre service teachers' and youth's experiences of an activist sport pedagogical model. *Physical Education & Sport Pedagogy, 24*(6), 629–646. https://doi.org/10.1080/17408989.2019.1663499.

Mandalaywala, T. M., Tai, C., & Rhodes, M. (2020). Children's use of race and gender as cues to social status. *PloS one, 15*(6), e0234398. https://doi.org/10.1371/journal.pone.0234398.

Martin, C. L., & Ruble, D. N. (2010). Patterns of gender development. *Annual Review of Psychology, 61*, 353–381. https://doi.org/10.1146/annurev.psych.093008.100511.

McGlothlin, H., & Killen, M. (2006), Intergroup attitudes of European American children attending ethnically homogeneous schools. *Child Development, 77*, 1375–1386. https://doi.org/10.1111/j.1467-8624.2006.00941.x.

Miller, E. T. (2015). Discourses of whiteness and blackness: An ethnographic study of three young children learning to be white. *Ethnography and Education, 10*(2), 137–153. https://doi.org/10.1080/17457823.2014.960437.

Mistry, R. S., Brown, C. S., Chow, K. A., & Collins, G. S. (2012). Increasing the complexity of young adolescents' beliefs about poverty and inequality: Results of an 8th grade social studies curriculum intervention. *Journal of Youth and Adolescence, 41*(6), 704–716. https://doi.org/10.1007/s10964-011-9699-6.

Mistry, R. S., Brown, C. S., White, E. S., Chow, K. A., & Gillen-O'Neel, C. (2015). Elementary school children's reasoning about social class: A mixed-methods study. *Child Development, 86*(5), 1653–1671. https://doi.org/10.1111/cdev.12407.

Ngai, P. B., & Koehn, P. H. (2011). Indigenous education for critical democracy: Teacher approaches and learning outcomes in a K-5 Indian education for all program. *Equity & Excellence in Education, 44*(2), 249–269. https://doi.org/10.1080/10665684.2011.559414.

Olson, K. R., Dweck, C. S., Spelke, E. S., & Banaji, M. R. (2011). Children's responses to group-based inequalities: Perpetuation and rectification. *Social Cognition, 29*(3), 270–287. https://doi.org/10.1521/soco.2011.29.3.270.

Olson, K. R., Shutts, K., Kinzler, K. D., & Weisman, K. G. (2012). Children associate racial groups with wealth: Evidence from South Africa. *Child Development, 83*(6), 1884–1899. https://doi.org/10.1111/j.1467-8624.2012.01819.x.

Osborne, K. R., Caughy, M. O., Oshri, A., Smith, E. P., & Owen, M. T. (2021). Racism and preparation for bias within African American families. *Cultural Diversity and Ethnic Minority Psychology, 27*(2), 269–279. https://doi.org/10.1037/cdp0000339.

Osorio, S. L. (2018). Toward a humanizing pedagogy: Using Latinx children's literature with early childhood students. *Bilingual Research Journal, 41*(1), 5–22. https://doi.org/10.1080/15235882.2018.1425165.

Overstreet, N. M., Rosenthal, L., & Case, K. A. (2020). Intersectionality as a radical framework for transforming our disciplines, social issues, and the world. *Journal of Social Issues. 76*, 779–795. https://doi.org/10.1111/josi.12414.

Pahlke, E., Bigler, R. S., & Martin, C. L. (2014). Can fostering children's ability to challenge sexism improve critical analysis, internalization, and enactment of inclusive, egalitarian peer relationships? *Journal of Social Issues, 70*(1), 115–133. https://doi.org/10.1111/josi.12050.

Patterson, M. M., Bigler, R. S., Pahlke, E. et al. (2019). Toward a developmental science of politics. *Monographs of the Society for Research in Child Development, 84*(3), 7–185. https://doi.org/10.1111/mono.12410.

Patterson, M. M., Pahlke, E., & Bigler, R. S. (2013). Witnesses to history: Children's views of race and the 2008 United States presidential election. *Analyses of Social Issues and Public Policy, 13*, 186–210. https://doi.org/10.1111/j.1530-2415.2012.01303.x.

Pauker, K., Brey, E. L., Lamer, S. A., & Weisbuch, M. (2019). Cultural snapshots: A method to capture social contexts in development of prejudice and stereotyping. In J. B. Benson (Ed.), *Advances in child development and behavior* (Vol. 56). Elsevier Academic Press, pp. 141–181. https://doi.org/10.1016/bs.acdb.2018.11.002.

Pinetta, B. J., Blanco Martinez, S., Cross, F. L., & Rivas, D. D. (2020). Inherently political? Associations of parent ethnic–racial socialization and sociopolitical discussions with Latinx youths' emergent civic engagement. *American Journal of Community Psychology, 66*(1/2), 94–105. https://doi.org/10.1002/ajcp.12435.

Quintana, S. M. (1998). Children's developmental understanding of ethnicity and race. *Applied and Preventive Psychology, 7*(1), 27–45. https://doi.org/10.1016/S0962-1849(98)80020-6.

Quintana, S. M. (2008). Racial perspective taking ability: Developmental, theoretical, and empirical trends. In S. M. Quintana & C. McKown (Eds.), *Handbook of race, racism, and the developing child*. John Wiley & Sons, Inc., pp. 16–36.

Raabe, T., & Beelmann, A. (2011). Development of ethnic, racial, and national prejudice in childhood and adolescence: A multinational meta-analysis of age differences. *Child Development*, *82*(6), 1715–1737. https://doi.org/10.1111/j.1467-8624.2011.01668.x.

Rapa, L. J., Bolding, C. W., & Jamil, F. M. (2020). Development and initial validation of the Short Critical Consciousness Scale (CCS-S). *Journal of Applied Developmental Psychology*, *70*. https://doi.org/10.1016/j.appdev.2020.101164.

Rapa, L. J., & Geldhof, G. J. (2020). Critical consciousness: New directions for understanding its development during adolescence. *Journal of Applied Developmental Psychology*, *70*, 101187. https://doi.org/10.1016/j.appdev.2020.101187.

Rizzo, M. T., & Killen, M. (2020). Children's evaluations of individually and structurally based inequalities: The role of status. *Developmental Psychology*, *56*(12), 2223–2235. https://doi.org/10.1037/dev0001118.

Roberts, S. O., & Rizzo, M. T. (2020). The psychology of American racism. *American Psychologist*, *76*(3), 475–487. http://dx.doi.org/10.1037/amp0000642.

Rogers, L. O., Rosario, R. J., Padilla, D., & Foo, C. (2021). "[I]t's hard because it's the cops that are killing us for stupid stuff": Racial identity in the sociopolitical context of Black Lives Matter. *Developmental Psychology*, *57*(1), 87–101. https://doi.org/10.1037/dev0001130.

Rutland, A., Killen, M., & Abrams, D. (2010). A new social-cognitive developmental perspective on prejudice: The interplay between morality and group identity. *Perspectives on Psychological Science*, *5*(3), 279–291. https://doi.org/10.1177/1745691610369468.

Sabol, T. J. , Busby, A. K. , & Hernandez, M. W. (2021). A critical gap in early childhood policies: Children's meaning making. *Translational Issues in Psychological Science*, *7*(1), 9–20. https://doi.org/10.1037/tps0000024.

Shedd, C. (2015). *Unequal city: Race, schools, and perceptions of injustice*. Russell Sage Foundation. https://www.jstor.org/stable/10.7758/9781610448529.

Short, G. (1991). Perceptions of inequality: Primary school children's discourse on social class. *Educational Studies*, *17*(1), 89–106. https://doi.org/10.1080/0305569910170107.

Shutts, K. (2015). Young children's preferences: Gender, race, and social status. *Child Development Perspectives*, *9*(4), 262–266. https://doi.org/10.1111/cdep.12154.

Shutts, K., Brey, E. L., Dornbusch, L. A., Slywotzky, N., & Olson, K. R. (2016). Children use wealth cues to evaluate others. *PLoS ONE*, *11*(3), 1–21. https://doi.org/10.1371/journal.pone.0149360.

Shutts, K., Roben, C. K. P., & Spelke, E. S. (2013). Children's use of social categories in thinking about people and social relationships. *Journal of Cognition and Development*, *14*(1), 35–62. https://doi.org/10.1080/15248372.2011.638686.

Silva, J. M. (2012). Critical classrooms: Using artists' lives to teach young students social groups, power, and privilege. *Urban Education*, *47*(4), 776–800. https://doi.org/10.1177/0042085912441187.

Skinner, A. L., & Meltzoff, A. N. (2019). Childhood experiences and intergroup biases among children. *Social Issues and Policy Review, 13*(1), 211–240. https://doi.org/10.1111/sipr.12054.

Stockstill, C. (2021). The "stuff" of class: How property rules in preschool reproduce class inequality. *Social Problems*. https://doi.org/10.1093/socpro/spab019.

Sullivan, J. N., Eberhardt, J. L., & Roberts, S. O. (2021). Conversations about race in Black and White US families: Before and after George Floyd's death. *Proceedings of the National Academy of Sciences, 118*(38). https://doi.org/10.1073/pnas.2106366118.

Suyemoto, K. L., & Hochman, A. L. (2021). "Taking the empathy to an activist state": Ally development as continuous cycles of critical understanding and action. *Research in Human Development, 18*(1–2), 105–148. https://doi.org/10.1080/15427609.2021.1928453.

Thornton, M. C., Chatters, L. M., Taylor, R. J., & Allen, W. R. (1990). Sociodemographic and environmental correlates of racial socialization by Black parents. *Child Development, 61*(2), 401–409. https://doi.org/10.2307/1131101.

Tintiangco-Cubales, A., Daus-Magbual, A., Desai, M., Sabac, A., & Torres, M. V. (2016). Into our hoods: Where critical performance pedagogy births resistance. *International Journal of Qualitative Studies in Education, 29*(10), 1308–1325. https://doi.org/10.1080/09518398.2016.1201165.

Van Deth, J. W., Abendschön, S., & Vollmar, M. (2011). Children and politics: An empirical reassessment of early political socialization. *Political Psychology, 32*(1), 147–174. https://doi.org/10.1111/j.1467-9221.2010.00798.x.

Vilkin, E., Einhorn, L., Satyanarayana, S., Eisu, A., Kimport, K., & Flentje, A. (2020). Elementary students' gender beliefs and attitudes following a 12-week arts curriculum focused on gender. *Journal of LGBT Youth, 17*(1), 70–88. https://doi.org/10.1080/19361653.2019.1613282.

Vittrup, B. (2016). Early childhood teachers' approaches to multicultural education & perceived barriers to disseminating anti-bias messages. *Multicultural Education*, 23, 37–41.

Vittrup, B. (2018). Color blind or color conscious? White American mothers' approaches to racial socialization. *Journal of Family Issues, 39*(3), 668–692. https://doi.org/10.1177/0192513X16676858.

Watts, R. J., Diemer, M. A., & Voight, A. M. (2011). Critical consciousness: Current status and future directions. Critical consciousness: Current status and future directions. *New Directions for Child and Adolescent Development, 134*, 43–57. https://doi.org/10.1002/cd.310.

Woods, T. A., Kurtz-Costes, B., & Rowley, S. J. (2005). The development of stereotypes about the rich and poor: Age, race, and family income differences in beliefs. *Journal of Youth and Adolescence, 34*(5), 437–445. https://doi.org/10.1007/s10964-005-7261-0.

Zucker, J. K., & Patterson, M. M. (2018). Racial socialization practices among white American parents: Relations to racial attitudes, racial identity, and school diversity. *Journal of Family Issues, 39*(16), 3903–3930.https://doi.org/10.1177/0192513X18800766.

# 5

# Adolescents' Developmental Pathways to Critical Consciousness in the Contexts of Racial Oppression and Privilege

LAURA WRAY-LAKE, JASON A. PLUMMER, AND LAUREN ALVIS

Adolescents are key leaders in recognizing and challenging the pressing social and racial injustices of our time. Continued structural violence against Black, Latinx, Asian, and Indigenous communities and the visible rise of white supremacy in the United States have renewed racial justice uprisings and spurred greater awareness of structural racism for individuals across racial and ethnic backgrounds (Barroso & Minkin, 2020). These contexts are an important backdrop for the critical consciousness development of many adolescents today, yet some, particularly youth with white privilege, remain relatively unfazed by racial injustices or believe that racism no longer exists (Hagerman, 2018). Critical consciousness has long been understood as a process of moving from oppression to liberation (Freire, 1970) and, likewise, because of their contemporary and historical experiences of racial oppression, research has largely focused on Black and Latinx youth's critical consciousness (Heberle et al., 2020). However, to dismantle systems of oppression, people from all backgrounds – even those who have not directly experienced oppression – must become critically conscious: that is, reflective, motivated, and active in challenging systems of inequality and oppression.

Our chapter is premised on the idea that society's racial hierarchy and pervasive systemic racism create very different developmental contexts for youth of color and white[1] youth to become critically conscious. The idea that race and racism shape development is certainly not new (e.g., García Coll et al., 1996; Spencer, 1995). Our aim is to bring together conceptual and empirical work that speaks to how and why developmental pathways to critical consciousness across adolescence differ for youth with different experiences of racial oppression and privilege. This chapter has three main

[1] In line with the Associated Press and others, we capitalize Black, Latinx, Asian, and Indigenous because these terms refer to racial and ethnic groups with particular histories, cultures, and collective identities. We do not capitalize white because "white" came to exist by marginalizing other groups and white supremacists claim the capital "W." We believe it is crucial to name white as a racial group and call attention to the ways whiteness operates.

sections. First, we situate critical consciousness within a developmental perspective and discuss tenets of relational developmental systems theory and critical race and intersectional theories that can advance understanding of how youth become critically conscious. We then draw on these perspectives to consider contexts and processes of critical consciousness development. Specifically, the second section positions racism and whiteness as primary contexts that shape youth's critical consciousness development, and the third section considers heterogeneity in critical consciousness developmental processes in contexts of racial oppression and privilege. We end by looking ahead to future research.

We acknowledge that discussing many different racial and ethnic groups as "youth of color" grossly oversimplifies the complex, nuanced, and distinct histories of racial oppression that minoritized[2] racial and ethnic groups have experienced in the United States (Sánchez-Jankowski, 2002). This broad terminology draws out our main points of contrast with white youth, but ultimately this generality is a gap in the literature and this chapter. We also acknowledge our own positionalities. The first, second, and third authors, respectively, identify as a white cisgender woman, a Black first-generation American cisgender man, and a Latinx and white cisgender woman. We bring different personal experiences and histories with multiple systems of oppression, and we endeavored to elevate each other's unique expertise and perspective and challenge our own and each other's biases in writing this chapter. The chapter centers on adolescents, including some research with young adults, primarily within the United States, and does not comprehensively cover factors undergirding critical consciousness development. We excluded proximal contexts such as schools, families, and neighborhoods in critical consciousness development, as they are outside of the scope of our work here (see, however, Godfrey & Rapa, in press). Despite these caveats, this chapter sets a course for a developmentally informed research agenda to understand distinct pathways to critical consciousness development for adolescents that vary based on positions and experiences in systems of racial oppression.

## INTEGRATING CRITICAL AND DEVELOPMENTAL THEORIES

The chapter first reviews several theoretical perspectives with insights for research on youth's developmental paths to critical consciousness. We begin by briefly overviewing critical consciousness theory itself, conceptualizing the three key dimensions of critical consciousness from a developmental lens. Next, we highlight tenets of relational developmental systems (RDS) theory

[2] We use the terms "marginalized" and "minoritized" interchangeably to refer to social groups that are devalued in society through dynamics created by dominant groups. Minoritized is preferred over "minority group" to acknowledge power dynamics and recognize that subjugated groups are not always numerical minorities (Sensoy & DiAngelo, 2012).

that can inform the study of dynamic and heterogeneous processes of youth's critical consciousness development. Much of the existing research on critical consciousness lacks a developmental framing, and RDS theory offers a set of developmental principles that can spur research on critical consciousness as a set of dimensions that change in complex ways over time, interact with other developmental systems, result from individuals' reciprocal exchanges in contexts, and vary across individuals. Finally, we turn to critical race theories, which are crucial for situating youth's critical consciousness development in the context of systems of racism and other forms of oppression. Critical race, critical whiteness, and intersectionality theories are useful lenses for conceptualizing and analyzing systems of power and privilege, which are important contexts for youth's critical consciousness development as well as targets for transformative change, which can result from young people's critical reflection, motivation, and action.

## CRITICAL CONSCIOUSNESS THEORY AND CONCEPTS

Born from Paulo Freire's (1970) work documenting the education and liberation of Brazilian farm workers from oppressive conditions, critical consciousness embodies a process by which individuals become critically aware of inequalities and empowered to dismantle systems of oppression. Developmental scientists emphasize three main dimensions of critical consciousness: critical reflection, critical motivation, and critical action (Watts et al., 2011). Examining critical consciousness *development* requires situating each dimension within a developmental perspective. First, critical reflection is a cognitive dimension of critical consciousness, defined as awareness of societal inequalities and analysis of the structural and historical roots of inequalities (Watts et al., 2011). Critical reflection includes viewing social problems from a systems level, and thus structural attributions of inequalities are an important, understudied component of critical reflection (Bañales et al., 2020; Godfrey & Wolf, 2016). Developmentally, youth from across different racial and ethnic groups demonstrate increasingly complex understandings of inequality and its structural roots across adolescence (Flanagan et al., 2014). Cognitive growth in abstract thinking and perspective taking likely facilitate critical perspectives on the world (Van der Graaff et al., 2014). Critical reflection about racial and societal inequalities overlaps with moral reasoning and judgments regarding justice, fairness, and equality; yet, cognitive growth in moral reasoning can be nonlinear (Krettenauer et al., 2014), and this complexity may partly explain why some youth of color and white youth are critically reflective about some systems of oppression but not others, or why some simultaneously hold opposing views about inequality (Godfrey & Wolf, 2016; Moffitt et al., 2021).

Second, critical motivation is broadly defined as individuals' perceived abilities to advance equity and justice, either individually or collectively, and desires and commitments to make such change (Jemal 2017; Rapa et al., 2020). This dimension has also been called critical efficacy, which entails feeling able to effectively participate in politics and effect political change (Diemer & Rapa, 2016; Watts et al., 2011); similar terms include civic or political efficacy or agency, internal efficacy, sociopolitical control, and emotional empowerment (Seider et al, 2020). The broader conceptualization of critical motivation may be advantageous from a developmental perspective in its potential to clarify youth's multiple motivations for challenging oppression that go beyond personal competence and include collective agency as well as values, goals, and hopes. Adolescents' critical reflection on social hierarchies and their racial and ethnic identity development may be foundational for critical motivation development (Kiang et al., 2021). The limited available evidence points to developmental growth in critical motivation (or related constructs) for Black and Latinx adolescents (Seider et al., 2020) and majority white samples (Zaff et al., 2011), yet research on social justice values in a Swiss sample showcased upward and downward patterns of change during adolescence (Daniel et al., 2014), suggesting wide variation in patterns of critical motivation development.

Third, critical action is broadly defined as actions that challenge inequalities and systems of oppression (Diemer et al., 2021) and is often operationalized as political protesting, organizing, and other forms of activism. Yet, critical action can encompass a wider range of resistance behaviors, such as refuting stereotypes and reframing narratives about one's historically marginalized group, reclaiming history or spaces, or noncompliance. Critical actions increasingly take place on social media, which are becoming central youth-led civic spaces (Conner & Slattery, 2014; Reynolds & Mayweather, 2017; Wilf & Wray-Lake, 2021). Watts and Hipolito-Delgado (2015) frame critical action as occurring at three levels: personal action, group action, and mass action. Adopting this multilevel framework could address a gap in research by emphasizing both individual and collective forms of critical actions. Additionally, the extant literature commonly measures political actions without expressly considering whether these actions challenge systems of oppression, yet promising approaches address this limitation, such as the Anti-Racism Action Scale (Aldana et al., 2019) and the Black community activism orientation scale, which focuses on advocating for the Black community or challenging anti-Black racial injustices (Hope et al., 2019). Considered developmentally, youth across racial and ethnic groups become more politically engaged during adolescence and young adulthood (Wray-Lake et al., 2017, 2020). These trends are typically attributed to increasing access to opportunities to take political actions, greater knowledge and awareness of issues, and consolidation of personal beliefs about social issues. Yet, the development of critical actions can also vary substantially across race, gender, and social class (Wray-Lake et al., 2020).

The study of youth critical consciousness is interdisciplinary, with different fields using various terminology and conceptual models (Christens et al., 2016; Jemal, 2017; Thomas et al., 2014). Although research is exponentially growing and has advanced theory and practice in many ways, we still lack knowledge of longitudinal, developmental processes for youth critical consciousness and know little about how critical consciousness develops for youth with different experiences of racial privilege and oppression (Heberle et al., 2020). We next turn to relational developmental systems theory and then to critical race and intersectionality theories, which can advance thinking on how critical reflection, motivation, and action develop for adolescents from different racial and ethnic groups in the context of racial oppression and privilege.

## RELATIONAL DEVELOPMENTAL SYSTEMS THEORY

Several principles of relational developmental systems (RDS) theory (Lerner et al., 2014; Overton, 2015) can help situate youth critical consciousness within a developmental perspective. First, RDS assumes that developmental change unfolds over time and can be multidirectional and nonlinear, and that all youth have potential for positive plasticity. In other words, all youth are capable of positive change in critical reflection, motivation, and action, and their developmental trajectories can take various shapes, including upward or downward directions, across adolescence. Embracing this principle alone would transform research on youth critical consciousness in recognizing that *any* young person is capable of becoming critically conscious (regardless of racial oppression or privilege) and that cross-sectional snapshots of critical consciousness tell us little about development. Second, developmental processes are assumed to be dynamic and transactional, suggesting that dimensions of critical consciousness may be bidirectionally related over time and that changes in critical consciousness inform and are informed by other domains of development, such as cognition, social and emotional functioning, and identity. Applying this principle suggests that research would benefit from examining the dynamic interplay of critical reflection, motivation, and action across adolescence, and as we discuss later, this approach may be especially useful for illuminating different entry points and processes of critical consciousness development in contexts of oppression and privilege.

A third relevant RDS principle is that development arises from individual–context exchanges that unfold over time: Critical consciousness development results from experiences in proximal environments and interactions with societal systems including institutions, policies, and cultural norms. An RDS perspective emphasizes influential roles of contexts on individuals and individuals as active agents who shape contexts, and the ongoing interactions between individuals and contexts form the foundation for development. One obvious implication for critical consciousness development is that these processes must be situated within culture and context, as we illustrate later in discussing the role of racism and whiteness as contexts for critical consciousness development. Additionally, processes of critical consciousness development embody the RDS assertion that adolescents are powerful agents of their own development: through critical reflection, motivation, and action, youth can actively construct, dismantle, contribute, and navigate everyday contexts and larger institutional forces. As another example of individual–context exchanges relevant to critical consciousness, racial identity development is one set of agentic processes, among many, that illuminates how youth make sense of their racial oppression and privileges and define themselves in ways that challenge or uphold oppression; these identity processes are intertwined with critical consciousness development and situated in context (Mathews et al., 2020).

Finally, a key RDS principle is heterogeneity of development (Lerner et al., 2014). Youth can differ substantially in developmental trajectories and processes related to critical consciousness. Embracing heterogeneity would mean examining variations in specific dimensions of critical consciousness for youth with different identities and backgrounds who experience different oppressions and privileges across systems. An important way to highlight heterogeneity in critical consciousness development involves examining how the developmental sequencing of – and interrelationships between – critical reflection, motivation, and action look different for different youth, a topic we explore later in the chapter. Although little research thus far has focused on differences in critical consciousness developmental processes across subgroups of youth (Heberle et al., 2020), the field is ripe for identifying specific patterns and processes as well as highlighting the role of individual–context interactions in shaping these processes. In summary, RDS theory offers a foundation for examining dynamic, youth-led, contextually influenced, and specific developmental pathways to critical consciousness. Despite its breadth and flexibility, however, RDS theory does not explicitly articulate the role of systems of oppression such as racism (Santos & Toomey, 2018).

## CRITICAL RACE AND INTERSECTIONALITY THEORIES

Critical race theory, across its multiple forms and articulations, fundamentally argues that race is socially constructed rather than biologically rooted and that racism is a powerful and pervasive organizing force in US society (Crenshaw, 1991; Delgado & Stefancic, 2017). We argue, like many before us, that racism and racial hierarchies shape adolescents' critical consciousness in important ways (e.g., Anyiwo et al., 2018; Hope & Spencer, 2017; Watts &

Flanagan, 2007). Critical race theory emphasizes that racial oppression normalizes the dehumanization of people of color, systematically excludes them from desirable social resources on the basis of racial or ethnic background, and secures white advantage as privilege or social standing (Olson, 2004). Racism is deeply entrenched in societal institutions such as the educational, financial, health, child welfare, and justice systems (Feagin, 2013; Miller & Garran, 2017), plays out in everyday interactions of adolescents' lives (Brown, 2017), and has numerous deleterious consequences for the health and development of youth of color (Causadias & Umaña-Taylor, 2018). The conceptual link from systemic racism to critical consciousness is, we hope, obvious: Critical consciousness has been called the "antidote to oppression" and framed as a process by which youth of color become agents of change in analyzing racial and other inequalities and advancing their own and others' liberation from oppression (Watts et al., 1999). Research often focuses on youth critical consciousness in the context of racial oppression among Black and Latinx youth, with much less attention to Asian or Indigenous youth (Heberle et al., 2020). Sometimes research utilizes race and ethnic self-identification as crude markers of contexts of racial oppression, yet critical race theory calls for recognizing that race and ethnicity are rough proxies for the dynamic processes of racialization, discrimination, and systematic exclusion (Hochschild et al., 2012), suggesting that, when possible, systems of oppression should be conceptualized and studied explicitly (Godfrey & Burson, 2018).

Critical whiteness studies is a branch of critical race theory that emphasizes white supremacy and privilege as root causes of racism (Cabrera et al., 2017; Leonardo, 2013). Whiteness goes beyond skin color and is a social construction that upholds hierarchies of power and dominance among racial and ethnic groups, from which whites systematically and continuously benefit (Applebaum, 2016). White supremacy has been pervasive and destructive since the country's inception up to the present day because whiteness is rendered invisible, normal, and privileged at all levels of society. A critical whiteness perspective argues that whiteness must be made visible and explicitly challenged to disrupt and dismantle systems of power and dominance (Helms, 2020). White youth and adults, even those with "good intentions," benefit from white supremacy and are thus complicit in upholding racist systems (Applebaum, 2016). White youth's development of critical reflection on racial injustice and whiteness, critical motivation, and antiracist critical actions are key to rejecting notions of white supremacy and resisting racial oppression in social structures (Aldana et al., 2019). Scholars are increasingly examining white youth's critical reflection on whiteness (e.g., Hazelbaker et al., 2021; Hershberg & Johnson, 2019; Tyler, Geldhof, et al., 2020). The field should continue to move beyond an exclusive emphasis on critical consciousness among youth of color, which implies that these youth bear the brunt of combating oppression and runs the risk of absolving individuals from privileged backgrounds from taking responsibility for sustaining and perpetuating systems of oppression (Miller & Garran, 2017). However, embracing a critical whiteness perspective risks recentering whiteness and further marginalizing youth of color. Thus, scholars who incorporate this perspective must remain vigilant and critical of the ways that research and practice, including their own, can uphold racial power and privilege (Applebaum, 2016). Seriously contending with whiteness can advance the ultimate goal of supporting all youth in developing awareness, motivation, and actions to dismantle racism and other systems of oppression.

Intersectionality is a sister perspective to critical race theory that rests on the idea that multiple, interlocking systems of power and oppression exist outside of individuals and operate together to create unique experiences of marginalization (Cole, 2009; Collins, 2014). Intersectionality originated from Black feminist activists and scholar activists, some of whom were also lesbian or queer, and expanded from there (Combahee River Collective, 1974; Collins, 2019; Crenshaw, 1991; hooks, 1984). Although our chapter focuses primarily on the role of race, racism, and whiteness in shaping processes of critical consciousness development, forms of marginalization due to gender and sexuality, immigration status, social class, and (dis)ability status also operate in interlocking ways to harm youth from these marginalized groups while privileging others. Intersectionality calls for analysis of how power operates alongside how marginalization is experienced when understanding impacts of systems of oppression (Moradi & Grzanka, 2017). For example, white youth who hold lesbian, gay, bisexual, or queer (LGBQ+) identities move through systems where white privilege and marginalization due to sexuality alternately or simultaneously operate to influence critical consciousness. Likewise, Black boys' experiences of anti-Black racism and male privilege in school or other contexts may uniquely shape their critical consciousness development. Intersectionality can offer conceptual and analytic tools with which to consider how access to oppression and privilege simultaneously shapes critical consciousness development (Godfrey & Burson, 2018). In summary, infusing a relational developmental systems perspective with critical race, whiteness, and intersectionality theories offers new directions for the study of youth's critical consciousness development.

## RACISM AND WHITENESS AS CONTEXTS OF CRITICAL CONSCIOUSNESS DEVELOPMENT

From a critical race theory lens, it is important to consider the multitiered impact of racism in the lives of young people of color in the United States. This focus also aligns with the RDS principle that development arises from individual–context exchanges that unfold over time. Blending these theoretical perspectives, we argue that systems of racism and white privilege create very different contexts for youth's critical consciousness development that depend on their racial positions in society. Research has increasingly documented racism's pernicious and lasting harms on health, mental health, educational attainment, and economic well-being across the lifespan for Black, Latinx, Asian, and Indigenous individuals (Carter et al., 2017; Paradies et al., 2015; Priest et al., 2013); this research largely focuses on interpersonal racism, with less attention given to systemic racism. Occurring alongside these harms is critical consciousness development: processes that youth oppressed by racism engage in to cope with, survive, resist, and challenge racism. We highlight empirical work on how youth of color's critical consciousness development occurs in response to systemic as well as interpersonal racism. We then consider research and thinking about white youth's processes of critical consciousness development in the context of racial privilege.

## SYSTEMIC RACISM

Youth of color's recognition of and experiences with systems that harm and disadvantage them are undoubtedly detrimental for their well-being, yet critical consciousness offers a way of responding that can enable youth of color to cope or heal and can also build political power and stimulate social and political change (Hope & Spencer, 2017). Black youth's stress from institutional and cultural racism predicts more engagement in critical political actions such as protesting, some of which entail high personal risk, as well as higher critical reflection and motivation (Hope et al., 2019; 2020). Youth from minoritized racial and ethnic groups, such as Black and Latinx youth, also engage in critical actions in response to policies that perpetuate racism and exclusion, such as unjust policing and hostile immigration laws (Hope et al., 2016; Wray-Lake et al., 2018). Often, links from systemic racism to youth of color's critical actions are theorized – and sometimes demonstrated – to be mediated by critical reflection or motivation (Hope et al., 2020), underscoring that dimensions of critical consciousness are developing in a dynamic process over time. Systemic racism in these studies is often measured as youth's awareness of or reports of stress from racist policies and/or practices embedded in institutions.

Youth of color vary in their understandings of systemic racism based on many factors, such as the history of their racial or ethnic group, their ethnic/racial socialization experiences, and their personal experiences of racial discrimination (Anyiwo et al., 2018). Critical responses to systemic racism also vary. For example, for Black college students at predominantly white institutions, the likelihood of taking critical action in response to institutionalized and cultural racism was predicted by complex interactions between critical reflection, efficacy, and gender (Leath & Chavous, 2017). Such findings underscore the RDS idea that critical consciousness development is heterogeneous and dynamic. Other work shows that some youth of color join intergroup coalitions in racial justice movements targeting systemic racism, such as Black youth engaged in the movement to support the Deferred Action for Childhood Arrivals (DACA) Act (Hope et al., 2016). Thus, some youth of color are galvanized to combat oppression directed toward other groups, recognizing shared liberation goals in combating systemic oppressions. In examining youth's critical consciousness development in the context of systemic racism, it is important to understand youth's exposure to and understandings of intersecting systems of oppression.

## PERSONAL EXPERIENCES OF RACIAL DISCRIMINATION

Individual–context exchanges are fundamental drivers of development (e.g., Lerner et al., 2014), and interpersonal racism is a common daily experience in youth of color's everyday lives (e.g., Huynh et al., 2016; Ortega-Williams et al., 2022). Likewise, youth of color's personal experiences with racial oppression are part of what drives their critical reflection, motivation, and action to challenge injustices. For example, Latinx and Asian youth who experienced racial discrimination reported more critical views of government (Ballard, 2016), and Black youth who experienced racial stress from personal discrimination had higher critical reflection, motivation, and action (Hope et al., 2020). Black youth are disproportionately more likely to be stopped, targeted, and brutalized by the police; for some, these experiences produce a form of carceral knowledge and motivation for critical action (Cohen & Luttig, 2020). Encounters with racism can prompt Black and Latinx youth to reconsider or redefine what it means to be a member of their racial or ethnic group (Neville & Cross, 2017). These same encounters with racism are theorized as starting points for critical consciousness development (Watts et al., 2011). Indeed, Black youth and other youth of color are theorized to have a "second sight" or unique vantage point that comes from experiences of racism that helps to navigate power and privilege and offers deeper insights into injustice and systems of oppression (Cammarota, 2016). This second sight predisposes youth of color to become critically conscious, but does not guarantee it. As Tyler, Olsen, et al. (2020) point out through mixed methods research, interpersonal discrimination predicts critical action, on average, for youth across ethnic/racial groups, but if, when, and how youth choose to respond via critical action depends on their ethnic/racial and social positionalities as well as their attributions about inequalities, resources, and opportunities.

Youth of color cope with the burdens of racism and whiteness in numerous ways that may or may not include critical action, again indicating that critical consciousness development is heterogeneous.

When youth of color have more positive private regard, or positive affirmation of, pride in, and belonging to one's racial or ethnic group, they may be more protected from negative effects of racial discrimination (Umaña-Taylor et al., 2014). Pride in one's ethnic/racial group can be a source of resistance to oppression in itself (Love, 2019), and belonging to a collective can inspire critical motivation to challenge oppression (Martinez et al., 2012). Although racism and racialized experiences may help explain how youth of color come to be critically conscious around race and racism, other explanatory processes may be needed to understand youth of color's critical consciousness development around other forms of oppression (Diemer et al., 2015). Intriguingly, however, among college students identifying as Indigenous people and people of color, ethnic identity exploration was positively associated with ally identity – that is, commitments and behaviors to support the social change efforts of other minoritized groups (Fish et al., 2021). Thus, for some, one's own interpersonal experiences with racism can expand desires to dismantle oppression more broadly.

## WHITE PRIVILEGE

The socialization and institutionalization of whiteness presents significant obstacles to white youth's development of critical race consciousness. White youth often lack developmental opportunities to observe, learn about, and discuss racial inequalities in their everyday environments (Hazelbaker et al., 2021) owing to the socialization of color-blind racial ideology and reproduction of whiteness (Bonilla-Silva, 2003; Hagerman, 2018). White youth may be implicitly or explicitly taught not to acknowledge racism, and critical reflection may be actively countered in white spaces by messages about meritocracy that frame individuals as responsible for their own problems rather than recognizing systemic sources of inequality and that communicate white supremacy in tacitly or explicitly upholding and maintaining oppressive systems (Hagerman, 2018; Olson, 2004). Whiteness can manifest for youth in various ways, including psychologically (e.g., remaining ignorant or in denial of racism), behaviorally (e.g., racial discrimination or microaggressions), and emotionally (e.g., guilt, anger, and fragility; Coleman et al., 2021). These aspects of whiteness stifle critical reflection about racism and other inequalities, thereby reifying systems of oppression. Supporting this idea, awareness of oppression was found to be lower among white college students than among Black college students (Thomas et al., 2014). Longitudinally, white youth were higher in awareness of inequality than Latinx or Asian youth in sixth grade, but their awareness did not change across adolescence and ended up lower than Black, Latinx, and Asian youth in late adolescence (Wray-Lake et al., 2022). This overall lack of growth in white youth's awareness of inequality contrasts with cognitive developmental expectations of increases in critical reflection skills with age, a pattern that does not appear for white youth on average. Given RDS perspectives that all youth are capable of growth in critical consciousness and that such development stems from person–environment interactions, parents, educators, and others have serious work to do in restructuring white youth's everyday developmental contexts in ways that fully acknowledge how racism and whiteness operate. Research is urgently needed that pinpoints how contexts and socialization of whiteness operate as barriers to white youth's development of critical reflection, motivation, and action, and how socialization approaches that embrace critical race perspectives are adopted.

White identity development, which describes white youth's understandings of and relationship to white privilege, white supremacy, and racism, is key to understanding white youth's antiracist critical consciousness development. Although not often studied with youth, Helms' (2020) White Racial Identity Development (WRID) model proposes two broad categories of white identity that span internalized racism to evolving nonracist (now commonly termed antiracist) identity, with antiracist identity including thinking, motivations, and actions that counter racism, white supremacy, and white privilege. The development of antiracist white identity may parallel critical consciousness development for white youth. For example, antiracist activists seek opportunities to learn how systems of oppression are rooted in whiteness and explore personal identity in relation to racism, privilege, and proximity to whiteness (Collins et al., 2019). Youth activists' definitions of antiracism overlap with white identity development and emphasize reflecting on and rejecting white privilege and power, elevating marginalized voices, and actively resisting racial oppression through action (Toraif et al., 2021). Witnessing racism and the harm it causes can lead white youth to rethink their white identity and move from internalizing to challenging racism (Moffitt et al., 2021). Thus, critical reflection on racial inequalities informs and is informed by white identity development, reflecting a dynamic developmental process. White guilt, empathetic responding to others' experiences of racism, and social responsibility values may spur the development of antiracist attitudes and behaviors (Dull et al., 2021; Spanierman et al., 2006). Unfortunately, qualitative studies suggest that many white youth hold color -blind racial beliefs that race does not matter or that racism no longer exists and feel uncomfortable talking about race, which are facets of white identity reflecting internalized racism (Hagerman, 2018; Moffitt et al., 2021). Aligned with RDS theory, developing an antiracist white identity requires lifelong vigilance and self-work, as white individuals can shift expressions of white identity across time and contexts (Helms, 2020).

Individuals holding social identities that are differentially privileged may be able to draw on their marginalized identity to help them recognize the privilege they receive for other aspects of their identity (Cole, 2009). For example, in a predominantly white sample of heterosexual college students, women demonstrated a greater awareness of heterosexual privilege compared to men (Montgomery & Stewart, 2012). Thus, experiences of marginalization perhaps enhance recognition of others' oppression and spark reflection on one's own privilege. Among cisgender heterosexual Chinese young adults in Hong Kong, critical reflection on sexual and gender inequalities was associated with lower internalized domination of LGBT groups (Chan & Mak, 2020). This finding underscores that critical reflection on oppression and privilege may be key to shifting critical motivations and actions among dominant groups. Research that takes an intersectional perspective may help us better understand the multifaceted experiences that prompt white youth's antiracist critical consciousness development.

## HETEROGENEITY IN CRITICAL CONSCIOUSNESS DEVELOPMENTAL PROCESSES

The prior section laid out how racial oppression and white privilege serve as contexts for critical consciousness development. Now, we turn our attention to heterogeneity in developmental processes, as youth within and across racial and ethnic groups vary in how they become critically conscious. Indeed, RDS theory emphasizes heterogeneity in development, and one way to examine heterogeneity is to consider variation in the ways in which critical reflection, motivation, and action emerge and overlap for different youth. In merging RDS and critical theories, we argue that youth's varying patterns of critical consciousness development may have different meanings and explanations when considered in the context of racial oppression and privilege. To illustrate this point, we consider potential explanations for youth's levels of critical reflection, motivation, and action through critical race and whiteness lenses.

Some youth are low across critical reflection, motivation, and action (Godfrey et al., 2019; Suzuki, 2021), and reasons may tie to systems of oppression and privilege. For youth of color, it may be temporarily adaptive to justify existing systems rather than critically challenge them, although these system-justifying beliefs can have longer-term negative consequences for well-being (Godfrey et al., 2017). White youth can often easily remain comfortable with white privilege and its benefits, especially when their everyday environments uphold systems of whiteness, and never come to critique or challenge oppression (Hagerman, 2018).

Other youth may show critical reflection by recognizing the structural roots of social problems yet report low critical motivation and action. These youth may be on a journey through critical consciousness development that begins with critical reflection (Watts et al., 2011). Some youth in urban neighborhoods characterized by poverty, community violence, and state violence are critically reflective about these problems but feel disempowered to act due to the overwhelming nature of these problems, highlighting contextual barriers, including systemic and interpersonal racism, to critical motivation and action (Wray-Lake & Abrams, 2020). Critical motivation and action may be low among some critically reflective white youth because they lack personal incentive to challenge systems from which they benefit. White allyship and antiracist identity development requires an abstract and personalized understanding of systemic inequality (Helms, 2020); studies show that educational experiences can enhance white individuals' critical reflection, especially when they understand racism emotionally and psychologically (Coleman et al., 2021; Smith & Redington, 2010).

Some youth are highly critically reflective and motivated, yet low on action. Christens et al. (2018) called these youth "critical and hopeful," whereas others have named them "armchair activists" (Watts & Guessous, 2006) or "civic sympathizers" (Voight & Torney-Purta, 2013; Wray-Lake & Shubert, 2019). Referring to youth as "armchair activists" is unnecessarily pejorative as structural barriers often reduce opportunities for critical action and youth can play important roles in identifying historical-structural roots of racial equity while being otherwise inactive in challenging systems of oppression (Mayorga-Gallo, 2019). These youth may be poised to act critically to challenge inequalities when or if opportunities arise. However, youth of color face substantially more barriers in being heard and seen as legitimate by adults in civic spaces (Gordon, 2007), and adolescents more broadly often lack access to formal channels of political action (Wray-Lake, 2019). Thus, youth's critical action may often be the last piece to fall into place. In a longitudinal national sample of adolescents, Wray-Lake and Shubert (2019) found that civic sympathizers were likely to lower their civic values over time, pointing to challenges of sustaining critical values and motivation without any action. Furthermore, some critically conscious youth may step back from critical action, yet maintain their critical reflection and motivation, to avoid feelings of burden or burnout due to psychological stress or to competing demands like academics (Ballard & Ozer, 2016). Youth of color may experience heightened racial battle fatigue – that is, burdens of everyday racism through their activism that prompt them to pause critical actions (Gorski, 2019).

Finally, some youth of color are highly critically motivated and active, yet low on critical reflection (Godfrey et al., 2019; Suzuki, 2021). Youth engaged in racial justice movements or other critical actions who are low on critical reflection may gain exposure over time to knowledge of historical oppression and deeper structural roots of social problems (Bañales et al., 2021). Such educational opportunities are often lacking in schools, so youth must find them elsewhere, such as through community-based organizations, movement spaces, or on social media (Kirshner, 2015). Youth from any racial or ethnic background who lack a critical lens but are motivated and engaged in addressing problems may endorse racially color-blind approaches and lean on individual explanations for inequalities (Desante & Smith, 2020). Some

Black youth adhere to respectability politics, seeking to survive white dominance and defy negative stereotypes by adopting behaviors that white culture views as respectful rather than challenging the system (Obasogie & Newman, 2016). Such beliefs may lead to being acritical yet civically motivated and engaged. White youth in this group may have internalized messages about white supremacy or may lack awareness of their own white identity (Helms, 2020). A challenge for engaging white youth in allyship is the potential for well-intentioned allies to operate from a "savior complex" and behave paternalistically toward communities of color (Spanierman & Smith, 2017). Such paternalism can convey a sense of superiority, cause harm by dehumanizing people of color, and reify white dominance and sustain white privilege (Trepagnier, 2010). Racial justice allyship requires antiracist critical reflection (i.e., recognizing the power and privilege afforded based on whiteness) that also prioritizes a focus on racial justice and equity (Smith & Redington, 2010).

Taken together, these empirical examples demonstrate considerable variation in youth's critical consciousness at particular points in time, given that most research in this area is cross-sectional. Couching developmental processes of critical consciousness within the contexts of racial oppression and privilege can offer important and divergent explanations for developmental patterns among youth from different racial and ethnic backgrounds and experiences. Future research is ripe for examining the role of racial oppression and privilege in shaping youth's critical reflection, motivation, and action. Finally, it is worth emphasizing the practical benefit of examining the three dimensions of critical consciousness holistically: To dismantle racism and other systems of oppression, we need youth who are critically reflective, motivated, and active in challenging multiple, overlapping systems.

## FUTURE DIRECTIONS

The main point of this chapter is that research on youth's critical consciousness would benefit from being more developmental *and* more contextualized within systems of racial oppression and privilege. Integrating relational developmental systems principles with critical race, whiteness, and intersectional lenses offers important directions for future research on youth's critical consciousness development. Although we hope this chapter pushes the field forward in numerous ways, here we highlight a few promising next steps for research.

From an RDS perspective, critical consciousness develops as a result of individual–context exchanges that dynamically unfold over time and differ across people. Clear ways to embrace this thinking include, among others: (1) greater use of longitudinal designs, (2) more focus on dynamic interactions between youth and their contexts, and (3) more recognition of complexity and heterogeneity in processes of critical consciousness development. It is worth stating explicitly that these future directions could be taken up in quantitative or qualitative research. As our examination of the dynamic codevelopment of critical consciousness dimensions underscored, any of the three dimensions – whether reflection, motivation, or action – could be a launching point for critical consciousness development. This idea has implications for innovations in educational and intervention research, which could consider multipronged strategies that emphasize critical reflection, motivation, action, or all three simultaneously (Watts & Hipolito-Delgado, 2015). More broadly, we believe it is time for the field to move beyond unidirectional conceptual models, which are often tested with cross-sectional data, and embrace more of the multidirectional and heterogeneous complexity in critical consciousness development.

The study of youth's critical consciousness would greatly benefit from explicitly incorporating systems of racial oppression and privilege into theory and research on critical consciousness development. Research examining youth's reports of cultural and institutional racism represent clear examples of incorporating systems of oppression into research on critical consciousness development (e.g., Hope et al., 2019, 2020). White supremacy and privilege has been largely absent in research on youth critical consciousness despite the pernicious ways these forces operate in society and in youth's lives to uphold racial hierarchies (Applebaum, 2016). The field should seek to strengthen conceptualization and operationalization of systems of oppression and privilege in developmental research. For example, examining school-, neighborhood-, state-, or country-level analyses of oppressive policies and practices may provide insight into the systems contexts in which youth of color and white youth develop critical consciousness. A society's institutional and cultural structures, norms, and hierarchies of power and privilege often are translated to adolescents through mediating institutions wherein adolescents directly interact with others (Flanagan et al., 2011). Hence, youth's reactions to policies and rhetoric that are oppressive to particular groups offers a way to get at how systems of oppression and privilege filter into youth's experiences and then shape their critical consciousness (e.g., Kennedy et al., 2020). Research should further examine messages conveyed to adolescents about race, racism, and whiteness by families, schools, peers, and community-based organizations and how these messages inform adolescents' critical consciousness. Evidence already demonstrates that parents' racial socialization and school racial messages relate to youth's critical consciousness (Bañales et al., 2020; 2021) and can be expanded to include analyses of dynamic, longitudinal processes, distinct patterns for youth of different racial and ethnic groups, and other mediating institutions. To advance this line of inquiry, the field clearly needs to ramp up research that focuses on different racially minoritized groups (with various Asian and Indigenous groups particularly underrepresented in the literature) and that includes attention on white youth from a lens of critical whiteness.

We are certainly not the first to point out that an intersectionality lens could greatly enhance understanding of youth's critical consciousness development (e.g., Godfrey & Burson, 2018). Intersectionality can be applied in considering youth's critical reflection, motivation, and action in ways that reflect attention to multiple systems of oppression. How youth come to reflect on and act to change multiple systems of oppression and understand their overlaps, including oppressions they do not personally experience, remains an unanswered question for the field. Intersectionality can also be applied in understanding youth's simultaneous experiences of oppression and/or privilege across domains of oppression such as racism, sexism, classism, ableism, xenophobia, homophobia, and transphobia (Godfrey & Burson, 2018). It is important for research to examine how youth's critical consciousness grows out of navigating multiple systems of oppression as well as the implications of experiencing oppression alongside privilege.

When considering racial oppression and privilege as contexts that inform critical consciousness development, it is clear that youth's racial and ethnic identities are core to understanding the development of critical race consciousness. Racial and ethnic identity embodies youth's agentic interpretations of themselves in social contexts and systems and thus reflects a dynamic individual–context exchange. We echo the sentiments of Mathews et al. (2020) that the field needs to better recognize synergies between racial and ethnic identity and critical reflection, motivation, and action. Although some research linking racial and ethnic identity and critical consciousness already exists, the field would benefit from more work that explicitly includes racial and ethnic identity in conceptual, developmental models and empirical inquiries of youth's critical consciousness, especially when applying critical race, intersectionality, or whiteness perspectives.

Finally, an underexplored area of research is the role of youth's critical consciousness, and particularly collective critical actions, in creating change in mediating institutions and larger systems of oppression. Such efforts would align with RDS theory in centering youth's agency in changing their contexts and with critical theories' roots in transformative activism toward liberation. We know that many social movements in the United States and globally have been youth-led and responsible for ideological and policy changes (Earl et al., 2017). Building on research showing the impact of youth activism on social change (e.g., Stornaiuolo & Thomas, 2017; Terriquez et al., 2020), future research could expand evidence showing how youth's critical consciousness development prompts systems change at micro and macrolevels.

## CONCLUSION

Critical consciousness is fundamentally about liberation from oppression, and it is everyone's responsibility to create a society free from dominance, exploitation, and dehumanization of any groups (Freire, 1970). Young people should not be primarily charged with fixing society's long-standing problems of racism and white dominance, yet through critical consciousness development, young people from all racial and ethnic groups can play meaningful roles in dismantling systems of oppression now and into the future. The field of critical consciousness development is growing rapidly, and we expect the next five to ten years of research to exponentially advance knowledge of how youth who experience racial oppression and youth with racial privilege come to be critically conscious in challenging racial injustices and reimagining societal systems that ensure racial equity and inclusion.

## REFERENCES

Aldana, A., Bañales, J., & Richards-Schuster, K. (2019). Youth anti-racist engagement: Conceptualization, development, and validation of an anti-racism action scale. *Adolescent Research Review*, *4*, 369–381. https://doi.org/10.1007/s40894-019-00113-1.

Anyiwo, N., Bañales, J., Rowley, S. J., Watkins, D. C., & Richards-Schuster, K. (2018). Sociocultural influences on the sociopolitical development of African American youth. *Child Development Perspectives*, *12*(3), 165–170. https://doi.org/10.1111/cdep.12276.

Applebaum, B. (2016). *Critical whiteness studies*. Oxford Research Encyclopedia of Education.

Ballard, P. J. (2016). Longitudinal links between discrimination and civic development among Latino and Asian adolescents. *Journal of Research on Adolescence*, *26*(4), 723–737. https://doi.org/10.1111/jora.12221.

Ballard, P. J., & Ozer, E. J. (2016). The implications of youth activism for health and well-being. In J. Conner & S. M. Rosen (Eds.), *Contemporary youth activism: Advancing social justice in the United States* (pp. 223–244). Praeger.

Bañales, J., Aldana, A., Richards-Schuster, K. et al. (2021). Youth anti-racism action: Contributions of youth perceptions of school racial messages and critical consciousness. *Journal of Community Psychology*, *49*(8), 3079–3100. https://doi.org/10.1002/jcop.22266.

Bañales, J., Marchand, A. D., Skinner, O. D. et al. (2020). Black adolescents' critical reflection development: Parents' racial socialization and attributions about race achievement gaps. *Journal of Research on Adolescence*, *30*, 403–417. https://doi.org/10.1111/jora.12485.

Barroso, A., & Minkin, R. (2020, June 24). Recent protest attendees are more racially and ethnically diverse, younger than Americans overall. *Pew Research Center*. www.pewresearch.org/fact-tank/2020/06/24/recent-protest-attendees-are-more-racially-and-ethnically-diverse-younger-than-americans-overall/.

Bonilla-Silva, E. (2003). Racial attitudes or racial ideology? An alternative paradigm for examining actors' racial views. *Journal of Political Ideologies*, *8*(1), 63–82. https://doi.org/bcx3jf.

Brown, C. S. (2017). *Discrimination in childhood and adolescence: A developmental intergroup approach*. Routledge.

Cabrera, N. L., Franklin, J. D., & Watson, J. S. (2017). Whiteness in Higher Education: The Invisible Missing Link in Diversity and Racial Analyses: ASHE Higher Education Report, Volume 42, Number 6. John Wiley & Sons.

Cammarota, J. (2016). The praxis of ethnic studies: Transforming second sight into critical consciousness. *Race Ethnicity and Education*, *19*(2), 233–251. https://doi.org/gddxtv.

Causadias, J. M., & Umaña-Taylor, A. J. (2018). Reframing marginalization and youth development: Introduction to the special issue. *American Psychologist*, *73*(6), 707–712. http://dx.doi.org/10.1037/amp0000336.

Carter, R. T., Lau, M. Y., Johnson, V., & Kirkinis, K. (2017). Racial discrimination and health outcomes among racial/ethnic minorities: A meta-analytic review. *Journal of Multicultural Counseling and Development*, 45(4), 232–259.

Chan, R. C. H., & Mak, W. W. S. (2020). Liberating and empowering effects of critical reflection on collective action in LGBT and cisgender heterosexual individuals. *American Journal of Community Psychology*, *65*(1/2), 63–77. https://doi.org/10.1002/ajcp.12350

Christens, B. D., Byrd, K., Peterson, N. A., & Lardier, D. T. (2018). Critical hopefulness among urban high school students. *Journal of Youth and Adolescence*, *47*(8), 1649–1662. https://doi.org/10.1007/s10964-018-0889-3.

Christens, B. D., Winn, L. T., & Duke, A. M. (2016). Empowerment and critical consciousness: A conceptual cross-fertilization. *Adolescent Research Review*, *1*(15), 15–27. https://doi.org/gsbd.

Cohen, C. J., & Luttig, M. D. (2020). Reconceptualizing political knowledge: Race, ethnicity, and carceral violence. *Perspectives on Politics*, *18*(3), 805–818. https://doi.org/gg958r.

Cole, B. A. (2009). Gender, narratives and intersectionality: Can personal experience approaches to research contribute to "undoing gender"? *International Review of Education*, *55*(5), 561–578. https://doi.org/10.1007/slll59-009-9.

Coleman, B. R., Collins, C. R., & Bonam, C. M. (2021). Interrogating whiteness in community research and action. *American Journal of Community Psychology*, *67*, 486–504. https://doi.org/10.1002/ajcp.12473.

Collins, C. R., Kohfeldt, D., & Kornbluh, M. (2019). Psychological and political liberation: Strategies to promote power, wellness, and liberation among anti-racist activists. *Journal of Community Psychology*, *48*(2), 369–386. https://doi.org/10.1002/jcop.22259.

Collins, P. H. (2014). Toward a new vision: Race, class, and gender as categories of analysis and connection. In M. S. Kimmel & A. L. Ferber (Eds.), *Privilege: A Reader* (pp. 240–257). Westview Press.

Collins, P. H. (2019). *Intersectionality as critical social theory*. Duke University Press.

Combahee River Collective. 1974. "The Combahee River Collective Statement." Accessed January 26 2022. https://americanstudies.yale.edu/sites/default/files/files/Keyword%20Coalition_Readings.pdf.

Conner, J., & Slattery, A. (2014). New media and the power of youth organizing: Minding the gaps. *Equity & Excellence in Education*, *47*(1), 14–30. https://doi.org/gsbf.

Crenshaw, K. (1991). Mapping the margins: Intersectionality, identity politics, and violence against women of color. *Stanford Law Review*, *43*, 1241–1299. https://doi.org/dn82xw.

Daniel, E., Dys, S. P., Buchmann, M., & Malti, T. (2014). Developmental relations between sympathy, moral emotion attributions, moral reasoning, and social

justice values from childhood to early adolescence. *Journal of Adolescence*, *37*(7), 1201–1214. https://doi.org/10.1016/j.adolescence.2014.08.009.

Delgado, R., & Stefancic, J. (2017). *Critical race theory*. New York University Press.

Desante, C. D., & Smith, C. W. (2020). *Racial stasis: The millennial generation and the stagnation of racial attitudes in American politics*. The University of Chicago Press.

Diemer, M. A., McWhirter, E. H., Ozer, E. J., & Rapa, L. J. (2015). Advances in the conceptualization and measurement of critical consciousness. *The Urban Review*, *47*, 809–823. https://doi.org/10.1007/s11256-015-0336-7.

Diemer, M. A., Pinedo, A., Bañales, J. et al. (2021). Recentering action in critical consciousness. *Child Development Perspectives*, *15*(1), 12–17. https://doi.org/10.1111/cdep.12393.

Diemer, M. A., & Rapa, L. J. (2016). Unraveling the complexity of critical consciousness, political efficacy, and political action among marginalized adolescents. *Child Development*, *87*(1), 221–238. https://doi.org/10.1111/cdev.12446.

Dull, B. D., Hoyt, L. T., Grzanka, P. R., & Zeiders, K. H. (2021). Can white guilt motivate action? The role of civic beliefs. *Journal of Youth and Adolescence*, *50*(6), 1081–1097. https://doi.org/10.1007/s10964-021-01401-7.

Earl, J., Maher, T. V., & Elliott, T. (2017). Youth, activism, and social movements. *Sociology Compass*, *11*(4), e12465. https://doi.org/10.1111/soc4.12465.

Feagin, J. (2013). *Systemic racism: A theory of oppression*. Routledge.

Fish, J., Aguilera, R., Ogbeide, I. E., Ruzzicone, D. J., & Syed, M. (2021). When the personal is political: Ethnic identity, ally identity, and political engagement among Indigenous people and people of color. *Cultural Diversity and Ethnic Minority Psychology*, *27*(1), 18–36. https://doi.org/10.1037/cdp0000341.

Flanagan, C. A., Kim, T., Pykett, A. et al. (2014). Adolescents' theories about economic inequality: Why are some people poor while others are rich? *Developmental Psychology*, *50*(11), 2512–2525. http://dx.doi.org/10.1037/a0037934.

Flanagan, C. A., Martínez, M. L., Cumsille, P., & Ngomane, T. (2011). Youth civic development: Theorizing a domain with evidence from different cultural contexts. *New Directions for Child and Adolescent Development*, 2011(134), 95–109. https://doi.org/10.1002/cd.313.

Freire, P. (1970). *Pedagogy of the oppressed*. Continuum.

García Coll, C., Lamberty, G., Jenkins, R. et al. (1996). An integrative model for the study of developmental competencies in minority children. *Child Development*, *67*(5), 1891–1914. https://doi.org/10.1111/j.1467-8624.1996.tb01834.x.

Godfrey, E. B., & Burson, E. (2018). Interrogating the intersections: How intersectional perspectives can inform developmental scholarship on critical consciousness. In C. E. Santos & R. B. Toomey (Eds.), *Envisioning the Integration of an Intersectional Lens in Developmental Science. New Directions for Child and Adolescent Development*, *161*, 17–38. https://doi.org/10.1002/cad.20246.

Godfrey, E. B., Burson, E. L., Yanisch, T. M., Hughes, D., & Way, N. (2019). A bitter pill to swallow? Patterns of critical consciousness and socioemotional and academic well-being in early adolescence. *Developmental Psychology*, *55*(3), 525–537. https://doi.org/gf3nm8

Godfrey, E. B., & Rapa, L. J. (in press). *Developing critical consciousness in youth: Contexts and settings*. Cambridge: Cambridge University Press.

Godfrey, E. B., Santos, C. E., & Burson, E. (2017). For better or worse? System-justifying beliefs in sixth-grade predict trajectories of self-esteem and behavior across early adolescence. *Child Development*, *90*(1), 180–195. https://doi.org/10.111/cdev.12854.

Godfrey, E. B., & Wolf, S. (2016). Developing critical consciousness or justifying the system? A qualitative analysis of attribution of poverty and wealth among low-income racial/ethnic minority and immigrant women. *Cultural Diversity and Ethnic Minority Psychology*, *22*(1), 93–103. https://doi.org/10.1037/cdp0000048.

Gordon, H. R. (2007). Allies within and without: How adolescent activists conceptualize ageism and navigate adult power in youth social movements. *Journal of Contemporary Ethnography*, *36*(6), 631–668. https://doi.org/10.1177/0891241606293608.

Gorski, P. C. (2019). Racial battle fatigue and activist burnout in racial justice activists of color at predominately white colleges and universities. *Race Ethnicity and Education*, *22*(1), 1–20. https://doi.org/10.1080/13613324.2018.1497966.

Hagerman, M. A. (2018). *White kids*. New York: New York University Press.

Hazelbaker, T., Spears Brown, C., Nenadal, L., & Mistry, R. S. (2021). Raising white resisters: Studying the development of anti-racist white children and youth. *PsyArXiv*. https://doi.org/10.31234/osf.io/ej9a5.

Heberle, A. E., Rapa, L. J., & Faragó, F. (2020). Critical consciousness in children and adolescents: A systematic review, critical assessment, and recommendations for future research. *Psychological Bulletin*, *146*(6), 525–551. https://doi.org/10.1037/bul0000230.

Helms, J. E. (2020). *A race is a nice thing to have: A guide to being a white person or understanding the white persons in your life*. Cognella.

Hershberg, R. M., & Johnson, S. K. (2019). Critical reflection about socioeconomic inequalities among White young men from poor and working-class backgrounds. *Developmental Psychology*, *55*(3), 562–573. https://doi.org/10.1037/dev0000587.

Hochschild, J., Weaver, V., & Burch, T. (2012). *Creating a new racial order: How immigration, multiracialism, genomics, and the young can remake race in America*. Princeton University Press.

hooks, b. (1984). *Feminist theory: From margin to center*. South End Press.

Hope, E. C., & Spencer, M. B. (2017). Civic engagement as an adaptive coping response to conditions of inequality: An application of Phenomenological Variant of Ecological Systems Theory (PVEST). In N. J. Cabrera, & B. Leyendecker (Eds.), *Handbook on positive development of minority children and youth* (pp. 421–435). Springer.

Hope, E. C., Gugwor, R., Riddick, K. N., & Pender, K. N. (2019). Engage against the machine: Institutional and cultural racial discrimination and racial identity as predictors of activism orientation among Black youth. *American Journal of Community Psychology*, *63*, 61–72. https://doi.org/10.1002/ajcp.12303.

Hope, E. C., Keels, M., & Durkee, M. I. (2016). Participation in Black Lives Matter and Deferred Action for Childhood Arrivals: Modern activism among Black and Latino college students. *Journal of Diversity in Higher Education*, *9*(3), 203–215. https://doi.org/10.1037/dhe0000032.

Hope, E. C., Smith, C. D., Cryer-Coupet, Q. R., & Briggs, A. S. (2020). Relations between racial stress and critical consciousness for black adolescents. *Journal of Applied Developmental Psychology*, *70*, 101184. https://doi.org/10.1016/j.appdev.2020.101184.

Huynh, V. W., Guan, S. S. A., Almeida, D. M., McCreath, H., & Fuligni, A. J. (2016). Everyday discrimination and diurnal cortisol during adolescence. *Hormones and Behavior*, 80, 76–81. https://doi.org/10.1016/j.yhbeh.2016.01.009.

Jemal, A. (2017). Critical consciousness: A critique and critical analysis of the literature. *Urban Review*, *49*, 602–626. https://doi.org/10.1007/s11256-017-0411-3.

Kennedy, H., Matyasic, S., Schofield Clark, L. et al. (2020). Early adolescent critical consciousness development in the age of Trump. *Journal of Adolescent Research*, *35*(3), 279–308. https://doi.org/10.1177/0743558419852055.

Kiang, L., Christophe, N. K., & Stein, G. L. (2021). Differentiating pathways between ethnic-racial identity and critical consciousness. *Journal of Youth and Adolescence*, *50*(7), 1369–1383. https://doi.org/10.1007/s10964-021-01453-9.

Kirshner, B. (2015). *Youth activism in an era of education inequality*. New York: New York University Press.

Krettenauer, T., Colasante, T., Buchmann, M., & Malti, T. (2014). The development of moral emotions and decision-making from adolescence to early adulthood: A 6-year longitudinal study. *Journal of Youth and Adolescence*, *43*(4), 583–596. https://doi.org/10.1007/s10964-013-9994-5.

Leath, S., & Chavous, T. (2017). "We really protested": The influence of sociopolitical beliefs, political self-efficacy, and campus racial climate on civic engagement among Black college students attending predominantly White institutions. *The Journal of Negro Education*, *86*(3), 220–237. https://doi.org/gdcxb3.

Leonardo, Z. (2013). *Race frameworks: A multidimensional theory of racism and education*. Teachers College Press.

Lerner, R. M., Wang, J., Chase, P. A. et al. (2014). Using relational developmental systems theory to link program goals, activities, and outcomes: The sample case of the 4-H Study of Positive Youth Development. *New Directions for Youth Development*, 2014(144), 17–30. https://doi.org/10.1002/yd.20110.

Martínez, M. L., Peñaloza, P., & Valenzuela, C. (2012). Civic commitment in young activists: Emergent processes in the development of personal and collective identity. *Journal of Adolescence*, *35*(3), 474–484. https://doi.org/10.1016/j.adolescence.2011.11.006.

Mathews, C. J., Medina, M. A., Bañales, J. et al. (2020). Mapping the intersections of adolescents' ethnic-racial identity and critical consciousness. *Adolescent Research Review*, *5*(4), 363–379. https://doi.org/10.1007/s40894-019-00122-0.

Mayorga-Gallo, S. (2019). The white-centering logic of diversity ideology. *American Behavioral Scientist*, *63*(13), 1789–1809. https://doi.org/10.1177/0002764219842619.

Miller, J., & Garran, A. M. (2017). *Racism in the United States: Implications for the helping professions*. Springer Publishing Company.

Moffitt, U., Rogers, L. O., & Dastrup, K. R. (2021). Beyond ethnicity: Applying Helms's White Racial Identity Development Model among White youth. *Journal of Research on Adolescence*, *32*, 1140–1159. https://doi.org/10.1111/jora.12645.

Montgomery, S. A., & Stewart, A. J. (2012). Privileged allies in lesbian and gay rights activism: Gender, generation, and resistance to heteronormativity. *Journal of Social Issues*, *68*(1), 162–177. https://doi.org/10.1111/j.1540-4560.2012.01742.x.

Moradi, B., & Grzanka, P. R. (2017). Using intersectionality responsibly: Toward critical epistemology, structural analysis, and social justice activism. *Journal of Counseling Psychology*, *64*(5), 500–513. https://doi.org/10.1037/cou0000203.

Neville, H. A., & Cross, W. E. , Jr. (2017). Racial awakening: Epiphanies and encounters in Black racial identity. *Cultural Diversity and Ethnic Minority Psychology*, *23* (1), 102–108. https://doi.org/10.1037/cdp0000105.

Obasogie, O. K., & Newman, Z. (2016). Black Lives Matter and respectability politics in local news accounts of officer-involved civilian deaths: An early empirical assessment. *Wisconsin Law Review*, *2016*(3), 541–574.

Olson, J. (2004). *The abolition of white democracy*. University of Minnesota Press.

Ortega-Williams, A., Booth, J., Fussell-Ware, D. et al. (2022). Using ecological momentary assessments to understand Black youths' experiences of racism, stress, and safety. *Journal of Research on Adolescence*, *32*, 270–289. https://doi.org/10.1111/jora.12733

Overton, W. F. (2015). Process and relational developmental systems. In W. F. Overton & P. C. M. Molenaar (Eds.) and R. M. Lerner (Editor-in-Chief), *Theory and method. Vol. 1: The handbook of child psychology and developmental science* (7th ed., pp. 9–62). Wiley.

Paradies, Y., Ben, J., Denson, N. et al. (2015). Racism as a determinant of health: A systematic review and meta-analysis. *PloS one*, *10*(9), e0138511. https://doi.org/10.1371/journal.pone.0138511.

Priest, N. , Paradies, Y. , Trenerry, B. et al. (2013). A systematic review of studies examining the relationship between reported racism and health and wellbeing for children and young people. *Social Science & Medicine*, *95*, 115–127. https://doi.org/10.1016/j.socscimed.2012.11.031.

Rapa, L. J., Bolding, C. W., & Jamil, F. M. (2020). Development and initial validation of the Short Critical Consciousness Scale (CCS-S). *Journal of Applied Developmental Psychology*, *70*, 101164. https://doi.org/ghd3pj.

Reynolds, R., & Mayweather, D. (2017). Recounting racism, resistance, and repression: Examining the experiences and# hashtag activism of college students with critical race theory and counternarratives. *The Journal of Negro Education*, *86*(3), 283–304. https://doi.org/10.7709/jnegroeducation.86.3.0283.

Sánchez-Jankowski, M. (2002). Minority youth and civic engagement: The impact of Group Relations. *Applied Developmental Science*, *6*(4), 237–245. https://doi.org/dc3wxm.

Santos, C. E., & Toomey, R. B. (2018). Integrating an intersectionality lens in theory and research in developmental science. *New Directions for Child and Adolescent Development*, 2018(161), 7–15. https://doi.org/10.1002/cad.20245.

Seider, S., El-Amin, A., & Kelly, L. L. (2020). The development of critical consciousness. In L. A. Jensen (Ed.), *The Oxford handbook of moral development* (pp. 202–221). Oxford University Press. https://doi.org/10.1093/oxfordhb/9780190676049.013.11.

Sensoy, O. , & DiAngelo, R. (2012). *Is everyone really equal? An introduction to key concepts in social justice education*. Teacher's College Press.

Smith, L., & Redington, R. M. (2010). Lessons from the experiences of White antiracist activists. *Professional Psychology: Research and Practice, 41*(6), 541–549. https://doi.org/dqkrh2.

Spanierman, L. B., Poteat, V. P., Beer, A. M., & Armstrong, P. I. (2006). Psychosocial costs of racism to whites: Exploring patterns through cluster analysis. *Journal of Counseling Psychology, 53*(4), 434–441. https://doi.org/10.1037/0022-0167.53.4.434.

Spanierman, L. B., & Smith, L. (2017). Roles and responsibilities of white allies: Implications for research, teaching, and practice. *The Counseling Psychologist, 45*(5), 606–617. https://doi.org/10.1177/0011000017717712.

Spencer, M. B. (1995). Old issues and new theorizing about African American youth: A phenomenological variant of ecological systems theory. In R. L. Taylor (Ed.), *African American youth: Their social and economic status in the United States* (pp. 37–69). Praeger.

Stornaiuolo, A., & Thomas, E. E. (2017). Disrupting educational inequalities through youth digital activism. *Review of Research in Education, 41*(1), 337–357. https://doi.org/10.3102/0091732X16687973.

Suzuki, S. (2021). *Critical consciousness and positive youth development: A group-differential longitudinal study among youth of color in the United States* (Doctoral dissertation, Boston College; Available from ProQuest Dissertations & Theses Global [2525622882]).

Terriquez, V., Villegas, R., Villalobos, R., & Xu, J. (2020). The political socialization of Latinx youth in a conservative political context. *Journal of Applied Developmental Psychology, 70*, 101188. https://doi.org/10.1016/j.appdev.2020.101188.

Thomas, A. J., Barrie, R., Brunner, J. et al. (2014). Assessing critical consciousness in youth and young adults. *Journal of Research on Adolescence, 24*(3), 485–496. https://doi.org/10.1111/jora.12132.

Toraif, N., Augsberger, A., Young, A. et al. (2021). How to be an antiracist: Youth of Color's critical perspectives on antiracism in a youth participatory action research context. *Journal of Adolescent Research, 36*(5), 467–500. https://doi.org/07435584211028224.

Trepagnier, B. (2010). *Silent racism: How well-meaning white people perpetuate the racial divide*. Paradigm.

Tyler, C. P., Geldhof, G. J., Black, K. L., & Bowers, E. P. (2020). Critical reflection and positive youth development among white and Black adolescents: Is understanding inequality connected to thriving? *Journal of Youth and Adolescence, 49*(4), 757–771. https://doi.org/10.1007/s10964-019-01092-1.

Tyler, C. P., Olsen, S. G., Geldhof, G. J., & Bowers, E. P. (2020). Critical consciousness in late adolescence: Understanding if, how, and why youth act. *Journal of Applied Developmental Psychology, 70*, 101165. https://doi.org/10.1016/j.appdev.2020.101165.

Umaña-Taylor, A. J., Quintana, S. M., Lee, R. M. et al. (2014). Ethnic and racial identity during adolescence and into young adulthood: An integrated conceptualization. *Child development, 85*(1), 21–39. https://doi.org/10.1111/cdev.12196.

Van der Graaff, J., Branje, S., De Wied, M. et al. (2014). Perspective taking and empathic concern in adolescence: Gender differences in developmental changes. *Developmental Psychology, 50*(3), 881–888. https://doi.org/f5zrq8.

Voight, A., & Torney-Purta, J. (2013). A typology of youth civic engagement in urban middle schools. *Applied Developmental Science, 17*(4), 198–212. https://doi.org/gsbg.

Watts, R. J., Diemer, M. A., & Voight, A. M. (2011). Critical consciousness: Current status and future directions. *New Directions for Child and Adolescent Development, 134*, 43–57. https://doi.org/10.1002/cd.310.

Watts, R. J., & Flanagan, C. (2007). Pushing the envelope on youth civic engagement: A developmental and liberation psychology perspective. *Journal of Community Psychology, 35*(6), 779–792. https://doi.org/10.1002/jcop.20178.

Watts, R. J., Griffith, D. M., & Abdul-Adil, J. (1999). Sociopolitical development as an antidote for oppression – theory and action. *American Journal of Community Psychology, 27*(2), 255–271. https://doi.org/10.1023/A:1022839818873.

Watts, R. J., & Guessous, O. (2006). Sociopolitical development: The missing link in research and policy on adolescents. In S. Ginwright, P. Noguera, & J. Cammarota (Eds.), *Beyond resistance! Youth activism and community change: New democratic possibilities for practice and policy for America's youth* (pp. 59–80). Routledge.

Watts, R. J., & Hipolito-Delgado, C. P. (2015). Thinking ourselves to liberation? Advancing sociopolitical action in critical consciousness. *The Urban Review, 47*, 847–867. https://doi.org/10.1007/s11256-015-0341-x.

Wilf, S., & Wray-Lake, L. (2021). "That's How Revolutions Happen": Psychopolitical resistance in youth's online civic engagement. *Journal of Adolescent Research*. https://doi.org/10.1177/07435584211062121.

Wray-Lake, L. (2019). How do young people become politically engaged? *Child Development Perspectives, 13*(2), 127–132. https://doi.org/10.1111/cdep.12324.

Wray-Lake, L., & Abrams, L. S. (2020). Pathways to civic engagement among urban youth of color. *Monographs of the Society for Research in Child Development, 85*(2), 7–154. https://doi.org/10.1111/mono.12415.

Wray-Lake, L., Alvis, L., Plummer, J. A., Shubert, J. , & Syvertsen, A. K. (2022). *Adolescents' developing awareness of inequality: Racial and ethnic differences in trajectories. Child Development, 0*(0), 1–19. https://doi.org/10.1111/cdev.13870.

Wray-Lake, L., Arruda, E. H., & Schulenberg, J. E. (2020). Civic development across the transition to adulthood in a national US sample: Variations by race/ethnicity, parent education, and gender. *Developmental Psychology, 56*(10), 1948–1967. https://doi.org/10.1037/dev0001101.

Wray-Lake, L., Metzger, A., & Syvertsen, A. K. (2017). Testing multidimensional models of youth civic engagement: Model comparisons, measurement invariance, and age differences. *Applied Developmental Science, 21*(4), 266–284. https://doi.org/gfttnq.

Wray-Lake, L., & Shubert, J. (2019). Understanding stability and change in civic engagement across adolescence: A typology approach. *Developmental Psychology, 55*(10), 2169–2180. https://doi.org/10.1037/dev0000772.

Wray-Lake, L., Wells, R., Alvis, L. et al. (2018). Being a Latinx adolescent under a Trump presidency: Analysis of Latinx youth's reactions to immigration politics. *Children and Youth Services Review, 87*, 192–204. https://doi.org/gdcxb3.

Zaff, J. F., Kawashima-Ginsberg, K., Lin, E. S. et al. (2011). Developmental trajectories of civic engagement across adolescence: Disaggregation of an integrated construct. *Journal of Adolescence, 34*(6), 1207–1220. https://doi.org/bxztph.

# 6

# Making Reflection Critical

## *Structural and Historical Attributions for Inequity*

ESTHER BURSON, ERIN B. GODFREY, RIANA M. BROWN, AND DEANNA A. IBRAHIM

In this chapter, we consider the roles of structural and historical thinking in critical consciousness (CC), a key process of sociopolitical development. CC is an important developmental competency that seeds social change by empowering young people to combat injustice and navigate the oppression present in their daily lives. In addition to facilitating broader social change, CC also has important consequences for shorter-term, individual positive developmental outcomes among youth facing persistent marginalization. Since CC was suggested as an "antidote for oppression" (Watts et al., 1999) two decades ago, a spate of studies has demonstrated links between CC and positive outcomes for Black, Latinx, and low-socioeconomic status youth (Heberle et al., 2020). This work has found that CC predicts increased occupational goals and attainment (Diemer, 2009; Diemer & Blustein, 2006; Diemer & Hsieh, 2008; Heberle et al., 2020; Olle & Fouad, 2015; Rapa et al., 2018; Uriostegui et al., 2021) and academic success (El-Amin, et al. 2017; Godfrey et al., 2019; Seider et al., 2020) among low-socioeconomic status ethnic/racial minority youth and has linked CC to increased well-being (Christens & Peterson, 2012; Zimmerman et al., 1999), collective action (Conlin et al., 2021), and community engagement (Carlson et al., 2006).

CC is a promising paradigm for both short-term thriving and longer-term social change. The construct's theoretical breadth, however, poses a challenge to researchers' ability to reach definitive causal conclusions about CC's impact on positive outcomes and to design interventions to foster CC for the sake of positive youth development. CC is difficult to measure through quantitative assessment. Over the past decade, researchers have confronted this challenge with increasing success (see Rapa et al., 2020 for an excellent review of existing measures and discussion of measurement challenges; also see Chapter 7 [this volume]). Yet, the creation of a generalizable measure of underlying awareness of social and political attitudes, divorced from political ideology and specific social issues, is a complicated proposition.

CC is typically conceptualized as three interrelated subcomponents of critical reflection, political efficacy, and critical action (Diemer et al., 2015, Godfrey & Grayman, 2014; Watts et al., 2011), although historically there has been debate about the type and number of components present in CC (Jemal, 2017). Critical reflection represents a systemic understanding and moral rejection of social inequity (Christens et al., 2016; Watts et al., 2011). Political efficacy, also referred to as critical motivation, refers to an individual's interest and perceived ability to change social or political inequalities (Rapa et al., 2020). Finally, critical action represents individual or collective action directed at challenging and reforming unjust aspects of society (Diemer et al., 2021). These components were articulated and formalized by Watts et al. (2011) based on Freire's articulation of CC as a praxis of liberation comprising "the action and reflection of men and women upon their world in order to transform it" (Freire, 1970, p. 79), with attention as well to Freire's later discussion (1973) of the role of perceiving possibilities for action (Watts et al., 2011). Watts and colleagues (2011) synthesized these ideas into the reflection, efficacy, and action subcomponents of CC most often studied today.

## CURRENT ISSUES IN MEASUREMENT

These subcomponents are not simple to measure (Chapter 7 [this volume]). For example, there is debate over the value of measuring motivations to make social change versus an individual's perceived ability to do so, and over distinguishing between actions to support general community wellness versus actions aimed specifically at changing an unjust status quo (Diemer et al., 2021). Definitions of critical reflection in particular vary across studies. This lack of clarity presents a challenge in understanding *how* critical consciousness predicts positive developmental outcomes; this challenge is especially pronounced given that critical reflection is a unique contribution of CC theory (Burson & Godfrey, 2020), whereas the associations between positive developmental outcomes and CC's other components (political efficacy and critical action) are explored to some extent in the literatures on empowerment (Christens et al., 2016; Christens & Peterson, 2012) and collective action and civic engagement (e.g., Van Zomeren et al., 2008), respectively. More definitional clarity and better measurement of critical reflection will help illuminate how this unique aspect of CC manifests in relation to developmental outcomes.

## THEORETICAL ISSUES: THE NEED FOR STRUCTURAL AND HISTORICAL THINKING

In measuring critical reflection, it is difficult to distinguish between a general awareness of hot-button social issues and "critical reflection on the root causes of social conditions" (Westheimer & Kahne, 2003). The importance of this distinction is also debated, as scholars continue to explore the definition of critical reflection itself. While all formulations of critical reflection include an awareness of oppression or inequality, scholars place varying levels of emphasis on the need for systemic, structural, and historical thinking as part of this reflection (see Jemal, 2017 for a review). As such, measuring critical reflection faces not only the theoretical challenge of defining the term but also the empirical challenge of accurate measurement.

In response to these theoretical questions, we argue that an understanding of the historical origins of current inequities – and an analysis of their evolution and enactment over time and through institutional structures, laws, and policies – is key in making reflection truly critical. Freire emphasizes the necessity of these facets of reflection in *Pedagogy of the Oppressed* (1970), noting that "to surmount the situation of oppression, people must first critically recognize its causes" (p. 47). Freire repeatedly discussed how this reflection involves identifying the "concrete historical dimensions" (p. 99) of an unjust reality as well as the social structures through which oppression operates. Freire (1970) envisioned both reflection and action to be directed not at individuals but "at the structures to be transformed" (p. 126), thereby highlighting the need for critical reflection to consider the social structures that perpetuate injustice rather than focusing exclusively on the injustice itself. Throughout his discussions of CC, Freire highlighted not just awareness of inequality but also an understanding of the historical and structural forces that allow it to develop and evolve – that is, a "reading" of the sociohistorical, sociocultural, and sociopolitical realities of the world.

Early developmental and community psychology studies on CC incorporated this focus on the structural and historical aspects of reflection. For example, Watts and colleagues' "Young Warriors Program" aimed to foster sociopolitical development through critical discussions of rap music, with the hope that these conversations might connect themes present in rap to structural issues of exploitation, such as overpolicing of poor Black communities, and their historical roots (Watts et al., 1999, 2002). Subsequent theoretical work has echoed the importance of a structural and historical perspective in critical reflection (Burson & Godfrey, 2020; Christens et al, 2016). This work argues that critical reflection focuses on an understanding of systemic inequality that is rooted in knowledge of the origins and development of economic, political, and social inequities and the ways they are enforced through policies, laws, cultural norms, and other social institutions (Burson & Godfrey, 2020; Christens et al, 2016; Watts et al., 2011). For reflection to be truly critical, in other words, it requires attributions that acknowledge how systemic, macrolevel forces, such as government policies and laws, have acted over time to shape both past and present inequity (Christens et al., 2016; Watts et al., 2011).

This focus on structural and historical thinking can help transform general awareness of, and interest in, current affairs into action for a more just society (Westheimer & Kahne, 2003). Understanding the structural and historical aspects of oppression helps young people situate inequity in the larger social world, thereby directing blame away from individuals and onto the social systems that drive inequity (Burson & Godfrey, 2020; Watts et al., 2011). This type of reflection can also highlight the intersectionality of oppressions, casting light on the ways different forms of oppression overlap and reinforce each other (Godfrey & Burson, 2018). This process leads to a more comprehensive understanding of oppression as not one single issue affecting one group of people but rather as a tangle of related issues embedded in larger power structures over time. This conceptualization of critical reflection also points out avenues for intervention and action to increase equity. Ultimately, a structural and historical dimension of reflection is necessary to inform the liberatory praxis Freire (1970) envisioned.

## EMPIRICAL ISSUES: CURRENT MEASURES

Despite the theoretical centrality of structural and historical understandings of inequality, most measures of critical reflection do not explicitly assess structural and historical dimensions. For example, perhaps the most frequently employed measure of critical reflection in developmental research, the Critical Consciousness Scale (CCS; Diemer et al., 2017), assesses critical reflection along the dimensions of awareness of inequality and rejection of inequality (also called egalitarianism). To measure awareness of inequality, this scale measures agreement with statements asserting that three specific marginalized populations (women, poor people, and racial/ethnic minority groups) have a harder time in education, the workplace, and generally "getting ahead" in life. One recently validated short version of this scale (CCS-S; Rapa et al., 2020) similarly assesses egalitarianism and awareness of the existence of challenges for women, racial/ethnic minorities, and poor people.

The CCS is seminal in providing a reliable and valid scale to assess both awareness of inequality and the rejection thereof. As such, it has been widely applied to further our understanding of causes and consequences of youth CC. Notably, however, this scale does not address broader structural attributions for inequality nor does it address inequality's historical roots. One limitation to measuring awareness of inequality, as opposed to structures and historical dimensions of oppression, is that the former is confined to assessing inequality faced by specifically named social groups only, thereby omitting discrimination on the basis of other characteristics such as sexual orientation, gender presentation, or disability. Moreover, this approach does not assess attitudes toward or awareness of the underlying systemic forces driving group-based inequities such as sexism, classism, and racism. As we have argued earlier, for reflection to be truly critical it must involve recognition of these driving forces and structures, their origins, and their effects – that is, a measure must move beyond assessing endorsement of the statement that individuals face hardship based on membership in a social group to gauging the extent to which the respondent sees these hardships as systemic throughout time. Furthermore, focusing on specific single categories of marginalization precludes the possibility of recognizing inequities existing or experienced as a result of intersecting systems of oppression.

Other less widely adopted measures of critical reflection have attempted to incorporate an intersectional measurement perspective with a broader focus on oppressive systems. For example, the creators of the Contemporary Critical Consciousness Measure (CCCM; Shin et al., 2016) and the CCCMII (Shin et al., 2018) acknowledge the value of measuring intersectional reflection that considers systems of oppression and their overlaps. The Critical Consciousness Inventory (CCI; Thomas et al., 2014) also aims to measure awareness of oppression and hierarchy, drawing from aspects of sociopolitical development theory. Neither of these scales has been widely adopted, however, and they have yet to be replicated or validated among diverse populations (for emerging work in this area, however, see Chapter 11 [this volume]).

An examination of these scales illustrates the difficulty of measuring an intersectional awareness of structural oppression. The CCCM scale items assess attitudes toward Black, Latinx, Asian, and white people, toward poverty and poor people, and toward LGBTQ people. Items are a mix of individual attributions (e.g. "Overall, whites are the most successful racial group because they work the hardest" [reverse-coded]) and structural attributions (e.g., "the overrepresentation of Blacks and Latinos in prison is directly related to racist disciplinary policies in public schools"). Each separate item assesses a single issue such that intersectional measurement comes from the diversity of topics in the scale as a whole, as opposed to intersectionality represented in any one item. While some items refer to structural issues, there is no broader articulation of structural attributions or systemic thinking because these measures assess specific examples rather than broader thought patterns; it can therefore be difficult to separate whether these scale items assess a critical style of reflection or a more general progressive ideology. If a limitation of the CCCM and the CCCMII is their focus on specific, concrete examples, the CCI is possibly overly general, asking quite broadly about fairness and oppression. These items may not directly activate ideas about specific forces of oppression such as racism or sexism. Furthermore, the unusual format of this measure, which utilizes a Guttman scale, may deter researchers from employing it. Indeed, a recent adaptation of the CCI eliminated the use of Guttman scaling altogether (Chan, 2022).

Finally, none of these measures of critical reflection explicitly measure structural or historical thinking, perhaps because of the difficulty involved in assessing these types of attributions. Because structural and historical thinking are not usually measured directly in current CC instruments, evidence for the role of *truly critical* "critical reflection" in CC scholarship is lacking despite its theoretical import.

## CHALLENGES IN INCORPORATING STRUCTURAL AND HISTORICAL THINKING

Given our opinion that critical reflection must be structurally and historically rooted, we now consider methods to assess the construct in this way. There are several major challenges to the measurement of structural and historical thinking. First, there is the definitional issue of what we mean by structural and historical thinking. In the current chapter, we use the term "thinking" to refer to a range of attributions, cognitions, rationalizations, and understandings of inequality that in some way reference historical and/or structural knowledge or thought patterns. We understand "structural thinking" as attributing inequity to macrolevel factors such as laws, policies, institutional norms, and social norms rather than to individual characteristics or decisions. "Historical thinking" refers to an awareness of the historical origins of inequity, its development, and its multiple manifestations over time. Given a lack of agreement and definitional clarity in the CC literature, we use the broader catch-all term "thinking" because little is currently known about the nuances and distinctions among these different terms

Second, it is unclear whether structural and historical thinking should be conceptualized as one subdimension of critical reflection, or if they are better understood as two separate subdimensions, and, if so, how each should be defined. Within the CC literature, discussions of the topic view structural–historical thinking as one combined process. Freire, along with later theorists who emphasize the need for structural and historical thinking, viewed these types of thought as a joint process, such that historical knowledge is nearly always linked to or conflated with structural attributions (Burson & Godfrey, 2020). These writings use the terms "structural" and "historical" interchangeably to refer to a type of attribution that is in fact both structural and historical in scope (see Christens et al., 2016; Godfrey & Burson, 2018).

Other literatures, such as social psychology, separate these ideas, focusing on structural thinking as an attribution style, while history is treated as either factual knowledge or opinions about how relevant the past is to understanding the present day. This research explores historical and structural thinking in theoretical isolation from each other despite their conceptual overlaps (Burson & Godfrey, 2020). In the social psychology literature, structural attributions refer to thinking about policies and institutions either situated in or devoid of historical context. One such study found that for white Americans, attributing anti-Black racism to structural and institutional policy, as opposed to interpersonal prejudice, was associated with greater awareness of anti-Black racism in the wake of Hurricane Katrina (O'Brien et al., 2009), suggesting that more structural thinking led to greater critical reflection on inequality.

Conversely, this research explores historical thinking in isolation from structural thinking. This work offers multiple ways to measure historical thinking. Two possibilities emerge: first, to measure concrete historical knowledge, and second, to measure endorsement of the past as relevant to present social issues. As mentioned earlier, historical knowledge about racism has been linked to an increased ability to identify instances of present-day racism among both Black and white Americans (Adams et al., 2006), indicating that historical knowledge plays a role in awareness of inequality in the present day. Similarly, refusal to endorse the relevance of historical injustices against the Maori to present-day inequalities is associated with opposition to redistributive policies among white New Zealanders (Sibley & Liu, 2012; Sibley et al., 2008). Increased endorsement of history as relevant may therefore facilitate critical reflection's goal of rejecting inequality in favor of liberation. In neither of these approaches, however, does historical thinking require attention to the structural ways policies, laws, and institutions develop and enact inequity over time.

These examples all ultimately illustrate some form of structural or historical thinking driving critical reflection on oppression, even though each of these traditions defines structural and historical thinking differently. In the CC literature, structural-historical thinking is one combined attribution style. In the social psychological literature, however, structural attributions can occur in the absence of historical perspective, while historical thinking is not explicitly linked to structural attributions. Furthermore, historical thinking can be measured with concrete knowledge or endorsing the past as relevant. It is unclear which of these types of structural or historical thinking would be most valuable to incorporate into measures of critical reflection.

Given a lack of definitional clarity around what structural and historical thinking and attributions actually entail, and a paucity of empirical evidence for the roles of these thinking styles in critical reflection, the roles of structural and historical thinking in CC are currently ambiguous. This omission has consequences for both theory and intervention. Arguments for the role of structural and historical thinking in CC are predominately theoretical rather than empirical and, as noted, tend not to distinguish between structural and historical thought. Other literatures, including social psychology, have demonstrated a range of positive individual and intergroup outcomes associated with structural or historical thinking, in isolation, that are in line with the goals of CC. It remains unclear, however, whether structural and historical thinking have distinct results from each other, or if they exert different effects separately and in tandem. For example, it is possible to focus on historical thinking alone, without focusing explicitly on the role of policy and institutions; or to think about structural factors such as laws and organizations without historical context; or to focus specifically on the interplay of structural and historical forces in creating present inequities. It is also possible that all these orientations are in fact features of a shared underlying cognitive latent construct. Clarifying how structural and historical thinking manifest and interplay in critical reflection will support the creation of more effective CC measures and, eventually, interventions focused on individual well-being or intergroup solidarity, both outcomes that have been linked to structural and historical thinking.

Third, there is the question of what particular structural and historical knowledge we are seeking to measure. Should critical reflection be defined by a general tendency to make attributions that are structural and/or historical in nature or toward structural attributions and historical knowledge of a specific issue? This question of specificity echoes a larger debate in CC research about the value of treating CC as a domain-specific or general construct (e.g., Diemer et al., 2016). Existing measures of critical reflection usually focus on one or more explicitly articulated domains such as racism or sexism (see the CCS, CCCM, and CCCMII). Given both the theoretical arguments for treating CC as a domain-specific construct and the empirical difficulty of creating one broad measure that applies to all situations and domains of oppression, we suggest that it may be more practical and useful to measure structural and historical attributions applied to a specific issue than to attempt to capture more general patterns of thought.

A final question in incorporating structural and historical thinking into the measurement of critical reflection is that it is unclear how these theoretical components fit with existing subdimensions of critical reflection. As discussed earlier, the most commonly applied measure of critical reflection assesses awareness of inequality and egalitarian ideology. It is conceivable that measures of structural and historical thinking would not correlate at all with these subdimensions, as assessed through current instrumentation. Conversely, it is possible that there would be complete empirical overlap among one or more of these subdimensions, such that adding structural and historical thinking scales would be redundant to currently used scales. Understanding the associations among these constructs will aid in building a more comprehensive measure of critical reflection.

In the following section, we conduct a proof-of-concept empirical study that examines how best to measure orientations to structural and historical thinking and situates these constructs alongside more commonly and successfully measured dimensions of critical reflection. We focus on one major domain of inequality for the purposes of this study. Specifically, we examine racial critical reflection due to its prevalence in CC research and in research on historical thinking. In addition to measuring awareness of inequality and egalitarianism, we pilot new subscales focused on structural attributions, combined structural/historical attributions, and endorsement of historical relevance in an attempt to clarify how these subdimensions interact with each other and with previously validated measures of critical reflection.

## EMPIRICAL CASE STUDY

Thus far, we have argued for the importance of assessing structural and historical thinking styles within critical reflection. We now explore options for adding these measures to current instruments that focus on awareness of inequality and egalitarianism. We aim to empirically explore our theoretical supposition that structural and historical thinking are key subdimensions of critical reflection. We also seek to gain conceptual clarity around the empirical functioning of these subdimensions by examining whether structural and historical thinking about inequality are part of the same overarching construct or if they are, in fact, separate subdimensions. To explore these questions, we conduct measurement work and compare a series of theoretically driven confirmatory factor analyses. Through these analyses, we investigate whether measures of structural and historical thinking can be added to measures of egalitarianism and awareness of inequality that typically form measures of critical reflection in order to create a more comprehensive measure. We also determine how best to conceptualize the dimensions comprising this new, expanded version of critical reflection. As discussed, existing measures of CC often address inequality based on race/ethnicity, gender, and social class. In the interest of both parsimony and theoretical clarity, we focused our preliminary exploration on racial critical reflection.

## PARTICIPANTS

Following the precedent of earlier measure validation in CC (McWhirter & McWhirter, 2016), we recruited 329 English-speaking US-based Latinx participants via Amazon Mechanical Turk ($N$ = 140) and Prolific.ac ($N$ = 189). Measures were identical on both platforms. After eligibility checks to confirm ethnicity, age, and nationality, we retained a sample of 292 (173 male, 96 female, 2 "other"). Participants ranged in age from 18 to 35 ($M$ = 24.39, SD = 3.37). All participants identified as both US American and Latinx. This group was chosen for its inclusion in the CC literatures as a group that faces discrimination in education, employment, and wealth. We recognize that this group faces specific challenges around language and immigration that are not addressed in the current study, which may affect the generalizability of findings.

## PROCEDURE

Participants completed a battery of items designed to assess awareness of inequality, egalitarianism, structural attributions, historical relevance, and combined structural/historical thinking. These three types of structural and historical thinking were chosen to reflect CC theory and current research on structural and historical thinking, as discussed earlier. All items focused on racial inequality in the United States. Participants then responded to questions assessing basic demographic information.

## MEASURES

All measures are discussed in the following sections and can also be found in the chapter appendix. We included measures from the validated and widely used CCS as well as new measures we created to capture the three different types of structural and historical thinking discussed earlier.

### AWARENESS OF INEQUALITY

Awareness of inequality was measured with six items from the Critical Reflection Subscale of the CCS. This subscale is often used in CC research to assess awareness of inequality and has been validated for use with racial/ethnic minority youth (sample item: "Certain racial or ethnic groups have fewer chances to get good jobs"). More specifically, we utilized the three items of the CCS Perceived Inequality subscale that focused on racial inequality, excluding items asking about gender- and class-based inequality. For each item used, we made slight adaptations so that respondents were asked about racism directed at both Latinx and Black people in the United States (e.g., "Latinx people have fewer chances to get a good high school education than white people" and "Black people have fewer chances to get a good high school education than white people"), for a total of six items. Response options ranged from 1 (*Very Untrue*) to 5 (*Very True*). Cronbach's alpha for this scale was 0.95.

### EGALITARIANISM

We measured the second major component of critical reflection, egalitarian ideology, with the egalitarianism subscale of the CCS. This five-item subscale assesses the extent to which an individual supports social hierarchies (sample item: "All social groups should be given an equal chance in life"). No specific groups or types of inequality are mentioned in this subscale. Response options ranged from 1 (*Strongly Disagree*) to 5 (*Strongly Agree*). Cronbach's alpha for this scale was 0.82.

### STRUCTURAL ATTRIBUTIONS

A measure of structural attributions was created with items drawn from the social psychological literature intended to measure awareness of structural versus interpersonal attributions for inequality (Cortland et al., 2017; Craig et al., 2020). Additional items were adapted from the CCS to highlight the structural nature of inequality. Two items adapted from Cortland et al. (2017) ask the extent to which discrimination is structural in nature (sample item: "Most of the inequality that Latinx people face stems from policies that disproportionately disadvantage Latinx people"). Two further items were inspired by the types of inequality mentioned in the CCS, which asks about contexts for inequality (e.g., work and school; sample item: "Many businesses intentionally keep Black people from gaining positions of power"). Each item was repeated in regard to both anti-Black and anti-Latinx racism for a total of eight items assessing structural thinking. Response options ranged from 1 (*Strongly Disagree*) to 5 (*Strongly Agree*). Cronbach's alpha for this scale was 0.92.

### STRUCTURAL-HISTORICAL THINKING

Combined structural/historical thinking was measured with six items asking about the historical roots of structural inequality. These items were generated based on themes from the CCS and measures of historical knowledge and structural attributions from the social psychological literature on historical thinking (Bonam et al, 2017; Nelson et al., 2013). These items aimed to assess combined structural and historical thinking about inequality (sample item: "Years of slavery followed by Jim Crow laws – which legally enforced segregation, limited job opportunities, and kept Black Americans from voting – have created a racial wealth gap in the United States"). Three items concerned Black history and three focused on Latinx history in the United States. Cronbach's alpha for this scale was $\alpha = 0.88$. Response options ranged from 1 (*Strongly Disagree*) to 5 (*Strongly Agree*).

### HISTORICAL RELEVANCE

The extent to which history is seen as important to understanding current events was measured with two items following the structural and historical questions. These items asked "How relevant are events like these to issues [Black, Latinx] people face today?" Response options ranged from 1 (*Not at all Relevant*) to 5 (*Extremely Relevant*). These two items were correlated at $r = 0.62$, $p < 0.01$.

## ANALYTIC PLAN

We conducted a series of theoretically driven confirmatory factor analyses examining the factor structure that best represented interrelations between these items and scales. We used the maximum likelihood estimator and used Bayesian Information Criterion (BIC) values to compare fit among models. For factor analyses, $N = 50$ is suggested as appropriate for a model with more than six indicator variables per factor, and $N = 100$ for models with three to four indicators per factor (Wang & Wang, 2012). Our sample was $N = 292$ for proposed factors ranging from 5 to 13 indicators, giving us confidence in the power and precision of our estimates.

We hypothesized four theoretically likely factor structures for our model of structural and historical racial critical reflection. Factor structures for each model are displayed in Figure 6.1. We first estimated a five-factor model (model 1) in which all items were specified to load onto constructs representing their respective scales, leading to factors of awareness of inequality, egalitarianism, structural attributions, structural-historical thinking, and historical relevance. We then explored a three-factor model (model 2) with the traditionally employed factors of awareness of inequality and egalitarianism alongside a third factor composed of all newly introduced items: structural attributions, structural-historical thinking, and historical relevance. We next estimated a one-factor model (model 3) in which all items were specified to load onto only one factor. Finally, we estimated a second-order latent factor model (model 4) with higher-order factors of awareness of inequality, egalitarianism, and a factor composed of latent factors of structural attributions, structural-historical thinking, and historical relevance. Latent factors were allowed to correlate in all models with more than one latent factor.

Model 1. Five factors (factor 1 = awareness of inequality, factor 2 = egalitarianism, factor 3 = structural attributions, factor 4 = structural-historical thinking, factor 5 = historical relevance).

Model 2. Three-factor model with factors of awareness of inequality (factor 1), egalitarianism (factor 2), and all structural and historical items (factor 3).

Model 3. All indicators load onto one single factor.

Model 4. Latent factor model with higher-order factors of awareness of inequality (factor 1), egalitarianism (factor 2), and a higher-order factor (factor 6) composed of latent factors of structural attributions (factor 3), historical relevance (factor 4), and structural-historical thinking (factor 5).

We followed established guidelines to evaluate model fit, specifically: (1) Root Mean Square Error of Approximation (RMSEA) below 0.05 (a higher

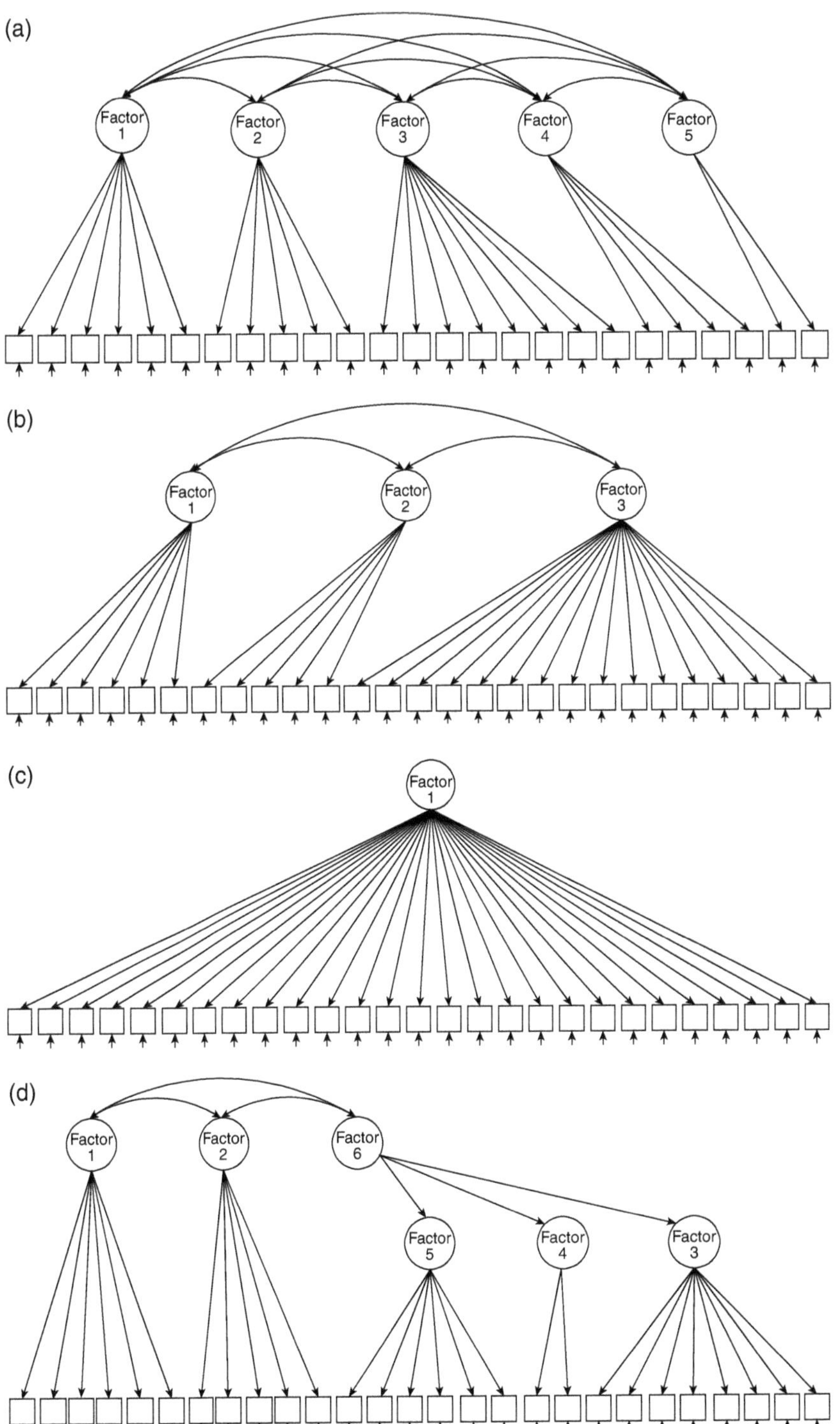


FIGURE 6.1 Confirmatory factor analysis models.

RMSEA may be acceptable as long as it does not exceed 0.10 and if all other fit statistics are good); (2) the Benton Comparative Fit (CFI) above 0.95; and (3) the Standardized Root Mean Square Residual (SRMR) below 0.08 (Kline, 2011). BIC can be used to compare non-nested models using the same observed variables. In the present case, BIC was necessary to compare the latent factor model to the single-order models, and can be applied to nested models as well (Muthén, 2010). A difference in BIC of greater than 10 is considered "very strong" evidence that the model with the lower BIC is a better fit to the data (Kass & Raftery, 1995; Muthén, 2010; Raftery, 1995). After establishing the best-fitting factor structure for our data, we examined correlations among the factors in our best-fitting model to determine if there are associations among these scales. Medium correlations ($0.25 < r < 0.75$) would suggest associations without complete conceptual overlap.

## RESULTS

We conducted the four theoretically driven confirmatory factor analyses described earlier in Mplus to test the hypothesized relations among structural and historical thinking and related subdimensions of critical reflection. Model fit statistics are presented in Table 6.1 and factor structures in Figure 6.1. BIC comparisons provided strong evidence that Model 1 (the five-factor, higher-order model) was the best model for our data. After selecting this five-factor model as the best-fitting factor structure, we explored the factor structure in greater detail. We began by calculating item loadings onto factors (see the Appendix, Table 6.A.1). All items loaded onto their specified factor at or above 0.68, with the exception of one reverse-coded item that loaded onto the specified factor at 0.47.

We then calculated the correlations among these five factors. Correlations between factors ranged from $r = 0.46$ to $r = 0.82$ (Table 6.2). Notably, structural attributions were highly correlated with awareness of inequality ($r = 0.82$) and structural-historical thinking ($r = 0.81$).

TABLE 6.1 Fit statistics for main models

| Variable | CFI | RMSEA | SRMR | $\chi^2$ (*df*) | BIC |
|---|---|---|---|---|---|
| Five-Factor Model | 0.91 | 0.07 | 0.06 | 727.47(314)** | 15679.80 |
| Three-Factor Model | 0.87 | 0.08 | 0.07 | 900.80(321)** | 15813.76 |
| One-Factor Model | 0.74 | 0.11 | 0.09 | 1478.74(324)** | 16081.29 |
| Latent-Factor Model | 0.90 | 0.07 | 0.06 | 761.63(318)** | 15691.47 |

*$p < 0.05$, **$p < 0.01$

TABLE 6.2 Standardized factor correlations

| | 1 | 2 | 3 | 4 |
|---|---|---|---|---|
| 1. Awareness of Inequality | | | | |
| 2. Egalitarianism | 0.50*** | | | |
| 3. Structural Attributions | 0.82*** | 0.59*** | | |
| 4. Historical Relevance | 0.66*** | 0.46*** | 0.75*** | |
| 5. Structural-Historical Thinking | 0.72*** | 0.76*** | 0.81*** | 0.76*** |

*Notes:* Standardized correlations presented; all items were significant at $p < 0.001$.

## DISCUSSION

In this chapter, we discussed the rationale for incorporating structural and historical thinking into the ways we understand and measure critical reflection. Structural and historical thinking are key to theory on critical reflection as liberatory practice. These patterns of thinking can facilitate an understanding of the ways systems of oppression evolve over time, interact with each other, and manifest in the lives of individuals and communities. This awareness may better empower youth to fight inequality and shed light on key points of intervention.

Through our empirical analyses, we demonstrated that structural and historical thinking can be operationalized as subdimensions of racial critical reflection. We added new measures of structural attributions for inequality, structural-historical thinking about current inequality, and endorsement of the past as relevant to present inequity to a measure of critical reflection. After testing several theoretically driven factor structures, we obtained a well-fitting model that included each of these new subscales as separate factors alongside currently employed factors of awareness of inequality and egalitarianism. The best-fitting model specified five separate factors based on each subscale. A latent factor model in which all structural and historical thinking items loaded onto one higher-order factor displayed meaningfully worse model fit, suggesting that these new factors represent fundamentally different constructs. Factor loadings were all high on their respective factors, suggesting that our indicators meaningfully represent their factors. The resultant factor structure suggested that we can think of structural attributions, structural-historical thinking, and historical relevance as distinct, individual subdimensions of critical reflection rather than as components of the same higher-order subdimension.

The suggestion that egalitarianism, awareness of inequality, structural attributions, structural-historical thinking, and endorsement of historical relevance all form discrete dimensions of critical reflection is complicated by high correlations among some of these subscales, as all of the specified factors in the five-factor model were meaningfully correlated (see Table 6.2). However, strong correlations ($r > 0.75$) between structural-historical thinking and egalitarianism, structural attributions, and historical relevance suggest there may be some theoretical overlap among these constructs. Similarly, structural attributions and awareness of inequality were highly correlated ($r = 0.82$), also suggesting some possible redundancy among awareness of inequality, structural attributions, historical relevance, and structural-historical thinking – despite factor analytic results indicating that these measures form separate factors.

The high correlation between awareness of inequality and structural attributions suggests that the awareness of inequality scale does perhaps capture a degree of structural thinking. For general measurement, therefore, the widely used CCS may sufficiently capture the structural thinking inherent in critical reflection. Given the popularity of this measure, it is a good sign for the field that the CCS may implicitly tap into structural attributions. That said, depending on the goals of a particular study, researchers may well wish to include more nuanced measures of structural and historical thinking, and will likely want to do more work to distinguish between its different types. Studies with predictors or outcomes that have a theoretical link to structural or historical thinking should still consider measurement approaches that more explicitly prioritize these ideas. For example, an understanding of structural manifestations and historical roots of oppression may be central to research that considers systemic change and liberation.

Our finding of high correlations between constructs, despite factor analytic results suggesting that these scales represent discrete concepts, may reflect an inherent difficulty in operationalizing or measuring these complicated constructs, which often overlap in the real world. It may be impossible to completely separate these constructs. For instance, traditional measures of awareness of inequality may pick up on some structural attributions. Indeed, while awareness of inequality items have not necessarily been framed to highlight structural thinking explicitly, it seems that structural attributions would lead to an endorsement of these items. For example, items that ask about educational or occupational success (e.g., "Black people have fewer chances to get good jobs than white people") could tap into a range of interpersonal, situational, and structural attributions about job candidates, employers, and industries. It would not be surprising if structural and historical attributions for inequality underpin an awareness of inequality or endorsement of egalitarian ideology. Similarly, awareness of inequality may drive youth to seek a range of explanations for a social issue, leading to a higher awareness of structural and historical factors.

Many of these constructs are difficult to operationalize and measure in their own right, and may be inherently or tangentially connected. Different types of structural and historical thinking in particular are difficult to disentangle. It is difficult to imagine historical knowledge of inequality that does not rely on awareness of past laws, policies, and institutions. Conversely, structural attributions often entail an awareness of the origin of unjust social structures. Measuring these constructs presents a further difficulty, as awareness of structural and historical factors driving inequity must necessarily be specific to the instance of inequity in question, posing a problem in the creation of consistent measurement. Compare this need for domain-specific measurement to constructs of endorsement of historical relevance and egalitarianism, which may be uniformly assessed across situations.

## LIMITATIONS

We explored how to define structural and historical thinking and how to incorporate these ideas into a measure of critical reflection. We did not, however, explore what outcomes these types of thinking are important *for*, or how they might be differentially important in a range of contexts. It remains unclear from our empirical exploration whether structural and historical thinking in racial critical reflection indeed add necessary subdomains to existing measures. While confirmatory factor analysis suggested that structural attributions, historical awareness, and combined structural-historical thinking form discrete subdimensions of critical reflection, alongside traditional measures of awareness of inequality and egalitarianism, the correlations among these subscales may limit the unique added value these new subscales might provide. One source of this limitation may be the omission of outcomes from our data collection. Without linking our newly generated subdimensions of racial critical reflection to outcomes of interest, it is unclear what these factors add to our understanding of processes related to critical reflection. Future work should explore how these measures relate to a range of predictors and outcomes of CC.

It is also worth noting that our empirical sample was predominately male (59%), which may impact generalizability. Furthermore, this study explored racial critical reflection items only among a young Latinx sample. There is theoretical and empirical precedence for validating CC scales in this way (McWhirter & McWhirter, 2016), but it is important to assess this new, expanded racial critical reflection instrument's validity with other demographic groups. The current study did not account for diversity of race, language, and immigration status – all potentially important factors with a Latinx sample.

## CLOSING THOUGHTS

In this chapter we developed and tested a new, expanded racial critical reflection measure that more closely embodies the theoretical aims of critical reflection by emphasizing structural and historical thinking about racial inequity. The addition of these subdimensions may enable us to better assess the extent to which reflection considers the ways power and hegemony shape past and current inequities. We developed a five-factor model in which egalitarianism, awareness of inequality, structural attributions, endorsement of historical relevance, and structural-historical thinking served as distinct subdimensions of racial critical reflection. While correlations among some factors were high, confirmatory factor analyses suggested the existence of distinct factors.

Conceiving of critical reflection as a construct that comprises these new subcomponents has implications for well-being, social change, and intervention. First, structural and historical reflection may affect mental health. The association between CC and mental health is complicated. Critical reflection is not always associated with positive mental health outcomes (Godfrey et al., 2019). An awareness of inequality in general can evoke negative emotions. Focusing on the structural factors driving inequality in particular may make inequity seem intractable. In this way, structural thinking could be overwhelming and ultimately disempowering for youth. A nuanced understanding of structural forces of inequality that points to areas for intervention may help disrupt this process. Relatedly, understanding these structures as situated in history may give youth a better sense of the process of social change over time. This knowledge may buffer negative mental health outcomes associated with awareness of inequality by reassuring youth that social change does happen, even if it is a slow process, and by normalizing both setbacks and victories as part of this process.

Structural and historical attributions may also motivate social change, a key goal of CC. A structural understanding of inequality may drive a sense of moral outrage and provide a target for this anger, such that frustration is aimed at structures and systems to be reformed instead of at individuals or social groups. A historical understanding of how inequality has been enforced over time may give youth perspective on how social change has been achieved in the past, and how it can continue to evolve in the future. Furthermore, a deeper understanding of the history of different social groups and how similar structures of inequality have affected different groups over time may increase intersectional awareness, thereby stoking solidarity among diverse groups to work together for increased equity.

Taken together, these suppositions have consequences for intervention and future research. They suggest that structural and historical thinking may have benefits for mental health and social change. Freire and later scholars of sociopolitical development emphasized the importance of structural and historical knowledge about inequality, and some early interventions emphasized these discussions. It is still unclear, however, how these factors empirically relate to well-being or social change, or even compose aspects of critical reflection itself. Our empirical case study found high correlations among awareness of inequality and both structural attributions and structural-historical thinking. Future research should assess potential causal connections among these constructs in order to determine the most effective interventions targeting CC development. More evidence is needed to better understand potential causal links between structural and historical thinking and awareness of inequality and egalitarianism, and among these subdimensions of racial critical reflection and positive outcomes for youth facing oppression. A better understanding of the unique contribution of each of these subdimensions of racial critical reflection will highlight the most meaningful directions for future intervention work.

## CHAPTER 6 APPENDIX
## MEASURES

### The Critical Consciousness Scale (CCS; Diemer et al., 2017)

Response options range from 1 (Strongly Disagree) to 6 (Strongly Agree).

1. Certain racial or ethnic groups have fewer chances to get a good high school education.
2. Poor children have fewer chances to get a good high school education.
3. Certain racial or ethnic groups have fewer chances to get good jobs.
4. Women have fewer chances to get good jobs.
5. Poor people have fewer chances to get good jobs.
6. Certain racial or ethnic groups have fewer chances to get ahead.
7. Women have fewer chances to get ahead.
8. Poor people have fewer chances to get ahead.
9. It is a good thing that certain groups are at the top and other groups are at the bottom (reversed).
10. It would be good if groups could be equal.
11. Group equality should be our ideal.
12. All groups should be given an equal chance in life.
13. We would have fewer problems if we treated people more equally.

### Awareness of Inequality Scale, adapted from Critical Reflection Subscale of the Critical Consciousness Scale (Diemer et al., 2017)

How true are the following statements?
Response options range from 1 (Strongly Disagree) to 5 (Strongly Agree).

1. Black people have fewer chances to get a good high school education than White people.
2. Black people have fewer chances to get good jobs than White people.
3. Black people have fewer chances to get ahead than White people.
4. Latinx people have fewer chances to get a good high school education than White people.

5. Latinx people have fewer chances to get good jobs than White people.
6. Latinx people have fewer chances to get ahead than White people.

**Egalitarianism scale, from Critical Reflection Subscale of the Critical Consciousness Scale (Diemer et al., 2017)**

How much do you agree with the following statements?
Response options range from 1 (Strongly Disagree) to 5 (Strongly Agree).

1. It is a good thing that certain social groups are at the top and other social groups are at the bottom (reversed).
2. It would be good if social groups could be equal.
3. Group equality should be our ideal.
4. All social groups should be given an equal chance in life.
5. We would have fewer problems if we treated people more equally.

**Structural attribution scale, items 1, 2, 4, and 6 adapted from Craig et al., 2020; items 3, 4, 7, and 8 generated based on Diemer et al., 2017**

How much do you agree with the following statements?
Response options range from 1 (Strongly Disagree) to 5 (Strongly Agree).

1. Most of the inequality that Black people face stems from policies that disproportionately disadvantage Black people.
2. Anti-Black discrimination is primarily caused by institutional practices that disadvantage Black people.
3. Many businesses intentionally keep Black people from gaining positions of power.
4. Racism in the educational system limits the success of Black people.
5. Most of the inequality that Latinx people face stems from policies that disproportionately disadvantage Latinx people.
6. Anti-Latinx discrimination is primarily caused by institutional practices that disadvantage Latinx people.
7. Many businesses intentionally keep Latinx people from gaining positions of power.
8. Racism in the educational system limits the success of Latinx people.

**Structural-historical thinking, inspired by measures from Nelson et al., 2013; Bonam et al., 2017**

How useful are the following statements in understanding present-day inequality?
Response options range from 1 (Not at all Useful) to 5 (Very Useful).

1. Years of slavery followed by Jim Crow laws – which legally enforced segregation, limited job opportunities, and kept Black Americans from voting – have created a racial wealth gap in the United States.

2. The United States criminal justice system has historically delivered longer sentences to Black Americans than White Americans who commit the same crimes, leading to high numbers of incarcerated Black Americans.
3. The Supreme Court ruling in *Plessy v. Ferguson* (1896), namely that separate facilities for Whites and Blacks were constitutional, encouraged discriminatory laws, leading to direct consequences on present-day school and residential segregation.
4. A history of redlining and denying home loans to Latinx families has contributed to a racial wealth gap in which White American families have more than eight times that of Hispanic and Latinx families.
5. American foreign policy and CIA involvement in Central America during the Reagan administration led to the rise of state and drug violence in countries including, but not limited to El Salvador, Guatemala, Honduras, and Nicaragua, creating the conditions that cause many Central Americans to seek refugee status in the US today.
6. Despite a treaty guaranteeing full US citizenship to Mexicans living on land that was annexed by the US during the Mexican–American War, the US government did not protect Latinx families from violence and displacement by White settlers, leading to a loss in property and wealth with intergenerational impacts.

### Historical Relevance

Response options range from 1 (Not at all Relevant) to 5 (Very Relevant).

1. How relevant are events like these [those listed in the preceding measure of structural-historical thinking] to issues Black people face today?
2. How relevant are events like these [those listed in the preceding measure of structural-historical thinking] to issues Latinx people face today?

## FACTOR LOADINGS

TABLE 6.A.1. Standardized factor loadings for five-factor model

| Variable | Loading | SE |
|---|---|---|
| Awareness of Inequality | | |
| Black people have fewer chances to get a good high school education than White people | 0.857 | 0.019 |
| Black people have fewer chances to get good jobs than white people | 0.851 | 0.019 |
| Black people have fewer chances to get ahead than white people | 0.894 | 0.015 |
| Latinx people have fewer chances to get a good high school education than White people | 0.852 | 0.021 |
| Latinx people have fewer chances to get good jobs than white people | 0.868 | 0.019 |
| Latinx people have fewer chances to get ahead than white people | 0.851 | 0.021 |
| Egalitarianism | | |

TABLE 6.A.1. *(cont.)*

| Variable | Loading | SE |
|---|---|---|
| It is a good thing that certain social groups are at the top and other social groups are at the bottom (reverse-coded) | 0.472 | 0.052 |
| It would be good if social groups could be equal | 0.779 | 0.03 |
| Group equality should be our ideal | 0.768 | 0.032 |
| All social groups should be given an equal chance in life | 0.677 | 0.038 |
| We would have fewer problems if we treated people more equally | 0.768 | 0.032 |
| Structural Attributions | | |
| Most of the inequality that Black people face stems from policies that disproportionately disadvantage Black people | 0.842 | 0.021 |
| Anti-Black discrimination is primarily caused by institutional practices that disadvantage Black people | 0.772 | 0.027 |
| Many businesses intentionally keep Black people from gaining positions of power | 0.709 | 0.033 |
| Racism in the educational system limits the success of Black people | 0.808 | 0.024 |
| Most of the inequality that Latinx people face stems from policies that disproportionately disadvantage Latinx people | 0.786 | 0.029 |
| Anti-Latinx discrimination is primarily caused by institutional practices that disadvantage Latinx people | 0.753 | 0.033 |
| Many businesses intentionally keep Latinx people from gaining positions of power | 0.688 | 0.039 |
| Racism in the educational system limits the success of Latinx people | 0.741 | 0.034 |
| Structural-Historical Thinking | | |
| Years of slavery followed by Jim Crow laws – which legally enforced segregation, limited job opportunities, and kept Black Americans from voting – have created a racial wealth gap in the United States | 0.725 | 0.033 |
| The United States criminal justice system has historically delivered longer sentences to Black Americans than White Americans who commit the same crimes, leading to high numbers of incarcerated Black Americans | 0.704 | 0.035 |
| The Supreme Court ruling in Plessy v. Ferguson (1896), namely that separate facilities for Whites and Blacks were constitutional, encouraged discriminatory laws, leading to direct consequences on present day school and residential segregation | 0.744 | 0.032 |
| A history of redlining and denying home loans to Latinx families has contributed to a racial wealth gap in which White American families have more than eight times that of Hispanic and Latinx families | 0.75 | 0.035 |
| American foreign policy and CIA involvement in Central America during the Reagan administration led to the rise of state and drug violence in countries including, but not limited to El Salvador, Guatemala, Honduras, and Nicaragua, creating the conditions that cause many Central Americans to seek refugee status in the US today | 0.773 | 0.032 |

TABLE 6.A.1. *(cont.)*

| Variable | Loading | SE |
|---|---|---|
| Despite a treaty guaranteeing full US citizenship to Mexicans living on land that was annexed by the US during the Mexican–American War, the US government did not protect Latinx families from violence and displacement by White settlers, leading to a loss in property and wealth with intergenerational impacts | 0.687 | 0.036 |
| Historical Relevance | | |
| How relevant are events like these [those listed in the preceding measure of structural-historical thinking] to issues Black people face today? | 0.763 | 0.043 |
| How relevant are events like these [those listed in the preceding measure of structural-historical thinking] to issues Latinx people face today? | 0.794 | 0.041 |

*Notes:* Standardized loadings presented; all items were significant at $p < 0.001$.

## REFERENCES


Adams, G., O'Brien, L. T., & Nelson, J. C. (2006). Perceptions of racism in Hurricane Katrina: A liberation psychology analysis. *Analyses of Social Issues and Public Policy*, *6*(1), 215–235. https://psycnet.apa.org/doi/10.1111/j.1530-2415.2006.00112.x.

Bonam, C. M., Nair Das V., Coleman, B. R., & Salter, P. (2017). Ignoring history, denying racism: Mounting evidence for the Marley hypothesis and epistemologies of ignorance. *Social Psychological and Personality Science*, *10*(2), 257–265.

Burson, E., & Godfrey, E. B. (2020). Intraminority solidarity: The role of critical consciousness. *European Journal of Social Psychology*, *50*(6), 1362–1377.

Carlson, E. D., Engebretson, J., & Chamberlain, R. M. (2006). Photovoice as a social process of critical consciousness. *Qualitative Health Research*, *16*(6), 836–852.

Chan, R. C. (2022). Development and validation of the Critical Reflection Scale for youth in China: Factor structure and measurement invariance across age, gender, and sexual orientation. *Applied Developmental Science*, 1–13.

Christens, B. D., & Peterson, N. A. (2012). The role of empowerment in youth development: A study of sociopolitical control as mediator of ecological systems' influence on developmental outcomes. *Journal of Youth and Adolescence*, *41*(5), 623–635.

Christens, B. D., Winn, L. T., & Duke, A. M. (2016). Empowerment and critical consciousness: A conceptual cross-fertilization. *Adolescent Research Review*, *1*(1), 15–27.

Conlin, S. E., Douglass, R. P., Moradi, B., & Ouch, S. (2021). Examining feminist and critical consciousness conceptualizations of women's subjective well-being. *The Counseling Psychologist*, *49*(3), 391–422. https://doi.org/10.1177/0011000020957992.

Cortland, C. I., Craig, M. A., Shapiro, J. R. et al. (2017). Solidarity through shared disadvantage: Highlighting shared experiences of discrimination improves relations between stigmatized groups. *Journal of Personality and Social Psychology*, 113(4), 547.

Craig, M. A., Rucker, J., & Brown, R. M. (2020). Structural solidarity: Lay theories of discrimination and coalitional attitudes among stigmatized groups. *PsyArXiv*.

Diemer, M. A. (2009). Pathways to occupational attainment among poor youth of color: The role of sociopolitical development. *The Counseling Psychologist*, *37*(1), 6–35.

Diemer, M. A., & Blustein, D. L. (2006). Critical consciousness and career development among urban youth. *Journal of Vocational Behavior*, *68*(2), 220–232. https://doi.org/10.1016/j.jvb.2005.07.001.

Diemer, M. A., & Hsieh, C. A. (2008). Sociopolitical development and vocational expectations among lower socioeconomic status adolescents of color. *The Career Development Quarterly*, *56*(3), 257–267.

Diemer, M. A., McWhirter, E. H., Ozer, E. J., & Rapa, L. J. (2015). Advances in the conceptualization and measurement of critical consciousness. *The Urban Review*, *47*(5), 809–823.

Diemer, M. A., Pinedo, A., Bañales, J., Mathews, C. J., Frisby, M. B., Harris, E. M., & McAlister, S. (2021). Recentering action in critical consciousness. *Child Development Perspectives*, 0, 1–6. https://doi.org/10.1111/cdep.12393.

Diemer, M. A., Rapa, L. J., Park, C. J., & Perry, J. C. (2017). Development and validation of the Critical Consciousness Scale. *Youth & Society*, *49*(4), 461–483.

Diemer, M. A., Rapa, L. J., Voight, A. M., & McWhirter, E. H. (2016). Critical consciousness: A developmental approach to addressing marginalization and oppression. *Child Development Perspectives*, *10*(4), 216–221.

El-Amin, A., Seider, S., Graves, D. et al. (2017). Critical consciousness: A key to student achievement. *Phi Delta Kappan*, 98(5), 18–23.

Friere, P. (1970). *Pedagogy of the oppressed*. Bloomsbury Publishing.

Freire, P. (1973). *Education for critical consciousness*. Bloomsbury Publishing.

Godfrey, E. B., & Burson, E. (2018). Interrogating the intersections: How intersectional perspectives can inform developmental scholarship on critical consciousness. *New Directions for Child and Adolescent Development*, 2018(161), 17–38.

Godfrey, E. B., Burson, E. L., Yanisch, T. M., Hughes, D., & Way, N. (2019). A bitter pill to swallow? Patterns of critical consciousness and socioemotional and academic well-being in early adolescence. *Developmental Psychology*, *55*(3), 525.

Godfrey, E. B., & Grayman, J. K. (2014). Teaching citizens: The role of open classroom climate in fostering critical consciousness among youth. *Journal of Youth and Adolescence*, *43*(11), 1801–1817. https://doi.org/10.1007/s10964-013-0084-5.

Heberle, A. E., Rapa, L. J., & Faragó, F. (2020). Critical consciousness in children and adolescents: A systematic review, critical assessment, and recommendations for future research. *Psychological Bulletin*, *146*(6), 525–551. https://doi.org/10.1037/bul0000230.

Jemal, A. (2017). Critical consciousness: A critique and critical analysis of the literature. *The Urban Review*, *49*(4), 602–626.

Kass, R. E., & Raftery, A. E. (1995). Bayes factors. *Journal of the American Statistical Association*, *90*(430), 773–795.

Kline, R. (2011). *Principles and Practice of Structural Equation Modeling*. The Guilford Press.

McWhirter, E. H., & McWhirter, B. T. (2016). Critical consciousness and vocational development among Latina/o high school youth: Initial development and testing of a measure. *Journal of Career Assessment*, *26*(3), 543–558. https://doi.org/10.1177/1069072715599535.

Muth én, B. O. (2010, July 15). Using BIC for SEM. Discussion posted on www.statmodel.com/discussion/messages/11/5682.html.

Nelson, J. C., Adams, G., & Salter, P. S. (2013). The Marley hypothesis: Denial of racism reflects ignorance of history. *Psychological Science*, *24*(2), 213–218.

O'Brien, L. T., Blodorn, A., Alsbrooks, A. et al. (2009). Understanding white Americans' perceptions of racism in hurricane Katrina-related events. *Group Processes & Intergroup Relations*, *12*(4), 431–444. https://doi.org/10.1177/1368430209105047.

Olle, C. D., & Fouad, N. A. (2015). Parental support, critical consciousness, and agency in career decision making for urban students. *Journal of Career Assessment*, *23*(4), 533–544. https://doi.org/10.1177/1069072714553074.

Raftery, A. E. (1995). Bayesian model selection in social research. *Sociological Methodology*, *25*, 111–163.

Rapa, L. J., Bolding, C. W., & Jamil, F. M. (2020). Development and initial validation of the Short Critical Consciousness Scale (CCS-S). *Journal of Applied Developmental Psychology*, *70*, 101164.

Rapa, L. J., Diemer, M. A., & Bañales, J. (2018). Critical action as a pathway to social mobility among marginalized youth. *Developmental Psychology*, *54*(1), 127–137. https://doi.org/10.1037/dev0000414.

Seider, S., Clark, S., & Graves, D. (2020). The development of critical consciousness and its relation to academic achievement in adolescents of color. *Child Development*, *91* (2), e451–e474. https://doi-org.proxy.library.nyu.edu/10.1111/cdev.13262.

Shin, R. Q., Ezeofor, I., Smith, L. C., Welch, J. C., & Goodrich, K. M. (2016). The development and validation of the Contemporary Critical Consciousness Measure. *Journal of Counseling Psychology*, *63*(2), 210.

Shin, R. Q., Smith, L. C., Lu, Y. et al. (2018). The development and validation of the Contemporary Critical Consciousness Measure II. *Journal of Counseling Psychology*, 65(5), 539.

Sibley, C. G., & Liu, J. H. (2012). Social representations of history and the legitimation of social inequality: The causes and consequences of historical negation 1. *Journal of Applied Social Psychology*, *42*(3), 598–623. https://doi.org/10.1111/j.1559-1816.2011.00799.x.

Sibley, C. G., Liu, J. H., Duckitt, J., & Khan, S. S. (2008). Social representations of history and the legitimation of social inequality: The form and function of historical negation. *European Journal of Social Psychology*, *38*(3), 542–565. https://doi.org/10.1002/ejsp.449.

Thomas, A. J., Barrie, R., Brunner, J. et al. (2014). Assessing critical consciousness in youth and young adults. *Journal of Research on Adolescence*, *24*(3), 485–496.

Uriostegui, M., Roy, A. L., & Li-Grining, C. P. (2021). What drives you? Black and Latinx youth's critical consciousness, motivations, and academic and career activities. *Journal of Youth and Adolescence*, *50*(1), 58–74.

Van Zomeren, M., Postmes, T., & Spears, R. (2008). Toward an integrative social identity model of collective action: A quantitative research synthesis of three socio-psychological perspectives. *Psychological Bulletin*, *134*(4), 504.

Wang, J., & Wang, X. (2012). *Structural equation modeling: Applications using Mplus*. John Wiley & Sons.

Watts, R. J., Abdul-Adil, J. K., & Pratt, T. (2002). Enhancing critical consciousness in young African American men: A psychoeducational approach. *Psychology of Men & Masculinity*, *3*(1), 41.

Watts, R. J., Diemer, M. A., & Voight, A. M. (2011). Critical consciousness: Current status and future directions. *New Directions for Child and Adolescent Development*, *134*, 43–57. https://doi.org/10.1002/cd.310

Watts, R. J., Griffith, D. M., & Abdul-Adil, J. (1999). Sociopolitical development as an antidote for oppression – theory and action. *American Journal of Community Psychology*, *27*(2), 255–271. https://doi.org/10.1023/A:1022839818873.

Westheimer, J., & Kahne, J. (2003). What kind of citizen? Political choices and educational goals. *Encounters in Theory and History of Education*, *4*.

Zimmerman, M. A., Ramirez-Valles, J., & Maton, K. I. (1999). Resilience among urban African American male adolescents: A study of the protective effects of socio-political control on their mental health. *American Journal of Community Psychology*, *27*(6), 733–751. https://doi.org/10.1023/A:1022205008.

# PART II

# MEASUREMENT

# 7

# Critical Consciousness Measurement

## *A Brief History, Current Status, and New Directions*

LUKE J. RAPA, SARAH E. MCKELLAR, AND ERIN B. GODFREY

As other chapters in this volume have noted, there has been a surge in critical consciousness scholarship in recent years (Heberle et al., 2020). Indeed, just as empirical research in the area of critical consciousness has been expanding, so too has scholarship focused on the measurement of critical consciousness. In this chapter, we provide a brief history of critical consciousness measurement, detail its current status, and highlight promising new directions for research in this area. Many of these promising new directions are explored more extensively in subsequent chapters of this collection. Our goal in this chapter is to set the stage for continued work in this area by centralizing and synthesizing where the quantitative measurement of critical conscious has been and where it is going.

Critical consciousness is particularly challenging to measure because there is considerable variation in how its three canonical dimensions – critical reflection, critical motivation (sometimes referred to as political or sociopolitical efficacy), and critical action – have been conceptualized and operationalized (Heberle et al., 2020; Jemal, 2017; Watts et al., 2011). This issue has marked critical consciousness scholarship since its initial theorization (Freire, 1973, 1968/2000). As we have argued elsewhere (Diemer et al., 2015), the development of instrumentation designed to assess critical consciousness could possibly bring together the field and unite scholars who use divergent approaches to studying it. Heberle et al. (2020) recently pointed this out:

> The development and validation of critical consciousness scales in recent years has the potential to unify critical consciousness conceptualization and measurement, but until the use of these scales becomes more prevalent, differences in the measurement of critical consciousness may obfuscate conclusions about how it develops, changes over time, and shapes other outcomes of interest. (p. 543)

Even with the recent rise in the prevalence and use of critical consciousness scales, however, tension still exists. The different foci deployed in various critical consciousness instruments may continue to complicate our understanding of what exactly critical consciousness is, what supports its growth and development, and what outcomes it fosters.

Advancements in critical consciousness measurement are nonetheless being made, leading to new insights and new directions for future research. In this chapter, we review the quantitative measurement of critical consciousness that has emerged within developmental and applied research over the last few decades. Our focus on quantitative measurement should not be taken to imply a preference for quantitative techniques over qualitative or other techniques to assess critical consciousness. Rather, quantitative measurement lends itself to this kind of review, given the push for standardization and psychometric validation of these kinds of measures. With this in mind, we provide a brief history and an overview of the current status of critical consciousness measurement. Specifically, we organize the extant literature into four overlapping "phases" of measurement, which we refer to as (1) proxy measurement; (2) scale development; (3) scale expansion and (re)specification; and (4) scale refinement and adaptation. Due to their central role in critical consciousness measurement, we pay particular attention to instruments appearing in phase two, the scale development phase. After summarizing each phase, we identify opportunities for advancement and innovation in critical consciousness measurement and point to important new directions for work in this area of scholarship (many of which are addressed more fully in the chapters that follow). These advancements are likely to shape research in this area for years to come.

## FOUR "PHASES" OF CRITICAL CONSCIOUSNESS MEASUREMENT: FROM PROXY MEASURES TO SCALE DEVELOPMENT AND BEYOND

Previous reviews of critical consciousness measurement highlighted the use of proxy measures and called attention to emerging instruments designed explicitly to measure critical consciousness (Diemer et al., 2015; Heberle et al., 2020). Building on this previous work, and considering the abundance of research that has recently appeared, we now suggest that quantitative critical consciousness measurement has evolved through four primary phases (Figure 7.1). Studies reflective of the first phase of critical consciousness measurement are those that have utilized proxy measures to assess critical consciousness. The earliest studies of this kind laid the groundwork for the eventual development of instrumentation designed to measure critical consciousness in more explicit ways (Diemer et al., 2015, Heberle et al., 2020), giving rise to the second phase. The second phase of critical consciousness measurement reflects a period of intensive work on instrument development. Studies emerging in this phase report on the development and validation of scales designed specifically to measure critical consciousness and/or its component parts. The third phase reflects a period of expansion and (re)specification, with studies bearing efforts

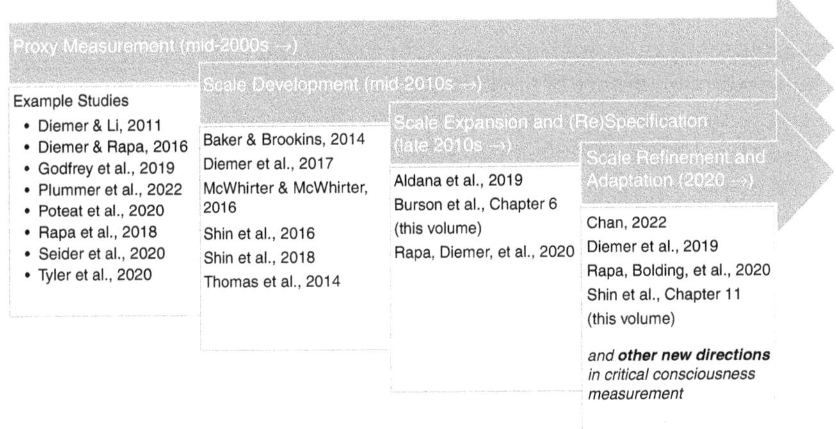


FIGURE 7.1 The four phases of quantitative critical consciousness measurement.

to add to, clarify, or introduce greater precision regarding conceptual aspects of critical consciousness measurement. The last phase reflects further scale refinement, with efforts made to adapt, modify, or streamline instrumentation – either to create more parsimonious or more comprehensive measures of critical consciousness or to adapt or enhance critical consciousness instrumentation for use within particular contexts.

While every phase is relatively distinct from the other, each has no specific endpoint; scholarship within each phase is still ongoing, at least to some degree. For example, studies are still being published that align with or reflect measurement efforts tied to the first phase: proxy measurement. Indeed, empirical studies are emerging that entail the use of proxy measures or introduce novel applications of such proxy measures; these studies are extremely valuable in addressing substantively meaningful questions about critical consciousness's development and functioning despite not using measures explicitly designed to assess critical consciousness.[1] Scholarship tied to the first phase, proxy measurement, is quite expansive, so we call attention to just a few studies that exemplify this approach. Scholarship tied to the other phases – scale development, scale expansion and (re)specification, and scale refinement and adaptation – is more limited although, as noted, there is the potential for research to continue in each of these phases (as a few chapters in this volume illustrate; see, for example, Chapters 6 and 11 [this volume]).

1 Of course, other scales exist and/or are emerging that assess constructs "adjacent" to critical consciousness as well. Such scales measure knowledge, skills, thoughts, behaviors, dispositions, or orientations that are much like the canonical dimensions of critical consciousness but are not explicit measures of critical consciousness per se. Byrd (2017), Hope et al. (2019), and Suyemoto et al. (2022) are three recent examples.

## PHASE ONE: PROXY MEASUREMENT (MID-2000S →)

As noted, early quantitative measurement of critical consciousness was carried out through the use of proxy measures (Diemer et al., 2015; Heberle et al., 2020).[2] Using this approach, scholars typically repurposed items that were included in large-scale quantitative data collection in order to approximate elements of critical consciousness, operationalizing critical consciousness through compilations of items reflecting its canonical dimensions. Pooling items together that "roughly" measure critical reflection, critical motivation, and/or critical action has thus been a viable approach to measuring critical consciousness for many years (Heberle et al., 2020).

As an example, Diemer and Li (2011) used items from the Civic and Political Health Survey of 2006 to assess the critical action behaviors of adolescents. Similarly, Diemer and Rapa (2016) drew from the Civic Education Study of 1999 to assess linkages between critical reflection, critical motivation (operationalized as internal and external political efficacy), and critical action among a nationally representative sample of American ninth-grade youth. Rapa et al. (2018) drew on data collected from a community sample, with original data collection spanning 1991–2009, to consider the longitudinal associations between critical action and occupational expectancies in adolescence and eventual career attainment in adulthood. Godfrey et al. (2019) used data from the Early Adolescent Cohort of the Center for Research, Culture, Development, and Education – a study that began during the 2004–2005 and 2005–2006 school years – to assess marginalized early adolescents' critical consciousness across critical reflection, motivation (sociopolitical efficacy), and action dimensions. Just as these studies illustrate, early quantitative critical consciousness measurement relied wholly on the use of proxy measures to assess critical consciousness, as no validated scales existed to measure it when source data were collected.

The use of proxy measures assessing critical consciousness is limited neither to these examples nor to studies cataloged in prior reviews. For instance, very recently, Plummer et al. (2022) utilized data from the Roots of Engaged Citizenship Project, which carried out data collection from 2012 to 2018, to explore the longitudinal relations between critical reflection (operationalized as awareness of societal inequality), prosocial values (i.e., social responsibility), and civic engagement (including political and prosocial behaviors). Similarly, Poteat et al. (2020) recently collected data in partnership with thirty-eight gender-sexuality alliances (GSAs) in Massachusetts to examine the longitudinal associations between GSA engagement and sociopolitical

[2] By "early" here, we are referring to studies that were initiated, carried out, and/or published before critical consciousness instruments became widely available for use. Because Heberle et al. (2020) cataloged a number of studies like this in their recent review, we only provide a few brief examples here.

efficacy (akin to critical motivation) at both individual and collective levels. Other recent examples abound, some using data elements and reporting findings from larger-scale data collection efforts (e.g., Tyler et al., 2020) and others reporting results from smaller-scale, more localized data collection efforts (e.g., Seider et al., 2020).

These few examples illustrate the robust body of research that has utilized proxy measurement of critical consciousness, be it because scales did not yet exist, were not used in large-scale secondary datasets, or did not fully capture nuanced conceptualizations of critical consciousness or its component parts. This research has contributed greatly to critical consciousness scholarship, elucidating the antecedents and consequences of critical consciousness and establishing it as an important developmental competency and process. However, it has also led to a lack of conceptual and operational clarity regarding the dimensions that compose critical consciousness, along with their definitions, interplay, and associations with its antecedents and consequences. Nevertheless, proxy measurement of critical consciousness laid the groundwork for the future measurement work that emerged during the scale development phase – scholarship aiming to create consolidated measures of critical consciousness in order to codify measurement approaches and move toward greater unification within the field.

## PHASE TWO: SCALE DEVELOPMENT (MID-2010S →)

In the mid-2010s, six scales were developed to measure critical consciousness (or its component parts) explicitly. These scales vary in their focus on critical consciousness dimensions and in their specificity. That is, each operationalizes critical consciousness slightly differently than the others, attends to canonical aspects of critical consciousness in different and nuanced ways, and/or assesses critical consciousness in either relatively more global or relatively more specific ways. The scales were validated with samples reflecting a broad range of sociodemographic characteristics, with some emphasizing the inclusion of individuals experiencing relatively more versus relatively less marginalization or oppression. The six initial studies developing and validating critical consciousness measures were predominantly carried out in the United States, with one exception (i.e., Baker & Brookins, 2014). Across studies, validation samples included a mix of youth and adults and a mix of ethnic/racial groups (see Table 7.1).

### The Sociopolitical Consciousness Scale

One of the earliest scales developed to measure critical consciousness was the Sociopolitical Consciousness Scale (Baker & Brookins, 2014). The scale was developed through participatory engagement between researchers and

TABLE 7.1 Scale and validation sample characteristics of critical consciousness scales

| | Scale Characteristics | | | Validation Sample Characteristics | | | |
|---|---|---|---|---|---|---|---|
| **Scale** | **# of Items** | **Reported Dimensions Measured** | **Specificity** | **Sample Size** | **Reported Gender** | **Reported Age** | **Reported Race/ Ethnicity** |
| Sociopolitical Consciousness Scale Baker & Brookins, 2014 | 35 | (1) Sociopolitical Awareness; (2) Global Belief in a Just World-Modified; (3) Collective Responsibility for the Poor; (4) Equality and Rights; (5) Belief in Collective Action; (6) Localized Community Efficacy; (7) Problem-Solving Efficacy | General | Stage 1: 11 Stage 2: 682 | Stage 1: 36% female and 64% male Stage 2: 47% female and 53% male | Stage 1: mean: 11.6 (five 11–14) and 17.7 (six 17–19) Stage 2: mean: 16.9 (SD = 1.5) range: 14–22 | Stage 1 & Stage 2: Latinx (El Salvadoran youth) |
| Critical Consciousness Scale (CCS) Diemer et al., 2017 | 22 | (1) Critical Reflection (perceived inequality and egalitarianism); (2) Critical Action (sociopolitical participation) | General | Study 1: 163 Study 2: 163 | Study 1 & 2: 56.9% female | Study 1 & 2: mean: 15.47 (SD = 1.34) range: 13–19 | Study 1 & 2: Black/ African American (63%) or as bi- or multiracial (24.6%), White (7.7%), Latino (2%), American Indian/Native American (1%), or as, Asian/Asian American (0.3%), self-identified "other" (1.3%) |

| | | | | | | | |
|---|---|---|---|---|---|---|---|
| Measure of Adolescent Critical Consciousness (MACC)<br>McWhirter & McWhirter, 2016 | 10 | (1) Critical Agency (motivation); (2) Critical Behavior (action) | Specific: racial inequity | Study 1: 476<br>Study 2: 870 | Study 1: 71% female and 29% male<br>Study 2: 64% female and 36% | Study 1: mean: 16.4 (SD = 1.10)<br>range: 14–19<br>Study 2: mean: 16.3 (SD = 1.26)<br>range: 13–20 | Study 1 & 2: 100% Latina/o |
| Contemporary Critical Consciousness Measure<br>Shin et al., 2016 | 19 | (1) Critical Reflection | Specific: (1) racism; (2) classism; (3) heterosexism | Study 1: 210<br>Study 2: 406 | Study 1: 64.8% female<br>Study 2: 53.8% female | Study 1: mean: 33.9<br>Study 2: mean: 33.7 | Study 1: Caucasian/ European American (68.1%)<br>Study 2: Caucasian/ European American (71.2%) |
| Contemporary Critical Consciousness Measure II<br>Shin et al., 2018 | 37 | (1) Critical Reflection | Specific: (1) cis-sexism; (2) ableism; (3) sexism | Study 1 & 2: 569 total<br>Study 1: 270<br>Study 2: 299 | Study 1 & 2: 65.7% female, 0.4% gender binary | Study 1 & 2: 38.5 years | Study 1 & 2: white (75.6%); African American (8.6%); Asian American (5.8%); Latino (5.6%); Native American (.5%); multiracial or multiethnic (3.0%), and "other" (.9%) |
| Critical Consciousness Inventory<br>Thomas et al., 2014 | 9 | (1) Critical Reflection (sociopolitical development and social perspective-taking) | General | 206 | 67.5% women & 32.5% men | 43.7% 18 years, 36.4% 19 years, 10.2% 20 years, 4.9% 21 years, 5% between 22 and 25 years | white (32.2%); Latino (11.2%); Asian/Pacific Islander (3.9%); African American (40%); multiracial (11.2%) |

a sample of Latinx youth in El Salvador. A two-stage process was used to develop the instrument. First, photovoice (e.g., Wang & Burris, 1997) was used to engage participants about their perceptions and experiences of concepts tied to sociopolitical development (cf. Watts et al., 2003; Watts & Flanagan, 2007) and create an original item-pool of thirty-six items measuring sociopolitical consciousness. Second, items were tested and refined for use with a second, independent sample. After refinement, the scale was validated using exploratory and confirmatory factor analyses and resulted in a 35-item instrument assessing seven dimensions of sociopolitical consciousness, most of which relate directly to critical consciousness' critical reflection and critical motivation dimensions. The seven dimensions of sociopolitical consciousness are: (1) sociopolitical awareness; (2) global belief in a just world; (3) collective responsibility for the poor; (4) equality and rights; (5) belief in collective action; (6) localized community efficacy; and (7) problem-solving efficacy. Sample items for a few of these dimensions include "In this society everyone has the same chance for success" (Global Beliefs in a Just World-Modified), "Women deserve the same rights as everyone else in society" (Equality and Rights), and "We need to participate in efforts such as demonstrations, protests, and community organizing in order to change society" (Belief in Collective Action).

The El Salvadorian youth who composed the sample for the development and initial validation of the Sociopolitical Consciousness Scale predominantly identified as boys. The sample was also mostly composed of adolescents, though some preadolescents and young adults were included (age range: 11–22 years). Unique among other measures of critical consciousness, the Sociopolitical Consciousness Scale was designed to explicitly incorporate youths' understandings of their sociocultural and sociopolitical contexts via their engagement in photovoice and other mixed methods research processes (Baker & Brookins, 2014). Also unique among other measures of critical consciousness, particularly those cataloged in this phase of critical consciousness measurement, is the fact that this instrument was developed for use with a population outside the United States.

## The Critical Consciousness Scale

The Critical Consciousness Scale (CCS; Diemer et al., 2017), one of the more frequently used instruments measuring critical consciousness, first became available in 2014. The CCS is a 22-item scale assessing two dimensions of critical consciousness: critical reflection and critical action. The critical reflection dimension itself comprises two subdimensions, perceived inequality and egalitarianism, designed to assess an individual's general awareness of racial/ethnic, class, and gender inequalities and supportive beliefs about group and societal equality, respectively. The critical action dimension is unitary, designed to assess the frequency of action taken over the past one-year period to address inequities via conventional (e.g., voting) and activist (e.g., protest) sociopolitical participation. Sample items include "Certain racial or ethnic groups have fewer chances to get ahead" (critical reflection: perceived inequality), "It would be good if groups could be equal" (critical reflection: egalitarianism), and "Joined in a protest march, political demonstration, or political meeting" (critical action: sociopolitical participation). The scale utilizes 6-point Likert-type scaling for the critical reflection dimension (1 = *strongly disagree*, 6 = *strongly agree*) and 5-point Likert-type scaling for the critical action dimension (1 = *never did this*, 5 = *at least once a week*).

The CCS was initially validated with an adolescent sample that was approximately balanced across gender and was composed predominantly of respondents who identified as youth of color. Rigorous exploratory and confirmatory factor analyses were utilized during the development and validation stages, with two distinct, independent samples used for each phase. Subsequent use of the CCS with varied samples demonstrates the broad utility of the instrument as a measure of critical consciousness, and since its development it has been used in a variety of settings and in numerous studies focused on examining the antecedents, consequences, and development of critical consciousness (e.g., Diemer et al., 2019; Marchand et al., 2021).

Despite its affordances, the CCS is somewhat limited by the fact that it only accounts for the reflection and action dimensions of critical consciousness. That is, it does not include an assessment of the critical motivation dimension. In addition, its critical reflection dimension focuses primarily on the awareness of and attitudes toward inequity and does not as readily assess historical, structural, or systemic attributions for inequity. Likewise, its critical action dimension does not explicitly reference challenging various systems of oppression. As will be discussed in greater detail, the CCS was the foundation of three additional scales. One was designed to assess critical motivation (Rapa, Diemer, et al., 2020) and emerged in the scale expansion and (re) specification phase. The other two emerged during the scale refinement and adaptation phase: the CCS-S (Rapa, Bolding et al., 2020) and the ShoCCS (Diemer et al., 2022). The latter two scales are streamlined versions of the original CCS, but they also address some of the limitations of the original CCS instrument by incorporating the critical motivation scale developed by Rapa, Diemer, et al. (2020).

## The Measure of Adolescent Critical Consciousness

The Measure of Adolescent Critical Consciousness (MACC; McWhirter & McWhirter, 2016) focuses specifically on issues related to racial inequity and assesses two dimensions of critical consciousness, namely critical motivation (referred to as critical agency) and critical action (referred to as critical behavior). Sample items include "I am motivated to try to end racism and discrimination" (critical agency) and "I am involved in activities and groups against racism and discrimination" (critical behavior). The scale utilizes 4-point Likert-type scaling (1 = *strongly agree*, 6 = *strongly disagree*), with scores reversed such that higher scores reflect higher levels of critical consciousness.

Like the CCS, the MACC was initially validated with an adolescent sample though all respondents in the validation study identified as Latinx and most identified as girls. Also like the CCS, the development and validation of the MACC included rigorous exploratory and confirmatory factor analysis procedures, with two distinct, independent samples used for the exploratory and confirmatory phases. Notably, the validation of the MACC included the development of a Spanish translation of the scale, making it accessible to and validated for use by those for whom Spanish is a preferred language. Because of the MACC's particular focus on racial inequities, the scale is less useful for the assessment of inequities across domains – for example, class and gender – or for explication of other specific disparities such as inequities with regard to dis/ability or immigrant status, among others. In addition, it does not incorporate a dimension focusing on critical reflection.

## The Contemporary Critical Consciousness Measure

The Contemporary Critical Consciousness Measure (CCCM; Shin et al., 2016) is a 19-item instrument measuring critical reflection vis-à-vis three specific forms of oppression: racism, classism, and heterosexism. It is the only Critical Consciousness Scale designed to assess these three forms of oppression explicitly and simultaneously. Sample items include "Most poor people are poor because they are unable to manage their expenses well" (reverse-coded; classism), "All whites receive unearned privilege in US society" (racism), and "Discrimination against gay persons is still a significant problem in the United States" (heterosexism). Grounded in an intersectionality framework (Collins, 1993; Combahee River Collective, 1977/2014; Crenshaw, 1989; see also Godfrey & Burson, 2018), the CCCM aims to assess critical consciousness at the nexus of these forms of oppression, taking all the included forms of oppression into account. Through its item composition, it is also focused more explicitly on the structural and systemic nature of marginalization and oppression relative to other critical consciousness scales. The CCCM utilizes 7-point Likert-type scaling (1 = *strongly agree*, 7 = *strongly disagree*), with scores reversed such that higher scores reflect higher levels of critical consciousness.

Like the CCS and the MACC, the CCCM utilized exploratory and confirmatory analyses during the development and validation process. Unlike the CCS and the MACC, however, the validation sample used to develop the CCCM was composed only of adults, most of whom were women and most of whom identified ethnically/racially as white (note: this category was designated as "Caucasian/European American" during the data collection process). According to Shin et al. (2016), the CCCM was designed for use with clinical mental health care and counseling providers to assess their consciousness or awareness of various forms of oppression that may be experienced by those in their care and to provide insights about the need to enhance understanding of the forms of social injustice relevant to the work of counseling psychologists. While the scale could be useful beyond this context – that is, with individuals who are not counseling psychology trainees – the specific focus of the scale on critical reflection alone perhaps makes it less broadly applicable as a measure of critical consciousness than some of the other instruments developed during this phase.

### The Contemporary Critical Consciousness Measure II

Building on the foundation of the CCCM, Shin et al. (2018) developed the 37-item Contemporary Critical Consciousness Measure II (CCCMII) to assess critical reflection in terms of three different forms of oppression: cis-sexism, ableism, and sexism. These foci are unique to the CCCMII, as no other Critical Consciousness Scale considers these multiple forms of marginalization or oppression explicitly. Sample items include "Discrimination against transgender persons in our society is severe" (cis-sexism), "People with disabilities are generally treated more poorly in US society than those without disabilities" (ableism), and "US society has yet to reach a point where women and men have equal opportunities for achievement" (sexism). The CCCMII, also grounded in an intersectionality framework, aims to assess critical consciousness at the nexus of these three forms of oppression and accounts for the systemic and structural nature of oppression across these areas. The scale utilizes 7-point Likert-type scaling (1 = *strongly agree*, 7 = *strongly disagree*), with scores reversed such that higher scores reflect higher levels of critical consciousness.

Similar to the approach used to develop and validate the CCCM, Shin et al. (2018) conducted rigorous exploratory and confirmatory analyses during the development and validation stages of their work to create the CCCMII. The validation sample for the CCCMII was again composed of adults, with respondents identifying predominantly as women and predominantly as white. The CCCMII was designed for use with clinical mental health care and counseling providers, as was the original CCCM. The scale's specific focus on cis-sexism, ableism, and sexism again perhaps makes it less broadly applicable as a measure of critical consciousness than some of the other critical consciousness instruments, but its granularity and precision in assessing these "-isms" may be advantageous if the specific forms of oppression are of central interest to researchers or those working in applied settings. Both the

CCCM and the CCCMII can also be leveraged to empirically unpack core questions in the field as to whether critical consciousness develops in domain-specific or domain-general ways. As noted earlier, however, by design, the CCCM and the CCCMII both attend only to critical reflection, and they lack assessment of the critical motivation and critical action dimensions of critical consciousness.

## The Critical Consciousness Inventory

The Critical Consciousness Inventory (CCI; Thomas et al., 2014) is a 9-item measure of critical reflection that assesses two distinct components: sociopolitical development and social perspective-taking. The sociopolitical development component of the CCI aligns with the typical conceptualization of critical reflection in terms of critical social analysis of societal inequities, while the social perspective-taking subdimension falls somewhat outside of the canonical conceptualizations of critical reflection or of the other critical consciousness dimensions: motivation and action (Diemer et al., 2015).

The CCI utilizes Guttman scaling to allow for the measurement of growth in critical consciousness across what Thomas et al. (2014) refer to as "pre-critical" and "post-critical" stages. This makes the CCI unique among the other critical consciousness scales, which otherwise each use Likert-type scaling. Reinforced by their chosen measurement approach, Thomas et al. (2014) suggest that critical consciousness develops in a stage-like manner, from precritical to postcritical and from reflection toward action and/or awareness of the need for societal change. Items across two sample sets of indicators from the CCI illustrate this. The first sample shows increasingly greater critical consciousness regarding educational opportunities: "(3a) I think that education gives everyone an equal chance to do well"; "(3b) I think that education gives everyone who works hard an equal chance"; "(3c) I think the educational system is unequal"; and "(3d) I think the educational system needs to be changed in order for everyone to have an equal chance." The second sample shows increasingly greater critical consciousness of prejudice: "(6a) I don't notice when people make prejudiced comments"; "(6b) I notice when people make prejudiced comments and it hurts me"; "(6c) It hurts me when people make prejudiced comments, but I am able to move on"; and "(6d) When someone makes a prejudiced comment, I tell them what they said is hurtful." Rasch analyses carried out during the initial scale development and validation processes supported the viability of differentiating low versus high critical consciousness using the CCI, as reflected in the different stages of development – though there remains considerable debate as to whether critical consciousness develops in this stage-like fashion and additional empirical inquiry about this is warranted (see Diemer et al., 2015 for discussion).

The CCI was validated with a college-aged sample of adults, whose ages ranged from 18 (47% of the sample) to between 22 and 25 (5%). The sample was diverse in terms of ethnic/racial composition, while a higher proportion of the sample identified as women (67.5%) versus men. The CCI served as the foundation of a new instrument that emerged during the scale refinement and adaptation phase (Chan, 2022). However, as detailed further in the related section, that new instrument abandoned the Guttman scaling approach used in the original CCI in favor of the Likert-type scaling used in other critical consciousness instruments. It also focused specifically on assessing critical reflection among youth in China.

Overall, scholarship in this phase has made considerable new advances in critical consciousness measurement by introducing and validating a number of new scales designed explicitly to measure critical consciousness. The challenges that characterize this phase – including inconsistent inclusion of all three canonical dimensions of critical consciousness and differences in the nuance of how each dimension is conceptualized – illustrate how transitioning from proxy measurement to specific measurement had the potential to clarify and unify scholarly understanding of what critical consciousness is; yet, at the same time, they reveal the complexity of this endeavor and signify how disparate critical consciousness measurement actually still is. The development of these scales nevertheless laid groundwork for further empirical and conceptual expansion and (re)specification of critical consciousness measurement, which is the focus of studies appearing in phase three.

## PHASE THREE: SCALE EXPANSION AND (RE)SPECIFICATION (LATE 2010S →)

Scholars have continued their measurement efforts in recent years, expanding and (re)specifying critical consciousness instruments in follow-up to initial scale development. In particular, instruments have been developed to better target specific aspects of critical consciousness – aspects either absent from or not sufficiently accounted for during initial scale development processes. Three scales exemplify critical consciousness measurement research carried out during this phase: the Anti-Racist Action Scale (Aldana et al., 2019), an expanded critical reflection scale (Chapter 6 [this volume]), and a scale assessing critical motivation (Rapa, Diemer, et al., 2020).

### The Anti-Racism Action Scale

The assessment of critical action within the critical consciousness instruments developed during the scale development phase did not, perhaps, sufficiently attend to the extent to which critical action targets the systemic or structural nature of inequity/ies or the extent to which critical action targets certain forms of oppression. In light of this, the Anti-Racist Action Scale was developed. The Anti-Racist Action Scale more fully assesses adolescents' actions to counter racism, in particular, and it captures the multidimensional nature of the action that is, in fact, taken.

Like the Sociopolitical Consciousness Scale (Baker & Brookins, 2014), the development of the Anti-Racism Action Scale proceeded in two stages. The first stage entailed engagement with youth in a participatory process to identify ways they engaged in action to oppose racism encountered in their lives; exploratory factor analysis was then used to identify items that reflected the various dimensions associated with youths' antiracist action. The second stage entailed validating that factor structure and refining items for inclusion in the finalized instrument; confirmatory factor analysis was used in this second stage, and the resulting scale was tested with an independent, nationally representative youth sample. The final 16-item Anti-Racist Action Scale assesses action along three dimensions – interpersonal action, communal action, and political change action – and asks respondents to indicate their engagement in various actions at any point over the previous two months. Answers from respondents are recorded using binary "yes"/"no" responses. Sample items include "Challenged or checked a family member who uses a racial slur or makes a racial joke" (interpersonal action), "Joined a club or group working on issues related to race, ethnicity, discrimination, and/or segregation" (communal action), and "Attended a protest on an issue related to race, ethnicity, discrimination, and/or segregation" (political change action).

The Anti-Racism Action Scale was validated with youth (Study 1 $M_{age}$ = 16.00, Study 2 $M_{age}$ = 17.00). The two samples were composed of slightly more girls than boys (Study 1 = 61.7% girls, Study 2 = 51.0% girls), and they included a broad range of ethnic/racial groups; Study 2 comprised a nationally representative sample. Notably, Aldana et al.'s (2019) analyses included an assessment of convergent validity between the Anti-Racism Action Scale and the CCS, with results suggesting the Anti-Racist Action Scale captures dimensions of youths' engagement in critical action targeting systemic and structural forms of inequities – namely, racism – in ways that are multidimensional and distinct from the CCS's more generally assessed critical action.

## An Expanded Measure of Critical Reflection

Another effort to target specific aspects of critical consciousness that were not sufficiently accounted for in critical consciousness instruments during the scale development phase is the exploratory work carried out by Burson et al. (Chapter 6 [this volume]) to test an expanded measure of critical reflection. Burson and colleagues sought to extend measures of critical reflection in order to assess more precisely both awareness of inequality and various aspects of structural attributions for these inequities and historical thinking about inequality as experienced by people of color. First, items from the CCS were revised to focus more on the awareness of inequality shaping the experiences of members of Black and Latinx ethnic/racial groups. Sample items from the respecified measure of critical reflection: perceived inequality include: "Black people have fewer chances to get a good high school education than white people" and "Latinx people have fewer chances to get ahead than white people." Other items were developed to focus on structural attributions for these inequities and historical thinking about inequality. Sample items from the new structural attributions subscale include "Most of the inequality that Black people face stems from policies that disproportionately disadvantage Black people" and "Racism in the educational system limits the success of Latinx people." Similarly, sample items from the new structural-historical thinking subdimension include "Years of slavery followed by Jim Crow laws – which legally enforced segregation, limited job opportunities, and kept Black Americans from voting – have created a racial wealth gap in the United States" and "American foreign policy and CIA involvement in Central America during the Reagan administration led to the rise of state and drug violence in countries including, but not limited to El Salvador, Guatemala, Honduras, and Nicaragua, creating the conditions that cause many Central Americans to seek refugee status in the US today."

From a theoretical standpoint, critical consciousness entails recognition of both the systemic and the structural causes of societal inequity; however, prior instruments have failed to capture these elements in their assessment of critical reflection. Consequently, according to Burson et al. (Chapter 6 [this volume]), measures of critical reflection should be expanded and/or (re) specified to include the explicit assessment of structural and historical thinking. The authors contend that if measures are to truly assess critical reflection, then attention to the structural and historical aspects of societal inequity must be more fully and more explicitly accounted for. Through their work, Burson and colleagues present compelling new evidence for the utility and importance of measuring structural and historical thinking alongside existing – if not also slightly expanded or respecified – measures of critical reflection.

## Critical Motivation

Rapa, Diemer, et al. (2020) developed and validated a scale measuring critical motivation using items created during the initial development of the CCS (Diemer et al., 2017; see also Rapa, 2016). In particular, the authors created a 10-item critical motivation scale capturing respondents' motivation to change perceived societal inequalities and their efficacy beliefs about whether it is possible for such inequalities to be rectified. As noted elsewhere (Rapa, Bolding, et al., 2020), this conceptualization of critical motivation is slightly different from some conceptualizations that are focused more on an individual's efficacy beliefs about being able to promote change (e.g., Diemer & Rapa, 2016) and instead accounts for an individual's interest in and perceptions of the importance of promoting such change (see also Heberle et al., 2020; Watts et al., 2011). Such differences merit attention in future scholarship, both theoretical and empirical. Notwithstanding, sample items from the current critical motivation scale include "It is important for young people to speak out when an injustice has occurred," "It is important to confront someone who says something that you think is racist or prejudiced," and "It is my responsibility to get involved and make things better for society." In alignment with the scale used for the critical reflection dimension of the CCS, the critical motivation scale utilizes 6-point Likert-type scaling (1 = *strongly disagree*, 6 = *strongly agree*).

The critical motivation scale was initially tested and validated with a sample of adolescents enrolled in the ninth and tenth grades ($M_{age}$ = 14.97). The sample was predominantly composed of girls (58%), while a minority of the sample identified as youth of color, defined within the study as Black, Latinx, or multiracial (34%). As noted earlier in this chapter, and discussed in further detail later, the critical motivation scale was incorporated into the CCS-S and the ShoCCS. Both of these instruments streamlined the original CCS while also incorporating the critical motivation dimension of critical consciousness to create more holistic measures of critical consciousness capturing all three of its dimensions.

These expansion and (re)specification efforts continue to push the field even further toward unified and comprehensive measurement of critical consciousness, representing all dimensions of the construct and incorporating additional nuances into their operationalization. Such nuances better represent the theoretical origins of and lived experiences pertaining to critical consciousness, and they serve to further differentiate critical consciousness dimensions from other related constructs. For example, expanding the operationalization of critical motivation to include the importance of and perceived responsibility to take action against inequity distinguishes this dimension from conceptualizations of internal and external political efficacy proffered by political scientists – though additional theoretical and empirical work is still needed to tease apart where these constructs may converge and diverge from or compose different facets of critical motivation. It also better positions critical motivation to serve as a moderator or mediator of the reflection–action praxis cycle. Similarly, youth-driven operationalizations of critical action incorporate forms of action (e.g., interpersonal action) that expand and differentiate this dimension from the conceptualization of collective action in social psychological literature. Additional work to continue expanding and (re)specifying may be merited to support sustained movement toward conceptual clarity and more precise measurement of critical consciousness and its component parts. This is true even while additional refinement and adaptation of existing critical consciousness measures is underway, such as that which is occurring in phase four.

## PHASE FOUR: SCALE REFINEMENT AND ADAPTATION (2020 →)

The final phase of critical consciousness measurement accounts for ways in which critical consciousness instruments have very recently been further streamlined, refined, and adapted to be more easily implemented across multiple populations and/or to account for more holistic assessments of the construct. Four instruments comprise critical consciousness measurement research carried out during this phase: the Critical Reflection Scale for Youth in China, the ShoCCS and the CCS-S – both streamlined versions of the original CCS – and the CCCM-S, a scale integrating the CCCM and the CCCMII.

### The Critical Reflection Scale for Youth in China

Recently, Chan (2022) developed the Critical Reflection Scale for Youth in China. Most contemporary critical consciousness scholarship – focused on measurement or otherwise – has been carried out within Western contexts. However, such contexts have different sociopolitical realities than other contexts, including those characterized as less democratic societies. The Critical Reflection Scale for Youth in China assesses critical reflection across two distinct subdimensions: (1) recognition of social inequity and (2) awareness of everyday oppression. Notably, the scale was developed by testing an adapted version of the CCI. Reductions were made to the scope of each item set, incorporating just the first statement within each of the nine original CCI indicators. This resulted in the abandonment of the Guttman scaling; instead, the scale used the Likert-type scaling typical of other critical consciousness instruments in order "to assess the extent to which individuals recognize and how they feel about the oppression and inequity in society" (Chan, 2022, p. 4). Sample items include "I think that education gives everyone an equal chance to do well" (reverse-coded; recognition of social inequity) and "When people tell a joke that makes fun of a social group, I laugh and don't really think about it" (reverse-coded; awareness of everyday oppression). The scale utilizes 4-point Likert-type scaling, with some items reverse-coded (1 = *strongly disagree*, 4 = *strongly agree*).

Like a number of other critical consciousness instruments, the Critical Reflection Scale for Youth in China was initially validated with a youth sample, which was recruited from secondary schools throughout a few regions of the nation. Exploratory and confirmatory factor analyses were used during the development and validation stages, with distinct independent samples used for the exploratory ($n$ = 1,601) and confirmatory ($n$ = 1,414) phases of analysis. According to sociodemographic data reported, the sample was fairly balanced across gender (51.4% identified as young men) and the majority identified as heterosexual (73.2%). The mean age of respondents was 15.71 ($SD$ = 1.54 years). Once the scale's factor structure was established during the exploratory phase and validated during the confirmatory phase, Chan (2022) utilized multiple-indicators multiple-causes (MIMIC) analyses to test the equivalence of the measure across age, gender, and sexual orientation, with results revealing two of the scale's items functioning differentially between youth identifying as boys versus those identifying as girls. Notably, the Critical Reflection Scale for Youth in China forges new ground in that it represents the development of instrumentation to measure the critical reflection dimension of critical consciousness in non-Western societies – an important advancement in the field of critical consciousness measurement that has not been undertaken since Baker and Brookins' (2014) work in El Salvador. However, it is still subject to limitations in that it only measures one dimension of critical consciousness – critical reflection – and it does so using more basic indicators of awareness of inequality.

## The "ShoCCS" Short Critical Consciousness Scale

The "ShoCCS" Short Critical Consciousness Scale (Diemer et al., 2022) is a streamlined version of the CCS that includes items from the critical reflection: perceived inequality and critical action scales of the CCS along with critical motivation items from the critical motivation scale (Rapa, Diemer, et al., 2020). Items for the critical reflection: egalitarianism subscale were excluded from analyses in the development of the ShoCCS due in part to the tenuous link between egalitarianism and other critical consciousness subdimensions in some empirical research. To develop the ShoCCS, Diemer and colleagues utilized item response theory methods to reduce the longer-form instruments to smaller item sets that provide maximally useful and efficient measurement of each included critical consciousness dimension. The short scales were developed in a first study and then replicated with an independent sample in a second study. Youth in Study 1 averaged 16.9 years of age and just over half (55.7%) were girls. Youth in Study 2 were middle and high school aged students (reporting grade level as opposed to age, specifically) and were predominantly girls (56.8%). Across both studies, most respondents identified as youth of color.

The ShoCCS is a 13-item instrument that includes four items assessing critical reflection: perceived inequality, five items assessing critical action, and four items assessing critical motivation. All items were derived from the longer-form instruments and were not otherwise adapted or refined. A sample critical reflection: perceived inequality item is "Women have fewer chances to get ahead." A sample critical action item is "Participated in a civil rights group or organization." A sample critical motivation item is "It is important to correct social and economic inequality." Like the original CCS, the scale utilizes 6-point Likert-type scaling for the critical reflection and critical motivation dimensions (1 = *strongly disagree*, 6 = *strongly agree*) and 5-point Likert-type scaling for the critical action dimension (1 = *never did this*, 5 = *at least once a week*).

## The "CCS-S" Short Critical Consciousness Scale

Like the ShoCCS, the "CCS-S" Short Critical Consciousness Scale (Rapa, Bolding, et al., 2020) is a validated, adapted, and streamlined version of the original CCS. The CCS-S includes items from the critical reflection and critical action scales of the CCS, along with critical motivation items from the critical motivation scale (Rapa, Diemer, et al., 2020). Contrary to the ShoCCS, however, the CCS-S includes items from the CCS's critical reflection: egalitarian subdimension. To develop and validate the CCS-S, two separate studies were carried out. In the first study, Rapa, Bolding, et al. (2020) identified and extracted items from the original scales, creating the 14-item CCS-S while maintaining the strong psychometric properties of the original subscales and attending to the contents of the constructs measured by the original item sets. In the second study, Rapa, Bolding, et al. (2020) validated the CCS-S with a large-scale, independent sample ($n$ = 4,901; $M_{age}$ = 14.69). Respondents in Study 1 predominantly identified as girls (56.9%) and as youth of color, spanning high school grades nine through twelve. Respondents in Study 2 also predominantly identified as girls (51.8%) and as youth of color. However, youth in Study 2 spanned fourth through twelfth grade. Rapa, Bolding, et al. (2020) tested measurement invariance of the CCS-S across ethnic/racial, age, and gender groups, with equivalence supported for each group, making it the first of the critical consciousness instruments for which measurement equivalence was tested and demonstrated.

The CCS-S has fourteen items. Three items assess critical reflection: perceived inequality, three items assess critical reflection: egalitarianism, four items assess critical action, and four items assess critical motivation. As with the ShoCCS, all items were derived from the longer-form instruments and were not otherwise adapted or refined. While the approach taken to streamline the longer-form scales to develop the CCS-S was different from the approach taken by Diemer et al. (2022), the CCS-S and the ShoCCS are remarkably similar, with only a few items differing across subdimensions. Each sample item referenced earlier for the ShoCCS also appears in the CCS-S. A sample critical reflection: egalitarianism item is "All groups should be given an equal chance in life." Like the original CCS, the CCS-S utilizes 6-point Likert-type scaling for critical reflection (1 = *strongly disagree*, 6 = *strongly agree*) and

5-point Likert-type scaling for the critical action dimension (1 = *never did this*, 5 = *at least once a week*). Like the original critical motivation scale (Rapa, Diemer, et al., 2020), 6-point Likert-type scaling is used for the critical motivation dimension (1 = *strongly disagree*, 6 = *strongly agree*). Both the ShoCCS and the CCS-S are notable for their brevity, ease of administration, strong psychometric properties, and inclusion of items tapping each dimension of critical consciousness. However, they are still subject to some of the concerns inherent to the measures on which they were based: notably, the lack of items assessing more structural and systemic understanding of inequity along with the varied and specific ways individuals take action to challenge inequity.

### The Contemporary Critical Consciousness Measure-Short

Similar to the recent efforts by Diemer et al. (2022) and Rapa, Bolding, et al. (2020) to create streamlined versions of their previously developed critical consciousness measures, Shin et al. (Chapter 11 [this volume]) also developed a streamlined, integrated measure combining their two previously published scales, the CCCM and the CCCMII. The new Contemporary Critical Consciousness Measure-Short (CCCM-S) is a 24-item instrument that provides a general index of critical reflection that also captures critical reflection vis-à-vis five specific forms of oppression: racism, classism, heterosexism, ableism, and sexism/cis-sexism.

All items for the CCCM-S were derived from the longer-form instruments and were not otherwise adapted or refined. Similarly, like the original CCCM and the CCCMII, the CCCM-S utilizes 7-point Likert-type scaling (1 = *strongly agree*, 7 = *strongly disagree*), with scores reversed such that higher scores reflect higher levels of critical reflection. The CCCM-S remains solely focused on the critical reflection dimension of critical consciousness, like the CCCM and the CCCMII, in line with Shin and colleagues' goal to develop a tool to assess and support the development of critical consciousness among mental health professionals. However, it is the only validated scale to assess critical reflection in an intersectional manner across five different forms of oppression.

## OTHER NEW DIRECTIONS: OPPORTUNITIES FOR ADVANCEMENT AND INNOVATION IN CRITICAL CONSCIOUSNESS MEASUREMENT

In the preceding sections of this chapter, we presented a brief history and an overview of the current status of critical consciousness measurement. More specifically, we cataloged the progression of critical consciousness measurement from proxy measurement (phase one) to scale development (phase two), to scale expansion and (re)specification (phase three) and finally to scale refinement and adaptation (phase four). As noted at the outset, scholarship within each phase is still ongoing, with studies emerging that newly expand, respecify, refine, or adapt extant critical consciousness measures – or even provide new applications of proxy measures in ways that push the boundaries of how the field accounts for critical consciousness and its dimensions. Numerous scales now exist to measure critical consciousness, each with various foci, affordances (and constraints), and target populations. Scholars studying critical consciousness have no dearth of choices to make when selecting instrumentation for critical consciousness measurement. We encourage scholars to consider how various measures match their study purposes and align with the conceptual and theoretical foundations of their work.

While we expect research to continue across each of these phases, scholars working in the area of critical consciousness measurement are also pursuing new directions. Indeed, numerous opportunities exist for further advancement and innovation. As documented throughout this chapter, new directions for critical consciousness measurement have often arisen to address the limitations of extant instrumentation despite their various affordances. However, current new directions largely emanate from the need to better match critical consciousness measurement with critical consciousness theory and the need to address the conceptual, theoretical, and/or measurement-related issues identified through empirical work carried out in recent years – issues we have tried to elucidate up to this point within our review. A few of the promising new directions for work in the area of critical consciousness measurement are worth consideration here; however, we note that many of these are addressed more fully in the chapters that follow.

## MORE REFINED INTERSECTIONAL MEASUREMENT

Current measures of critical consciousness are limited by the fact that they do not holistically or extensively account for intersectional experiences of, or attributions for, marginalization and oppression (Godfrey & Burson, 2018; Heberle et al., 2020). While the CCCM (Shin et al., 2016) and the CCCMII (Shin et al., 2018) explicitly draw on intersectional theory, even they are limited by the extent to which they adequately account for marginalization or oppression experienced at the nexus of certain marginalizing forces. Nor do they holistically attend to the systemic or structural realities that govern experiences of marginalization or oppression at such intersections (cf. "Axis 3"; see Introduction [this volume]). This blind spot also manifests through the sociodemographic characteristics of samples used to develop and validate extant scales, no doubt reflecting distinct and varied experiences with oppressive forces. When comparing participants across studies, it is clear that some focused on youth of color and others on white adults; some studies had a balanced ratio of girls to boys while others had one gender group that was vastly overrepresented. Most failed to attend to measurement differences that may be present across groups. For example, only two instruments to date – the CSS-S (Rapa, Bolding, et al., 2020) and the Critical Reflection Scale for Youth in China (Chan, 2022) – examined measurement invariance in critical consciousness items across sociodemographic groups during the scale development and initial validation process.

The CCCM-S (Chapter 11 [this volume]) reflects advancement in the area of intersectional critical consciousness measurement, as the new scale captures more extensive critical reflection about varied forms of oppression, including racism, classism, heterosexism, ableism, and sexism/cis-sexism. Shin and colleagues are leading the way in this area, and they are helping scholars and practitioners alike envision better ways of implementing intersectional critical consciousness measurement. Yet, more expansive intersectional critical consciousness measurement is still needed. By design, the CCCM-S only accounts for the critical reflection dimension of critical consciousness (cf. "Axis 1"; see Introduction [this volume]). While scholars interested in critical consciousness measurement should continue to develop and test instrumentation that captures reflection about various forms of oppression, they also should develop instrumentation that more explicitly attends to the systemic, structural, and interlocking nature of these forms of oppression (Godfrey & Burson, 2018). Scholars should also consider how the critical motivation and critical action dimensions of critical consciousness might be measured in ways that support intersectional analysis or incorporate an intersectional frame. As suggested by Godfrey and Burson (2018), more refined measures might be developed that better account for the conceptualization and examination of multiple interlocking systems of oppression, with instrumentation providing item sets that include follow-up questions allowing respondents to share the reflection–motivation–action they exhibit regarding certain types of issues and systems related to marginalization and oppression (cf. "Axis 1," "Axis 3," and "Axis 5"; see Introduction [this volume]).

## DEEPER ASSESSMENT OF STRUCTURAL-HISTORICAL KNOWLEDGE AND/OR THINKING

Extant measures of critical reflection are generally lacking in their assessment of the historical-structural knowledge and the historical-structural nature of contemporary societal inequities. Burson et al. (Chapter 6 [this volume]) take up this issue explicitly in their refined and expanded measure of critical reflection, which introduces new dimensions of critical reflection that are intended to capture structural attributions for, and historical thinking related to, inequality. As critical consciousness theory clearly recognizes both the systemic and structural causes of societal inequity – but current measures lack this specific focus – more research is needed to continue to bear out the extent to which structural-historical knowledge and/or thinking should be captured as an additional subdimension(s) of critical reflection. This would ensure that measures of critical reflection adequately assess the construct in full alignment with critical consciousness theory. While less explicitly focused on measurement, Rapa, Bolding, et al. (Chapter 3 [this volume]) also move us toward this accounting of structural-historical knowledge through their exploration of how social empathy (which includes awareness and contextual understanding of systemic barriers faced by marginalized groups) associates with and moderates pathways between dimensions of critical consciousness. Future work should continue to explore the extent to which structural-historical thinking is adequately captured in critical consciousness measures (cf. "Axis 3"; see Introduction [this volume]).

## IMPLEMENTATION OF LONGITUDINAL MEASUREMENT USING CRITICAL CONSCIOUSNESS INSTRUMENTS

Longitudinal studies focused on critical consciousness have emerged over the past decade, and they are continuing to emerge. However, to date, these have been primarily – if not exclusively – reliant upon proxy measurement (e.g., Diemer & Li, 2011; Godfrey et al., 2019; Rapa et al., 2018). Longitudinal research that uses explicitly designed critical consciousness measures has not been carried out. The use of critical consciousness instruments in longitudinal research will help further enhance our understanding of how critical consciousness develops and operates over time and will reveal how its dimensions interrelate, while also potentially solidifying or raising issues as to where critical consciousness theory (and, perhaps, measurement itself) needs further refinement (cf. Rapa, Bolding, et al., 2020). The development of shorter, more parsimonious, and yet more comprehensive scales such as the ShoCCS and the CCS-S will allow for new opportunities to complete this sort of longitudinal critical consciousness measurement in empirical studies while also reducing participant burden tied to extensive or very lengthy instruments.

### Utilization of More Intensive Measurement Approaches

Somewhat relatedly, we do not fully understand the interaction between various temporal aspects of critical consciousness's operation and development as measured with current instruments. As Tyler et al. point out (Chapter 9 [this volume]), there are likely dynamic and reciprocal relations between an individual's "state-like," in-the-moment level of critical consciousness and their more "trait-like" level of critical consciousness manifesting over time. Indeed, someone's critical consciousness at a given moment is likely to be influenced by both proximal and distal contexts that shape its development and functioning (see also Bañales et al., in press). However, existing measures do not yet allow us to capture the fine-grained nuances between "micro" and "macro" assessments of critical consciousness. Tyler and colleagues provide a blueprint for how scholars might forge new ground with critical consciousness measurement, using intensive measurement approaches that capture critical consciousness both in the moment and over time. They also provide several postulates for how critical consciousness measured at the microlevel may be related to critical consciousness at the macrolevel. Such nuances cannot be captured through current instrumentation. The utilization of more intensive critical consciousness measurement approaches, as proposed by Tyler and colleagues, may lead to additional new insights and new directions for how critical consciousness measurement can be adapted or expanded to capture reflection–motivation–action praxis, or the processes related to the development and operation of critical consciousness within individuals, in the moment and longitudinally.

## Breadth vs. Depth, Domain-Specific vs. Domain-General, and More Granular Measurement

Existing critical consciousness measures represent various degrees of specificity in terms of the dimensions of critical consciousness they capture. Likewise, they represent various degrees of specificity in terms of the types of inequality they assess – that is, some are more general, expansive, or holistic measures, while others are narrower and more specific (Table 7.1). Scholars have noted for some time that a tension exists around whether critical consciousness development is domain specific as opposed to domain general and for whom it is applicable (e.g., Diemer et al., 2015, 2016; also see "Axis 4"; see Introduction [this volume]). The variation in breadth and depth, and domain-specificity and domain-generality, in extant critical consciousness measures is an obstacle to a wholly unified conceptualization and measurement of critical consciousness within the field. Scholars should continue to (re)assess how critical consciousness theory aligns with existing measures and should be willing to further adapt or adjust measures where misalignment or disconnects exist.

At the same time, new opportunities exist for scholars to explore critical consciousness within certain contexts – that is, to further operationalize and measure critical consciousness of certain types of societal inequities or specific forms of oppression. Doing so allows for subsequent exploration of how reflection–motivation–action praxis operates to address specific inequities and promote positive societal change in certain domains; it also supports the development of understanding about whether these processes vary for different forms of oppression. For example, pilot work has been carried out within the context of undergraduate civil engineering to assess students' critical consciousness of infrastructure inequities, in particular (Bolding et al., 2021). Other work is underway to measure specific aspects of critical consciousness development and operation related to teaching and parenting practices (Heberle et al., 2022). The application of critical consciousness to these areas and the development of measures designed specifically to capture dynamic processes related to critical consciousness development and operation within certain contexts (e.g., within the undergraduate civil engineering classroom, within the role of parenting, or within the role of teaching, among others) represents opportunities for continued advancement in the field.

## DEVELOPMENT OF OTHER NOVEL APPROACHES

Other novel approaches to critical consciousness measurement are emerging as well. Mixed methods research may be well suited to support continued growth in critical consciousness measurement, as data collection across quantitative and qualitative strands allows researchers to consider areas of convergence and divergence in the conceptualization and operationalization of critical consciousness instruments as they currently exist. The work of Baker and Brookins (2014) and Aldana and colleagues (2019), as highlighted earlier, may be especially exemplary in this regard, given their use of participatory approaches and analyses that incorporated both quantitative and qualitative data during their scale development processes. Future measurement work in critical consciousness should employ mixed methods research approaches to expand, (re)specifiy, refine, and adapt extant critical consciousness instruments.

Likewise, approaches that capture contextual dynamics more comprehensively may also help advance critical consciousness measurement. For example, Johnson et al. (Chapter 10 [this volume]) consider the dynamic interplay between "systems" and "selves" and make recommendations for how quantitative critical consciousness measurement can be enhanced to better account for complex person ←→ environment interactions. Similarly, Kornbluh et al. (Chapter 8 [this volume]) propose new approaches to assess critical consciousness by suggesting that social network analysis might be useful for assessing person ←→ environment interactions to account for people's understanding of power and power dynamics within certain settings. Less emphasized this chapter, but no less important, measurement of critical consciousness at the collective level versus the individual level must also be explored further (Heberle et al., 2020; Sánchez Carmen et al., 2015; also see "Axis 2"; see Introduction [this volume]).

## CONCLUDING THOUGHTS

Despite the advancement of critical consciousness measurement in recent decades, questions remain about the extent to which current critical consciousness instruments adequately capture what critical consciousness is – conceptually (i.e., theoretically) or as it manifests and operates within individuals and collectives, across contexts and over time. As we have demonstrated throughout this chapter, there is variation in how critical consciousness scholars have conceptualized and operationalized critical consciousness in current instrumentation. Most existing instruments focus on one or two dimensions of critical consciousness, with a predominant focus on critical reflection; yet, emergent work suggests that even instrumentation focused on critical reflection may need to be expanded or respecified (see Chapter 6 [this volume]). Two of the newer scales that have been developed include all three dimensions of critical consciousness: reflection, motivation, and action (Diemer et al., 2022; Rapa, Bolding et al., 2020). Additionally, other newer scales are specific to particular settings (e.g., Chan, 2022) or were designed for use with particular populations (see Chapter 11 [this volume]). All but two were developed and validated in the United States.

We have argued that critical consciousness measurement has evolved across four phases. We refer to these as (1) proxy measurement; (2) scale development; (3) scale expansion and (re)specification; and (4) scale refinement and adaptation. We have also argued that, while these phases are somewhat distinct, critical consciousness measurement work is still unfolding within each phase, meaning none of these phases has reached its terminus. This no doubt complicates critical consciousness measurement, along with the empirical work carried out using critical consciousness instrumentation, adding complexity that will not too soon be resolved. Yet, it also represents the rich and innovative ways critical consciousness scholarship continues to advance to better understand and promote individuals' navigation of and resistance to societal inequity. Our hope is that this brief history of critical consciousness measurement, along with our overview of the current status and a few new directions for research in this area, is helpful to readers as they themselves navigate this highly active and complex area of scholarship.

## REFERENCES

Aldana, A., Bañales, J., & Richards-Schuster, K. (2019). Youth anti-racist engagement: Conceptualization, development, and validation of an anti-racism action scale. *Adolescent Research Review*, 4, 369–381. https://doi.org/10.1007/s40894-019-00113-1.

Baker, A. M., & Brookins, C. C. (2014). Toward the development of a measure of sociopolitical consciousness: Listening to the voices of Salvadoran youth. *Journal of Community Psychology*, 42, 1015–1032. http://doi.org/10.1002/jcop.21668.

Bañales, J., Aldana, A., & Hope, E. C. (in press). Critical race consciousness: Conceptualizing a model of race-specific critical consciousness among youth. In E. B. Godfrey & L. J. Rapa (Eds.), *Developing Critical Consciousness in Youth: Contexts and Settings*. Cambridge University Press.

Bolding, C. W., Ogle, J., & Rapa, L. J. (2021). Exploring undergraduate civil engineering students' perceptions of infrastructure inequities: A pilot study. 2021

American Society for Engineering Education Annual Conference & Exposition. https://par.nsf.gov/servlets/purl/10336901.

Byrd, C. M. (2017). The complexity of school racial climate: Reliability and validity of a new measure for secondary students. *British Journal of Educational Psychology, 87*, 700–721. https://doi.org/10.1111/bjep.12179.

Chan, R. C. H. (2022). Development and validation of the critical reflection scale for youth in China: Factor structure and measurement invariance across age, gender, and sexual orientation. *Applied Developmental Science*. Advanced online publication. https://doi.org/10.1080/10888691.2022.2059481.

Crenshaw, K. (1989). Demarginalizing the intersection of race and sex: A Black feminist critique of antidiscrimination doctrine, feminist theory and antiracist politics. *University of Chicago Legal Forum, 140*(1), 139–167. http://chicagounbound.uchicago.edu/uclf/vol1989/iss1/8.

Collins, P. H. (1993). Toward a new vision: Race, class, and gender as categories of analysis and connection. *Race, Sex, & Class, 1*(1), 25–45.

Combahee River Collective. (1977/2014). A Black feminist statement. *Women's Studies Quarterly, 42*, 271-280.

Diemer, M. A., Frisby, M. B., Pinedo, A. et al. (2022). Development of the Short Critical Consciousness Scale (ShoCCS). *Applied Developmental Science, 26*(3), 409–425. https://doi.org/10.1080/10888691.2020.1834394.

Diemer, M. A., & Li, C. H. (2011). Critical consciousness development and political participation among marginalized youth. *Child Development, 82*, 1815–1833. https://doi.org/10.1111/j.1467-8624.2011.01650.x.

Diemer, M. A., McWhirter, E., Ozer, E., & Rapa, L. J. (2015). Advances in the conceptualization and measurement of critical consciousness. *The Urban Review, 47*, 809–823. https://doi.org/10.1007/s11256-015-0336-7.

Diemer, M. A., & Rapa, L. J. (2016). Unraveling the complexity of critical consciousness, political efficacy, and political action among marginalized adolescents. *Child Development, 87*, 221–238. https://doi.org/10.1111/cdev.12446.

Diemer, M. A., Rapa, L. J., Park, C. J., & Perry, J. C. (2017). Development and validation of the Critical Consciousness Scale. *Youth & Society, 49*(4), 461–483. https://doi.org/10.1177/0044118X14538289.

Diemer, M. A., Rapa, L. J., Voight, A. M., & McWhirter, E. H. (2016). Critical consciousness: A developmental approach to addressing marginalization and oppression. *Child Development Perspectives, 10*(4), 216–221. https://doi.org/10.1111/cdep.12193.

Diemer, M. A., Voight, A. M., Marchand, A. D., & Bañales, J. (2019). Political identification, political ideology, and critical social analysis of inequality among marginalized youth. *Developmental Psychology, 55*(3), 538–549. https://doi.org/10.1037/dev0000559.

Freire, P. (1973). *Education for critical consciousness*. Continuum.

Freire, P. (1968/2000). *Pedagogy of the oppressed*. Continuum.

Godfrey, E. B., & Burson, E. (2018). Interrogating the intersections: How intersectional perspectives can inform developmental scholarship on critical consciousness. In C. E. Santos & R. B. Toomey (Eds.), *Envisioning the Integration of an*

*Intersectional Lens in Developmental Science. New Directions for Child and Adolescent Development, 161*, 17-38. https://doi.org/10.1002/cad.20246.

Godfrey, E. B., Burson, E. L., Yanisch, T. M., Hughes, D., & Way, N. (2019). A bitter pill to swallow? Patterns of critical consciousness and socioemotional and academic well-being in early adolescence. *Developmental Psychology, 55*(3), 525–537. https://doi.org/10.1037/dev0000558.

Heberle, A. E., Esposito, A., & Stewart, A. (2022, May). Measurement of Parent and Teacher Critical Consciousness. [Roundtable discussion of Spencer Foundation funded project on critical consciousness measurement]. Clark University.

Heberle, A. E., Rapa, L. J., & Faragó, F. (2020). Critical consciousness in children and adolescents: A systematic review, critical assessment, and recommendations for future research. *Psychological Bulletin, 146*(6), 525–551. https://doi.org/10.1037/bul0000230.

Hope, E. C., Pender, K. N., & Riddick, K. N. (2019). Development and validation of the Black Community Activism Orientation Scale. *Journal of Black Psychology, 45*(3), 185–214. https://doi.org/10.1177/0095798419865416.

Jemal, A. (2017). Critical consciousness: A critique and critical analysis of the literature. *The Urban Review, 49*, 602–626. https://doi.org/10.1007/s11256-017-0411-3.

Marchand, A. D., Frisby, M. B., Kraemer, M. et al. (2021). Sociopolitical participation among marginalized youth: Do political identification and ideology matter? *Journal of Youth Development, 16*(5), 41–63. https://doi.org/10.5195/jyd.2021.1089.

McWhirter, E. H., & McWhirter, B. T. (2016). Critical consciousness and vocational development among Latina/o high school youth: Initial development and testing of a measure. *Journal of Career Assessment, 24*(3), 543–558. https://doi.org/10.1177/1069072715599535.

Plummer, J. A., Wray-Lake, L., Alvis, L., Metzger, A., & Syvertsen, A. (2022). Assessing the link between adolescents' awareness of inequality and civic engagement across time and racial/ethnic groups. *Journal of Youth and Adolescence, 51*, 428–442. https://doi.org/10.1007/s10964-021-01545-6.

Poteat, V. P., Godfrey, E. B., Brion-Meisels, G., & Calzo, J. P. (2020). Development of youth advocacy and sociopolitical efficacy as dimensions of critical consciousness within gender-sexuality alliances. *Developmental Psychology, 56*(6), 1207–1219. https://doi.org/10.1037/dev0000927.

Rapa, L. J. (2016). Fostering marginalized youths' academic achievement and critical consciousness through a values-affirmation intervention. Unpublished doctoral dissertation, Department of Counseling, Educational Psychology, and Special Education, Michigan State University.

Rapa, L. J., Bolding, C. W., & Jamil, F. M. (2020). Development and initial validation of the Short Critical Consciousness Scale (CCS-S). *Journal of Applied Developmental Psychology, 70*, 101164. https://doi.org/10.1016/j.appdev.2020.101164.

Rapa, L. J., Diemer, M. A., & Bañales, J. (2018). Critical action as a pathway to social mobility among marginalized youth. *Developmental Psychology, 54*, 127–137. https://doi.org/10.1037/dev0000414.

Rapa, L. J., Diemer, M. A., & Roseth, C. J. (2020). Can a values-affirmation intervention bolster academic achievement and raise critical consciousness? Results from a small-scale field experiment. *Social Psychology of Education, 23*(2), 537–557. https://doi.org/10.1007/s11218-020-09546-2.

Sánchez Carmen, S. A., Domínguez, M., Greene, A. C. et al. (2015). Revisiting the collective in critical consciousness: Diverse sociopolitical wisdoms and ontological healing in sociopolitical development. *The Urban Review, 47*, 824–846. https://doi:10.1007/s11256-015-0338-5.

Seider, S., Clark, S., & Graves, D. (2020). The development of critical consciousness and its relation to academic achievement in adolescents of color. *Child Development, 91*(2), e451–e474. https://doi.org/10.1111/cdev.13262.

Shin, R. Q., Ezeofor, I., Smith, L. C., Welch, J. C., & Goodrich, K. M. (2016). The development and validation of the contemporary critical consciousness measure. *Journal of Counseling Psychology, 63*, 210–223. https://doi.org/10.1037/cou0000137.

Shin, R. Q., Smith, L. C., Lu, Y. et al. (2018). The development and validation of the contemporary critical consciousness measure II. *Journal of Counseling Psychology, 65*, 539–555. https://doi.org/10.1037/cou0000302.

Suyemoto, K. L., Abdullah, T., Godon-Decoteau, D. et al. (2022). Development of the Resistance and Empowerment Against Racism (REAR) Scale. *Cultural Diversity and Ethnic Minority Psychology, 28*(1), 58–71. https://doi.org/10.1037/cdp0000353.

Thomas, A. J., Barrie, R., Brunner, J. et al. (2014). Assessing critical consciousness in youth and young adults. *Journal of Research on Adolescence, 24*(3), 485–496. https://doi.org/10.1111/jora.12132.

Tyler, C. P., Olsen, S. G., Geldhof, G. J., & Bowers, E. P. (2020). Critical consciousness in late adolescence: Understanding if, how, and why youth act. *Journal of Applied Developmental Psychology, 70*, 101165. https://doi.org/10.1016/j.appdev.2020.101165.

Wang, C., & Burris, M. (1997). Photovoice: Concept, methodology, and use for participatory needs assessment. *Health Education & Behavior, 24*(3), 369–387. http://doi.org/10.1177/109019819702400309.

Watts, R. J., Diemer, M. A., & Voight, A. M. (2011). Critical consciousness: Current status and future directions. In C. A. Flanagan & B. D. Christens (Eds.), *Youth civic development: Work at the cutting edge. New Directions for Child and Adolescent Development, 134*, 43–57. https://doi.org/10.1002/cd.310.

Watts, R. J., & Flanagan, C. (2007). Pushing the envelope on youth civic engagement: A developmental and liberation psychology perspective. *Journal of Community Psychology, 35*(6), 779–792. https://doi.org/10.1002/jcop.20178.

Watts, R. J., Williams, N. C., & Jagers, R. J. (2003). Sociopolitical development. *American Journal of Community Psychology, 31*, 185–194. https://doi.org/10.1023/A:1023091024140.

# 8

# Using Social Network Analysis to Identify Individual and Structural Precursors for Promoting Critical Consciousness in Childhood and Adolescence

MARIAH KORNBLUH, JENNIFER WATLING NEAL, AND MACKENZIE HART

Critical consciousness (CC) refers to an individual's awareness of systems of structural inequities within society (*critical reflection*), a sense of agency to work against oppressive structures (*critical motivation*), and engagement in individual or collective action to challenge social inequities (*critical action*; Freire, 1973; Watts et al., 2011). Central to CC is the ability to recognize the power structures that uphold unjust conditions (Ilten-Gee & Manchanda, 2021). The concept of power consists of control over desired resources (Gaventa, 1980; Speer & Hughey, 1995). Such control can be exhibited through multiple avenues, including: (1) using resources for rewards and punishment; (2) dictating what issues or interests are addressed in a particular setting (Bachrach & Baratz, 1962); and (3) shaping shared consciousness and collective narratives (Lukes, 2005; Prilleltensky, 2008). An overarching theme surrounding these dimensions of power is their inherently relational nature (Serrano-Garcia, 1994). In short, the relationships within a setting can shape an individual's ability to exercise power and have direct implications for equitable resource distribution. Vollhardt and Sinayobye (2016) argue that measures of power are key to exploring individual and structural precursors to CC. Such inquiries can illuminate the connections between structural conditions (specifically, power differences) in relation to individual thoughts, beliefs, and behaviors.

In a recent metareview, Heberle and colleagues (2020) noted key gaps in measurement designed to capture relational and setting-level processes in relation to CC development. Such areas of inquiry could further expand our understanding of the various ecological environments and interpersonal experiences that can foster or hinder CC "readiness" or engagement. Furthermore, measures of CC have been mainly developed for adolescent and young adult populations (Heberle et al., 2020). This focus makes sense developmentally, as key milestones such as the emergence of abstract thinking as well as civic aspirations and identity formation often occur in adolescence (Flanagan, 2009; Watts et al., 2011). However, developmental researchers have argued that children also possess complex but often overlooked understandings of social inequality and dehumanizing conditions (Langhout & Thomas, 2010; Ruck et al., 2019). Capturing such information has important implications for developmental theory building and educational intervention efforts further promoting CC programming within primary school contexts (Ilten-Gee & Manchanda, 2021).

Social Network Analysis (SNA) researchers operationalize power as resulting from an advantageous position within a sequence of relationships in which value-added resources (e.g., information and support) are exchanged among actors (Neal & Neal, 2011). Thus, SNA focuses on identifying relational patterns (e.g., friendship, communication, and resource sharing) among sets of actors (e.g., students and youth organizers) within a bounded system (e.g., classroom, afterschool program; Borgatti et al., 2009; Wellman, 1988). SNA can be utilized to measure how an individual thinks about and perceives relational power at the individual, dyadic, and setting levels. CC researchers may tap into SNA to explore how children's and adolescents' awareness of and ability to access resources in their proximal environment (individual level), perceptions of resources shared between pairs of actors (dyadic level), and distribution of relational power within a setting (setting-level conditions) act as precursors that can be used to engage in CC before a fuller analysis of larger social conditions emerges developmentally. At the individual level, children's or adolescents' awareness of their own and others' access to social resources could serve as a precursor to a further analysis of macrolevel understandings of social inequity reflected within the construct of critical reflection. Children's or adolescents' ability to navigate and access such resources may also be an early precursor to developing sentiments of critical motivation. Children's or adolescents' cognizance of their own social privilege may also act as individual precursors to critical action that emerges over time. At the dyadic level, perceptions of access to key relationships within a setting in association to power may impact the desire or motivation for children and adolescents to engage in social action. Perceived access to relational supports may serve as a precursor to understandings of social issues (critical reflection), commitment to social transformation (critical motivation), and civic engagement (critical action). At the setting level, the extent to which social support is perceived as equitably distributed or available to all children and adolescents may serve as a structural precursor to critical reflection and critical action.

SNA offers a developmentally inclusive lens that consists of children and adolescents reporting on the relationships within their everyday environments. It provides the opportunity to quantify early developmental understandings and savviness in assessing multiple components of CC. SNA measures consist of tangible language and everyday questions (e.g., "Who are your friends?"), thus avoiding complex terminology often associated with capturing perceptions of macrolevel concepts. Cognitive social structure (CSS), an SNA method introduced in this chapter, has been used with children as young as seven years old through late adolescence (Neal et al., 2016; Kornbluh et al., 2016) and provides the opportunity to capture understandings of individual and setting-level relational contexts by comparing individual perceptions to benchmarks of power relations within a proximal setting (via aggregating relationships through consensus). In sum, we argue that SNA can expand our understanding of CC theory by identifying precursors that capture children's and adolescents' early CC conceptualizations and understandings at multiple levels of analysis, yielding implications for expanding developmental theory.

For CC researchers new to SNA, conducting such analyses involves several steps. First, researchers must define the boundary of the system they would like to study by determining which actors (i.e., individuals and organizations) should be included in the network (Laumann et al., 1992). Developmental researchers often bound their networks to include all children in a classroom, grade, youth organizing program, or school (Neal, 2020). Second, researchers conceptualize and operationally define the relationships that they plan to assess in the network (Marsden, 1990). Developmental researchers most commonly study friendships (Neal, 2020), but other types of relationships like "hanging out," communication, resource sharing, or "liking" may also be important. Relationships can be defined as *binary* (i.e., a friendship either exists or does not exist between two children) or *weighted* where values of the relationship reflect strength (i.e., friendship on a scale of 0–5 where higher values reflect a closer friendship). Additionally, some types of relationships are *directed* in nature, whereby resources or affection flow from one individual to another (e.g., Child A shares a resource with Child B), while other types of relationships are *undirected* (e.g., Child A and Child B hang out together). Third, researchers collect social network data on the relationships between each pair of actors in the system and use specialized methods and models to analyze these data. Developmental researchers commonly use self-reported or peer-reported surveys and interviews or observations to collect these data (adams, 2020; Neal, 2020).

In the following sections, we explore the potential of SNA to identify individual and setting-level precursors in relation to CC development in children and adolescents. First, we provide a brief overview of prominent methods used to explore CC. Next, we discuss the use of SNA to capture dimensions of power within a setting and provide illustrative examples within the primary settings of children/adolescents (i.e., classroom and afterschool program). We conclude with considerations for future research employing SNA as well as ethical considerations.

## HISTORY OF METHODS EMPLOYED TO EXPLORE CRITICAL CONSCIOUSNESS WITH CHILDREN AND ADOLESCENTS

There has been growing interest and perceived potential in CC as a concept that may promote thriving in ethnically and racially minoritized children and adolescents (Heberle et. al., 2020; Seider & Graves, 2020) in the domains of mental health, academic engagement, higher enrollment in higher education, resistance against racial trauma, and career development (Diemer et al., 2016; Mosley et al., 2021; Uriostegui et al., 2021). CC has been also identified as an important phenomenon to study among individuals occupying positions of power who utilize the structural advantages afforded to them as an avenue for facilitating understandings of injustice, allyship, and social justice organizing (Deutsch, 1974; Hershberg & Johnson, 2019; Jemal, 2017; Stoudt, 2012). Furthermore, Godfrey and Burson (2018) stress that individuals have intersecting identities, some with more access to social privilege than others. While such discussions are beyond the scope of this chapter, we stress that CC development is unique for every child or adolescent. Furthermore, such consciousness is inevitably linked to one's positionality in relation to systems of power and the intersecting identities they embody. Thus, we put forth the argument that CC is a critical phenomenon to explore with diverse children and adolescent populations. In the literature review section, we: (1) offer an overview of prior measures of CC and the role of power; (2) further describe the added value of exploring contexts associated with CC development for children; and (3) highlight precursors of CC development.

## MEASURES OF CC AND THE ROLE OF POWER

Notably, the most commonly used quantitative measures of CC were developed and validated using samples of high school students (e.g., the Critical Consciousness Scale [CCS; Diemer et al., 2017], the Short Critical Consciousness Scale [CCS-S; Rapa et al., 2020], the Measure of Adolescent Critical Consciousness [MACC; McWhirter & McWhirter, 2016], the Anti-Racism Action Scale [ARAS; Aldana et al., 2019]) or university students (e.g., the Critical Consciousness Inventory [CCI; Thomas et al., 2014]). Each of these measures asks participants to report on their personal behaviors and beliefs, such as the frequency and nature of their civic participation and their perception of society as fair or unfair. For example, the CCS asks respondents to rate their agreement, from 1 (*strongly disagree*) to 6 (*strongly agree*), with statements such as "Poor people have fewer chances to get ahead." Such quantitative measures of CC have predominantly relied on self-reporting, which may be vulnerable to social desirability response patterns and typically involves individual-level analyses.

Qualitative methods (e.g., ethnographic studies, focus groups and interviews, and photovoice) have also been employed to broaden theory and expand or specify contextual foci regarding CC in youth (Heberle et al., 2020; Silva, 2012). For instance, a mixed methods project by Tyler and colleagues (2020) identified contextual factors that led to adolescents' critical action (e.g., a sense of connectedness to inequality through beliefs/values, others, or self) and employed interviews to query how adolescents become aware of and subsequently responded to inequalities. In another study, Groves Price and Mencke (2013) employed youth participatory action research (YPAR) to promote CC through a weeklong summer camp designed for Native American adolescents (ages 13–17 years old) focused on cultural reclaiming and well-being, thereby expanding the study of CC to different cultural populations. Educational and developmental researchers have further stressed the value of process-oriented data to capture evolving socialization processes (e.g., group discussions and informal conversations) and activities (e.g., written reflections and skits) in relation to CC development (Freedman et al., 2016; Ilten-Gee & Manchanda, 2021). The use of these methods demonstrates how qualitative work can generate new themes surrounding CC (e.g., ways in which critical action is exercised beyond traditional outlets, such as challenging offensive comments or jokes). Indeed, there have been recent calls to use mixed methods and qualitative frameworks to expand the measurement of CC (Godfrey & Burson, 2018; Heberle et al., 2020).

Diverse measurement methods may be particularly well suited to strengthen the field's understanding of power dynamics in relation to development of CC among children and adolescents. Power dynamics are inherently embedded in the social structures that drive inequality and have direct implications in shaping individuals' cognitions, feelings, and actions (Vollhardt & Sinayobye Twali, 2016). CC requires an awareness of and desire to engage in social change. Thus, CC consists of recognizing and understanding systems of power (Bozalek & Biersteker, 2010). Such awareness is inevitably situated in how power operates within one's everyday lived experiences (Vollhardt & Sinayobye Twali, 2016). Sakamoto and Pitner (2005) highlight the value of CC in identifying and challenging potentially oppressive power differentials, and Bozalek and Biersteker (2010) cite CC-building approaches (e.g., participatory learning and action) as ways to explore power. Ilten-Gee and Manchanda (2021) further stress, from a developmental lens, that awareness of proximal power may provide novel opportunities in fostering children's CC development.

## EXPLORATION OF CC IN CHILDREN

Studying precursors to CC among children (e.g., elementary school students) is particularly valuable, given their developing understandings of power, social groups, and social justice (Hawkins, 2014; Mistry et al., 2016; Silva, 2012). Evidence also suggests that promoting CC from a young age can positively affect developmental trajectories (Diemer et al., 2016; El-Amin et al., 2017). For instance, adolescents with higher CC often demonstrate greater academic achievement and attainment (McWhirter & McWhirter, 2016) as well as resilience (Luginbuhl et al., 2016), leading to career development (Diemer et al., 2010; Luginbuhl et al., 2016) and other positive outcomes both civically and personally (Heberle et al., 2020).

Research indicates that while children may not be able to identify complex societal forces and patterns (i.e., racism, sexism, ableism), they do demonstrate an attentiveness to social identity and differences in relation to wealth, age, gender, and race (Dunham & Emory, 2014; Mistry, 2016). Children are especially attuned to noticing power differences within interpersonal contexts and may associate such behaviors based on these understandings (Ilten-Gee & Manchanda, 2021). Lapsley (2006) found that children as young as five years old provided rationales surrounding fairness based on concepts of equality and equity. For instance, Hazelbaker and colleagues (2018) documented that children (aged five to eight years) employed social markers to assess the social stratification within their neighborhoods. Furthermore, over half the children exhibited evidence-based reasoning to note that extreme ends of the spectrum (i.e., "the very poor" and "the very rich") were considered unjust. Social domain theory stresses that there are key developmental transitions in which children encounter social contradictions that require them to refine and modify their thinking (Darder, 2014). Specifically, between the ages of eight and nine, children note that rules are not equally enforced and thus begin to question such rules, igniting a re-examination of complex scenarios and contradictions within society. Ilten-Gee and Manchanda (2021) stress that such encounters create opportunities for "CC breakthroughs" (p. 21) consisting of changes in conceptualizations of moral, conventional, and personal issues. Exploring the individual and structural precursors that facilitate children's opportunities for exposure to such "breakthroughs" may further expand CC developmental theory generation and illuminate implications for earlier intervention efforts surrounding CC raising. In the following sections, we provide an overview of CC research highlighting potential precursors of CC development and discuss specific implications within the context of SNA.

## INDIVIDUAL AND STRUCTURAL PRECURSORS OF CC DEVELOPMENT

### Individual Precursors

CC researchers have stressed particular skills, competencies, and character traits that may be associated with CC development (Corning & Myers, 2002; Seider et al., 2017; Watts et al., 1999). Regarding skills, critical thinking is considered a foundational block to critical reflection (Seider et al., 2017; Watts et al., 1999). Elements of critical thinking include the ability to recognize power differences, analyze unjust conditions, and reflect on one's own positionality in relation to such systems (Darder, 2014; Ilten-Gee & Manchanda, 2021; Stoudt, 2012). Flexible and adaptive thinking are key competencies associated with critical motivation (Seider et al., 2017; Watts et al., 1999). Seider and colleagues (2017) argue that such thinking requires "a degree of social intelligence and savviness" (pg. 114) to identify others' motivations, biases, and prejudices and leverage such understandings to advocate for and navigate social situations (Osyerman et al., 2001). A commitment to civic engagement and enhanced sentiments of social responsibility have been identified as key individual traits facilitating critical action (Corning & Myers, 2002; Seider et al., 2017; Pancer et al., 2007). In the context of SNA, a child's or adolescent's ability to recognize their own relational power, identify key individuals who have access to valued resources, and leverage relationships to navigate their social settings may further illuminate critical thinking, social awareness, and savviness in relation to early understandings of multiple aspects of CC before a fuller analysis of larger social conditions emerges developmentally.

## Structural Precursors

At the dyadic level, children and adolescents have connections to various socializing agents (i.e., teachers, parents, peers, staff, and community members) within their daily lives that can provide or restrict access to valuable resources and capital (Parsons et al., 1982). Socialization is one relational process that has been explored in association with CC development (Bañales et al., 2020; Diemer, 2012) encompassing everyday conversations (Kurtz-Costes et al., 2019). These conversations can include discussions of social inequities (Diemer, 2012), political conversations about recent current events (Diemer et al., 2006; Diemer, 2012), and ethnic/racial socialization that includes implicit and explicit messages about race, including messages of racial pride and alertness to racial discrimination (Bañales et al., 2020, Bañales et al., 2021). Research has found that these conversations can predict critical reflection (Bañales et al., 2020, 2021; Diemer et al., 2006), critical motivation (Diemer et al., 2009), and critical action (Bañales et al., 2021; Diemer & Li, 2011) among Black families, low-income youth, working-class youth, youth of color, and white youth. Notably, although access to socialization processes has been examined as a predictor to CC, we argue that SNA can help us understand children's and adolescents' awareness of *who has access to socializing agents*, which may be an important precursor of CC.

Interpersonal social exchanges can also reinforce differential treatment of children and adolescents based on social categorization in an explicit or implicit effort to uphold existing power structures. When probed around perceptions of power and oppression, children and adolescents often center their analyses around relational power by noting experiences of differential treatment at the dyadic level (adult to youth, youth to youth) within their proximal environments (Joseph et al., 2016; Tatum, 1997). Furthermore, awareness of and experience with interpersonal discrimination (i.e., discriminatory remarks, racial profiling) has also been found to be associated with critical action for both Black and Latino college students (Cronin et al., 2012; Hope et al., 2016; White-Johnson, 2012). Hope and Spencer (2017) posit that such activism serves as an "adaptive coping strategy" (p. 421) to combat and resist existing systems of power. Applying an SNA approach, we stress that children's and adolescents' ability to identify who is receiving preferential treatment by adults within their proximal environments could be a noteworthy precursor to various aspects of CC.

At the setting level, children and adolescents spend a substantial portion of their weekly time in schools (Hofferth, 2009) and afterschool programs (Afterschool Alliance, 2014), making them pivotal social environments to explore surrounding CC development (Diemer & Li, 2011; Hope et al, 2015). Such environments are inherently embedded within power structures (i.e., school environments) and often uphold policies, practices, and resource allocations that perpetuate existing systems of power (Baldridge et al., 2017; Hope & Jagers, 2014; Kornbluh et al., 2021). Children's and adolescents' exploration and understanding of how power is enacted within their primary environments is often a key cognitive step in their understanding and development of CC (Hope et al., 2015). For instance, CC researchers have found that children's and adolescents' awareness of the lack of institutional support and discriminatory racial-stigmatizing practices analyzed through meaningful opportunity structures can foster critical reflection (Fine & Ruglis, 2009; Hope et al., 2015; Kornbluh, 2020, 2021). Using YPAR with Black high school students, Hope and colleagues (2015) questioned school policies in relation to institutional discrimination, fostering critical reflection. Kornbluh (2020) highlighted similar findings among Black and Latino(a) middle school students through the analysis of educational budget cuts that disproportionately targeted schools consisting of Black and Latino(a) students. In the context of SNA, a child or adolescents' awareness of *setting-level power dynamics via relationships* may be an early precursor to CC development at multiple levels, with such analyses being later applied to larger macrosystems and structures.

## Summary

Diemer (2020) challenged researchers to move beyond dichotomous and quantitative measures of CC, highlighting that oppression and privilege exist on a dynamic spectrum and in multiple domains (e.g., ableism, racism, sexism, and socioeconomic status). An expert in CC scholarship, he states that "further integrating intersectional perspectives in what critical consciousness means, and how it is measured, particularly among young people, remains territory that critical consciousness [studies have] incompletely explored" (Diemer, 2020, p. 3). Such studies may expand on and strengthen existing CC research by examining its development in younger children (i.e., before high school or college age) and by moving beyond individual queries and toward exploring dimensions of power and inequality at the relational and setting levels. In response to those calls, the present chapter posits the value of SNA to explore how perceptions of individual, relational, and setting-level power serve as precursors to CC development. The proposed approach may also enable exploration of CC to become more inclusive of populations with intersectional or relative privilege (Hershberg & Johnson, 2019) as well as younger populations. In sum, past quantitative scales of CC are useful for capturing adolescents' broader critical reflection, motivation, and action with respect to societal inequalities and oppression. Additionally, qualitative methods are useful for broadening theory surrounding CC. However, existing research may be enhanced when conducted with SNA to further illuminate multilevel precursors of CC with an explicit focus on relational power dynamics.

## USING SNA TO EXPLORE POWER DYNAMICS

SNA provides the opportunity to explore individual and structural precursors related to CC development by capturing children's and adolescents' awareness of: (1) relational power dynamics within their everyday setting (e.g., "Are children/adolescents cognizant of existing power dynamics?"); (2) access to valued resources (e.g., "What access do children/adolescents have to such resources?"); and (3) setting level dynamics (e.g., "How do resources flow via relationships?").

## MEASURING PERCEPTIONS OF POWER DYNAMICS

Children and adolescents have distinct perceptions of the social networks within everyday settings such as classrooms or afterschool programs that shape their understanding of power dynamics and resource distribution in those settings. Traditionally, SNA methods involve the use of survey, interview, or observational methods to assess the presence or strength of relationships among all individuals in a setting. These methods yield social network data in the form of a two-dimensional adjacency matrix, $\mathbf{R}$, where each cell $R_{ij}$ indicates the presence or strength of a relationship between a pair of individuals ($i$ and $j$) in the setting (adams, 2020; Marin & Wellman, 2011). However, these traditional SNA methods do not capture individuals' perceptions of relationships, a unique and potential precursor of CC.

CSS is a method for collecting social network data that is specifically designed to assess a respondent's perception of an entire social network in a setting (e.g., all possible relationships between individuals in a classroom or afterschool program; Krackhardt, 1987; Neal, 2008; Neal & Kornbluh, 2016). CSS is an accessible and suitable methodology for collecting network data with children and adolescents (Neal, 2008; Neal & Kornbluh, 2016). Notably, CSS has been employed to explore demographic trends in children's "hanging out" relationships (Neal, 2010), peer relational behaviors (prosocial and aggressive behaviors) (Kornbluh & Neal, 2016), and the role of classroom context (Cappella et al., 2012). We stress in this chapter that CSS can provide a developmentally inclusive measure to explore individual and structural precursors of children's and adolescents' CC development by tapping into their understanding, awareness, and access to social relationships in association with the relational dynamics distributed within their primary settings.

To collect CSS data, researchers employ survey or interview methods that ask respondents to identify the presence or strength of a relationship between each pair of individuals within the entire setting. Because CSS involves gathering data on respondents' perceptions of the entire social network within a setting, it results in social network data that takes the form of a three-dimensional adjacency matrix, **R**, where each cell $R_{ijk}$ indicates the presence or strength of a relationship between individuals $i$ and $j$ as perceived by respondent $k$ (Krackhardt, 1987; Neal & Kornbluh, 2016). The rich three-dimensional data provided by CSS are complex and can be aggregated in different ways to reflect individuals' self-reported relationships (i.e., locally aggregated structures), individuals' perceptions of the entire social network (i.e., slices), or a consensus across respondents about the presence or absence of relationships in the network (i.e., consensus and aggregation; Krackhardt, 1987; Neal & Kornbluh, 2016). These different aggregations offer flexibility for exploring individual children's and adolescents' perceptions of social networks in their everyday settings. In addition, aggregations allow researchers to explore the unique setting-level contexts in relationship distribution (i.e., social cliques, equality in relational distributions within a bounded setting) that may facilitate or hinder CC development. In sum, CSS offers promise for assessing relational power at the individual, dyadic, and setting levels with implications for CC development (see Table 8.1 for a summary).

In this chapter, we focus on applying SNA to explore individual and structural precursors within their primary settings (e.g., classroom, and afterschool/community-based programs) to assess early understandings and savviness of CC across multiple domains, before a fuller analysis of larger social conditions that emerge developmentally. Specifically, children's and adolescents' perceptions of these social environments can provide a venue to understand forms of power within a proximal context.

## POWER AT THE INDIVIDUAL LEVEL

At the individual level, it may be useful to capture children's and adolescents' perceptions of who has the ability to control resources via their position in the network. Informed by Emerson's (1962) resource dependence model,

TABLE 8.1 Utilizing SNA to explore individual and structural precursors of critical consciousness

| Level | Definition | Measurement | Research Questions | Precursors Promoting Critical Consciousness |
|---|---|---|---|---|
| Individual | Perceptions of the ability of classmates or peers to control resources via their position in the network | Network Power (Bonacich, 1987; Neal & Neal, 2011) | Do children/adolescents identify certain classmates/peers that have control over valued resources? Are children and adolescents aware of their own control and access to social resources? | Child/adolescents' awareness of who has access to resources within their proximal environments, ability to navigate and leverage social connections, and cognizance of their own privilege may act as individual precursors to CC development. |
| Teacher–Student Dyads | Perceived teacher/staff rewards and punishments toward classmates | Student report of teacher–classmate relationships | Who has access to key socializing agents?<br>Do children/adolescents perceive differences in teacher/staff behavior toward students?<br>How might these perceptions impact learning and health outcomes? | Child/adolescents' awareness of who has access to socializing agents as well as their ability to who is receiving preferential treatment by adults within their proximal environments could be a noteworthy precursor to various aspects of CC. |
| Setting | Distribution of social relationships across students in a classroom or program | Network Equality (Cappella et al., 2013) or Network Power (Neal, 2014) in a Setting | Do children/adolescents perceive the network as egalitarian? Are such perceptions accurate?<br>How does network equality relate to child/adolescent behaviors? | Child/adolescents' awareness of the extent to which social support is equitably distributed within a setting may serve as a structural precursor to CC development. |

| | | | | |
|---|---|---|---|---|
| Setting | Cliques or divides within the classroom or program network limiting access to social support | Community Detection (Fortunato & Hric, 2016)<br>E-I Index (Krackhardt & Stern, 1988) | Do cliques exist within the setting? Are children/adolescents cognizant of such cliques?<br>How do cliques impact children and adolescent behaviors? | Child/adolescents' awareness of group-level power dynamics via relationships may be an early precursor to CC development in multiple domains. |

measures of *network power* provide information about the extent to which certain individuals hold network positions that necessitate others' dependence on them for valued resources (Bonacich, 1987; Neal & Neal, 2011). When combined with CSS, measures of network power can be calculated within children's and adolescents' perceptions (or slices) of the network to determine which individuals they identify as more or less able to control resources.

CSS network questions can capture children's perceptions of whether particular peers or adults (i.e., teachers, youth workers, and staff) have control over valued resources within the classroom or afterschool setting. These resources could include access to desired social contacts that can help navigate academics as well as opportunities to engage in civic conversations and activities (e.g., "Who hangs out with whom? Who has friends that can help with class assignments? With whom can one discuss current events?"). Children's and adolescents' cognizance surrounding who has access to social resources or supports can illuminate potential class or racial inequities within their proximal environments that are inherently situated within larger systemic structures (Williams & Hamm, 2018). Researchers have stressed that such critical thinking may serve as an individual precursor to critical reflection (Hope et al., 2015; Seider et al., 2017). For instance, Hope and colleagues (2015) found that Black high school students' awareness of discriminatory practices enacted by teachers and staff through critical analysis fostered a structural understanding of race-based educational experiences.

An awareness of one's relational power and ability to strategically navigate social connections to access desired resources (i.e., engaging in strategic acts of bridging and brokering) may demonstrate key competencies in social savviness. Such skill sets have been linked within the literature to critical motivation (Garcia & Ramirez, 2018; Kirshner & Ginwright, 2012; Seider et al., 2017). For instance, Seider and colleagues (2017) conducted qualitative interviews with predominantly Black and Latino(a) high school students. Interviews illustrated the benefits of utilizing social intelligence to navigate various social situations in pursuit of higher education.

Furthermore, consciousness of one's own social power and network location may facilitate understandings of privilege and heightened sentiments of empathy and social responsibility for others. Such sentiments have been found to be associated with critical action (Hershberg & Johnson, 2019; Kornbluh et al., 2021). For example, Stoudt (2012) documented high school students' exploration of gendered privilege at a predominately white, wealthy preparatory school, which he noted served as a launching pad for their own school-based activism surrounding bullying.

## POWER AT THE DYADIC LEVEL

At the dyadic level, it may be useful to capture children's and adolescents' perceptions of key relationships within a setting. For example, children's and adolescents' perceptions of teachers' rewards and punishments toward classmates could provide important information about the extent to which teachers treat students equally within the classroom. Within school and afterschool settings, children's and adolescents' perceptions of who has access to civic information, resources, and social support from peers or staff (i.e., relational power) can serve as a precursor to CC. These data can be collected directly via student report of dyadic relationships (e.g., teacher–student and adult staff–youth) or by incorporating the teacher/adult staff as a member of the bounded network (e.g., classroom/afterschool program) in CSS data.

Utilizing CSS, students have the opportunity to identify who has access to social supports and resources from adults (e.g., "Who tends to get support from adult staff? Who tends to talk to adult staff about current events?"). An awareness at the dyadic level of who has access to socializing agents who provide specific information and resources (i.e., political and ethnic/racial socialization) via peers and adults may illuminate structural precursors to critical reflection (Bañales et al., 2020, 2021; Diemer et al., 2006), critical motivation (Diemer, 2012; Diemer et al., 2009), and critical action (Bañales et al., 2021; Diemer & Li, 2011). SNA provides an avenue to explore how a meta-awareness of relational power in access to socializing agents can relate to CC development. Such analyses could further explore if children and adolescents' awareness of their own and peers' access to socializing agents within their proximal environment impact their CC development across multiple domains.

CSS may also illuminate potential power differences in treatment of children and adolescents within their proximal settings (e.g., "Are certain kids more likely to get in trouble?"). SNA questions may also identify precursors to early awareness of proximal inequality. By collecting simple relational survey data, CSS allows researchers to explore trends in students' perceptions of their teachers' behaviors to other students. For example, using an aggregated consensus of the social relationships within a classroom allows researchers to examine where students are located within the network and how their location may relate to their perceptions of their teachers' behaviors. Furthermore, CSS data can provide the opportunity to explore associations in perceptions of fairness surrounding teacher behavior and educational outcomes. Identifying differential treatment in an adult's behavior, not just for oneself but for others, may be a potential cognition associated with critical reflection development (Hope et al., 2015; Thomas et al., 2014). Thomas and colleagues (2014) developed a CCI scale that assesses discrimination and marginalization at an interpersonal level, which they stress is an important developmental component of critical reflection. Such awareness has also been found to be associated with critical action for Black children and adolescents (Hope & Spencer, 2017). SNA may add to our understanding of perceived proximal inequality by exploring children's and adolescents' social position within their primary settings in relation to perceived power dynamics, for instance, in examining children's and adolescents' perceived relational power in association with understandings of interpersonal discrimination and a desire for social betterment.

## POWER AT THE SETTING LEVEL

At the setting level, it may be useful to capture children's and adolescents' perceptions of the distribution of relationships across all individuals in the network and how resources flow within their proximal environments. Cappella and colleagues (2013) proposed a measure of network equality that uses a coefficient of variation to measure the extent to which the number of relationships in the network are distributed equally across individuals in a setting. Likewise, Neal (2014) proposed using a Gini coefficient to measure the extent to which network power is distributed equally across individuals in a setting. The Gini coefficient was originally proposed to measure income inequality (Gini, 1912) but can be applied to measure the inequality of any finite resource in a setting. It ranges from 0, which reflects total equality (e.g., all actors in the setting have the same amount of network power) to 1, which reflects total inequality (e.g., all network power is held by only one actor in the setting). When combined with CSS, distributional measures such as network equity or the Gini coefficient can be calculated within children's and adolescents' perceptions (or slices) of the network to determine the extent to which they perceive relationships and power within the setting as egalitarian. Measures calculated within perceptual slices can also be compared to the consensus aggregation in order to determine whether children and adolescents perceive the distribution of relationships similarly to their peers.

Specifically, network questions can capture children's perceptions of who is friends with whom within their proximal settings (i.e., capturing desired social support and contacts). These questions may include "Who hangs out with whom? or Who is friends with whom?" Employing CSS allows the researcher to examine the extent to which the classroom or afterschool program is egalitarian in the context of social support and relational access. Furthermore, CSS allows CC researchers to explore associations between an individual student's perception of power at the setting level compared to an aggregated understanding of power (i.e., based on consensus across students). These analyses open a window for novel areas of inquiry because they can identify which students might be most attuned to setting-level inequalities in social relationships. In particular, it might be useful to assess whether a student's own network position is tied to their ability to pick up on and identify setting-level power dynamics.

To illustrate, we provide a visual example of using network equality (see Figure 8.1). Network equality, as described earlier, is a setting-level measure based on the distribution of degree centrality across a setting, thereby employing the coefficient of variation: $-1 \times (SD_{degree} / M_{degree})$ (Cappella et al., 2013).[1] A value of 0 indicates complete network equality within the classroom setting (i.e., all students have the same number of peers), whereas lower values indicate less equality (i.e., certain students may have more peers as compared to other classmates). We can employ CSS to compare an individual's perception of network equality to network equality captured through classroom consensus. Referring to Figure 8.1 (panel 1), say an individual perceives the classroom to be more equal in distribution (e.g., each student has two friends), yet an aggregated perception of the network among classmates reflects an unequal distribution (e.g., each student has a number of friendships that range from one to four peers). When calculating the student's perception of network equality they perceive the classroom as completely equal (i.e., 0; see panel 2), whereas the classroom consensus network equality reflects greater inequality in friendship distribution (i.e., −0.48; see panel 3). The difference between an individual's perception of network equity and the classroom consensus may capture proximal indicators of inequality. Such awareness of proximal inequities may be tied to understanding of macrolevel concepts, serving as a potential precursor for critical reflection (Ilten-Gee & Manchanda, 2021; Flanagan & Kornbluh, 2019; Kornbluh et al., 2019). Kornbluh and colleagues (2019) conducted a study within a cross-sectional, socioeconomically and ethnically diverse sample of middle and high school students. Findings indicated positive associations between understandings of proximal inequities of distributive justice concerning classroom peers (via hypothetical vignettes) and structural understandings of poverty.

The network equality measure captures a child's or adolescent's perception surrounding social inequalities within their proximal environments. Additionally, this measure can be calculated to reflect the consensus of all children in the classroom to reflect classroom agreement on the level of equality in the distribution of relationships. For instance, a child may perceive their classroom to be equal in the domains of friendship and social support. However, this perception may greatly differ from the consensus of their peers, thereby illuminating the child's potential lack of awareness surrounding existing power differentials within the classroom (i.e., rating lower as a precursor to critical reflection).

1 Cappella et al., (2013) originally referred to this measure as "network equity," but we refer to it as "network equality" because the measure more accurately captures how equal the distribution of relationships is across a setting. Determining equity would require additional information about the relational needs of each participant in the setting.

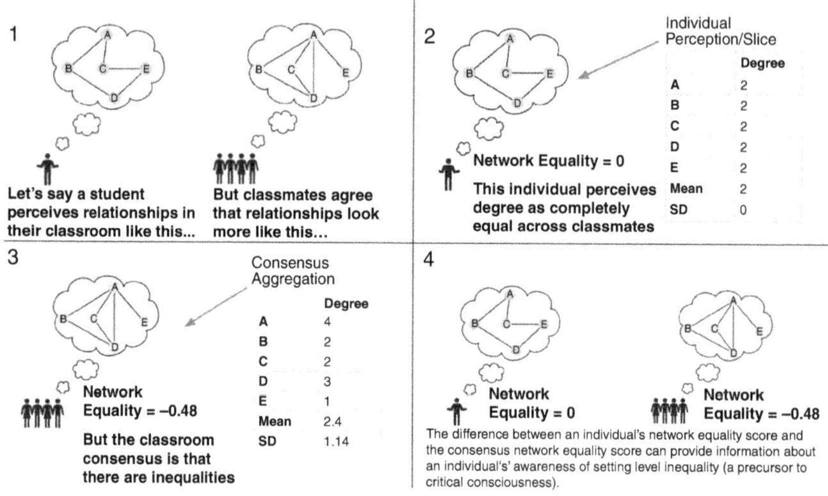


FIGURE 8.1 Illustrative example of Network Equality.

Furthermore, beyond individual perceptions of network equality, classmates' consensus about the distribution of relationships within their proximal setting (i.e., equal access to relationships) may hold implications for children's and adolescents' civic thoughts and behaviors. Research suggests primary environments that intentionally provide sociopolitical support via educator engagement in key pedagogical practices have implications in promoting critical reflection, critical motivation, and critical action (Diemer & Li, 2011; Godfrey & Grayman, 2014; Heberle et al., 2020; Rapa et al., 2020; Silva, 2012).

It may also be useful to capture children's and adolescents' perceptions of cliques within the network. Community detection algorithms can be used to identify cliques or clusters of connected individuals (e.g., Fortunato & Hric, 2016). The E-I index can be used to determine the extent to which the network is characterized by relationships within a particular demographic or social group (e.g., relationships among those of the same ethnicity) than relationships between groups (e.g., cross-ethnic relationships; Krackhardt & Stern, 1988). Combined with CSS, these measures can be applied within children's and adolescents' individual perceptions of the network to determine the extent to which they perceive relational divides within a particular setting that might limit access to social support. Follow-up qualitative probing could yield the opportunity to explore how cognizant students are of larger-scale trends in peer dynamics (e.g., "Do certain students tend to hang out with one another?"). Students who are able to report a "bird's-eye view" of setting-level dynamics and hierarchies in peer relationships may be more attuned to larger structural inequities or have greater developmental "readiness" to explore macrolevel issues.

Awareness of power at the setting level (i.e., degree of equity in relationship distribution or absence/presence of cliques) may be an early precursor to multiple domains of CC.

## CONCLUSION

SNA taps into the relational and contextual components of human behavior by providing a tangible method by which to assess the pattern of relationships between a set of actors (Luke, 2005; Neal & Christens, 2014). A notable benefit of SNA is the "bird's-eye view" that it uses to identify the pattern of relationships between actors within a bounded system. This bird's-eye view cannot easily be captured through more traditional self-report survey or interview methods (Kornbluh & Neal, 2016; Provan et al., 2005). The CC literature stresses the need for novel methods and measures that capture dynamic, relational, and setting-level processes surrounding issues of power and resource distribution (Diemer, 2020; Heberle et al., 2020).

In this chapter, we argued that SNA and the employment of CSS provide CC researchers with a multilevel lens through which to explore individual and structural precursors of CC (i.e., individual, dyadic, and setting level), tapping into perceptions of proximal injustice, access to resources, and relational power within the everyday settings (e.g., schools and afterschool programs) of children and adolescents. SNA has been successfully applied to both children and adolescent populations. Such measures are particularly beneficial for CC researchers interested in documenting children's and adolescents' developing understandings of inequality and power. Children's and adolescents' understanding of relational power and distribution inequities within their primary environment may serve as a precursor to a fuller analysis of macrolevel structures and systems that perpetuate larger-scale societal inequities.

Regarding intervention and practice, the act of filling out a CSS for one's proximal environment could facilitate children's and adolescents' recognition of proximal inequities within the context of relational power distribution. Such understandings could potentially provide linkages to understandings of larger macrolevel concepts (critical reflection), a desire to push for a more equitable environment (critical motivation), and engagement in social action (critical action). Furthermore, documenting distributions in relationships and the flow of resources within youth development settings can further allow educator and youth development worker insights into the types of environments that may promote CC development. Such insights could provide opportunities to track the impact of relationship-building social-emotional learning activities to further foster connections between peers and youth/adult relationships.

It is important to note that SNA also comes with methodological and real-world challenges. First, it is vulnerable to missing data, which can greatly impact the accuracy of study findings (Kossinets, 2006). However, because the CSS methods described in this chapter depend on individuals' perceptions of social networks and can capitalize on triangulating network data across respondents, these methods are less vulnerable to missing data than traditional network methods (Neal, 2008). Second, SNA presents unique ethical considerations regarding the lack of anonymity and use of secondary participants in the data collection procedures (Tubaro et al., 2021). Thus, researchers have to be conscious and intentional in how they present SNA findings to the larger public or community partners (e.g., schools and afterschool programs). Specifically, findings should be presented in a format in which children and adolescents are nonidentifiable (see Klovdahl, 2005 for an in-depth description). If researchers intend to provide schools or afterschool programs with identifiable data on children and adolescents, it is necessary to make sure they seek truly informed consent from parents and assent from students that specifies exactly what these data will look like and how they will be used (Borgatti & Molina, 2005). In our prior work, we did not present specific network actor positions back to schools and partnering nonprofits (see Kornbluh & Neal, 2016). Rather, we focused on how individual, dyadic, and setting-level features and trends influenced child and adolescent developmental outcomes and provided recommendations for strengthening connections in order to optimize intervention outcomes (Kornbluh et al., 2016, 2019; Kornbluh & Neal, 2016).

Despite these considerations, SNA has exciting potential to capture individual and structural precursors of CC development at multiple levels of analysis. Therefore, we hope this chapter motivates CC researchers to use SNA to explore precursors of CC.

## REFERENCES

adams, j. (2020). *Gathering social network data*. Sage Publications.

Afterschool Alliance. (2014). *Taking a deeper dive into afterschool: Positive outcomes and promising practices*. ERIC Clearinghouse.

Aldana, A., Bañales, J., & Richards-Schuster, K. (2019). Youth anti-racist engagement: Conceptualization, development, and validation of an anti-racist action scale. *Adolescent Research Review*, *4*(4), 369–381. https://doi.org/10.1007/s40894-019-00113-1.

Bachrach, P., & Baratz, M. S. (1962). Two faces of power. *American Political Science Review*, *56*(4), 947–952. https://doi.org/10.2307/1952796.

Baldridge, B. J., Beck, N., Medina, J. C., & Reeves, M. A. (2017). Toward a new understanding of community-based education: The role of community-based educational spaces in disrupting inequality for minoritized youth. *Review of Research in Education*, *41*(1), 381–402. https://doi.org/10.3102/0091732X16688622.

Bañales, J., Hope, E. C., Rowley, S. J., & Cryer-Coupet, Q. R. (2021). Raising justice-minded youth: Parental ethnic-racial and political socialization and Black youth's critical consciousness. *Journal of Social Issues*, *77*(4), 964–986. https://doi.org/10.1111/josi.12486.

Bañales, J., Marchand, A. D., Skinner, O. D. et al. (2020). Black adolescents' critical reflection development: Parents' racial socialization and attributions about race achievement gaps. *Journal of Research on Adolescence*, *30*, 403–417. https://doi.org/10.1111/jora.12485.

Bonacich, P. (1987). Power and centrality: A family of measures. *American Journal of Sociology*, *92*(5), 1170–1182. https://www.jstor.org/stable/27800.

Borgatti, S. P., Mehra, A., Brass, D. J., & Labianca, G. (2009). Network analysis in the social sciences. *Science*, *323*(5916), 892–895. https://doi.org/10.1126/science.1165821.

Bozalek, V., & Biersteker, L. (2010). Exploring power and privilege using participatory learning and action techniques. *Social Work Education*, *29*(5), 551–572. https://doi.org/10.1080/02615470903193785.

Cappella, E., Kim, H. Y., Neal, J. W., & Jackson, D. R. (2013). Classroom peer relationships and behavioral engagement in elementary school: The role of social network equity. *American Journal of Community Psychology*, *52*(3–4), 367–379. https://doi.org/10.1007/s10464-013-9603-5.

Cappella, E., Neal, J. W., & Sahu, N. (2012). Children's agreement on classroom social networks: cross-level predictors in urban elementary schools. *Merrill-Palmer Quarterly*, *58*(3), 285–313.

Corning, A. F., & Myers, D. J. (2002). Individual orientation toward engagement in social action. *Political Psychology*, *23*(4), 703–729. https://doi.org/10.1111/0162-895X.00304.

Cronin, T. J., Levin, S., Branscombe, N. R., van Laar, C., & Tropp, L. R. (2012). Ethnic identification in response to perceived discrimination protects wellbeing and promotes activism: A longitudinal study of Latino college students. *Group Processes & Intergroup Relations*, *15*, 393–407. https://doi.org/10.1177/1368430211427171.

Darder A (2014) *Freire and education*. Routledge Publications.

Deutsch, M. (1974). Awakening the sense of injustice. In M. Lerner & M. Ross (Eds.), *The Question for Justice: Myth, Reality, Ideal*. Holt, Rinehart and Winston.

Diemer, M. A. (2012). Fostering marginalized youths' political participation: Longitudinal roles of parental political socialization and youth sociopolitical development. *American Journal of Community Psychology*, *50*, 246–256. https://doi.org/10.1007/s10464-012-9495-9.

Diemer, M. A. (2020). Pushing the envelope: The who, what, when, and why of critical consciousness. *Journal of Applied Developmental Psychology*, *70*. https://doi.org/10.1016/j.appdev.2020.101192.

Diemer, M. A., Hsieh, C., & Pan, T. (2009). School and parental influences on sociopolitical development among poor adolescents of color. *The Counseling Psychologist*, *37*, 317–344. https://doi.org/10.1177/0011000008315971.

Diemer, M. A., Kauffman, A., Koenig, N., Trahan, E., & Hsieh, C. A. (2006). Challenging racism, sexism, and social injustice: Support for urban adolescents' critical consciousness development. *Cultural Diversity and Ethnic Minority Psychology*, *12*, 444–460. https://doi.org/10.1037/1099-9809.12.3.444.

Diemer, M. A., & Li, C. H. (2011). Critical consciousness development and political participation among marginalized youth. *Child Development, 82*, 1815–1833. https://doi.org/10.1111/j.1467-8624.2011.01650.x.

Diemer, M. A., Rapa, L. J., Park, C. J., & Perry, J. C. (2017). Development and validation of the Critical Consciousness Scale. *Youth & Society*, *49*(4), 461–483. https://doi.org/10.1177/0044118X14538289.

Diemer, M. A., Rapa, L. J., Voight, A. M., & McWhirter, E. H. (2016). Critical consciousness: A developmental approach to addressing marginalization and oppression. *Child Development Perspectives*, *10*(4), 216–221. https://doi.org/10.1111/cdep.12193.

Diemer, M. A., Wang, Q., Moore, T. et al. (2010). Sociopolitical development, work salience, and vocational expectations among low socioeconomic status African American, Latin American, and Asian American youth. *Developmental Psychology*, *46*(3), 619–635. https://doi.org/10.1037/a0017049.

Dunham, Y., & Emory, J. (2014) Of affect and ambiguity: The emergence of preference for arbitrary ingroups. *Journal of Social Issues 70*(1), 81–98. doi:10.1111/josi.12048.

El-Amin, A., Seider, S., Graves, D. et al. (2017). Critical consciousness: A key to student achievement. *Phi Delta Kappan*, *98*(5), 18–23. https://doi.org/10.1177/0031721717690360.

Emerson, R. M. (1962). Power-dependence relations. *American Sociological Review*, *27*, 31–41.

Fine, M. & Ruglis, J. (2009) Circuits and consequences of dispossession: The racialized realignment of the public sphere for US youth. *Transforming Anthropology*, *17*(1), 20–33. https://doi.org/10.1111/j.1548-7466.2009.01037.x.

Flanagan, C. (2009). Young people's civic engagement and political development. In A. Furlong (Ed.), *Handbook of youth and young adulthood* (pp. 309–316). Routledge Publications.

Flanagan, C. A., & Kornbluh, M. (2019). How unequal is the United States? Adolescents' images of social stratification. *Child Development*, *90*(3), 957–969. https://doi.org/10.1111/cdev.12954.

Fortunato, S., & Hric, D. (2016). Community detection in networks: A user guide. *Physics Reports*, *659*, 1–44. https://doi.org/10.1016/j.physrep.2016.09.002.

Freedman, S. W., Barr, D. J., Murphy, K., et al. (2016) The development of ethical civic actors in divided societies: A longitudinal case. *Human Development 59*(2–3), 107–127. https://doi.org/10.1159/000448229.

Freire, P. (1973). *Education for critical consciousness*. Continuum.

Garcia, G. A., & Ramirez, J. J. (2018). Institutional agents at a Hispanic serving institution: Using social capital to empower students. *Urban Education*, *53*(3), 355–381. https://doi.org/10.1177/0042085915623341.

Gaventa, J. (1980). *Power and powerlessness: Quiescence and rebellion in an Appalachian Valley*. University of Illinois Press.

Gini, C. (1912). *Variabilità e mutabilità*. Contributo allo studio delle Distribuzioni e della Relazioni Statistiche.

Godfrey, E. B., & Burson, E. (2018). Interrogating the intersections: How intersectional perspectives can inform developmental scholarship on critical consciousness. *New Directions for Child and Adolescent Development*, *161*, 17–38. https://doi.org/10.1002/cad.20246

Godfrey, E. B., & Grayman, J. K. (2014). Teaching citizens: The role of open classroom climate in fostering critical consciousness among youth. *Journal of Youth and Adolescence, 43*(11), 1801–1817. https://doi.org/10.1007/s10964-013-0084-5.

Groves Price, P., & Mencke, P. D. (2013). Critical pedagogy and praxis with Native American youth: Cultivating change through participatory action research. *Educational Foundations, 27*, 85–102. https://files.eric.ed.gov/fulltext/EJ1065661.pdf.

Hawkins, K. (2014). Teaching for social justice, social responsibility and social inclusion: A respectful pedagogy for twenty-first century early childhood education. *European Early Childhood Education Research Journal, 22*(5), 723–738. https://doi.org/10.1080/1350293X.2014.969085.

Hazelbaker, T., Griffin, K. M., Nenadal, L., & Mistry, R. S. (2018). Early elementary school children's conceptions of neighborhood social stratification and fairness. *Translational Issues in Psychological Science, 4*(2), 153–164. https://doi.org/10.1037/tps0000153.

Heberle, A. E., Rapa, L. J., & Faragó, F. (2020). Critical consciousness in children and adolescents: A systematic review, critical assessment, and recommendations for future research. *Psychological Bulletin, 146*(6), 525–551. https://doi.org/10.1037/bul0000230.

Hershberg, R. M., & Johnson, S. K. (2019). Critical reflection about socioeconomic inequalities among White young men from poor and working-class backgrounds. *Developmental Psychology, 55*(3), 562–573. https://doi.org/10.1037/dev0000587.

Hofferth, S. L. (2009). Changes in American children's time–1997 to 2003. *Electronic International Journal of Time Use Research, 6*(1), 26–47. https://www.ncbi.nlm.nih.gov/pmc/articles/PMC2939468/.

Hope, E. C., & Jagers, R. (2014). The role of sociopolitical attitudes and civic education in the civic engagement of Black youth. *Journal of Research on Adolescence, 24*, 460–470. https://doi.org/10.1111/jora.12117.

Hope, E. C., Keels, M., & Durkee, M. I. (2016). Participation in Black Lives Matter and deferred action for childhood arrivals: Modern activism among Black and Latino college students. *Journal of Diversity in Higher Education, 9*(3), 203–215. https://doi.org/10.1037/dhe0000032.

Hope, E. C., Skoog, A. B., & Jagers, R. J. (2015). "It'll never be the white kids, it'll always be us": Black high school students' evolving critical analysis of racial discrimination and inequity in schools. *Journal of Adolescent Research, 30*(1), 83–112. https://doi.org/10.1177/0743558414550688.

Hope, E. C., & Spencer, M. B. (2017). Civic engagement as an adaptive coping response to conditions of inequality: An application of phenomenological variant of ecological systems theory (PVEST). In N. J. Cabrera, & B. Leyendecker (Eds.). *Handbook on positive development of minority children and youth* (pp. 421–435). Springer.

Ilten-Gee, R., & Manchanda, S. (2021). Using social domain theory to seek critical consciousness with young children. *Theory and Research in Education, 19*(3), 235–260. https://doi.org/10.1177/14778785211057485.

Jemal, A. (2017). Critical consciousness: A critique and critical analysis of the literature. *The Urban Review*, *49*(4), 602–626. https://doi.org/10.1007/s11256-017-0411-3.

Joseph, N. M., Viesca, K. M., & Bianco, M. (2016). Black female adolescents and racism in schools: Experiences in a colorblind society. *The High School Journal*, *100*(1), 4–25. https://doi.org/10.1353/hsj.2016.0018.

Kirshner, B., & Ginwright, S. (2012). Youth organizing as a developmental context for African American and Latino adolescents. *Child Development Perspectives*, *6*(3), 288–294. https://doi.org/10.1111/j.1750-8606.2012.00243.x.

Klovdahl, A. S. (2005). Social network research and human subjects protection: Towards more effective infectious disease control. *Social Networks*, *27*, 119–137. https://doi.org/10.1016/j.socnet.2005.01.006.

Kornbluh, M. (2020). Untold student stories: Examining educational budget cuts within urban school settings. *Journal of Urban Affairs*, *42*(5), 731–749. https://doi.org/10.1080/07352166.2019.1607748.

Kornbluh, M., Bell, S., Vierra, K., & Herrnstadt, Z. (2021). Resistance capital: Cultural activism as a gateway to college persistence for minority and first-generation students. *Journal of Adolescent Research*, *37*(4), 501–540. https://doi.org/10.1177/07435584211006920.

Kornbluh, M., Collins, C., & Kohfeldt, D. (2020). Navigating activism within the academy: Consciousness building and social justice identity formation. *Journal of Community & Applied Social Psychology*, *30*(2), 151–163. https://doi.org/10.1002/casp.2434.

Kornbluh, M., Johnson, L., & Hart, M. (2021). Shards from the glass ceiling: Deconstructing marginalizing systems in relation to critical consciousness development. *American Journal of Community Psychology*, *68*(1–2), 187–201. https://doi.org/10.1002/ajcp.12512.

Kornbluh, M., Neal, J. W., & Ozer, E. J. (2016). Scaling-up youth-led social justice efforts through an online school-based social network. *American Journal of Community Psychology*, *57*(3–4), 266–279. https://doi.org/10.1002/ajcp.12042.

Kornbluh, M. E., Pykett, A. A., & Flanagan, C. A. (2019). Exploring the associations between youths' explanations of poverty at the societal level and judgements of distributive justice. *Developmental Psychology*, *55*(3), 488. https://doi.org/10.1037/dev0000523.

Kossinets, G. (2006). Effects of missing data in social networks. *Social Networks*, *28*(3), 247–268. https://doi.org/10.1016/j.socnet.2005.07.002.

Krackhardt, D. (1987). Cognitive social structures. *Social Networks*, *9*(2), 109–134. https://doi.org/10.1016/0378-8733(87)90009-8.

Krackhardt, D., & Stern, R. N. (1988). Informal networks and organizational crises: An experimental simulation. *Social Psychology Quarterly*, *51*, 123–140. https://doi.org/2786835.

Kurtz-Costes, B., Hudgens, T. M., Skinner, O. D., Adams, E. A., & Rowley, S. J. (2019). Parents' racial beliefs and ethnic–racial socialization in African American families. *Merrill-Palmer Quarterly*, *65*(1), 54–80. https://doi.org/10.13110/merrpalmquar1982.65.1.0054.

Langhout, R. D., & Thomas, E. (2010). Imagining participatory action research in collaboration with children: An introduction. *American Journal of Community Psychology*, *46*(1), 60–66. https://doi.org/10.1007/s10464-010-9321-1.

Lapsley, D. K. (2006). Moral stage theory. In M. Killen & J. Smetana (Eds.), *Handbook of moral development* (pp. 37–66). Erlbaum

Laumann, E. O., Marsden, P. V., & Prensky, D. (1992). The boundary specification problem in network analysis. In L. C. Freeman, D. R. White, & A. K. Romney (Eds.), *Research methods in social network analysis* (pp. 61–87). Routledge.

Luginbuhl, P. J., McWhirter, E. H., & McWhirter, B. T. (2016). Sociopolitical development, autonomous motivation, and education outcomes: Implications for low-income Latina/o adolescents. *Journal of Latina/o Psychology*, *4*(1), 43–59. https://doi.org/10.1037/lat0000041.

Luke, D. A. (2005). Getting the big picture in community science: Methods that capture context. *American Journal of Community Psychology*, *35*, 185–200. https://doi.org/10.1007/s10464-005-3397-z.

Lukes, S. (2005). *Power: A radical view* (2nd ed.). Palgrave MacMillan.

Marin, A., & Wellman, B. (2011). *Social network analysis: An introduction.* In J. Scott & P.J. Carrington (Eds.), The SAGE handbook of social network analysis (pp. 11–25). Sage.

Marsden, P. V. (1990). Network data and measurement. *Annual Review of Sociology*, *16* (1), 435–463. https://doi.org/10.1146/annurev.so.16.080190.002251.

McWhirter, E. H., & McWhirter, B. T. (2016). Critical consciousness and vocational development among Latina/o high school youth: Initial development and testing of a measure. *Journal of Career Assessment*, *24*(3), 543–558. https://doi.org/10.1177/1069072715599535.

Mistry, R. S., White, E. S., Chow, K. A., Nenadal, L., & Griffin, K. (2016). A mixed methods approach to equity and justice research: Insights from research on children's reasoning about economic inequality. In S. Horn, M. Ruck, & L. Liben (Eds.), *Equity and Justice in Developmental Science: Theoretical and Methodological Issues, Vol 50* (pp. 209–236), Advances in Child Development and Behavior Series. Elsevier, Academic Press.

Mosley D. V., Hargons, C. N., Meiller C., et al. (2021) Critical consciousness of anti-Black racism: A practical model to prevent and resist racial trauma. *Journal of Counseling Psychology*, *68*(1): 1–16. https://doi.org/10.1037/cou0000430.

Neal, J. W. (2008). "Kracking" the missing data problem: Applying Krackhardt's cognitive social structures to school-based social networks. *Sociology of Education*, *81*(2), 140–162. https://doi.org/10.1177/003804070808100202.

Neal, J. W. (2010). Hanging out: Features of urban children's peer social networks. *Journal of Social and Personal Relationships*, *27*(7), 982–1000. https://doi.org/10.1177/0265407510378124.

Neal, J.W. (2020). A systematic review of social network methods in high impact developmental psychology journals. *Social Development*, *29*, 923–944. https://doi.org/10.1111/sode.12442.

Neal, J. W., & Christens, B. D. (2014). Linking the levels: Network and relational perspectives for community psychology. *American Journal of Community Psychology*, *53*, 314–323. https://doi.org/10.1007/s10464-014-9654-2.

Neal, J. W. & Kornbluh, M. (2016). Using cognitive social structures to understand peer relations in childhood and adolescence. In Z. Neal (Ed.), *Handbook of systems science* (pp. 147–163). Routledge.

Neal, J. W., & Neal, Z. P. (2011). Power as a structural phenomenon. *American Journal of Community Psychology, 48*(3–4), 157–167. https://doi.org/10.1007/s10464-010-9356-3.

Neal, J. W., Neal, Z. P., & Cappella, E. (2016). Seeing and being seen: Predictors of accurate perceptions about classmates' relationships. *Social Networks, 44*, 1–8. https://doi.org/10.1016/j.socnet.2015.07.002.

Neal, Z. P. (2014). A network perspective on the processes of empowered organizations. *American Journal of Community Psychology, 53*(3–4), 407–418. https://doi.org/10.1007/s10464-013-9623-1.

Pancer, S., Pratt, M., Hunsberger, B., & Alisat, S. (2007). Community and political involvement in adolescence: What distinguishes the activists from the uninvolved? *Journal of Community Psychology, 35*(6), 741–759. https://doi.org/10.1002/jcop.20176.

Parsons, J. E., Adler, T. F., & Kaczala, C. M. (1982). Socialization of achievement attitudes and beliefs: Parental influences. *Child Development, 53*, 310–321. https://doi.org/10.2307/1128973.

Prilleltensky, I. (2008). The role of power in wellness, oppression, and liberation: The promise of psychopolitical validity. *Journal of Community Psychology, 36*(2), 116–136. https://doi.org/10.1002/jcop.20225.

Provan, K. G., Veazie, M. A., Staten, L. K., & Teufel-Stone, N. I. (2005). The use of network analysis to strengthen community partnerships. *Public Administration Review, 65*, 603–613. https://doi.org/10.1111/j.1540-6210.2005.00487.x.

Rapa, L. J., Bolding, C. W., & Jamil, F. M. (2020). Development and initial validation of the Short Critical Consciousness Scale (CCS-S). *Journal of Applied Developmental Psychology, 70*, 1–10. https://doi.org/10.1016/j.appdev.2020.101164.

Ruck, M. D., Mistry, R. S., & Flanagan, C. A. (2019). Children's and adolescents' understanding and experiences of economic inequality: An introduction to the special section. *Developmental Psychology, 55*(3), 449. https://doi.org/10.1037/dev0000069.

Sakamoto, I., & Pitner, R. O. (2005). Use of critical consciousness in anti-oppressive social work practice: Disentangling power dynamics at personal and structural levels. *The British Journal of Social Work, 35*(4), 435–452. https://doi.org/10.1093/bjsw/bch190.

Seider, S., & Graves, D. (2020). *Schooling for critical consciousness: Engaging Black and Latinx youth in analyzing, navigating, and challenging racial injustice.* Harvard Education Press.

Seider, S., Tamerat, J., Clark, S., & Soutter, M. (2017). Investigating adolescents' critical consciousness development through a character framework. *Journal of Youth & Adolescence, 46*(6), 1162–1178. https://doi.org/10.1007/s10964-017-0641-4.

Serrano-Garcia, I. (1994). The ethics of the powerful and the power of ethics. *American Journal of Community Psychology, 22*, 1–20.

Silva, J. M. (2012). Critical classrooms: Using artists' lives to teach young students social groups, power, and privilege. *Urban Education, 47*(4), 776–800. https://doi.org/10.1177/0042085912441187.

Speer, P. W., & Hughey, J. (1995). Community organizing: An ecological route to empowerment and power. *American Journal of Community Psychology*, *23*(5), 729–748. https://doi.org/10.1007/BF02506989.

Stoudt B. G. (2012). "This is exactly what this study is all about and it is happening right in front of me!" Using participatory action research to awaken a sense of injustice within a privileged institution. *Masculinities and Social Change*, *1*(2), 134–164. https://doi.org/10.4471/MCS.2012.09.

Tatum, B. D. (1997). *"Why are all the black kids sitting together in the cafeteria?" And other conversations about race*. Basic Books.

Thomas, A. J., Barrie, R., Brunner, J. et al. (2014). Assessing critical consciousness in youth and young adults. *Journal of Research on Adolescence*, *24*, 485–496. https://doi.org/10.1111/jora.12132.

Tubaro, P., Ryan, L., Casilli, A. A., & D'angelo, A. (2021). Social network analysis: New ethical approaches through collective reflexivity. Introduction to the special issue of Social Networks. *Social Networks*, 67, 1–8. https://doi.org/10.1016/j.socnet.2020.12.001.

Tyler, C. P., Olsen, S. G., Geldhof, G. J., & Bowers, E. P. (2020). Critical consciousness in late adolescence: Understanding if, how, and why youth act. *Journal of Applied Developmental Psychology*, *70*, 1–13. https://doi.org/10.1016/j.appdev.2020.101165.

Uriostegui, M., Roy, A. L., & Li-Grining, C. P. (2021). What drives you? Black and Latinx youth's critical consciousness, motivations, and academic and career activities. *Journal of Youth and Adolescence*, *50*(1), 58–74. https://doi.org/10.1007/s10964-020-01343-6.

Vollhardt, J. R., & Sinayobye Twali, M. (2016). Emotion-based reconciliation requires attention to power differences, critical consciousness, and structural change. *Psychological Inquiry*, 27(2), 136–143. https://doi.org/10.1080/1047840X.2016.1160762.

Watts, R. J., Diemer, M. A., & Voight, A. M. (2011). Critical consciousness: Current status and future directions. Critical consciousness: Current status and future directions. *New Directions for Child and Adolescent Development*, *134*, 43–57. http://dx.doi.org/10.1002/cd.310.

Watts, R. J., Griffith, D. M., & Abdul-Adil, J. (1999). Sociopolitical development as an antidote for oppression – theory and action. *American Journal of Community Psychology*, *27*(2), 255–271. https://doi.org/10.1023/A:1022839818873.

Wellman, B. (1988). Structural analysis: From method and metaphor to theory and substance. In B. Wellman & S.D. Berkowitz (Eds.), *Social structures: A network approach* (pp. 19–61). Cambridge University Press.

White-Johnson, R. L. (2012). Prosocial involvement among African American young adults: Considering racial discrimination and racial identity. *Journal of Black Psychology*, *38*(3), 313–341. https://doi.org/10.1177/0095798411420429.

Williams, J. L., & Hamm, J. V. (2018). Peer group ethnic diversity and social competencies in youth attending rural middle schools. *The Journal of Early Adolescence*, *38*(6), 795–782. https://doi.org/10.1177/0272431617699945.

# 9

# Conceptualizing Adolescents' Daily Critical Consciousness

## *A Model and Research Agenda*

CORINE P. TYLER, KELLY D. CHANDLER, SHAUNA L. TOMINEY, SVEA G. OLSEN, LINDA J. FENSKE, AND KARA MCELVAINE

Critical consciousness – the process of coming to understand and combat oppression – is an integral aspect of adolescents' sociopolitical development and is necessary for collective liberation (Freire, 1970; Heberle et al., 2020). Adolescents are engaging in and developing skills related to critical consciousness amid a complex and ever-changing sociopolitical landscape. For example, the current landscape is informed by the global COVID-19 pandemic, which caused a significant reorganization in the schooling, family life, and social worlds of adolescents while simultaneously exacerbating existing class- and race-based disparities. As another example, recent instances of police brutality – coupled with the ongoing work of movements such as Black Lives Matter – inform adolescents' sociopolitical context. Some US schools and communities have responded by reprioritizing racial justice, while others have introduced or doubled down on existing oppressive practices and policies. Within this evolving landscape, adolescents navigate if and how to participate in critical consciousness each day as they enter different spaces and find themselves in different situations. Additionally, just as the world is continuously changing, so too are individual youth; their thoughts, feelings, and behaviors are not fixed (Baltes et al., 1988). Only a small body of research has begun to explore the contextualized daily dynamics of adolescents' critical consciousness. This gap is significant given that most of people's time and attention center around their everyday experiences (Bolger et al., 2003; Wheeler & Reis, 1991).

In this chapter, we introduce a conceptual model and research agenda focused on the daily dynamics of critical consciousness. In the sections that follow, we provide an overview of critical consciousness scholarship and review past research explicitly on daily critical consciousness. Then, we introduce our model of daily critical consciousness rooted in this past work and describe how daily diary designs can be used to examine this model. We conclude by discussing implications for research, practice, and policy.

## ORIGINS OF CRITICAL CONSCIOUSNESS

The concept of critical consciousness is founded in the ideas of the educator and philosopher Paulo Freire (Freire, 1970). Freire initially developed this concept while working within the Brazilian educational system in the 1950s and 1960s to increase literacy among peasants and the working class. These individuals were disenfranchised due to lingering effects of slavery and Portuguese colonization, which was compounded by the fact that literacy requirements blocked them from voting in government elections (Díaz, n.d.). Freire noticed that many of the workers he interacted with felt powerless to change the conditions of their lives, which led them to see no reason for education (Diemer et al., 2016; Freire, 1970). Freire's literacy programs, therefore, aimed not only to increase students' ability to read and write but also to increase their political awareness. As individuals participated in his programs, he saw them develop skills of "reading" the social world around them – including understanding their marginalized status within it – and express a motivation to collectively change their life circumstances. Based on these observations, as well as on the work of philosophers and economists such as Karl Marx, Freire developed the idea of *conscientização* or "critical consciousness."

## EXISTING CRITICAL CONSCIOUSNESS THEORIES AND RELATED SCHOLARSHIP

### Components of Critical Consciousness

Developmental researchers who have built on Freire's work often conceptualize critical consciousness through the presence of and interplay between three main constructs: critical reflection, critical motivation, and critical action (Diemer et al., 2016, 2020; Jemal, 2017). *Critical reflection* refers to an individual's ability to examine their sociopolitical context and recognize how it is shaped by oppression. In this respect, critically reflective youth are able to identify how various social structures perpetuate inequalities. *Critical motivation* refers to one's perceived capacity to have an impact on oppressive conditions and one's expressed commitment to making change for social justice.[1] Lastly, *critical action* is marked by working to alter oppressive conditions.[2] Current critical consciousness theories largely focus on interrelations among these constructs. The general consensus is that critical reflection

1 Critical motivation has also been referred to as "sociopolitical efficacy" in past literature (Poteat et al., 2020).

2 Generally (and in this chapter), critical action is conceptualized as external behaviors, although some researchers have explored the concept of internal critical action (Watts & Hipolito-Delgado, 2015).

should promote critical action; however, it is not sufficient to promote critical action in and of itself (Diemer et al., 2021; Freire, 1970). Instead, theorists indicate that critical reflection will primarily promote critical action when combined with critical motivation (Watts & Flanagan, 2007).

## Emotions and Critical Consciousness

Beyond these three commonly cited constructs, some theorists have posited that critical consciousness also includes an emotional dimension (Wallin-Ruschman, 2018). This dimension refers to the emotional experience of engaging in critical reflection, motivation, and action. Emotions are expected to play a central role in critical consciousness processes and serve different functions. For example, youth may feel anger due to their analysis of oppression or hope in connection to critical action. Indeed, scholars indicate that experiencing an emotion such as anger "is a justified reaction to a realistic appraisal of an objectively unjust situation" (Vollhardt & Twali, 2016; p. 136). To this end, in a recent study by Bañales and colleagues (2021), anger toward injustice was positively associated with critical reflection and interpersonal critical action. Emotions such as hope are also expected to be positively connected to reflection, motivation, and action, whereas emotions such as fear or shame are expected to be a hindrance (DiAngelo, 2018; Freire, 1970; Wallin-Ruschman, 2018).

Given the relevance of emotions to critical consciousness, social and emotional development has recently been introduced as a potential promoter of this process. Social and emotional development refers to an individual's ability to understand their own and others' emotions, to manage and express their emotions effectively, and to form and sustain positive relationships with others (Salovey & Mayer, 1990). More specifically, social and emotional development has been conceptualized to include five competencies: self-awareness (e.g., identifying personal emotions), self-management (e.g., regulating emotions), social awareness (e.g., perspective-taking and understanding different cultures), relationship skills (e.g., communicating clearly, actively listening, and working collaboratively), and responsible decision-making (e.g., identifying and solving problems; CASEL, 2022; Jagers et al., 2019). Scholars argue that these skills should enable youth to acknowledge complex societal realities and critically engage with the world around them (Jagers et al., 2019; Vollhardt & Twali, 2016).

## Promotive Contexts

Contexts are understood to inform and structure youth's critical consciousness development. Indeed, inherent to theories of critical consciousness is the idea that contexts can serve oppressive functions that individuals must analyze and act against (Ginwright & James, 2002). Contexts which serve an oppressive function can be more proximal (e.g., noninclusive school policies) or more distal (e.g., national anti-immigration policies). Research on this topic has consistently linked oppression in one's context to critical consciousness development. For example, Tyler and colleagues (2020) found that youth often noticed disparities in their proximal contexts, such as those in their schools and communities, sometimes linking these disparities to larger systems. Kennedy and colleagues (2020) similarly found that discriminatory policies and rhetoric enacted by the Trump administration – a distal context – sparked some adolescents' critical reflection, motivation, and action.

Supportive contexts are likewise expected to lead to increased critical consciousness development. In this regard, Freire (1970) noted that classrooms could be key sites for instigating critical consciousness if teachers used a radical or revolutionary pedagogy. In this approach, teachers are not seen as "experts" but instead as coinvestigators who learn alongside students. Teachers focus on relationship-building and open dialogue, actively engaging with students' concerns and questions. Indeed, past research indicates that schooling factors connected to the Freirean approach, such as problem-posing education practices and an open classroom climate, are associated with higher critical reflection, motivation, and action among students (Godfrey & Grayman, 2014; Rapa et al., 2022; Schwarzenthal et al., 2022; Seider et al., 2021). Watts and Guessous (2006) similarly identified that other antioppressive socialization practices should promote youth's critical consciousness development as well. For instance, youth whose parents more frequently talked to them about politics and oppression also had higher levels of critical reflection (Bañales et al., 2020; Diemer, 2012; Diemer et al., 2009, 2006; Diemer & Li, 2011). More recently, Heberle and colleagues (2020) introduced the concept of a consciousness-raising system: an environment that is characterized by antioppressive norms and one where youth are regularly provided with the opportunity to engage in critical consciousness. These scholars suggested that youth's critical consciousness may manifest differently from one context to the next depending on the norms, values, and culture of that context.

## Daily Processes: A Missing Link

Existing theories offer an important framework for researchers to draw on when seeking to understand individual differences in long-term critical consciousness development. In other words, existing theories describe how and under what conditions critical consciousness is expected to develop within youth across a span of years. Yet, a core assumption of lifespan human development is that individuals and their contexts are not fixed but fluctuate over short time intervals (Baltes et al., 1988). Despite this, current theorists have yet to explicitly propose how critical consciousness manifests and changes within youth across a span of days, weeks, or months. Although current theories do not offer explicit models for how youth engage in critical consciousness across short time periods, the extant literature nonetheless describes critical consciousness in this way. For instance, Turner-Essel (2013) notes that people "use critical consciousness to navigate the settings and contexts of their daily lives" (p. 54).

Daily process models (e.g., Almeida, 2005) focus on describing the ebb and flow of daily life. The creation of a daily process model that is specific to critical consciousness can therefore be used to address the existing gap in theory. These models often are concerned with both between- and within-person differences. Between-person differences reference the ways in which one person might differ from another person in their daily experiences, beliefs, and behaviors. Within-person differences reference the ways in which a person might differ from themselves from one day to the next or from one situation to the next. Some research has explored daily between- and within-person aspects of critical consciousness, and this work can be used to inform a Daily Process Model of Critical Consciousness.

## RESEARCH ON DAILY CRITICAL CONSCIOUSNESS

### Qualitative Research

Most research that has explored daily critical consciousness has been qualitative. This research finds that some people engage in critical action in waves or cycles (Hagen et al., 2018). Indeed, young activists have described periods of time in which they spent countless hours planning social justice initiatives and other periods of time in which they focused their energy on different endeavors such as school or family (Vaccaro & Mena, 2011). Additionally, qualitative research has shown that the same individuals engage in critical consciousness in certain situations but not others (Bogart et al., 2017; Tyler et al., 2020; Vaccaro & Mena, 2011). Careful decisions about if and when to engage in critical action may be protective. To this end, youth may feel it is important to "pick their battles" and not respond to every instance of oppression via critical action to avoid burnout (Vaccaro & Mena, 2011).

Qualitative researchers have also taken an applied approach to actively promote youth's daily engagement in critical consciousness through facilitating youth participatory action research (YPAR) programs. YPAR programs provide youth with the opportunity to investigate and address social problems in partnership with researchers over the course of multiple weeks or months (Anyon et al., 2018). In this way, youth participate in scaffolded forms of daily critical consciousness throughout their involvement in the YPAR program. As an example, Smith and Hope (2020) facilitated a YPAR program among Black adolescent boys. Throughout this program, some youth began to acknowledge racial disparities present in their daily lives at their school – an important step toward critical reflection. Furthermore, YPAR programs have been found to promote youth's overall awareness of injustice in society and support larger feelings of efficacy to bring about social change (Anyon et al., 2018; Shamrova & Cummings, 2017). This extant qualitative research offers insight into the daily cadencing of critical consciousness as well as how daily processes might inform longer-term development.

## Quantitative Research

In addition, quantitative research has begun to explore how critical consciousness is a dynamic, situation-specific, and daily process (Hyers, 2007; Oosterhoff et al., 2020, 2021; Wray-Lake et al., 2019). For example, in a study conducted by Oosterhoff and colleagues (2020), young people were asked to report on whether they had engaged in standard political behavior (e.g., expressing a political opinion on social media) and social movement behavior (e.g., participating in a protest) once a day for seven consecutive days in the period surrounding the US 2018 midterm election. They found that individuals varied in their standard political and social movement behavior from one day to the next. Additionally, on days when individuals engaged in more standard political behavior and social movement behavior, they also had a stronger sense of purpose that day. Past research such as this highlights how daily variation in critical consciousness might connect to daily variation in other domains. Additionally, these examples further underscore the need for a theoretical model that is specific to microlongitudinal processes of critical consciousness.

## Daily Process Model of Critical Consciousness

We aim to extend existing theories and build on past research by introducing the Daily Process Model of Critical Consciousness. This model includes five testable propositions that can serve as a guiding path toward understanding and exploring daily critical consciousness. Figure 9.1 provides a visualization of this model. This model is by no means absolute but provides a framework and starting point for further investigation and refinement. Here, we detail each proposition included in the model and discuss the figure in depth.

### PROPOSITION 1: CRITICAL CONSCIOUSNESS VARIES WITHIN YOUTH FROM ONE DAY TO THE NEXT

As a foundational part of this proposition, we recognize that critical consciousness exists in both trait and state forms. *Critical consciousness traits* are the aspects of critical reflection, motivation, and action that represent defining

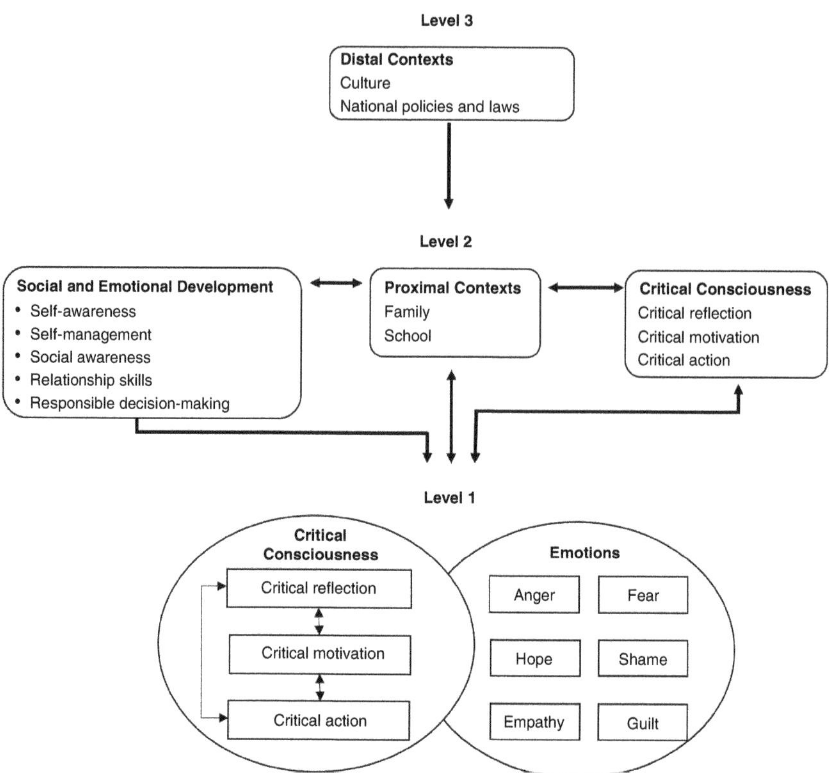


FIGURE 9.1 Conceptual model for studying daily critical consciousness.

*Note.* Level 1 depicts youth's day-to-day within-person experiences. Under Level 1 and to the left, the boxes labeled "critical reflection," "critical motivation," and "critical action" represent critical consciousness states. The double-headed arrows between these boxes represent daily interrelations (Proposition 1). Level 2 and 3 represent larger or slower-changing factors. The box labeled "critical consciousness" under Level 2 represents the idea that youth differ from one another in the trait-like development of critical consciousness. The double-headed arrow between this box and Level 1 represents the idea that critical consciousness traits inform states and vice versa (Proposition 2). The two overlapping circles under Level 1 (labeled "critical consciousness" and "emotions") represent the idea that critical consciousness states and emotional states connect to one another (Proposition 3). The boxes in the right circle are examples of emotional states. Under Level 2, the box labeled "social and emotional development" represents the idea that youth differ from one another in these skills. The single-headed arrow from this box to Level 1 depicts that between-persons differences in these skills shape youth's daily processes (Proposition 4). The boxes labeled "proximal contexts" and "distal contexts" under the Level 2 and 3 headings represent the idea that youth are embedded in contexts that have different characteristics. The single-headed arrow connecting Level 3 to Level 2 represents how distal contexts inform and structure Level 2 factors. The double-headed arrows between the boxes under Level 2 represent how these factors interact with one another. The double-headed arrow between the box labeled "proximal contexts" and Level 1 depicts the ways in which contextual characteristics shape youth's daily processes and vice versa (Proposition 5).

characteristics of a person and are relatively stable over time and across situations. In this regard, a trait-level form of critical reflection might pertain to the degree to which an individual acknowledges the existence of oppression overall in our society. This is the form of critical consciousness that has received the most attention in research and theory to date. In comparison, *critical consciousness states* refer to a person's engagement in critical reflection, motivation, and action on a particular day or in a particular situation. An example of a state-level form of critical reflection is when an adolescent recognizes that they are receiving misinformation about US history during a class lesson and attributes this practice to the larger cultural project of settler colonialism. We hypothesize that youth experience meaningful and significant within-person variation in critical consciousness states.

We further hypothesize that states of critical reflection, motivation, and action inform one another. For example, a person's engagement in critical action on one day should be connected to their other critical consciousness states on that day and/or in the surrounding days. Although microlongitudinal interrelations are not expected to perfectly mirror macrolongitudinal ones, we expect that the basic premise that these constructs support one another should hold at the state level as well. In Figure 9.1, Proposition 1 is represented under the Level 1 heading on the left. The boxes labeled "critical reflection," "critical motivation," and "critical action" represent the existence of critical consciousness states. The double-headed arrows between these boxes represent the idea that each of these states informs one another.

## PROPOSITION 2: DAILY CRITICAL CONSCIOUSNESS PROCESSES CONNECT TO LONG-TERM CRITICAL CONSCIOUSNESS DEVELOPMENT

As part of this proposition, we suggest that intraindividual variability in critical consciousness states informs larger critical consciousness change and development. For example, extreme oscillations between states of high critical motivation and low critical motivation may represent a risk factor and negatively impact youth's long-term critical consciousness development. Indeed, scholars in other fields have long emphasized how the cumulative effect of daily experiences and processes can impact individuals' overall development (see Almeida, 2005). As the second part of this proposition, we further hypothesize that trait-like development in critical consciousness informs intraindividual variability and change in critical consciousness states. For example, youth with a greater overall awareness of oppression (trait-like critical reflection) may be better able to identify and analyze oppression as it occurs in their daily lives (state-like critical reflection). In Figure 9.1, Proposition 2 is visualized under the Level 2 heading. The box labeled "critical consciousness" refers to the notion that adolescents differ from one another in terms of their long-term critical consciousness development (i.e., traits). The double-headed arrow connecting this box to the Level 1 heading represents the idea that critical consciousness traits and states both inform one another.

## PROPOSITION 3: EMOTIONS ARE AN INTEGRAL ASPECT OF DAILY CRITICAL CONSCIOUSNESS PROCESSES

Just as with Proposition 1, this proposition is built on the idea that the emotional dimension of critical consciousness exists in trait and state forms (e.g., Zelenski & Larsen, 2000). *Emotional traits* refer to the emotions that a person typically experiences when they engage in critical reflection, motivation, or action. For instance, Bañales and colleagues (2021) explored the emotional trait of anger toward injustice by asking youth to report on whether they typically feel angry when they think about inequalities. *Emotional states* are the emotions that a person experiences on a particular day or in a particular situation and can be applied to the emotional experience associated with participation in critical reflection, motivation, or action. In this regard, youth may experience an emotional state in the form of an immediate rush of anger after attributing their class lesson (from the previous example) to settler colonialism. We suggest that youth's engagement in daily critical consciousness can be best understood while also attending to youth's emotional states. More specifically, we posit that critical consciousness states both inform and are informed by emotional states. We further suggest that youth's emotional states impact the associations between daily critical reflection, motivation, and action. In Figure 9.1, Proposition 3 is visualized under the Level 1 heading on the right. The circle labeled "emotions" refers to adolescents' daily and situation-specific emotional states. This circle overlaps with the circle labeled "critical consciousness" to represent the connection between emotions and adolescents' daily engagement in critical consciousness. Boxes in this circle are examples of emotional states (though not all encompassing).

## PROPOSITION 4: BETWEEN-PERSON DIFFERENCES IN SOCIAL AND EMOTIONAL DEVELOPMENT IMPACT YOUTH'S DAILY CRITICAL CONSCIOUSNESS

As an underlying component of this proposition and the one that follows, we hypothesize that youth differ from one another in terms of their daily engagement in critical consciousness. In this regard, we suggest that critical consciousness states connect to and inform one another differently within different youth. Similarly, emotional states should connect to critical consciousness states differently within different youth. This is because human development is specific rather than universal (Bornstein, 2017). We further hypothesize that differences in within-person variation can be predicted by differences in the five core competencies of social and emotional development (CASEL, 2022). Youth who have a stronger social and emotional skill set overall should be better able to actively and effectively engage in daily critical consciousness compared to youth who have a less strong social and emotional skillset.

Skills such as self-awareness and self-management in particular should promote engagement in sustainable and healthy forms of critical action. Changing long-standing oppressive systems is difficult, and those who are attempting to do so fail many times, which can be disheartening and frustrating (e.g., Linder et al., 2019). Additionally, continuous participation in critical action can be emotionally draining and lead to burnout (Vaccaro & Mena, 2011). Self-awareness and self-management skills should enable youth to be better able to process disappointments associated with combatting systems of oppression, leading to more sustained engagement in action. These skills should also equip youth with the ability to identify the frequency and intensity of engagement in critical action that is most sustainable for them as well as decide if and when they might need to step back for a period of time to take care of themselves or reassess the healthiest way for them to engage in action. Relationship and decision-making skills should similarly enable youth to engage in critical action more effectively. In this regard, youth with these skills should be better able to work as a team with others on a critical action project, identify realistic and explicit goals for their critical action project, and understand how to achieve these goals.

For youth who experience privilege,[3] we posit that the skills of self-awareness, self-management, and social awareness should also support their ability to engage in critical reflection meaningfully and deeply. Phenomena such as white fragility and white centering highlight how people who experience privilege often struggle with authentic critical reflection, instead being consumed by their own emotions of fear, shame, entitlement, guilt, and the like (DiAngelo, 2018; Saad, 2020). As such, self-awareness, self-management, and social awareness should enable youth from positions of privilege to recognize their feelings and process them in order to instead focus on the feelings and experiences of people who are marginalized. In Figure 9.1, Proposition 4 is visualized under the Level 2 heading. The box labeled "social and emotional development" refers to the notion that adolescents differ from one another in these skill sets. The single-headed arrow connecting this box to the Level 1 heading represents the idea that differences in these skills should predict differences in youth's daily processes.

[3] Privilege refers to having unearned societal advantages. Youth are not uniformly "privileged" or "marginalized." Instead, they often experience privilege in some ways and marginalization in others.

## PROPOSITION 5: CHARACTERISTICS OF YOUTH'S CONTEXTS IMPACT THEIR DAILY CRITICAL CONSCIOUSNESS

We posit that youth will display different levels of engagement in daily critical consciousness depending on the overarching characteristics of the contexts in which they are embedded. More specifically, we expect that youth will be more actively involved in daily forms of critical reflection when they are situated in contexts (e.g., schools and communities) that are characterized by regularly occurring overt injustices and subordination. Contexts such as these necessitate critical reflection more often than those where injustices are less common. Additionally, overt forms of oppression (e.g., open hostility toward people of color) are easier to identify and analyze given their explicit nature than covert ones (e.g., using exclusively pictures of white students in educational materials). Youth may therefore actively recognize and critique oppressive dynamics, situations, and experiences as they are occurring in these contexts without significant intervention or support.

Although oppressive contexts might spur youth's daily critical reflection even without explicit support, we further posit that being embedded in a consciousness-raising system should lead youth to engage in more nuanced forms of daily critical reflection. These systems provide youth with the opportunity to have their critiques validated. Additionally, we expect that consciousness-raising systems will promote youth's daily critical motivation and action, enabling them to translate their reflection into action more readily. Although many contexts may be relevant, we focus on the school and family contexts as examples. A *consciousness-raising school* refers to a school where social justice and liberation are core values, where teachers use Freirean pedagogical practices (e.g., open dialogue and problem-posing), where students are provided information about injustice, where the social expectation is that injustice must be addressed through action (i.e., social justice norms; Torres-Harding et al., 2012), and where school leaders (e.g., teachers and administrators) are responsive to and welcoming of change efforts from students. Although some schools may display all these characteristics, it is likely that many schools only display some, if any. In these scenarios, we expect Freirean pedagogical practices and information about injustice to especially promote youth's daily critical reflection, responsive leadership to promote critical motivation, and social justice norms to promote critical action.

A *consciousness-raising family* similarly refers to a family in which the parents value social justice, regularly discuss the realities of oppression with their children, emphasize the importance of participating in critical action, and are actively engaged in critical consciousness themselves. Just as with schools, some parents may display all these characteristics, whereas others may only display one or two, if any. As such, we expect discussions about oppression to be particularly impactful on daily critical reflection, given that conversations and authentic dialogue are cornerstones of Freire's praxis. Additionally, we expect that adolescents will be better equipped to participate in critical action when their parents emphasize the importance of critical action and are actively involved in critical consciousness themselves. This is because parents' active engagement in critical consciousness can provide youth with an example of how to go about interacting with the world and creating change. Indeed, past research has found that some adolescents look to their parents as role models for how to respond to injustice (Tyler et al., 2020). Additionally, other work has found that adolescents who were engaged in critical action often had parents who were actively involved in social change efforts as well (Matlock & DiAngelo, 2015). Connections between contextual characteristics such as these and daily critical consciousness are similarly likely informed by the social and emotional skills discussed in Proposition 4 as well as by between-person differences in trait-level critical consciousness.

In Figure 9.1, Proposition 5 is visualized under the Level 2 and Level 3 headings. The boxes labeled "distal contexts" and "proximal contexts" under these headings refer to the notion that adolescents are embedded in different contexts: some of which are more immediate and others which are more broad. The single-headed arrow connecting Level 3 to Level 2 represents the idea that distal contexts can interact with and inform proximal contexts, trait-level critical consciousness, and the development of social and emotional skills. The double-headed arrows between the boxes "social and emotional development," "proximal contexts," and "critical consciousness" under the Level 2 heading represent how these factors interact with one another. The double-headed arrow connecting the box labeled "proximal contexts" to the Level 1 heading represents the idea that differences in these contexts should predict differences in youth's daily processes. This arrow also signifies that youth's daily processes inform and impact their contexts.

## STUDYING DAILY CRITICAL CONSCIOUSNESS USING INTENSIVE REPEATED MEASURES DESIGNS

The Daily Process Model of Critical Consciousness can be tested via intensive repeated measures designs,[4] or those that include five or more measurement occasions across a short time period, such as a week or a month (Bolger & Laurenceau, 2013). In these designs, individuals report their experiences, perspectives, and actions at each measurement occasion. Collecting densely spaced data using these designs could capture processes related to critical consciousness as they unfold in real time and could be used to model critical consciousness at a granular level (Bolger et al., 2003; Bolger & Laurenceau, 2013).

[4] Also referred to as "slice of life methods" (Smyth et al., 2017).

## TYPES OF DESIGNS

The two most common types of intensive repeated measures designs are ecological momentary assessments (EMA; Bolger & Laurenceau, 2013; Lischetzke, 2014; Smyth & Heron, 2014) and daily diaries. In EMA designs, data are collected from participants regarding their contexts, perspectives, and behaviors at a particular moment across a span of one or multiple weeks (Bolger & Laurenceau, 2013; Hektner et al., 2007; Smyth & Heron, 2014). EMA data can be collected in a time-based, event-based, or continuous format. Time-based approaches are the most common form of EMA and are those in which self-report data are collected at random or at pre-established measurement occasions multiple times per day (e.g., morning, afternoon, and evening). In event-based approaches, self-report data are collected every time an event takes place (e.g., when a stressor occurs). In continuous-format approaches, data are passively collected, usually across minutes or seconds (e.g., actigraphy).

In daily diary studies, self-report data are collected from participants once a day across one or more weeks. Typically, diary data are collected across consecutive days. At each measurement occasion, participants report on the last twety-four hours via methods such as telephone calls, journals, online surveys, and mobile apps. Data can be quantitative (e.g., fixed-response questions) or qualitative (e.g., open-ended questions). For example, the Daily Inventory of Stressful Experiences (DISE: Almeida et al., 2002) asks individuals whether or not a type of stressor occurred on that day (yes/no) and, if so, to describe what happened (subjective meaning of the stressors). Diary methods enable researchers to detect how processes fluctuate across days and for whom.

EMA and daily diary designs are useful for studying intraindividual and microlevel processes for several reasons. First, they can provide extremely fine-tuned information about the dynamic nature of phenomena across short time periods (Smyth et al., 2017). Second, these designs also often increase ecological validity because data are collected as individuals go about their lives within their natural environment, enabling researchers to truly understand a person's life "as it is lived" (Bolger et al., 2003). Third, the in-the-moment timeframe of EMA designs and the end-of-day reports in diary designs reduce recall bias and cognitive burden for participants reporting on their experiences.

Both EMA and daily diary designs would be appropriate approaches for studying microlevel processes of critical consciousness; however, our model focuses on day-to-day processes rather than within-day or moment-to-moment processes. Although within-day variability may be an important future direction in critical consciousness research, it is first crucial to understand daily-level processes and change. Therefore, we propose that daily diaries would be a particularly useful initial approach in understanding critical consciousness at a microlevel and we will focus on daily diaries moving forward. However, we encourage other researchers to theorize about momentary manifestations of critical consciousness and within-day processes.

## DATA COLLECTION CONSIDERATIONS

To ensure data quality and rigor, there are several factors related to data collection procedures that should be considered. In this regard, diary studies are only effective when data are collected across the time window in which the phenomenon of interest occurs and when enough data are collected within that time window to be powered to model said process (Hektner et al., 2007). Researchers therefore need to determine beforehand if there are specific time periods when daily engagement in critical consciousness is most likely to occur. We suggest that researchers collect data on days surrounding potential initiating events, including interventions, elections, and policy changes or initiatives. These events may occur in distal and/or proximal contexts. Indeed, events in youth's distal context can instigate critical consciousness both directly and indirectly through influencing the structure of and events taking place in youth's proximal contexts.

Researchers should also make an effort to proactively identify the needed spacing and minimum number of assessments necessary to answer their research questions pertaining to the Daily Process Model of Critical Consciousness. For example, researchers may choose to collect data once per day, once every few days, or once a week. Researchers may also choose to collect data, for example, across five measurement occasions, fourteen occasions, or over thirty occasions. Different research questions might lead to different decisions about the spacing and minimum number of assessments. Given the limited past scholarship explicitly on the pace of daily variability in critical consciousness, more frequent assessments are appropriate (Collins, 2006). Therefore, to start we recommend that researchers collect data once per day across multiple consecutive days.

Ideally, researchers would collect data across a span of at least two weeks (i.e., fourteen or more measurement occasions). A span of two or more weeks is more likely to capture the critical consciousness processes of interest than say, a span of five days. To this end, in the few quantitative studies that have explored daily critical consciousness, researchers found that youth typically engaged in critical action a few times per week (Oosterhoff et al., 2020). Studies that span two or more weeks are therefore better positioned to capture youth's engagement in critical action and to better estimate youth's person-means of critical action. Similarly, past qualitative research suggests that some people describe critical reflection as constant and impossible to turn off, while others note that they need to make an explicit effort to recognize issues of oppression (Turner-Essel, 2013). We propose that a span of two weeks should be able to capture and provide suitable estimates for both experiences. Further, statistically speaking, data collected each day across two weeks would allow for a broad range of analyses: from an exploration of person-means and variation to contemporaneous and lagged within-person associations to modeling trajectories. We also encourage researchers to solidify their plan for the spacing, minimum number of assessments, and time frame based on input from youth (e.g., interviews and focus groups) and based on pilot testing (Hektner et al., 2007).

Another key factor to consider when collecting data is obtaining participant input and buy-in and reducing participant burden. Taking part in a time-intensive study is another responsibility in participants' already busy lives, and unnecessarily densely spaced or thorough data collection may feel burdensome to participants and could result in high levels of missingness and attrition (Hektner et al., 2007). One strategy to maintain high response rates throughout data collection is to use a graded incentive scale, whereby participants receive a higher incentive once they meet a certain number of completed assessments. Similarly, finding ways to make data collection as simple and noninvasive as possible would be useful. For example, researchers might consider collecting data via phone apps and providing participants with text-based reminders. In addition, given the required investment, researchers may need to articulate the benefits of participation in this specific type of study design to obtain strong participant buy-in and to foster participant motivation to stay engaged.

## DAILY MEASUREMENT OF CRITICAL CONSCIOUSNESS

In addition to data collection procedures, adequate measurement is another essential factor influencing how effective daily diary studies are for testing the Daily Process Model of Critical Consciousness. There are a growing number of self-report measures that are designed to assess critical consciousness (e.g., Diemer et al., 2017; Johnson et al., 2019; Rapa et al., 2020), and other existing measures that could be used to assess components of critical consciousness (e.g., Social Issues Advocacy Scale; Marszalek et al., 2017). For example, critical reflection has been measured by asking youth to indicate how aware they are of various inequalities, and critical action has been measured by asking youth to indicate how frequently they have engaged in a range of behaviors over the past year (Diemer et al., 2017). Some measures of critical consciousness have pertained to a specific type of oppression, such as racism, whereas others have focused on social and political inequalities more generally. Although current measures have several strengths, they are only able to assess more trait-like forms of critical consciousness and cannot assess state-like forms.

Consequently, researchers will need to develop operational definitions for state-like forms of critical consciousness. For example, critical reflection states could be operationalized as the degree to which an individual thought about how inequalities and injustices were connected with larger structures that day. Using this operationalization, critical consciousness might be measured via an open-ended question addressing their experiences and thoughts that day about inequalities, which would then be coded for varying levels of critical reflection. In operationalizing and measuring daily critical consciousness, it is important to differentiate between the constructs themselves and constructs which tap into other related processes. For example, behaviors that support daily critical reflection (e.g., reading a book about oppression) should not be used themselves as a measure of critical reflection. Time spent thinking about an experience of racism would similarly not be a sufficient measure of critical reflection given that it may represent daily rumination. Instead, accurate operationalizations of critical reflection necessitate making a connection between conditions and larger oppressive systems or structures. In Table 9.1, we provide ideas for how researchers might define and operationalize critical reflection, motivation, and action at the daily level. In the first column, we list the three primary critical consciousness constructs. In the second column, we identify common trait-like operationalizations of each construct that are noted in the literature. In the third column, we take common trait-like operationalizations and provide suggestions for how they might be adapted or transformed to indicate state-like or daily operationalizations. In the final column, we offer examples of how researchers might go about measuring these constructs.

Ideally, researchers would also involve the population of interest in the measurement development process. Given the limited amount of daily critical consciousness research, a mixed method design could be a useful approach for measurement development. For example, by starting with semistructured interviews, researchers could learn about how youth define daily critical reflection, motivation, and action. In turn, researchers could use this information to create quantitative items or open-ended questions that best match youth's definitions and daily experiences. This kind of approach increases validity and minimizes potential sources of measurement error. Researchers may also consider carefully adapting existing measures of critical consciousness to meet these needs or may consider adapting existing daily measures of adjacent constructs, such as daily stressors and related affect measured in the Daily Inventory of Stressful Experiences (DISE; Almeida et al., 2002).

## TYPES OF ANALYSES THAT CAN BE CONDUCTED WITH DIARY DATA

Quantitative daily diary data are commonly analyzed via multilevel modeling (also known as hierarchical linear modeling; Hoffman & Stawski, 2009), which would be a useful approach for testing many aspects of the Daily Process Model of Critical Consciousness. Multilevel models are useful

TABLE 9.1 Examples of daily operationalizations of critical consciousness

| Construct | Construct Definition | Daily Operationalizations | Daily Diary Measurement Examples |
|---|---|---|---|
| Critical Reflection | Identifying, analyzing, and problematizing the oppressive features of reality. | Identifying how an experience, situation, or condition is connected to a larger system of oppression on a given day<br>Spending time on that day interrogating how one's own biases, reactions, and assumptions are rooted in oppression. | Open-ended questions which ask participants to describe any thoughts they had about social inequality that day as well as what instigated those thoughts. Responses could be coded for evidence of varying degrees of critical reflection. |
| Critical Motivation | Being committed to creating a more equitable reality.<br>Believing that one can have a positive impact on oppressive features of reality. | Feeling a sense of obligation or drive that day to engage in critical action.<br>Beliefs that day related to whether one could have a positive impact on oppressive features of reality. | Closed-ended question(s) pertaining to the degree to which youth felt obligated to challenge oppression or promote social justice that day.<br>Closed-ended question(s) pertaining to the degree to which youth felt like they could positively impact larger oppressive systems that day or effectively intervene in a situation that day. |
| Critical Action | Behaving in ways which are designed to have a positive impact on oppressive features of reality. | Spending time engaging in behaviors that day that are designed to promote social justice or address oppression. | Open-ended questions which ask participants to describe any actions or behaviors they engaged in that day that were designed to promote social justice or address oppression. Responses could be coded for the type and amount of participation in critical action.<br>A checklist of behaviors on which participants could mark which actions they participated in each day as well as how much time they spent engaging in each behavior. |

because they can partition variance into within-person and between-person components using two equations: the Level 1 equation and the Level 2 equation. The Level 1 equation is used to represent the smallest sampling unit, and the Level 2 equation represents a larger sampling unit in which Level 1 is nested. Take, for example, a daily diary study where youth complete self-report questionnaires once a day for two weeks. In this example, days (Level 1) are nested in youth (Level 2). Level 1 therefore pertains to the extent to which an individual youth deviates from their own average on any given day, also known as within-person variance. Level 2 represents between-person variance, or how average levels of a variable differ from one youth to another.

Researchers who wish to incorporate qualitative daily diary data (e.g., open-ended questions) into a multilevel model would first need to analyze it through an approach such as a content analysis. In a content analysis, researchers aim to identify and summarize the presence and prevalence of various words or core concepts and their meanings in text (Patton, 2002). For example, researchers could use content analysis to identify the prevalence, frequency, and depth of youth's daily critical reflection. This quantified information could then be included in a multilevel model. Qualitative data could also be used to explore the Daily Process Model of Critical Consciousness without quantification or incorporation into a multilevel model. In this regard, qualitative data from diaries each day can be used to understand daily processes in a more in-depth and exploratory manner.

## IMPLICATIONS FOR RESEARCH, PRACTICE, AND POLICY

Taken together, theories of critical consciousness and previous research largely focus on the long-term development of critical consciousness and differences between youth; however, little is known about how engagement in critical consciousness differs within youth from one day to the next. We developed a daily process model to address this gap. Our hope is that this model will be a useful tool for understanding the daily experiences of youth and inform future research, policy, and practice.

### Research

A focus on daily critical consciousness could significantly expand scholarship by providing information about intraindividual change, an essential component of human development (Baltes et al., 1988). Research guided by the model we put forth in this chapter could offer insight into the ways in which state-like manifestations of critical consciousness might be situation-specific and related to youth's emotions, social and emotional skills, and contexts. In this respect, the exploration of this model could further the field's understanding of how youth differ from themselves from one day to the next, as well as how their daily experiences differ from each other. Additionally, this line of research could offer insight into how youth engage in critical consciousness in different settings and how they respond to current events connected to oppression in real time. These events may occur in their proximal environments, such as a lesson at school. Events could also be larger, such as sociopolitical movements (e.g., Black Lives Matter), tragedies or crises (e.g., the Pulse nightclub shooting), or changes in programs and policies (e.g., Deferred Action for Childhood Arrivals [DACA]).

Daily diaries represent an underutilized methodological approach in critical consciousness scholarship that is particularly useful for exploring the model proposed in this chapter. Through the use of daily diary designs, researchers can be statistically powered to test this model, specifying how critical consciousness manifests in the short term within individuals and groups in a way that is responsive to emergent and changing contexts. Research using daily diaries could therefore contribute to further refinement and theory building. Additionally, a deeper understanding of the daily nuances of critical consciousness can inform both practice and policy.

## Practice

Research on our model can aid in the creation and refinement of interventions and practices that support youth's well-being and critical consciousness development as well as the goals of liberation. Findings from daily diary studies could be used to inform the implementation of efforts targeting various systems, including families and schools. For instance, research that identifies how parents help or hinder their children's critical consciousness as well as which antioppressive parenting practices are most effective, and for whom they could be useful, when creating parenting education programs. Parenting education program developers could use this information to create a curriculum that enables parents to best support their children. Similarly, in regard to schooling, research on daily critical consciousness could be used to inform the utilization of Freirean practices, curricula focused on social and emotional learning, and curricula focused on marginalized perspectives and the realities of oppression. Daily studies that are conducted within existing interventions and practice settings (e.g., classrooms, school clubs, and community organizations) would be especially able to provide detailed information regarding if and how program activities impact youth's engagement in critical consciousness. To this end, daily diary studies can help determine what works, when, for whom, and in what contexts so that practices across schools, homes, and communities can be enhanced to meet the needs of youth to combat oppression more effectively. Ultimately, developing and improving current practices to ensure sensitivity to individual youth's real-time experiences will support both youth well-being and larger efforts focused on collective liberation.

## Policy

Daily studies of critical consciousness also have the potential to impact policy. Policies exist at many levels (e.g., school district, state, and national) and often uphold the status quo. For example, zero-tolerance school policies and the presence of school resource officers contribute to funneling youth of color into prisons. Teachers and other authority figures consistently identify and interpret minor infractions by youth of color as more problematic than the same infractions by white youth, making it so that zero-tolerance policies largely serve to push youth of color out of schools and expose them to the criminal legal system (Palmer, 2019). As another example, recent legislation in a number of US states has banned the use of critical race theory in K-12 schools, which has translated to the banning of books that reflect diverse identities (e.g., LGBTQ+ youth) and to narrowing the lens through which subjects are taught so that the curriculum largely reflects racist narratives which exclude the perspectives, full histories, and experiences of people of color (Sawchuk, 2021). Decisions to uphold oppressive policies and limit antioppressive efforts such as these have often been informed by opinion and convenience rather than grounded in evidence and research. Research which speaks to how these issues connect to youth's daily lives could therefore be used in advocacy efforts.

More specifically, research that describes how youth engage in critical consciousness each day in the varying situations and contexts of their lives can highlight youth's perspectives about how certain policies contribute to oppression and areas where there are gaps in policy. This research can also provide empirical evidence regarding how policies impact youth, detailing which ones are supportive or harmful, why, and to whom. For instance, research could be used to highlight youth's experiences regarding zero-tolerance policies or the presence of school resource officers and how these factors can negatively impact youth's daily lives. In turn, this work could inform revised district policies related to discipline as well as policies regarding the relationship between law enforcement and schools.

To be most effective, researchers should ensure that findings from daily studies can be easily translated for and disseminated to policymakers. Additionally, researchers should make an effort to directly engage and collaborate with policymakers to identify meaningful and relevant questions as well as opportunities to share findings in a timely manner (Bogenschneider et al., 2019). In turn, having access to research on critical consciousness will better enable policy makers and others in positions of power to make informed decisions that contribute to the dismantling of oppression.

## CONCLUSION

In this chapter, we described how daily critical consciousness studies could be leveraged to strengthen the field's understanding of how youth conceptualize and interface with oppression as they move through life within an ever-evolving social and political landscape. Although youth interface with oppression continuously, little is known about how they engage in critical consciousness daily or how this process manifests across different situations and contexts. The conceptual model for studying daily critical consciousness presented in this chapter, including the model's five propositions, can be used to inform next directions in critical consciousness research with implications extending to practice and policy. Research that uses intensive repeated measures – specifically daily diary studies – can capture and reflect this complexity, thereby providing important information about how youth engage in this process and how to best support them across the contexts of their lives. Taken together, a focus on daily critical consciousness has the potential to positively impact scholarship toward the goal of collective liberation and ensuring that all youth can thrive.

## REFERENCES

Almeida, D. M. (2005). Resilience and vulnerability to daily stressors assessed via diary methods. *Current Directions in Psychological Science*, *14*(2), 64–68. https://doi.org/10.1111/j.0963-7214.2005.00336.x.

Almeida, D. M., Wethington, E., & Kessler, R. C. (2002). The daily inventory of stressful events: An interview-based approach for measuring daily stressors. *Assessment*, *9*(1), 41–55. https://doi.org/10.1177/1073191102091006.

Anyon, Y., Bender, K., Kennedy, H., & Dechants, J. (2018). A systematic review of youth participatory action research (YPAR) in the United States: Methodologies, youth outcomes, and future directions. *Health Education & Behavior*, *45*(6), 865–878. https://doi.org/10.1177/1090198118769357.

Bañales, J., Aldana, A., Richards-Schuster, K. et al. (2021). Youth anti-racism action: Contributions of youth perceptions of school racial messages and critical consciousness. *Journal of Community Psychology*, *49*(8), 3079–3100. https://doi.org/10.1002/jcop.22266.

Bañales, J., Marchand, A. D., Skinner, O. D. et al. (2020). Black adolescents' critical reflection development: Parents' racial socialization and attributions about race achievement gaps. *Journal of Research on Adolescence*, *30*(2), 403–417. https://doi.org/10.1111/jora.12485.

Baltes, P. B., Reese, H. W., & Nesselroade, J. R. (1988). *Introduction to research methods: Life-span developmental psychology*. Lawrence Erlbaum Associates.

Bogart, L. M., Dale, S. K., Christian, J. et al. (2017). Coping with discrimination among HIV-positive Black men who have sex with men. *Culture, Health & Sexuality*, *19*(7), 723–737. https://doi.org/10.1080/13691058.2016.1258492.

Bogenschneider, K., Corbett, T. J., & Parrott, E. (2019). Realizing the promise of research in policymaking: Theoretical guidance grounded in policymaker perspectives. *Journal of Family Theory & Review*, *11*(1), 127–147. https://doi.org/10.1111/jftr.12310.

Bolger, N., Davis, A., & Rafaeli, E. (2003). Diary methods: Capturing life as it is lived. *Annual Review of Psychology*, *54*(1), 579–616. https://doi.org/10.1146/annurev.psych.54.101601.145030.

Bolger, N., & Laurenceau, J-P. (2013) *Intensive longitudinal methods: An introduction to diary and experience sampling research*. The Guilford Press.

Bornstein, M. H. (2017). The specificity principle in acculturation science. *Perspectives in Psychological Science*, *12*(1), 3–45. https://doi.org/10.1177/1745691616655997.

Collaborative for Academic, Social, and Emotional Learning [CASEL] (2022). What Is the CASEL Framework? https://casel.org/fundamentals-of-sel/what-is-the-casel-framework/.

Collins, L. M. (2006). Analysis of longitudinal data: The integration of theoretical model, temporal design, and statistical model. *Annual Review of Psychology*, *57*, 505–528. https://doi.org/10.1146/annurev.psych.57.102904.190146.

DiAngelo, R., (2018). *White fragility: Why it's so hard for white people to talk about racism*. Beacon Press.

Díaz, K. (n.d.) *Paulo Freire*. https://iep.utm.edu/freire/.

Diemer, M. A. (2012). Fostering marginalized youths' political participation: Longitudinal roles of parental political socialization and youth sociopolitical development. *American Journal of Community Psychology*, *50*, 246–256. https://doi.org/10.1007/s10464-012-9495-9.

Diemer, M. A., Frisby, M. B., Pinedo, A. et al. (2020). Development of the Short Critical Consciousness Scale (ShoCCS). *Applied Developmental Science*, 1–17. https://doi.org/10.1080/10888691.2020.1834394.

Diemer, M. A., Hsieh, C., & Pan, T. (2009). School and parental influences on sociopolitical development among poor adolescents of color. *The Counseling Psychologist*, *30*(2), 317–344. https://doi.org/10.1177/0011000008315971.

Diemer, M. A., Kauffman, A., Koenig, N., Trahan, E., & Hsieh, C. A. (2006). Challenging racism, sexism, and social injustice: Support for urban adolescents' critical consciousness development. *Cultural Diversity and Ethnic Minority Psychology*, *12*(3), 444–460. https://doi.org/10.1037/1099-9809.12.3.444.

Diemer, M. A., & Li, C. H. (2011). Critical consciousness development and political participation among marginalized youth. *Child Development*, *82*(6), 1815–1833. https://doi.org/10.1111/j.1467-8624.2011.01650.x.

Diemer, M. A., Pinedo, A., Bañales, J. et al. (2021). Recentering action in critical consciousness. *Child Development Perspectives*, *15*(1), 12–17. https://doi.org/10.1111/cdep.12393.

Diemer, M. A., Rapa, L. J., Park, C. J., & Perry, J. C. (2017). Development and validation of the Critical Consciousness Scale. *Youth & Society*, *49*(4), 461–483. https://doi.org/10.1177/0044118X14538289.

Diemer, M. A., Rapa, L. J., Voight, A. M., & McWhirter, E. H. (2016). Critical consciousness: A developmental approach to addressing marginalization and oppression. *Child Development Perspectives*, *10*(4), 216–221. https://doi.org/10.1111/cdep.12193.

Freire, P. (1970). *Pedagogy of the oppressed* (M. B. Ramos, Trans.). Continuum.

Ginwright, S., & James, T. (2002). From assets to agents of change: Social justice, organizing, and youth development. *New Directions for Youth Development, 96* (2022), 27–46.

Godfrey, E. B., & Grayman, J. K. (2014). Teaching citizens: The role of open classroom climate in fostering critical consciousness among youth. *Journal of Youth and Adolescence, 43*(11), 1801–1817. https://doi.org/10.1007/s10964-013-0084-5.

Hagen, W. B., Hoover, S. M., & Morrow, S. L. (2018). A grounded theory of sexual minority women and transgender individuals' social justice activism. *Journal of Homosexuality, 65*(7), 833–859. https://doi.org/10.1080/00918369.2017.1364562.

Heberle, A. E., Rapa, L. J., & Faragó, F. (2020). Critical consciousness in children and adolescents: A systematic review, critical assessment, and recommendations for future research. *Psychological Bulletin, 146*(6), 525–551. https://doi.org/10.1037/bul0000230.

Hektner, J. M., Schmidt, J. A., & Csikszentmihalyi, M. (2007). *Experience sampling method: Measuring the quality of everyday life*. Sage.

Hoffman, L., & Stawski, R. S. (2009). Persons as contexts: Evaluating between-person and within-person effects in longitudinal analysis. *Research in Human Development, 6*(2–3), 97–120. https://doi.org/10.1080/15427600902911189.

Hyers, L. L. (2007). Resisting prejudice every day: Exploring women's assertive responses to anti-Black racism, anti-Semitism, heterosexism, and sexism. *Sex Roles, 56*(1), 1–12. https://doi.org/10.1007/s11199-006-9142-8.

Jagers, R. J., Rivas-Drake, D., & Williams, B. (2019). Transformative social and emotional learning (SEL): Toward SEL in service of educational equity and excellence. *Educational Psychologist, 54*(3), 162–184. https://doi.org/10.1080/00461520.2019.1623032.

Jemal, A. (2017). Critical consciousness: A critique and critical analysis of the literature. *The Urban Review, 49*(4), 602–626. https://doi.org/10.1007/s11256-017-0411-3.

Johnson, N. L., Walker, R. V., & Rojas-Ashe, E. E. (2019). A social justice approach to measuring bystander behavior: Introducing the critically conscious bystander scale. *Sex Roles, 81*(11), 731–747. https://doi.org/10.1007/s11199-019-01028-w.

Kennedy, H., Matyasic, S., Schofield Clark, L. et al. (2020). Early adolescent critical consciousness development in the age of Trump. *Journal of Adolescent Research, 35*(3), 279–308. https://doi.org/10.1177/0743558419852055.

Linder, C., Quaye, S. J., Stewart, T. J. et al. (2019). "The whole weight of the world on my shoulders": Power, identity, and student activism. *Journal of College Student Development, 60*(5), 527–542. https://doi.org/10.1353/csd.2019.0048.

Lischetzke, T. (2014). Daily diary methodology. In A. C. Michalos (Ed.), *Encyclopedia of quality of life and well-being research*. Springer, pp. 1413–1419.

Marszalek, J. M., Barber, C., & Nilsson, J. E. (2017). Development of the social issues advocacy scale-2 (SIAS-2). *Social Justice Research, 30*(2), 117–144. https://doi.org/10.1007/s11211-017-0284-3.

Matlock, S. A., & DiAngelo, R. (2015). "We put it in terms of not-nice": White antiracists and parenting. *Journal of Progressive Human Services, 26*(1), 67–92. https://doi.org/10.1080/10428232.2015.977836.

Oosterhoff, B., Hill, R. M., & Slonaker, N. J. (2020). Longitudinal associations between civic engagement and interpersonal needs during the 2018 US midterm elections. *Applied Developmental Science, 26*(2), 290–302. https://doi.org/10.1080/10888691.2020.1787169.

Oosterhoff, B., Whillock, S., Tintzman, C., & Poppler, A. (2021). Temporal associations between character strengths and civic action: A daily diary study. *The Journal of Positive Psychology*, 1–13. https://doi.org/10.1080/17439760.2021.1940247.

Palmer, G. (2019). Role of zero tolerance policies in school-to-prison pipeline: Does zero tolerance help or harm students of color? https://www.psychologytoday.com/us/blog/achieving-excellence-through-diversity-in-psychology-and-counseling/201905/role-zero-tolerance.

Patton, M.Q. (2002). *Qualitative, research & evaluation methods*. Sage Publications.

Poteat, V. P., Godfrey, E. B., Brion-Meisels, G., & Calzo, J. P. (2020). Development of youth advocacy and sociopolitical efficacy as dimensions of critical consciousness within gender-sexuality alliances. *Developmental Psychology, 56*(6), 1207–1219. https://doi.org/10.1037/dev0000927.

Rapa, L. J., Bolding, C. W., & Jamil, F. M. (2020). Development and initial validation of the Short Critical Consciousness Scale (CCS-S). *Journal of Applied Developmental Psychology, 70*, 1–10. https://doi.org/10.1016/j.appdev.2020.101164.

Rapa, L. J., Bolding, C. W., & Jamil, F. M. (2022). (Re)examining the effects of open classroom climate on the critical consciousness of preadolescent and adolescent youth. *Applied Developmental Science, 26*(3), 471–487. https://doi.org/10.1080/10888691.2020.1861946.

Saad, L. F. (2020). *Me and white supremacy: Combat racism, change the world, and become a good ancestor*. Sourcebooks, Inc.

Salovey, P., & Mayer, J. D. (1990). Emotional intelligence. *Imagination, Cognition and Personality, 9*(3), 185–211. https://doi.org/10.2190/DUGG-P24E-52WK-6CDG.

Sawchuk, S. (2021). What is critical race theory, and why is it under attack? www.edweek.org/leadership/what-is-critical-race-theory-and-why-is-it-under-attack/2021/05

Seider, S., Graves, D., El-Amin, A. et al. (2021). The development of critical consciousness in adolescents of color attending "opposing" schooling models. *Journal of Adolescent Research, 38*(1), 3–47. https://doi.org/10.1177/07435584211006466

Shamrova, D. P., & Cummings, C. E. (2017). Participatory action research (PAR) with children and youth: An integrative review of methodology and PAR outcomes for participants, organizations, and communities. *Children and Youth Services Review, 81*, 400–412. https://doi.org/10.1016/j.childyouth.2017.08.022.

Smith, C. D., & Hope, E. C. (2020). "We just want to break the stereotype": Tensions in Black boys' critical social analysis of their suburban school experiences. *Journal of Educational Psychology, 112*(3), 551–566. https://doi.org/10.1037/edu0000435.

Smyth, J. M., & Heron, K. E. (2014). Ecological momentary assessment (EMA) in family research. In S. McHale, P., Amato, & A. Booth (Eds), *Emerging methods in family research* (pp. 145–161). Springer.

Smyth, J. M., Juth, V., Ma, J., & Sliwinski, M. (2017). A slice of life: Ecologically valid methods for research on social relationships and health across the life span. *Social and Personality Psychology Compass*, *11*(10), e12356. https://doi.org/10.1111/spc3.12356.

Schwarzenthal, M., Juang, L. P., Moffitt, U., & Schachner, M. K. (2022). Critical consciousness socialization at school: Classroom climate, perceived societal islamophobia, and critical action among adolescents. *Journal of Research on Adolescence*, 1–18. https://doi.org/10.1111/jora.12713.

Torres-Harding, S. R., Siers, B., & Olson, B. D. (2012). Development and psychometric evaluation of the Social Justice Scale (SJS). *American Journal of Community Psychology*, *50*(1), 77–88. https://doi.org/10.1007/s10464-011-9478-2.

Turner-Essel, L. D. (2013). Critical consciousness development of black women activists: A qualitative examination (Doctoral dissertation, University of Akron; Order No. 10631300). Available from ProQuest Dissertations & Theses Global. (1923893084).

Tyler, C. P., Olsen, S. G., Geldhof, G. J., & Bowers, E. P. (2020). Critical consciousness in late adolescence: Understanding if, how, and why youth act. *Journal of Applied Developmental Psychology*, *70*, 1–13. https://doi.org/10.1016/j.appdev.2020.101165.

Vaccaro, A., & Mena, J. A. (2011). It's not burnout, it's more: Queer college activists of color and mental health. *Journal of Gay & Lesbian Mental Health*, *15*(4), 339–367. https://doi.org/10.1080/19359705.2011.600656.

Vollhardt, J. R. & Twali, M. S. (2016). Emotion-based reconciliation requires attention to power differences, critical consciousness, and structural change. *Psychological Inquiry*, *27*: 2, 136–143. https://doi.org/10.1080/1047840X.2016.1160762.

Wallin-Ruschman, J. (2018). "I thought it was just knowledge but it's definitely a lot of guts": Exploring emotional and relational dimensions of critical consciousness development. *The Urban Review*, *50*(1), 3–22. https://doi.org/10.1007/s11256-017-0427-8.

Watts, R. J., & Flanagan, C. (2007). Pushing the envelope on youth civic engagement: A developmental and liberation psychology perspective. *Journal of Community Psychology*, *35*(6), 779–792. https://doi.org/10.1002/jcop.20178.

Watts, R. J., & Guessous, O. (2006). Sociopolitical development: The missing link in research and policy on adolescents. *Beyond Resistance*, 59–80.

Watts, R. J., & Hipolito-Delgado, C. P. (2015). Thinking ourselves to liberation?: Advancing sociopolitical action in critical consciousness. *The Urban Review*, *47* (5), 847–867. https://doi.org/10.1007/s11256-015-0341-x.

Wheeler, L., & Reis, H. T. (1991). Self-recording of everyday life events: Origins, types, and uses. *Journal of Personality*, *59*(3), 339–354. https://doi.org/10.1111/j.1467-6494.1991.tb00252.x.

Wray-Lake, L., DeHaan, C. R., Shubert, J., & Ryan, R. M. (2019). Examining links from civic engagement to daily well-being from a self-determination theory perspective. *The Journal of Positive Psychology*, *14*(2), 166–177. https://doi.org/10.1080/17439760.2017.1388432.

Zelenski, J. M., & Larsen, R. J. (2000). The distribution of basic emotions in everyday life: A state and trait perspective from experience sampling data. *Journal of Research in Personality*, *34*(2), 178–197. https://doi.org/10.1006/jrpe.1999.2275.

10

# Measurement and Analysis in Quantitative Critical Consciousness Research

## *Attending to the Complexities of Systems and Selves*

SARA K. JOHNSON, MATTHEW N. GEE, AUTUMN DIAZ, AND RACHEL HERSHBERG

Contemporary American society is marked by high levels of inequality in health, education, and employment, among many other aspects (Grusky & Hill, 2017). Although these inequalities are rooted in institutions and systems (Caliendo, 2021), individuals have the power to identify and disrupt these systems in order to promote a more just and equitable society. These beliefs and actions have been the topic of research in many fields, including (but not limited to) youth development (Ginwright & James, 2002), developmental psychology (Thomas et al., 2014), and education (Akom, 2009; Cammarota, 2007). A considerable amount of this research has drawn on the framework of critical consciousness (CC; Freire, 1970/2018).

The CC concept originates from the writings of Brazilian educator and philosopher Paulo Freire (1970/2018). Freire worked with laborers in Brazil who were both poor and illiterate and, therefore, excluded from many aspects of society. He aimed to teach them how to "read" in two different ways: first, to read *words* (i.e., become literate), and second, as part of that process, to read the *world* (i.e., reflect on their social positions, the social injustices they experienced, and the reasons for them). He described the process of CC as "reflection and action upon the world in order to transform it" (1970/2018, p. 51). Scholars have operationalized Freire's work into models for empirical research. For in-depth information about the historical origins and contemporary uses of the CC framework, we encourage readers to consult the excellent available resources, including (but not limited to) Diemer and colleagues (2016), Heberle and colleagues (2020), Jemal (2017), Watts and colleagues (2011), and other chapters in this edited collection.

In this chapter, we start from what is (at the time of this writing) the most common operationalization of CC. It includes three components: critical reflection (identifying systemic roots of inequalities; e.g., Watts et al., 2011), critical actions (behaviors intended to change those systems; e.g., Diemer et al., 2021), and either critical efficacy (belief that critical actions may result in change; e.g., Watts et al., 2003) or critical motivation (a commitment to address perceived inequalities or the importance placed on equality and justice; e.g., Diemer et al., 2020). Considerable research conducted using these models has provided important insights about how youth who are marginalized make sense of, and act against, oppressive systems. This chapter builds on this strong body of work to suggest directions for future CC theory and research.

Our discussion centers on and expands the idea that the CC framework involves concepts about both **systems** and **selves**. For the former, we mean the multiple and intersecting systems of oppression (e.g., racism, sexism, and classism) that historically and currently operate in the United States and globally (e.g., Caliendo, 2021; Cho et al., 2013; Watts et al., 2003). For the latter, we are referring to individuals' understandings of themselves and their social locations (e.g., McLean & Syed, 2015; Schwartz et al., 2011; Velez & Spencer, 2018). Neither systems nor selves are simple; they both have layers of complexity which are further complicated by their interrelationship. Qualitative methods have long engaged with such complexity, and qualitative CC scholarship certainly does so (e.g., Godfrey & Wolf, 2016; Hershberg & Johnson, 2019; Hope & Bañales, 2019). However, the complexities of systems and selves have received less attention in quantitative CC research.

In this chapter, we describe aspects of the complexities of systems and selves and provide recommendations for how they can be attended to in quantitative CC research. This discussion is organized in three sections: (1) the complexity of systems, (2) the complexity of selves, and (3) the complexity of relationships between systems and selves. Within each section, we highlight several main points about complexity. After brief descriptions of the main points, we describe some of our observations about whether and how that complexity has been addressed within CC scholarship. These **observations** are based primarily on our interpretations of quantitative research that is explicitly labeled by the authors as being conducted from a CC framework and/or using measures that are designated as ones that measure CC. The discussion of insights about current quantitative CC research is followed by **recommendations** for how these aspects of complexity can be incorporated into future studies. These recommendations include the integration of measures from related fields as well as examples from other studies and some of our ongoing work. These points, observations, and recommendations are overviewed in Table 10.1.

As part of this discussion, we think it is important for researchers to consider how their own positionalities (i.e., their "selves") relate to their approach to CC (i.e., their views on systems) and similar constructs. We chose to address that in part by making our positionalities explicit. This chapter was written by two faculty members and two graduate students, with backgrounds in a range of fields (including family studies, community-based research, health equity, and

TABLE 10.1 Summary of chapter points, observations, and recommendations

| Point | Observations | Recommendations |
|---|---|---|
| | **Part 1. Complexities of Systems** | |
| Multiple Systems of Oppression Exist | 1. Most quantitative CC research acknowledges multiple systems conceptually but not analytically. | 1. Be intentional about how (and which) systems are incorporated. |
| | 2. Measures of CC focus on oppression in general. | 2a. Develop and/or evaluate measures of CC components about specific systems. |
| | | 2b. Consider views of privilege as well as oppression. |
| | 3. CC research focuses on relations among CC components generally and not about specific systems. | 3. Investigate CC components within and between systems. |
| Systems of Oppression Intersect | 4. Most quantitative CC research acknowledges intersecting systems conceptually but not analytically. | 4a. Develop and/or evaluate measures of intersectional awareness. |
| | | 4b. Study the role of intersectional awareness in CC. |

| Point | Observation | Recommendation |
|---|---|---|
| | **Part 2 Complexities of Selves** | |
| Social Identities Are Interpreted by Individuals | 5. Quantitative CC research often uses simplified measures of social group identifications. | 5. Facilitate participants' self-identifications. |
| Social Group Identities are Dynamic and Developing | 6. Much quantitative CC research includes social group memberships as static categories. | 6. Include information about identity processes relevant to social group memberships. |

| Point | Observation | Recommendation |
|---|---|---|
| | **Part 3. The Relationship Between Systems and Selves** | |
| Differences Between Groups in Their Views of Systems | 7. There has been limited attention to the equivalence of CC measures among groups. | 7. Conduct measurement invariance testing before group comparisons are made. |
| | 8. Group membership is often included as "controls" within analyses. | 8. Expand strategies for investigating between-group differences. |
| Differences Within Groups in Their Views on Systems | 9. Few quantitative CC studies examine within-group variation. | 9. Consider samples of specific groups. |

TABLE 10.1 (*cont.*)

| Part 3. The Relationship Between Systems and Selves | | |
|---|---|---|
| **Point** | **Observation** | **Recommendation** |
| Youth Make Meaning of Systems in Their Lives | 10. Quantitative CC research emphasizes youth's perceptions of systems as external to themselves. | 10. Incorporate youth's views of their own groups and their relations to systems. |

educational studies). We represent various racial identifications (white, Latinx, and Asian), gender identifications (three cisgender women and one cisgender man), religious identifications (one Jewish person, one nonreligious person, and one spiritual person), and socioeconomic backgrounds (from working to middle class). Our commitment to scholarship and action aimed at promoting a more socially just world is informed by our lived experiences and values and our recognition of the pervasive, intractable, and tangible nature of oppression. We have conducted research and collaborative work aimed at better understanding and promoting aspects of CC among young people with diverse identities and in diverse social locations. Throughout that process, we have learned more about our own experiences of CC as well as CC-related topics. In that spirit, we share these observations and ongoing goals for CC research.

## PART 1. COMPLEXITY OF SYSTEMS

Systems of oppression are a defining concept in CC research. The framework is built on the idea that oppression exists and is systemic. Accordingly, all parts of the framework include explicit attention to systems of oppression: to what extent people identify these systems (critical reflection), whether and how they feel efficacious and/or motivated to do something to change those systems (critical efficacy and motivation), and what things they do to change those systems (critical action). Systems have many facets of complexity, two of which we highlight in this chapter: there are multiple systems of oppression, and these systems intersect.

### MULTIPLE SYSTEMS OF OPPRESSION EXIST

For several decades, scholars in youth development (Ginwright & James, 2002; Watts et al., 2003), alongside those from many other disciplines, have been vocal about the need to name, identify, and interrogate – not as an afterthought, but as a core focus of our work – the various and interlocking systems of oppression that are present in the lives of youth. Watts and colleagues (2003) wrote that oppression

> is the unjust use of power by one socially salient group over another in a way that creates and sustains inequity in the distribution of coveted resources . . . maintained and propagated through overt or material violence (i.e., physical coercion and terror, denial of rights and resources, restriction of mobility, etc.) and by subtle or ideological violence (i.e., institutionally codified racism, sexism, classism, heterosexism, and related practices). (p. 188)

Interlocking systems of oppression that they pointed to included racism, sexism, classism, and heterosexism. CC research continues to emphasize these instances of oppression, and other scholars have pointed to the need to address ableism (Shin et al., 2018), ruralism (Murry et al., 2020), transphobia (Parent & Silva, 2018), and cis-sexism (Shin et al., 2018).

## OBSERVATION 1. MOST QUANTITATIVE CC RESEARCH ACKNOWLEDGES MULTIPLE SYSTEMS CONCEPTUALLY BUT NOT ANALYTICALLY

From a conceptual perspective, CC researchers often describe the framework as being about oppression generally while also acknowledging the multiplicity of systems operating within the US and other national contexts. We did not identify many *quantitative* CC studies wherein the authors explicitly stated in the paper that they were focusing on specific systems of oppression (cf. Bañales et al., 2021; Parent & Silva, 2018; Shin et al., 2018). Instead, in many cases the systems of oppression being focused on are implicit in the choice of sample. As many others have noted (e.g., Godfrey & Burson, 2018; Heberle et al., 2020), much CC research (but certainly not all) has been conducted with low-income youth of color. Accordingly, many studies emphasize racism as a system of oppression as a framing for the study, alongside the presentation of CC as a general framework for thinking about and acting against oppression. One interpretation of those studies, then, is that the authors are interested in CC about racism, but that is only an inference without explicit acknowledgment by the authors.

### Recommendation 1. Be Intentional About How (and Which) Systems Are Incorporated

We encourage CC researchers to be explicit about how multiple systems of oppression are included in studies, including why they are focusing on some and – if applicable – leaving others out. It is important for researchers to contemplate whether they want to investigate CC generally or focus on particular forms of oppression depending on where they are doing their work and who the participants are (see, e.g., Aldana et al., 2019), or perhaps the systems of inequity that may seem most harmful at particular moments and places.

We also recognize a need to listen to participants about the systems of oppression that are salient to their experiences to complement researcher-driven interests. Aldana and Richards-Shuster (2021) have argued for the value of a youth-led approach specifically in antiracism work. In our research (e.g., Hershberg et al., 2022; Johnson & Hershberg, 2017), we have included attention to ableism and ruralism, as these areas of inequity were identified by participants and student researchers as prominent features of young adults' lives. In other ongoing projects, we have included survey questions where participants can tell us about the systems of oppression that are important to their lived experiences. This approach does not mean sacrificing attention to systems of oppression that researchers identify as harmful to young people (e.g., racism), but it does require being broad, inclusive, and flexible in the areas of oppression that are asked about or attended to from the outset of a study.

## OBSERVATION 2. MEASURES OF CC FOCUS ON OPPRESSION IN GENERAL

A more general approach to systems of oppression is also present in most CC measures. As part of our work for this chapter, we evaluated whether and how multiple systems of oppression were incorporated into measures that are explicitly labeled by the authors as being about CC. We present these observations in the following three sections, organized by CC component. See Table 10.2 for an overview of the eight measures that we reviewed. Overall, references to specific systems of oppression are infrequent in CC measures but vary based on CC component and between measures. We note that there are other relevant measures available that are not explicitly labeled as being about CC, and we include some of these in later recommendations.

**Critical Reflection.** Of the three CC components, critical reflection has received the most measurement attention. Seven measures we reviewed included items related to critical reflection – broadly defined as critical analysis of oppressive sociopolitical inequity, often involving recognition of the systemic and structural nature of such inequalities (Jemal, 2017; Watts et al., 2011). Some models of CC include a singular critical reflection concept (e.g., Watts & Flanagan, 2007), whereas others treat it multidimensionally. For example, Diemer et al.'s (2017) Critical Consciousness Scale (CCS) includes two subcomponents: perceived inequality (a cognitive component of recognizing structural inequalities) and egalitarianism (an emotional component about a belief in social equality). In later scales, beliefs in the importance of social equality have been incorporated into measures of critical motivation, which we address later.

Subscales of critical reflection contain the most references to specific systems of oppression (in comparison to efficacy, motivation, and action subscales). The most referenced are racism, sexism, and classism (with some

TABLE 10.2 Critical consciousness measures

| Scale | # Items | Critical Reflection | Critical Efficacy/ Motivation | Critical Action |
|---|---|---|---|---|
| Sociopolitical Consciousness Measure Baker & Brookins (2014) | 35 | *Sociopolitical awareness, Global belief in a just world, Collective responsibility for the poor, Equality and rights, Belief in collective action* | Localized community efficacy, Problem-solving self-efficacy | N/A |
| Critical Consciousness Inventory (CCI) Thomas et al. (2014) | 9 | Sociopolitical Development: *Equity and justice in society, Equitable treatment across social groups, Access to resources or educational opportunities for various groups* Social Perspective-Taking: *Empathy, Emotional reactions to oppression and inequity* | N/A | N/A |
| Measure of Adolescent Critical Consciousness McWhirter & McWhirter (2016) | 10 | N/A | Critical Agency | Critical Behavior |
| Contemporary Critical Consciousness Measure I Shin et al. (2016) | 19 | Critical Reflection: *Classism, Racism, Heterosexism* | N/A | N/A |
| Critical Consciousness Scale Diemer et al. (2017) | 22 | Critical Reflection: *Perceived Inequality, Egalitarianism* | N/A | Sociopolitical Participation |

TABLE 10.2 (*cont.*)

| Scale | # Items | Critical Reflection | Critical Efficacy/ Motivation | Critical Action |
|---|---|---|---|---|
| Contemporary Critical Consciousness Measure II Shin et al. (2018) | 37 | Critical Reflection: *Classism, Racism, Heterosexism, Ableism, Cis-sexism, Sexism* | N/A | N/A |
| Critical Consciousness Scale-Short Rapa et al. (2020) | 14 | Critical Reflection: *Perceived Inequality, Egalitarianism* | Critical Motivation | Sociopolitical Participation |
| Short Critical Consciousness Scale Diemer et al. (2020) | 13 | Critical Reflection: *Perceived Inequality* | Critical Motivation | Sociopolitical Participation |

*Note.* Italic font indicates subscales.

exceptions, described later in the chapter; Shin et al., 2016; 2018). For six of the measures (Baker & Baker, 2014; Diemer et al., 2017, 2020; McWhirter & McWhirter, 2016; Rapa et al., 2020; Thomas et al., 2014), the subscales for critical reflection contain items that are a mix of references to different systems. For example, of the eight critical reflection items in the CCS (Diemer et al., 2017), three reference racial inequity (e.g., "certain racial or ethnic groups have fewer chances to get a good high school education"), three reference socio-economic inequity (e.g., "poor people have fewer chances to get ahead"), and two reference gendered inequity (e.g., "women have fewer chances to get good jobs"). For analytical purposes, one of two approaches is typically used. Sometimes the items are specified as indicators of a single critical reflection latent variable, whereas in other cases the items are averaged for a subscale score. Both approaches result in one overall critical reflection score, which obscures the (potentially more nuanced) system-specific information.

Two measures that we reviewed include subscales about single systems. The Contemporary Critical Consciousness Measure (Shin et al., 2016) includes classism, racism, and heterosexism. Its successor, the Contemporary Critical Consciousness Measure II (Shin et al., 2018), includes those as well as ableism, cis-sexism, and sexism. These measures were created to facilitate computation of an overall critical reflection score in addition to system-specific scores. However, in developing these scales, Shin and colleagues (2018) used a bifactor model where each item is decomposed into two sources of variance (here, the general critical reflection factor and the system-specific critical reflection factor). These types of models can only be used within structural equation modeling analyses, so Shin and colleagues (2018) recommend that if observed scores are computed, only the overall score should be used. These decisions make sense from a statistical perspective but have some unfortunate consequences. Many researchers work with sample sizes that are too small for structural equation modeling, which typically require several hundred participants (Kline, 2015), so they are therefore limited to using only an overall critical reflection score, which (as we noted earlier) conceals system-specific information.

**Critical Efficacy and Motivation.** These two components are relatively new with respect to being named as such and included in CC measures, although similar constructs (e.g., political efficacy: Watts et al., 2011; sociopolitical control: Zimmerman & Zahniser, 1991) have long been addressed in related research. Four measures we reviewed included efficacy and/or motivation. Overall, the items are generally phrased; few specifically reference inequity, and a small number of items refer to specific systems as the target of such efficacy or motivation.

The Sociopolitical Consciousness Measure (Baker & Brookins, 2014) has subscales for localized community *efficacy* (e.g., "I can help organize solutions to problems that my community faces") and problem-solving *efficacy* (e.g., "I am able to solve most problems"). These subscales provide information about collective and individual efficacy, which are important dimensions, but the items are phrased generally and therefore leave out information about the specific areas of social change work about which people may feel more efficacious. The Measure of Adolescent Critical Consciousness (MACC; McWhirter & McWhirter, 2016) includes critical agency, which the authors conceptualize as both *efficacy* (e.g., "I can make a difference in my community") and *motivation* (e.g., "It is important to fight against social and economic inequality" and "I am motivated to end racism and discrimination") for engaging in critical actions. The critical agency items of the MACC refer to inequality generally as well as economic inequality and racism more specifically.

Critical *motivation* subscales are included on the Short Critical Consciousness Scale (ShoCCS; Diemer et al., 2022) and the Critical Consciousness Scale-Short (CCS-S; Rapa et al., 2020). The ShoCCS includes four items: one specifically mentions economic inequality ("It is important to correct social and economic inequality"), whereas the other three reference general participation ("It is my responsibility to get involved and make things better for society"). The CCS-S includes three of the same items as the ShoCCS, with one different item: "It is important to confront someone who says something you think is racist or prejudiced." This last item is an example of how items can be made more specific.

**Critical Action.** Four measures that we reviewed contained subscales for critical action, defined in most CC research as behaviors intended to address inequalities in society through sociopolitical change (Jemal, 2017; Watts et al., 2011). Critical action items on these measures include particular behaviors but do not reference specific systems. McWhirter and McWhirter (2016)'s MACC includes three items about participation in activities related to equality and justice (e.g., "I am involved in activities or groups that promote equality and justice"). In the CCS, items assess how often adolescents engage in individual and/or collective actions that could bring about social change. For example, some of the items are participated in a civil rights group or organization; participated in a political party, club, or organization; contacted a public official by phone, mail, or email to tell him or her how you felt about a social or political issue; joined in a protest march, political demonstration, or political meeting; participated in a discussion about a social or political issue; and signed an email or written petition about a social or political issue. Subsets of these items are used for the critical action subscales in the two short forms (ShoCCS, CCS-S) that have been created from the original CCS.

### Recommendation 2a. Develop and/or Evaluate Measures of CC Components About Specific Systems

As already described, CC-specific measures do not, for the most part, target specific systems. Accordingly, if we want to know more about how youth think about specific systems, there is a need for work in this area. Future theoretical work should include conceptualizing what CC components may look like with respect to different systems. In some cases, researchers may be able to draw on measures from other fields, and we provide a few suggestions about potential measures in the sections that follow. In other cases, measures may need to be developed or more carefully teased apart with attention to which items target specific systems, which are more general in nature, and how to analyze them accordingly. Regardless of the source of measures, researchers should carefully evaluate new measures or those that are adapted or used outside of their original settings (e.g., McCoach et al., 2013).

**Critical Reflection.** Given the significant measurement attention to critical reflection, work on this CC component could build on the measures already available. To be able to make separate subscales for different systems, at least three items are needed for each (Kline, 2015): for example, at least three items would need to be specifically about racism. Some CC measures already include at least three items for specific systems (e.g., Diemer et al.'s [2017] CCS includes three items related to racism), so researchers with data collected using those measures could test the viability of modeling those items as separate subscales. Researchers could also investigate the conditions under which the CCCMII (Shin et al., 2018) subscales could be used on their own, or whether modifications could be made to the items to make that possible. Our research team is also working on several subscales that could be used separately (e.g., Gee & Johnson, 2022; Hershberg et al., 2022).

To guide these measurement decisions, researchers should consider whether they want to focus on participants' analyses of inequality more generally or with respect to specific systems. It places a high burden on participants to answer many questions with slight differences in wording (e.g., referencing racism rather than sexism). Accordingly, researchers could include subscales for only the systems of interest in their study (once they have identified what these specific systems are, which ones will not be emphasized within a particular study, and why).

Researchers focusing on specific systems may want to look outside of CC work and toward research in their specific area of interest. For example, researchers interested in participants' views of racism could consider the Modern Racism Scale (McConahay, 1986), the Symbolic Racism 2000 Scale (Henry & Sears, 2002), the Color-Blind Racial Attitudes Scale (Neville et al., 2000), or subscales of the Everyday Multicultural Competencies/Revised Scale of Ethnocultural Empathy (Mallinckrodt et al., 2014). Researchers interested in participants' critical reflection about sexism could consider the Modern Sexism Scale (Swim et al., 1995; Swim & Cohen, 1997) or the Neosexism Scale (Tougas et al., 1995).

In other studies, it may be useful to incorporate shorter measures of critical reflection about inequality more generally. We see two ways to approach that. The first is using a general critical reflection score that has been created by combining items that may reference specific systems; this is what most CC research does, currently by computing an overall score using items about racism, classism, and other systems. The second approach is to use measures with items that are intentionally phrased generally without reference to specific systems. Given the complexity of systems, we suspect that these two approaches tap different aspects of critical reflection – in other words, participants' average level of awareness across racism, sexism, and classism may not be equivalent to their overall awareness of inequality. However, we are not aware of empirical tests of this proposition, and more research is needed in this area.

**Critical Efficacy and Motivation.** Many of the recommendations we made regarding critical reflection also apply to efficacy and motivation. Specifically, researchers can consider whether they want to focus on general or system-specific efficacy or motivation and adjust their measurement plan accordingly. Beyond those recommendations, we offer a few additional considerations about these two constructs.

On an overall level, we note that, as the "third component" (along with reflection and action), the terms "efficacy" and "motivation" have been used inconsistently within CC research. In some models, efficacy is mentioned, whereas others use motivation, and sometimes they are referred to as efficacy/motivation (i.e., interchangeably). However, efficacy and motivation are distinct constructs, each with entire fields of research. Our view is that both motivation (feeling that addressing systems of oppression is necessary and important) and efficacy (feeling that one can act to change or dismantle systems) are important for CC development, so we encourage CC researchers to consider them as separate constructs with different measures and to consult their respective bodies of research. For example, research on efficacy often distinguishes between internal and external efficacy (e.g., Morrell, 2003) or individual and collective efficacy (e.g., van Zomeren et al., 2004). There is also a large body of research on motivation that researchers could draw from such as self-determination theory and regulatory focus theory (May, 2022).

**Critical Action.** Critical action has an additional layer to consider, given that it includes behaviors rather than beliefs, and the range of potential behaviors is quite large. It is impractical to ask participants to answer questions about numerous behaviors for many different systems: for example, whether they have attended a protest about sexism, a protest about racism, a protest about transphobia, and so on. It may also be difficult for the participants to identify a specific system being targeted through a behavior, and some behaviors may target multiple systems. We offer two ideas about how to approach this measurement challenge, depending on whether researchers are interested in critical actions toward specific systems.

Researchers interested in specific systems have a few options for developing and/or adapting items. Some critical reflection items could be made more specific: for example, the CCS question about how often participants had "Contacted a public official by phone, mail, or email to tell him or her how you felt about a social or political issue" could be adapted to wording along the lines of "Contacted a public official by phone, mail, or email to express your views about addressing racist policies and practices." More general items about civic engagement could be adapted in this way as well. Another option is to look to the literature regarding those systems. For example, the Anti-Racist Behavioral Inventory (Pieterse et al., 2016) includes items measuring individual activism and institutional activism, and the Anti-Racism Action Scale (Aldana et al., 2019) measures actions that youth may take to challenge racism in three areas: interpersonal action, communal action, and political change action. The Feminist Activities Scale measures involvement in seventeen activities (e.g., "I am involved in feminist teaching and/or mentoring activities") (Szymanski, 2004). DeBlaere and colleagues (2014) adapted the Feminist Activities Scale to measure LGBQ activism.

Researchers who are interested in critical action, broadly defined, could consider asking participants about their civic actions in a more general sense (e.g., "Did you participate in a protest?") and then asking them what it was about and coding whether a specific system was mentioned. In our lab, we have been pilot testing a measurement approach in which participants can name the social issues that they care about and then complete questions about actions that they are targeting toward those social issues (e.g., Johnson et al., 2021).

### Recommendation 2b. Consider Views of Privilege as Well as Oppression

In our review of the content of measures explicitly labeled by the authors as being about CC, we also noted that the majority of items reference awareness of inequity in terms of awareness of oppression or minoritization, but part of understanding that people experience oppression means understanding that other individuals and groups experience privilege. We acknowledge the ongoing discussion within the CC literature around whether – and how – people can have CC about aspects of oppression that they do not personally experience (e.g., whether white people can develop CC about race; Christens et al., 2016; Diemer et al., 2015; Jemal, 2017), and we return to those questions in Part 3. Relationships Between Systems and Selves.

In this section, which focuses on systems, we draw attention to the idea that systems of oppression include not only oppression and marginalization but also power and privilege (e.g., Johnson, 2006; McIntosh, 2000). CC items focus primarily on the former, however, rather than the latter. Accordingly, CC researchers may want to develop additional items or draw from the larger research tradition around awareness of privilege and oppression (e.g., McClellan et al., 2019). For example, the Awareness of Privilege and Oppression Scale-2 (McClellan et al., 2019) has subscales based on racism, sexism, heterosexism, and classism. There are also system-specific measures, such as those that address white privilege (Pinterits et al., 2009) or male privilege (Case, 2007).

## OBSERVATION 3. CC RESEARCH FOCUSES ON RELATIONS AMONG CC COMPONENTS GENERALLY AND NOT ABOUT SPECIFIC SYSTEMS

There is substantial literature about the relations between critical reflection and action as well as the moderating roles of efficacy and/or motivation (for an overview, please see Heberle et al., 2020). In large part, these analyses have been conducted using the measures reviewed earlier, which means that the constructs were measured at a general (rather than system-specific) level. This level of analysis may be in part related to the mixed nature of findings about the interrelationships among CC components.

## Recommendation 3. Investigate CC Components Within and Between Systems

More system-specific measurement will enable researchers to explore how CC components relate to each other within and between systems in their data analyses. These questions could be approached in many ways; here, we highlight a few we have begun to address in our work.

One branch of future research could focus on *specific CC components across systems*. For example, researchers could conduct in-depth explorations of the nature and perhaps the sequence of critical reflection development. Some questions that could guide this work are: Do young people on average show more critical reflection about some systems than others? Is there more variation in young people's views of one system as compared to others? How closely related are scores regarding critical reflection for each of the systems? Some young people may be more aware of certain kinds of oppression (e.g., those that are prominent in public discourse or salient to their experiences) and may even actively dismiss some systems while acknowledging others.

There are also important questions about developmental sequencing that could be addressed within research on specific CC components, such as critical reflection. For example, when (e.g., at what ages) do young people begin to understand the idea of inequality as related to different systems (e.g., for some, perhaps first related to income inequality, and then perhaps pervasive racism), rather than in a more general sense (e.g., living in an unequal society)? What are the different ways that such a developmental progression might unfold? Such research can serve as a foundation for questions about whether people must first identify various systems of oppression individually (e.g., racism and sexism) before they can see that the systems intersect. When addressing these kinds of developmentally oriented questions, researchers must also take individual differences into account, some of which may be related to youth's own positionality within systems of oppression (a point we return to in Part 3 of this chapter).

In our own work (e.g., Hershberg et al., 2019), described briefly earlier, we developed several subscales related to critical reflection (e.g., racism, sexism, ableism, heterosexism, classism, and ruralism), using a mixed-methods participatory research design with a diverse sample of college students. We then explored the variation within the sample in scores on critical reflection domains as well as how these scores might be related to well-being, and we selected five cases for more in-depth exploration. There was so much variation with respect to participant's critical reflection about different systems that it was difficult to highlight one salient pattern despite only focusing on five participants at one university.

Another branch of future research could involve *investigating "cross-over" between CC processes for different systems*. It is often theorized in CC research that reflection–action processes in one domain can "spill" over into another domain. For example, through engagement in activism about one area of inequity, individuals' critical reflection about that area deepens while they also learn about other systemic inequities impacting fellow activists (e.g., Mathews et al., 2019). These types of hypotheses have not frequently been tested quantitatively, however.

## SYSTEMS OF OPPRESSION INTERSECT

The idea that there are multiple systems of oppression leads into the idea that these systems are "distinct but interlocking" (Collins, 1993, p. 36). This idea has received significant attention in developmental science through the incorporation of an intersectional perspective (Crenshaw, 1989). Broadly, an intersectional perspective emphasizes that a person's experience is impacted by their membership in multiple minoritized groups: for example, a Black woman's experience is different from a Black man's experience, even if they both experience racism. Crenshaw (1989) articulated this reality by highlighting that neither Black men nor white women's experiences of discrimination within the legal system reflected the nature of discrimination that Black women faced. Thus, just treatment of Black women under the law requires an understanding of their unique experiences, particularly related to their multiple minoritized identities and social positions. Crenshaw and others' (e.g., Collins, 1990) attention to intersectionality has enhanced the rigor of scholarship across many fields as well as the ways in which such scholarship has led to more socially just action and policy change.

Murry and colleagues' (2020) work, aimed at promoting the health and well-being of rural Black families, illuminates the importance of understanding and examining development for minoritized individuals, families, and communities in the context of interlocking systems of oppression that include racism, classism, sexism, and ruralism (among others). They point to the unique ways rural Black families experience poverty, limited employment opportunities, educational inequities, and healthcare barriers, and that these experiences are different from the suffering, resistance, and resilience of Black families in lower-income urban areas. As they note, the meaning-making systems differently minoritized individuals experience cannot easily be generalized from one group to the next. Rural Black youth who grow up in poverty, for example, have different goals and aspirations with respect to education compared to Black youth in urban communities despite both groups likely experiencing racism and significant educational inequities (Murry et al., 2020). In other words, research with one oppressed community, though it may have some experiences of minoritization in common with another, cannot be easily extrapolated to understand the experiences of the other, particularly in so far as awareness of systemic inequities, motivations to address such inequities, and engagement in social justice work is concerned. More attention to various interlocking systems of oppression, and how they differentially impact minoritized groups, is needed. This attention will produce more robust scholarship, and it is also necessary to ensure that research results are optimally appliable and able to effectively address pervasive social injustices (Cho et al., 2013; Ghavami et al., 2016).

### OBSERVATION 4. MOST QUANTITATIVE CC RESEARCH ACKNOWLEDGES INTERSECTING SYSTEMS CONCEPTUALLY BUT NOT ANALYTICALLY

Although there is agreement that an intersectional perspective on systems of oppression is important in CC research (e.g., Godfrey & Burson, 2018; Santos & Toomey, 2018), this perspective has less often been translated into specific measurement or analysis strategies (for exceptions, see Shin et al., 2016, 2018). An intersectional perspective can be incorporated into CC research in several ways. In this section about systems, we focus on one facet: how much individuals are themselves aware of how systems intersect (in later sections we provide more examples; see Godfrey and Burson [2018] for more suggestions).

We highlight this aspect specifically because it is a logical extension of the concept of critical reflection. Within the CC framework, critical reflection focuses on identifying the existence of systems of oppression. This awareness may, for some youth and in some contexts, be a precursor to understanding that systems intersect (whereas it may not be a necessary precursor for other youth or in other contexts). Accordingly, intersectional awareness may be a particular type of critical reflection.

#### Recommendation 4a. Develop and/or Evaluate Measures of Intersectional Awareness

The first step to include intersectional awareness as a component of CC is to have measures that address it. We found two such measures that CC researchers could consider using or adapting. The Political Consciousness Measure (Greenwood, 2008) was designed to measure women's intersectional and singular political consciousness. The authors describe intersectional political consciousness as the recognition of "multiple grounds of identity" in one's social analysis and activism (p. 38). An example item is "In order to achieve the changes we seek, we must fight racism as well as sexism." Singular consciousness, on the other hand, is the prioritization of "a single axis of social relations" (e.g., gender). An example item is "Poor women experience sexism in ways that are the same as middle-class women." Curtin and colleagues (2015) expanded on Greenwood's (2008) work to develop a measure of intersectional awareness, which they define as the degree to which individuals view different social hierarchies as intersecting. Their measure, following Greenwood's (2008) structure, has two subscales: intersectional awareness (e.g., "Understanding the experiences of women from different ethnic groups is important") and singular awareness (e.g., "Gender is the most important issue in women's lives"). These measures were, however, not developed specifically within a CC framework, so they may need to be expanded or adapted for use in the CC framework.

### Recommendation 4b. Study the Role of Intersectional Awareness in CC

It is important to assess the extent to which individuals are aware of the ways that systems of inequity intersect to differentially impact people's lives, as Murry and colleagues' work (2020) with rural Black families describes. However, we also recognize that even if individuals can intellectually describe interlocking systems of heterosexism, racism, and ableism, for example, there may still be domains of inequity that they are more strongly committed to addressing. Indeed, this form of awareness may also be possible only after experiencing some form of sustained engagement in critical action (Cho et al., 2013) wherein individuals engage with the different groups of people who are affected by (or sincerely concerned with) different forms of marginalization. Moreover, people may have only enough energy to devote their critical action to one issue at a time. More research is needed to understand the edges of people's understandings of inequities, and if, for example, the inequities people put their energies into addressing are conceptualized through a lens of intersectionality or are more myopic and/or reflective of a highly salient identity.

## PART 2. COMPLEXITY OF SELVES

The second broad area of complexity we highlight is related to individual people and their identities (i.e., selves). Although the concept of identity is studied in many fields (Vignoles et al., 2011), given our backgrounds and training we draw primarily from the developmental psychological literature. Within this literature, identity is broadly defined as the answers that a person gives to the fundamental questions of "who am I?" and "who do I want to become?" (McLean & Syed, 2015). The answers that people give to these questions are, in keeping with the theme of the chapter, complex and include many types of information (Johnson et al., 2022; McLean & Syed, 2015). This chapter highlights two complexities of selves that may be especially relevant for CC research. First, social identities are always being interpreted by individuals; second, social identities are dynamic and developing. We hope that scholars with different perspectives on identity will engage with these points and offer suggestions for other ways to incorporate the complexities of selves into CC work.

## SOCIAL IDENTITIES ARE INTERPRETED BY INDIVIDUALS

Within a developmental science perspective on identity, group memberships that are relevant to systems of oppression are typically categorized as social identities (Spears, 2011). These include racial, gender, and sexual orientation identifications (among many others). All people have social group memberships that locate them within specific systems of oppression in their context, regardless of whether they consciously or frequently consider those group memberships. A primary point being grappled with within CC research is the relationship between these social group identities and individuals' CC (Hershberg & Johnson, 2019; Jemal, 2017; Tyler et al., 2020). We return to that point in Part 3. The Relationship between Systems and Selves; here, we focus only on self-related information because that forms the basis of being able to address questions about how selves are related to views of systems.

### OBSERVATION 5. QUANTITATIVE CC RESEARCH OFTEN USES SIMPLIFIED MEASURES OF SOCIAL GROUP IDENTIFICATIONS

CC research (along with research on many other topics) has traditionally incorporated oversimplified measures of group membership. For example, many quantitative studies of CC use predetermined categories for racial identification (e.g., the categories used on the US Census). These categories may facilitate comparisons with other studies and reduce the need for additional coding and analyses, but many young people may identify outside of the most commonly provided categories. Young people have their own views, and make their own meanings, of their social positions (Hope & Spencer, 2017; Velez & Spencer, 2018). Some identifications or social group memberships may not be visible (e.g., some disabilities), whereas others may be, and, in still other cases, particular group memberships may be ascribed to people who do not identify with them (e.g., light-skinned Latine individuals who might be considered white but more strongly identify with their ethnicity or nationality instead).

### Recommendation 5. Facilitate Participants' Self-Identifications

The ways in which youth describe their social group identifications is related to their sociohistorical context, including whether there is an ethos of support for or rejection of such identities (e.g., often referred to as public regard; Hughes et al., 2011). Accordingly, these identifications – and the terminology used to refer to them – are likely to change even within short periods of time. CC researchers must pay attention to activism and scholarship efforts that address the changing landscape of how participants identify themselves, as this is also an active area of research in and of itself (e.g., Diemer et al., 2013; Hughes et al., 2016; Johnston et al., 2014; Lindqvist et al., 2020; Suen et al., 2020; Wolff et al., 2017). Opportunities for self-identification are important, especially if the categories will be used for group comparisons.

### SOCIAL GROUP IDENTITIES ARE DYNAMIC AND DEVELOPING

Social group identifications are not only situated within the sociohistorical context – and thereby within systems of oppression – but also are a developmental process that youth experience. Group memberships are relevant in childhood (e.g., Bennett & Sani, 2008) and tend to become more prominent during adolescence as part of identity development (e.g., Tanti et al., 2008), where the self-categorizations of childhood (e.g., "I am a girl") become the identifications of adolescence and adulthood (knowing more about what being a girl means, both personally and in the world). During adolescence (and throughout life), the ways in which people think about, and make meaning of, these memberships can change. Considerable research has focused on these processes, especially regarding ethnic/racial identification (e.g., Williams et al. 2020), gender identification (e.g., Bussey, 2011), and sexual orientation (e.g., Morgan, 2013).

### OBSERVATION 6. MUCH QUANTITATIVE CC RESEARCH INCLUDES SOCIAL GROUP MEMBERSHIPS AS STATIC CATEGORIES

Very little CC research has addressed identity processes related to social group memberships. Instead, these identifications are often included as static or unchanging categories as part of the description of the sample or within analyses (addressed in Part 3). A prominent exception is the work by Mathews et al. (2019), who mapped the connections between ethnic/racial identity development and CC among youth of color.

#### Recommendation 6. Include Information About Identity Processes Relevant to Social Group Memberships

From a CC perspective, the ways that young people think about social identities may be especially relevant for group memberships that confer privilege and marginalization in connection with systems of oppression.

We urge CC researchers to become familiar with and incorporate information from the literatures regarding identity development, especially with respect to social group identities related to their CC work.

## PART 3. THE RELATIONSHIP BETWEEN SYSTEMS AND SELVES

The complexities of systems and selves come together in CC research, given its attention to how aspects of young people's positionalities (e.g., their marginalization within specific systems) are related to their views of oppression (e.g., their identification of the existence of systemic inequality and actions against it). In this section, we address three ways that quantitative CC research could investigate the connections between systems and selves while also incorporating the complexity of each. The first is investigating differences between groups in their views of systems, the second is exploring differences within groups in views of systems, and the third is addressing how young people make meaning of systems in their own lives.

### DIFFERENCES BETWEEN GROUPS IN THEIR VIEWS OF SYSTEMS

One way to think about how the complexities of systems and selves come together is the extent and nature of group differences in CC processes. Such research is critically important for many reasons, not the least of which is that social justice work requires coalition-building across groups, which is facilitated by a more nuanced understanding of CC in different groups.

#### OBSERVATION 7. THERE HAS BEEN LIMITED ATTENTION TO THE EQUIVALENCE OF CC MEASURES AMONG GROUPS

A major prerequisite for conducting comparisons when groups complete the same measures is whether the measures are statistically equivalent between the groups (in other words, whether the measures are invariant; e.g., van de Schoot et al., 2012). If the items are not functioning similarly, then group comparisons can be misleading (e.g., Guenole & Brown, 2014). However, the articles about CC measures we reviewed for this chapter did not often include the results of measurement invariance testing across the group memberships that are considered most relevant for CC research (e.g., racial or ethnic identification, gender identification, and subjective social class). For example, all ethnic/racial groups were combined in the validation studies of specific measures (e.g., Diemer et al., 2017, 2020; Shin et al., 2016, 2018; Thomas et al., 2014), except where the scale was created for a specific group (e.g., Baker & Brookins, 2014; McWhirter & McWhirter, 2016). More recently, however, Rapa et al. (2020) established measurement invariance on the CCS-S separately by ethnic/racial, gender, and age groups.

### Recommendation 7. Conduct Measurement Invariance Testing Before Group Comparisons Are Made

In prior sections of this chapter, we included recommendations for several areas of future measurement work. As this research progresses, we urge researchers to also investigate whether measures of views about systems (e.g., critical reflection about multiple systems) have similar psychometric properties in light of the complexity of selves present in specific studies. For example, in our work we are developing subscales specifically with respect to critical reflection about sexism (Gee & Johnson, 2022). We are testing the items for measurement invariance based on gender identification while also considering the racial identification of participants (given that, e.g., women of color likely have different experiences of sexism compared to white women). We do not believe that a quantitative measure captures these complexities fully, but we want to make sure that the items we are using can be meaningful compared across groups before we do so.

By making this recommendation, however, we do not mean that the same measures should always be used in all groups in a study, or that between-group comparisons are always meaningful to make. Indeed, researchers may decide to use different measures for different groups or that between-group comparisons are not meaningful, depending on the research questions they are asking and/or even the participants in their work. In many cases, in-depth research with one general population of participants may be more prudent and more needed than between-group research. However, *if* researchers want to do between-group comparisons, attention should be given to measurement properties beforehand.

### Observation 8. Group Membership is Often Included as "Controls" Within Analyses

Many quantitative studies of CC include group membership as categorical predictors, or as covariates or "statistical controls." Although that strategy is commonplace within many disciplines, there are significant downsides to including group membership in this way (e.g., Martin & Yeung, 2003). For example, these approaches imply that there are differences only in mean levels of an outcome between groups. However, group differences may also be related to processes or configurations of elements of CC.

## Recommendation 8. Expand Strategies for Investigating Between-Group Differences

We encourage CC researchers to carefully consider how group memberships are included in analyses. One way to investigate between-group differences is to conduct tests of moderation or use multiple-group models. For example, Bañales and colleagues (2020) tested the relations between critical reflection, voting likelihood, social media engagement, and sociopolitical action among Latinx and Black young adults. They found different pathways between the two ethnic/racial groups, specifically that voting likelihood mediated the relation between critical reflection and social media engagement for Latinx young adults, whereas it was unrelated to sociopolitical action and social media engagement for Black young adults. In another example, Wray-Lake and colleagues (2020) examined levels of community service, political interest, and electoral participation across twelve years. Compared to the Latinx, Asian, and white youth in the sample, Black youth started and remained highest in community service and showed the greatest growth in political interest and electoral participation. A race × gender analysis revealed that Black women had more accelerated growth in electoral participation compared to other women.

Another direction for future research about group memberships is related to the privilege and marginalization they confer. CC was originally conceived of as a way to promote the well-being of oppressed peoples through recognizing and resisting their own oppression, and the initial applications within youth development were consistent with that emphasis (e.g., Ginwright & James, 2002; Watts et al., 2011). Since then, researchers have become interested in whether, and how, people can have CC about aspects of oppression that they do not personally experience (e.g., Christens et al., 2016; Diemer et al., 2015; Jemal, 2017). Indeed, some intersectionality scholars (thought certainly not all) have highlighted a framing of intersectionality that recognizes that many individuals' salient identities include *both* elements of privilege and minoritization (Cho et al., 2013; Cole, 2009). Some research suggests that individuals may be able to become more critically reflective and active about injustices that they do *not* experience due to their personal experiences of oppression that they *do* experience (Mathews et al., 2019). Accordingly, important directions for future research relate to how an individual's understanding of their own privilege and oppression might be a necessary first step in being able to be part of a collective movement for justice, including as an aspiring ally or coconspirator for groups that they are not a part of (Dull et al., 2021; Mathews et al., 2019). This process has been highlighted with respect to white youth and adults from low-income backgrounds (e.g., Hershberg & Johnson, 2019; Rogers et al., 2020), but future research could explore more varied and complex constellations of privilege and oppression when conducting analyses focused on between-group questions.

### DIFFERENCES WITHIN GROUPS IN THEIR VIEWS ON SYSTEMS

Spencer and colleagues (e.g., Spencer et al., 2006; Velez & Spencer, 2018) have long recognized that young people's understandings of all aspects of their developmental contexts, including the systems of inequity that they are marginalized and/or privileged by, are filtered through their unique meaning-making systems. Thus, two youths who may technically have been exposed to the same sources of oppression (and/or privilege) throughout their development will view and react to these systems differently (Velez & Spencer, 2018). This perspective highlights the need to focus on within-group variation in CC processes.

#### Observation 9. Few Quantitative CC Studies Examine Within-Group Variation

Many quantitative studies of CC have focused specifically on low-income youth of color, but fewer of those studies have focused on within-group variation (instead focusing on averages across the entire sample). Many studies have aggregated across other social identities that are present: for example, sexual and gender minority youth are included alongside youth from majority groups. In a recent exception, Dull and colleagues (2021) showed that there was significant within-group variation among a sample of white college students with respect to their experiences of white guilt and the extent to which such experiences appeared to motivate civic action. Youth who identified as women or sexual minorities appeared to have significantly higher white guilt than men and heterosexual youth, and when such individuals also had a high sense of social responsibility, these affective experiences were related to more engagement in social change work. This example shows how young people who are similar with respect to one social identity nonetheless vary not only in their levels of CC-related constructs but also in CC-related process.

#### Recommendation 9. Consider Samples of Specific Groups

One way to be able to delve into within-group variation is to focus an entire study on a single group, as Dull and colleagues (2021) did (see also Jager et al., 2017). This approach allows for more representation of groups that may typically be smaller (e.g., sexual or gender minority youth) and accordingly not likely to be large enough if not specifically recruited. Focusing on single groups also enables researchers to include group-specific measures, such as the measure of white guilt included by Dull et al. (2021).

An analytic strategy that can be employed to investigate within-group variation is to focus on unobserved heterogeneity (e.g., Johnson, 2021). Many methods in developmental science and related fields rely on observed variables to differentiate groups (e.g., racial or gender identification). However, it is likely that within any given sample (even samples of youth who from the outside appear to be the same), there are distinct groups of youth who are more similar to each other with respect to the variables under study. For example, in a sample of white youth, some may have high levels of critical reflection about several systems, some may have high levels of critical reflection only about classism, and a third group may have low levels of critical reflection about all systems that were asked about. These groupings cannot be known a priori but must instead be inferred through participants' responses to quantitative questions and analyzed using techniques such as mixture modeling (e.g., latent class and latent profile analyses).

## YOUTH MAKE MEANING OF SYSTEMS IN THEIR LIVES

We end this chapter by zeroing in on individual youth, who make meaning of both their group memberships and the systems that they are located within. Qualitative research excels at more idiographic analyses that highlight the experiences of specific youth and CC research from that perspective has certainly done that as well (e.g., Gómez & Cammarota, 2022; Hope & Bañales, 2019). It can be more difficult to address these individual-level meaning-making process in quantitative studies, but we should at least attempt to do so! Even if we cannot do this for all subgroups or participants in our work, doing it for some will enhance our research. Moreover, centering individual meaning-making in future research may enable us to utilize information already in some of our data sets.

### OBSERVATION 10. QUANTITATIVE CC RESEARCH EMPHASIZES YOUTH'S PERCEPTIONS OF SYSTEMS AS EXTERNAL TO THEMSELVES

To more directly address meaning-making, we must also recognize that much of our measurement work does not directly inquire about how youth understand themselves and their experiences with respect to the systems of inequity we are asking about. The quantitative CC measures that we reviewed, for example, all include items – especially for critical reflection – that are phrased with respect to the existence of systems but without any references to the person answering the questions. For example, items on the CCS include "certain racial or ethnic groups have trouble getting ahead." These items do not include information about how youth themselves may think about their own positions or roles within those systems or the way in which such systems have affected their lives (cf. Hope & Bañales, 2019). These understandings likely play a very important role in, for example, how youth make decisions about becoming involved in actions.

### Recommendation 10. Incorporate Youth's Views of Their Own Groups and Their Relations to Systems

There are a few ways that CC researchers could incorporate youth's own views in quantitative research where they cannot provide long-form answers. One option is to include some previously developed quantitative questions. For example, the Intersectional Privilege Screening Inventory (Pester et al., 2020) addresses race, class, gender, sexual orientation, religious identity, and ability through two sets of subscales: Identity Privilege (the extent to which individuals are aware of their privileges) and Socially Referenced Privilege (the type of privileges that individuals have, including representation, access to resources, safety and security, and sense of belonging).

A second option is to develop questions that explicitly ask participants about their perceptions of their own group(s), the extent to which they think their group has been oppressed, and the way that this has oppression specifically affected their lives. In our own work with Black- and white-identifying college students in the United States, we have asked participants to describe their understandings of the words "racism," "sexism," and "classism" (in a survey that also includes other CC-related measures). We are analyzing these responses, both inductively and deductively, to better understand what these words mean to the participants, how their meanings match up with ideas present in the literature, and what, if anything, their responses may tell us about how they see themselves within the systems they discuss. One way that we plan to address this latter question is through quantizing these open-ended responses and relating them to other CC-related measures (such as critical reflection). Our initial analyses have shown that for some participants, these words immediately signal an understanding of the systemic nature of inequity, whereas for others, interpersonal dynamics – including their own experiences of interpersonal discrimination – come to the fore more readily. If and how such variation in meaning-making around racism (regarding both systems and selves) may differentially relate to CC development will be an important question for our future analyses.

Researchers could also consider assessing if and how young people identify with (or *resist* identifying with) various identities and social positions and why. For example, some white youth – such as youth who are Jewish – might be resistant to identifying "white" as their race for complex reasons (e.g., for Russian Jewish immigrants, having been expelled from their countries of origin because they were believed to be a lesser religious and racial group). Of course, these experiences do not mean that Jewish individuals do not experience white privilege in the United States, or deny experiences of class mobility for some, even if they or their parents experienced significant discrimination. There may, therefore, be complicated meaning-making around what it means to be white for members of these groups. Asking participants to explain the identifications they choose, and those that they do not, can shed light on these meaning-making process and how they may be related to CC development.

## CONCLUSION

The CC framework has provided a compelling and useful way to approach research about how young people think about and work toward creating a more just world. As this research continues to move forward, it is important for it to take into account that the systems of injustice that shape youth's experiences are complex, as are young people's own senses of who they are as people. In this chapter, we highlighted several ways in which that complexity could be incorporated into quantitative CC research. We hope others will use these recommendations as inspiration for developing other ways that complexities of systems and selves can be addressed.

We recognize that these recommendations to address and enhance complexity in CC scholarship are not easy to follow nor necessarily efficient. However, we believe they are needed in order to address many questions about CC development for different groups and to engage people in thoughtful and sustainable socially just action. Moreover, asking these questions as part of the process of developing quantitative measures will enhance the rigor of our work and is in keeping with the values of contemporary developmental science (e.g., Kornbluh et al., 2021). Specifically, attending to these areas of complexity will allow us to continue to prioritize and stay true to our knowledge of interindividual and intraindividual differences in development as well as the powerful ways in which youth voice and agency can improve our society. We also hope that these recommendations may help researchers be more reflective about their own CC development and areas of inequity that they may (unwittingly) ignore.

This topic requires continuous revisiting as the sociopolitical context is rapidly changing and the developmental processes related to CC change in tandem. Youth have been at the forefront of political movements throughout history – and certainly within recent times as well. Old narratives about youth disengagement are changing, and youth are being recognized as the leaders and change agents they have always been. Our scholarship needs to catch up – and try to keep up – with these changes. This process of "keeping up" is likely to be improved through mixed methods research that allows youth to describe these concepts and issues in their own words. By using all available methods, we can better understand the complexity of who develops CC, when, and under what conditions so that the ability of all youth to thrive and contribute to a more just world can be realized.

## REFERENCES


Akom, A. A. (2009). Critical hip hop pedagogy as a form of liberatory praxis. *Equity & Excellence in Education*, *42*(1), 52–66. https://doi.org/10.1080/10665680802612519.

Aldana, A., Bañales, J., & Richards-Schuster, K. (2019). Youth anti-racist engagement: Conceptualization, development, and validation of an anti-racism action scale. *Adolescent Research Review*, *4*(4), 369–381. https://doi.org/10.1007/s40894-019-00113-1.

Aldana, A., & Richards-Schuster, K. (2021). Youth-led antiracism research: Making a case for participatory methods and creative strategies in developmental science. *Journal of Adolescent Research*, *36*(6), 654–685. https://doi.org/10.1177/07435584211043289.

Baker, A. M., & Brookins, C. C. (2014). Toward the development of a measure of sociopolitical consciousness: Listening to the voices of Salvadoran youth. *Journal of Community Psychology*, *42*(8), 1015–1032. https://doi.org/10.1002/jcop.21668.

Bañales, J., Aldana, A., Richards-Schuster, K. et al. (2021). Youth anti-racism action: Contributions of youth perceptions of school racial messages and critical consciousness. *Journal of Community Psychology*, *49*(8), 3079–3100. https://doi.org/10.1002/jcop.22266.

Bañales, J., Mathews, C., Hayat, N., Anyiwo, N., & Diemer, M. A. (2020). Latinx and Black young adults' pathways to civic/political engagement. *Cultural Diversity and Ethnic Minority Psychology*, *26*(2), 176–188. https://doi.org/10.1037/cdp0000271.

Bennett, M., & Sani, F. (2008). Children's subjective identification with social groups: A group-reference effect approach. *British Journal of Developmental Psychology*, *26*(3), 381–387. https://doi.org/10.1348/026151007X246268.

Bussey, K. (2011). Gender identity development. In In S. J. Schwartz, K. Luyckx, & V. L. Vignoles (Eds.), *Handbook of identity theory and research* (pp. 603–628). Springer. https://doi.org/10.1007/978-1-4419-7988-9_25.

Caliendo, S. M. (2021). *Inequality in America: Race, poverty, and fulfilling democracy's promise* (3rd ed.). Routledge.

Cammarota, J. (2007). A social justice approach to achievement: Guiding Latina/o students toward educational attainment with a challenging, socially relevant curriculum. *Equity & Excellence in Education*, *40*(1), 87–96. https://doi.org/10.1080/10665680601015153.

Case, K. A. (2007). Raising male privilege awareness and reducing sexism: An evaluation of diversity courses. *Psychology of Women Quarterly*, *31*(4), 426–435. https://doi.org/10.1111/j.1471-6402.2007.00391.x.

Cho, S., Crenshaw, K. W., & McCall, L. (2013). Toward a field of intersectionality studies: Theory, applications, and praxis. *Signs: Journal of Women in Culture and Society*, *38*(4), 785–810. https://doi.org/10.1086/669608.

Christens, B. D., Winn, L. T., & Duke, A. M. (2016). Empowerment and critical consciousness: A conceptual cross-fertilization. *Adolescent Research Review*, *1* (1), 15–27. https://doi.org/10.1007/s40894-015-0019-3.

Cole, E. R. (2009). Intersectionality and research in psychology. *American Psychologist, 64*(3), 170–180. https://doi.org/10.1037/a0014564.

Collins, P. H. (1990). *Black feminist thought: Knowledge, consciousness, and the politics of empowerment*. Routledge.

Collins, P. H. (1993). Setting our own agenda. *The Black Scholar, 23*(3/4), 52–55.

Crenshaw, K. (1989). Demarginalizing the intersection of race and sex: A Black feminist critique of antidiscrimination doctrine, feminist theory and antiracist politics. *University of Chicago Legal Forum, 140*(1), 139–167. http://chicagounbound.uchicago.edu/uclf/vol1989/iss1/8.

Curtin, N., Stewart, A. J., & Cole, E. R. (2015). Challenging the status quo: The role of intersectional awareness in activism for social change and pro-social intergroup attitudes. *Psychology of Women Quarterly, 39*(4), 512–529. https://doi.org/10.1177/0361684315580439.

DeBlaere, C., Brewster, M. E., Bertsch, K. N. et al. (2014). The protective power of collective action for sexual minority women of color: An investigation of multiple discrimination experiences and psychological distress. *Psychology of Women Quarterly, 38*(1), 20–32. https://doi.org/10.1177/0361684313493252.

Diemer, M. A., Frisby, M. B., Pinedo, A. et al. (2022). Development of the Short Critical Consciousness Scale (ShoCCS). *Applied Developmental Science, 23*(6), 409–425. https://doi.org/10.1080/10888691.2020.1834394.

Diemer, M. A., McWhirter, E. H., Ozer, E. J., & Rapa, L. J. (2015). Advances in the conceptualization and measurement of critical consciousness. *The Urban Review, 47*(5), 809–823. https://doi.org/10.1007/s11256-015-0336-7.

Diemer, M. A., Mistry, R. S., Wadsworth, M. E., López, I., & Reimers, F. (2013). Best practices in conceptualizing and measuring social class in psychological research. *Analyses of Social Issues and Public Policy, 13*(1), 77–113. https://doi.org/10.1111/asap.12001.

Diemer, M. A., Pinedo, A., Bañales, J. et al. (2021). Recentering action in critical consciousness. *Child Development Perspectives, 15*(1), 12–17. https://doi.org/10.1111/cdep.12393.

Diemer, M. A., Rapa, L. J., Park, C. J., & Perry, J. C. (2017). Development and validation of the Critical Consciousness Scale. *Youth & Society, 49*(4), 461–483. https://doi.org/10.1177/0044118X14538289.

Diemer, M. A., Rapa, L. J., Voight, A. M., & McWhirter, E. H. (2016). Critical consciousness: A developmental approach to addressing marginalization and oppression. *Child Development Perspectives, 10*(4), 216–221. https://doi.org/10.1111/cdep.12193.

Dull, B. D., Hoyt, L. T., Grzanka, P. R., & Zeiders, K. H. (2021). Can white guilt motivate action? The role of civic beliefs. *Journal of Youth and Adolescence, 50*(6), 1081–1097. https://doi.org/10.1007/s10964-021-01401-7.

Freire, P. (2018). *Pedagogy of the oppressed* (M. B. Ramos, Trans.). Bloomsbury Academic. (Original work published 1970).

Gee, M. N., & Johnson, S. K. (2022). *Testing the psychometric properties of the Critical Reflection on Sexism Scale (CROSS) among young adults in the US* [Manuscript in preparation]. Department of Child Study and Human Development, Tufts University.

Ghavami, N., Katsiaficas, D., & Rogers, L. O. (2016). Toward an intersectional approach in developmental science: The role of race, gender, sexual orientation, and immigrant status. *Advances in Child Development and Behavior*, *50*, 31–73. https://doi.org/10.1016/bs.acdb.2015.12.001.

Ginwright, S., & James, T. (2002). From assets to agents of change: Social justice, organizing, and youth development. *New Directions for Youth Development*, 96, 27–46. https://doi.org/10.1002/yd.25.

Godfrey, E. B., & Burson, E. (2018). Interrogating the intersections: How intersectional perspectives can inform developmental scholarship on critical consciousness. In C. E. Santos & R. B. Toomey (Eds.), *Envisioning the Integration of an Intersectional Lens in Developmental Science. New Directions for Child and Adolescent Development*, *161*, 17–38. https://doi.org/10.1002/cad.20246.

Godfrey, E. B., & Wolf, S. (2016). Developing critical consciousness or justifying the system? A qualitative analysis of attributions for poverty and wealth among low-income racial/ethnic minority and immigrant women. *Cultural Diversity and Ethnic Minority Psychology*, *22*(1), 93–103. https://doi.org/10.1037/cdp0000048.

Gómez, R. F., & Cammarota, J. (2022). Taking the teachers to school! Critical consciousness emerging: A qualitative exploration of Mexican American youth's social justice orientation development. *The Urban Review*, *54*, 339–336. https://doi.org/10.1007/s11256-021-00623-0.

Greenwood, R. M. (2008). Intersectional political consciousness: Appreciation for intragroup differences and solidarity in diverse groups. *Psychology of Women Quarterly*, *32*(1), 36–47. https://doi.org/10.1111/j.1471-6402.2007.00405.x.

Grusky, D., & Hill, J. (Eds.). (2017). *Inequality in the 21st century: A reader*. Routledge.

Guenole, N., & Brown, A. (2014). The consequences of ignoring measurement invariance for path coefficients in structural equation models. *Frontiers in Psychology*, 5, 1–16. https://doi.org/10.3389/fpsyg.2014.00980.

Heberle, A. E., Rapa, L. J., & Faragó, F. (2020). Critical consciousness in children and adolescents: A systematic review, critical assessment, and recommendations for future research. *Psychological Bulletin*, *146*(6), 525–551. https://doi.org/10.1037/bul0000230.

Henry, P. J., & Sears, D. O. (2002). The Symbolic Racism 2000 Scale. *Political Psychology*, *23*(2), 253–283. https://doi.org/10.1111/0162-895X.00281.

Hershberg, R. M., Andringa, O., Camm, K. et al. (2019). Learning through doing: Reflections on the use of photovoice in an undergraduate community psychology classroom. *Global Journal of Community Psychology Practice*, *10*(2), 1–38. www.gjcpp.org/pdfs/4-HershbergEtAl-Final.pdf.

Hershberg, R. M., & Johnson, S. K. (2019). Critical reflection about socioeconomic inequalities among White young men from poor and working-class backgrounds. *Developmental Psychology*, *55*(3), 562–573. https://doi.org/10.1037/dev0000587.

Hershberg, R. M., Larsen, S., Webb, A. et al. (2022). *Presenting the six-domain measure of critical consciousness: Reflections and results from a participatory measurement design process* [Manuscript in preparation]. Division of Social, Behavioral, and Human Sciences, University of Washington, Tacoma.

Hope, E. C., & Bañales, J. (2019). Black early adolescent critical reflection of inequitable sociopolitical conditions: A qualitative investigation. *Journal of Adolescent Research, 34*(2), 167–200. https://doi.org/10.1177/0743558418756360.

Hope, E. C., & Spencer, M. B. (2017). Civic engagement as an adaptive coping response to conditions of inequality: An application of phenomenological variant of ecological systems theory (PVEST). In N. J. Cabrera & B. Leyendecker (Eds.), *Handbook on positive development of minority children and youth* (pp. 421–435). Springer.

Hughes, J. L., Camden, A. A., & Yangchen, T. (2016). Rethinking and updating demographic questions: Guidance to improve descriptions of research samples. *Psi Chi Journal of Psychological Research, 21*(3), 138–151. https://doi.org/10.24839/2164-8204.JN21.3.138.

Hughes, D., Way, N., & Rivas-Drake, D. (2011). Stability and change in private and public ethnic regard among African American, Puerto Rican, Dominican, and Chinese American early adolescents. *Journal of Research on Adolescence, 21*(4), 861–870. https://doi.org/10.1111/j.1532-7795.2011.00744.x.

Jager, J., Putnick, D. L., & Bornstein, M. H. (2017). II. More than just convenient: The scientific merits of homogeneous convenience samples. *Monographs of the Society for Research in Child Development, 82*(2), 13–30. https://doi.org/10.1111/mono.12296.

Jemal, A. (2017). Critical consciousness: A critique and critical analysis of the literature. *The Urban Review, 49*(4), 602–626. https://doi.org/10.1007/s11256-017-0411-3.

Johnson, A. G. (2006). *Privilege, power, and difference* (2nd ed.). McGraw-Hill.

Johnson, S. K., & Hershberg, R. M. (2017, November). *Measuring critical consciousness: Young adults' attributions about societal inequalities in the United States* [Paper presentation]. Society for the Study of Emerging Adulthood 8th Biennial Conference, Washington, DC.

Johnson, S. K., Odjakjian, K. O., & Park, Y. (2022). I am whatever I say I am: The salient identity content of US American adolescents. *Journal of Research on Adolescence*. Early View, *32*, 737–755. https://doi.org/10.1111/jora.12721.

Johnson, S. K., Park, Y., Hudani, N., Gee, M. N., & Otto, L. (2021, April). When is civic action critical? Exploring white young adults' actions against racism. In P. J. Ballard & L. T. Hoyt (Chairs), The development of "allyship" and critical action among white people over the lifecourse [Symposium]. Biennial Meeting of the Society for Research on Child Development, Virtual.

Johnston, M., Ozaki, C., Pizzolato, J. & Chaudhari, P. (2014). Which box(es) do I check? Investigating college students' meanings behind racial identification. *Journal of Student Affairs Research and Practice, 51*(1), 56–68. https://doi.org/10.1515/jsarp-2014-0005.

Kline, R. B. (2015). *Principles and practice of structural equation modeling* (3rd ed.). Guilford Publications.

Kornbluh, M., Rogers, L. O., & Williams, J. L. (2021). Doing anti-racist scholarship with adolescents: Empirical examples and lessons learned. *Journal of Adolescent Research, 36*(5), 427–436. https://doi.org/10.1177/07435584211031450.

Lindqvist, L., Gustafsson Sendén, M., & Renström, E. A. (2020) What is gender, anyway: a review of the options for operationalising gender. *Psychology & Sexuality*, *12*(4), 332–344. https://doi.org/10.1080/19419899.2020.1729844.

Mallinckrodt, B., Miles, J. R., Bhaskar, T. et al. (2014). Developing a comprehensive scale to assess college multicultural programming. *Journal of Counseling Psychology*, *61*(1), 133–145. https://doi.org/10.1037/a0035214.

Martin, J. L., & Yeung, K. T. (2003, December). The use of the conceptual category of race in American sociology, 1937–99. *Sociological Forum*, *18*(4), 521–543. https://doi.org/10.1023/B:SOFO.0000003002.90428.c2.

Mathews, C. J., Medina, M. A., Bañales, J. et al. (2019). Mapping the intersections of adolescents' ethnic-racial identity and critical consciousness. *Adolescent Research Review*, 5, 363–379. https://doi.org/10.1007/s40894-019-00122-0.

May, S. C. (2022). Motivation and commitment to activism: A group differential approach to investigating motivation and motivational change among Black and Latinx adolescents across high school. Unpublished doctoral dissertation; Boston College.

McClellan, M. J., Montross-Thomas, L. P., Remer, P., Nakai, Y., & Monroe, A. D. (2019). Development and validation of the Awareness of Privilege and Oppression Scale–2. *SAGE Open*, *9*(2), 1–15. https://doi.org/10.1177/2158244019853906

McCoach, D. B., Gable, R. K., & Madura, J. P. (2013). *Instrument development in the affective domain* (3rd ed.). Springer.

McConahay, J. B. (1986). Modern racism, ambivalence, and the Modern Racism Scale. In J. F. Dovidio & S. L. Gaertner (Eds.), *Prejudice, discrimination, and racism* (pp. 91–125). Academic Press.

McIntosh, P. (2000). White privilege and male privilege: A personal account of coming to see correspondences through work in women's studies. In A. Minas (Ed.), *Gender basics: Feminist perspectives on women and men* (2nd ed., pp. 30–38). Wadsworth.

McLean, K. C., & Syed, M. (2015). The field of identity development needs an identity: An introduction to the Oxford handbook of identity development. In K. C. McLean & M. Syed (Eds.), *The Oxford handbook of identity development* (pp. 1–10). Oxford University Press. https://doi.org/10.1093/oxfordhb/9780199936564.001.0001.

McWhirter, E. H., & McWhirter, B. T. (2016). Critical consciousness and vocational development among Latina/o high school youth: Initial development and testing of a measure. *Journal of Career Assessment*, *24*(3), 543–558. https://doi.org/10.1177/1069072715599535.

Morgan, E. M. (2013). Contemporary issues in sexual orientation and identity development in emerging adulthood. *Emerging Adulthood*, *1*(1), 52–66. https://doi.org/10.1177/2167696812469187.

Morrell, M. E. (2003). Survey and experimental evidence for a reliable and valid measure of internal political efficacy. *The Public Opinion Quarterly*, *67*(4), 589–602. https://doi.org/10.1086/378965.

Murry, V. M., Cooper, S. M., Burnett, M., & Inniss-Thompson, M. N. (2020). Rural African Americans' family relationships and well-being. In J. Glick, S. McHale, &

V. King (Eds.), *Rural families and communities in the United States* (pp. 169–200). Springer. https://doi.org/10.1007/978-3-030-37689-5_7.

Neville, H. A., Lilly, R. L., Duran, G., Lee, R. M., & Browne, L. (2000). Construction and initial validation of the Color-Blind Racial Attitudes Scale (CoBRAS). *Journal of Counseling Psychology*, *47*(1), 59–70. https://doi.org/10.1037/0022-0167.47.1.59.

Parent, M. C., & Silva, K. (2018). Critical consciousness moderates the relationship between transphobia and "bathroom bill" voting. *Journal of Counseling Psychology*, *65*(4), 403–412. https://doi.org/10.1037/cou0000270.

Pester, D. A., Lenz, A. S., & Watson, J. C. (2020). The development and evaluation of the Intersectional Privilege Screening Inventory for use with counselors-in-training. *Counselor Education and Supervision*, *59*(2), 112–128. https://doi.org/10.1002/ceas.12170.

Pieterse, A. L., Utsey, S. O., & Miller, M. J. (2016). Development and initial validation of the Anti-Racism Behavioral Inventory (ARBI). *Counselling Psychology Quarterly*, *29*(4), 356–381. https://doi.org/10.1080/09515070.2015.1101534.

Pinterits, E. J., Poteat, V. P., & Spanierman, L. B. (2009). The White Privilege Attitudes Scale: Development and initial validation. *Journal of Counseling Psychology*, *56*(3), 417–429. https://doi.org/10.1037/a0016274.

Rapa, L. J., Bolding, C. W., & Jamil, F. M. (2020). Development and initial validation of the Short Critical Consciousness Scale (CCS-S). *Journal of Applied Developmental Psychology*, *70*, 101164. https://doi.org/10.1016/j.appdev.2020.101164.

Rogers, L. O., Kiang, L., White, L. et al. (2020). Persistent concerns: Questions for research on ethnic-racial identity development. *Research in Human Development*, *17*(2–3), 130–153. https://doi.org/10.1080/15427609.2020.1831881.

Santos, C. E., & Toomey, R. B. (2018). Integrating an intersectionality lens in theory and research in developmental science. *New Directions for Child and Adolescent Development*, *2018*(161), 7–15. https://doi.org/10.1002/cad.20245.

Schwartz, S. J., Luyckx, K., & Vignoles, V. L. (Eds.). (2011). *Handbook of identity theory and research*. Springer. https://doi.org/10.1007/978-1-4419-7988-9.

Shin, R. Q., Ezeofor, I., Smith, L. C., Welch, J. C., & Goodrich, K. M. (2016). The development and validation of the Contemporary Critical Consciousness Measure. *Journal of Counseling Psychology*, *63*(2), 210–223. https://doi.org/10.1037/cou0000137.

Shin, R. Q., Smith, L. C., Lu, Y. et al. (2018). The development and validation of the Contemporary Critical Consciousness Measure II. *Journal of Counseling Psychology*, *65*(5), 539–555. https://doi.org/10.1037/cou0000302.

Spears, R. (2011). Group identities: The social identity perspective. In S. J. Schwartz, K. Luyckx, & V. L. Vignoles (Eds.), *Handbook of identity theory and research* (pp. 201–224). Springer. https://doi.org/10.1007/978-1-4419-7988-9_9.

Spencer, M. B., Harpalani, V., Cassidy, E. et al. (2006). Understanding vulnerability and resilience from a normative developmental perspective: Implications for racially and ethnically diverse youth. In D. Cicchetti & D. J. Cohen (Eds.), *Developmental psychopathology: Vol. 1. Theory and method* (2nd ed., pp. 627–672). Wiley. https://doi.org/10.1002/9780470939383.

Suen, L. W., Lunn, M. R., Katuzny, K. et al. (2020). What sexual and gender minority people want researchers to know about sexual orientation and gender identity questions: A qualitative study. *Archives of Sexual Behavior, 49*, 2301–2318. https://doi.org/10.1007/s10508-020-01810-y.

Swim, J. K., Aikin, K. J., Hall, W. S., & Hunter, B. A. (1995). Sexism and racism: Old-fashioned and modern prejudices. *Journal of Personality and Social Psychology, 68*(2), 199–214. https://doi.org/10.1037/0022-3514.68.2.199.

Swim, J. K., & Cohen, L. L. (1997). Overt, covert, and subtle sexism: A comparison between the attitudes toward women and modern sexism scales. *Psychology of Women Quarterly, 21*(1), 103–118. https://doi.org/10.1111/j.1471-6402.1997.tb00103.x.

Szymanski, D. M. (2004). Relations among dimensions of feminism and internalized heterosexism in lesbians and bisexual women. *Sex Roles, 51*(3), 145–159. https://doi .org/10.1023/B:SERS.0000037759.33014.55.

Tanti, C., Stukas, A. A., Halloran, M. J., & Foddy, M. (2008). Tripartite self-concept change: Shifts in the individual, relational, and collective self in adolescence. *Self and Identity, 7*(4), 360–379. https://doi.org/10.1080/15298860701665081.

Thomas, A. J., Barrie, R., Brunner, J. et al. (2014). Assessing critical consciousness in youth and young adults. *Journal of Research on Adolescence, 24*(3), 485–496. https://doi.org/10.1111/jora.12132.

Tougas, F., Brown, R., Beaton, A. M., & Joly, S. (1995). Neosexism: Plus ça change, plus c'est pareil. *Personality and Social Psychology Bulletin, 21*(8), 842–849. https://doi .org/10.1177/0146167295218007.

Tyler, C. P., Geldhof, G. J., Black, K. L., & Bowers, E. P. (2020). Critical reflection and positive youth development among White and Black adolescents: Is understanding inequality connected to thriving? *Journal of Youth and Adolescence, 49*(4), 757–771. https://doi.org/10.1007/s10964-019-01092-1.

van de Schoot, R., Lugtig, P., & Hox, J. (2012). A checklist for testing measurement invariance. *European Journal of Developmental Psychology, 9*(4), 486–492. https://doi.org/10.1080/17405629.2012.686740.

van Zomeren, M., Spears, R., Fischer, A. H., & Leach, C. W. (2004). Put your money where your mouth is! Explaining collective action tendencies through group-based anger and group efficacy. *Journal of Personality and Social Psychology, 87*(5), 649–664. https://doi.org/10.1037/0022-3514.87.5.649.

Velez, G., & Spencer, M. B. (2018). Phenomenology and intersectionality: Using PVEST as a frame for adolescent identity formation amid intersecting ecological systems of inequality. *New Directions for Child and Adolescent Development, 2018* (161), 75–90. https://doi.org/10.1002/cad.20247.

Vignoles, V. L., Schwartz, S. J., & Luyckx, K. (2011). Introduction: Toward an integrative view of identity. In S. J. Schwartz, K. Luyckx, & V. L. Vignoles (Eds.), *Handbook of identity theory and research* (pp. 1–27). Springer. https://doi.org/10 .1007/978-1-4419-7988-9_1.

Watts, R. J., Diemer, M. A., & Voight, A. M. (2011). Critical consciousness: Current status and future directions. *New Directions for Child and Adolescent Development, 2011*(134), 43–57. https://doi.org/10.1002/cd.310.

Watts, R. J., & Flanagan, C. (2007). Pushing the envelope on youth civic engagement: A developmental and liberation psychology perspective. *Journal of Community Psychology*, *35*(6), 779–792. https://doi.org/10.1002/jcop.20178.

Watts, R., Williams, N., & Jagers, R. (2003). Sociopolitical development. *American Journal of Community Psychology*, *31*, 185–194. https://doi.org/10.1023/A:1023091024140

Williams, C. D., Byrd, C. M., Quintana, S. M. et al. (2020) A lifespan model of ethnic-racial identity. *Research in Human Development*, *17* (2–3), 99–129. https://doi.org/10.1080/15427609.2020.1831882.

Wolff, M., Wells, B., Ventura-DiPersia, C., Renson, A., & Grov, C. (2017). Measuring sexual orientation: A review and critique of US data collection efforts and implications for health policy. *The Journal of Sex Research*, *54*(4–5), 507–531. https://doi.org/10.1080/00224499.2016.1255872.

Wray-Lake, L., Arruda, E. H., & Schulenberg, J. E. (2020). Civic development across the transition to adulthood in a national US sample: Variations by race/ethnicity, parent education, and gender. *Developmental Psychology*, *56*(10), 1948–1967. https://doi.org/10.1037/dev0001101.

Zimmerman, M. A., & Zahniser, J. H. (1991). Refinements of sphere-specific measures of perceived control: Development of a sociopolitical control scale. *Journal of Community Psychology*, *19*(2), 189–204. https://doi.org/10.1002/1520-6629(199104)19:2<189::AID-JCOP2290190210>.

# 11

# The Development of the Contemporary Critical Consciousness Measure-Short

RICHARD Q. SHIN, SHEREEN ASHAI, MANUEL TERAN HERNANDEZ, YUN LU, BRIAN KEUM, AND SARAH ESSNER

In this chapter, we present initial findings supporting the development of a brief, integrated measure of critical consciousness (CC). This project extends the authors' previous work on developing psychometrically sound measures of CC that are intended to capture individuals' awareness of various inequitable systems within contemporary US society. The new measure combines items from the CCCM (Shin et al., 2016) and CCCMII (Shin et al., 2018), which were developed to assess respondents' awareness of and attitudes about systemic, institutionalized manifestations of racism, classism, heterosexism, sexism, cis-sexism, and ableism. From the inception of these scale development projects, our ultimate goal was to develop a brief measure which captures elements of each form of oppression. This objective is consistent with our conviction that social justice efforts should not operate from a single-axis lens. Instead, liberation for all requires a commitment to dismantling each of the primary forms of oppression that are currently plaguing our society.

## THEORETICAL UNDERPINNINGS

The CCCM-S, like the CCCM and CCCMII, is inspired by the concept of CC or *conscientização*, a construct developed by Brazilian educator and philosopher Paulo Freire (Freire, 2000). CC represents the process by which oppressed people learn to think critically about their inequitable social conditions (critical reflection) and subsequently take action to change them (critical action). Contemporary scholars have expanded Freire's conceptualization of CC, suggesting that it is made up of three distinct but related elements: (1) critical reflection, which refers to the critical analysis of societal inequities; (2) critical motivation (also referred to as political agency or efficacy), which refers to the interest and agency one has to mobilize against such inequities; and (3) critical action, which refers to the individual or collective action that one engages in to facilitate the creation of a more equitable society (Watts et al., 2011). The CCCM-S accounts for the critical reflection component of Freire's theory, which he referred to as the process of people "coming to see critically *the way they exist* in the world *with which* and *in which* they find themselves" (Freire, 2000, italics original, p. 83). Freire argued that it is through critical reflection that the oppressed become engaged in the struggle for their own liberation. Some contemporary scholars conceptualize a reciprocal relationship between the components of CC, where participation in critical action stimulates critical reflection and motivation, and vice versa (Watts et al., 2011). In our own work, we operationalize CC as awareness of – and attitudes related to – the systemic, institutionalized manifestations of discrimination associated with various forms of oppression.

The CCCM-S is also inspired by the framework of intersectionality, which provides a critical theoretical lens through which to examine how systems of oppression manifested at individual, institutional, and structural levels intersect to produce unique experiences and outcomes for those who occupy multiple marginalized identities (Combahee River Collective, 1977/2014; Crenshaw, 1991). However, as we have argued previously (Shin et al., 2017), we believe that employing the powerful framework of intersectionality exclusively to study marginalized groups is problematic because it allows dominant social identities (e.g., white, male, temporarily able-bodied) to remain unacknowledged and uninterrogated. Never focusing on intersections involving dominant groups reinforces their normativity (Bowleg, 2008). As we have done since the conceptualization of our original CCCM, we deem intersectionality an ideal complement to CC theory because, at its core, intersectionality serves as a tool for interrogating intersecting forms of oppression and poses a mandate for the dismantling of socially unjust systems (e.g., Bowleg & Bauer, 2016; Shin et al., 2017). We also refer the reader to Godfrey and Burson's (2018) recent chapter, which provides an excellent rationale and guidelines for infusing intersectionality into CC scholarship.

## MEASUREMENT OF CC

A total of six quantitative instruments designed to assess CC and its subcomponents have been published in recent years (Heberle et al., 2020). A review of these measures is beyond the scope of this chapter (see Heberle et al., 2020; Rapa et al., 2020 for excellent reviews). The development and use of these measures has refined our understanding of CC, but limitations remain. Rapa et al. (2020) note the following important new directions for research focused on measuring CC: (1) the need for CC measures which include all three components of CC (reflection, motivation, and action); and (2) establishment of measurement invariance among CC scales in order to accurately determine differences across groups. Rapa and colleagues' (2020) development of the Short Critical Consciousness Scale (CCS-S) represents the first achievement in addressing these limitations. Our future goals for the CCCM do not include the addition of the motivation and action components of CC. While we value these essential aspects of CC, we continue to view critical reflection as a prerequisite for effective social justice action (Freire, 2000; Watts et al., 2011). We acknowledge that some scholars conceptualize a more reciprocal relationship between the components of CC, while others have noted an imbalance in the focus on critical reflection and insufficient attention paid to critical motivation or critical action among most CC measures (Rapa et al., 2020). Notwithstanding, our focus on critical reflection is consistent with our ultimate goal of the CCCM-S being an effective tool for facilitating the development of culturally competent mental health professionals. In 2015, the American Counseling Association endorsed the Multicultural and Social Justice Counseling Competencies (MSJCC; Ratts et al., 2015), which require counselors to develop CC of the power they hold in the counseling relationship, especially as it relates to privilege and oppression. Additionally, intersectionality theory is one of the theoretical pillars of the MSJCC (Singh et al., 2020). Because the CCCM-S is grounded in both CC and intersectionality theories, we believe it will serve as an ideal assessment tool for advancing these important professional competencies.

The samples used for the development and validation of the CCCM and CCCMII were both drawn from Amazon Mechanical Turk (MTurk). A strength of these samples is that they were representative of national demographics. A consistent limitation of the samples is that they were predominantly white, heterosexual, and cisgender. Since the publication of the CCCM, measurement invariance has been demonstrated by some research studies using the measure to assess support for the Black Lives Matter movement in a sample of college students in the Southwest United States (Yoo et al., 2021a), transphobic attitudes related to "bathroom bill" voting in college students (Parent & Silva, 2018), collective action and personal empowerment in samples of women (Conlin et al., 2021), sense of community in a sample of LGB individuals in Hong Kong (Yip & Chan, 2021), student engagement in a sample of undergraduate students (Faloughi & Herman, 2020), bicultural identity integration in a sample of bicultural people of color (Lee et al., 2021), and racial identity experiences in a sample of Asian American college students (Yoo et al., 2021b). To our knowledge, no evidence of measurement invariance for the CCCMII exists. While we are pleased to see that the CCCM has demonstrated adequate psychometric characteristics with samples that are divergent from the original scale development project, it has always been our goal to integrate the CCCM and CCCMII into one measure capturing elements of six pervasive forms of oppression in the United States. Ultimately, we hope this measure will enhance the education and training of mental health professionals to better serve marginalized individuals and communities. The development of the CCCM-S serves as our first step in this direction.

## REDUCING BIAS IN MENTAL HEALTH PRACTICE

Disparities in mental health status and access to quality mental health services for marginalized groups remains extensive, pervasive, and persistent (Barefoot et al., 2015; Flores, 2010; SAMHSA, 2015). Historically, minoritized clients have encountered multiple forms of oppression in the field of mental health, including difficulty accessing mental health services, receiving lower-quality mental health care, and terminating treatment prematurely (Farook, 2018). For instance, research continues to document that Black Americans experience (a) overdiagnoses and overmedication of psychological disorders, such as schizophrenia (Delphin-Rittmon et al., 2015); (b) underdiagnoses of other disorders, such as depression (Payne, 2014); (c) treatment delays in care (Fedewa et al., 2010); and (d) barriers to accessing mental health services (Kugelmass, 2016; Shin et al., 2016). Additionally, while lesbian, gay, bisexual, and queer (LGBQ) individuals have been found to engage in mental health services at higher rates than their heterosexual counterparts due to the cumulative stress that accompanies living within a heteronormative society, heterosexist bias continues to be documented among mental health professionals in covert (e.g., heterosexist microaggressions; Shelton & Delgado-Romero, 2011), overt (e.g., barriers to access; Shin et al., 2021), and institutional (Willging et al., 2006) ways. While these findings highlight the influence of racism and heterosexism in mental health disparities, classism, sexism, cissexism, and ableism are also undoubtedly perpetuated in individual and systemic ways within mental health professions.

To reduce the probability of biased clinical behaviors and to minimize disparities in treatment, psychologists have emphasized the need to increase multiculturally competent practice. The first and most prominent framework established to reduce discriminatory behaviors among mental health professionals was the Multicultural Counseling Competencies (MCC; Sue et al., 1992). The MCC framework conceptualizes culturally competent practice as the knowledge, awareness, and skills necessary for therapists to provide effective counseling services to individuals from diverse racial, ethnic, and cultural backgrounds. While each of the components of this tripartite model are considered important, MCC scholars have long considered the first pillar, which focuses on therapists' awareness of the assumptions, values, and biases that affect their worldview, to be of primary importance (Worthington et al., 2007).

The next most prominent framework developed to address biases in psychological practice is the social justice paradigm, which has been named as the "fifth force" alongside psychodynamic, cognitive-behavioral, existential-humanistic, and multicultural counseling paradigms (Ratts, 2009, p. 160). Social justice scholars emphasize the ways in which systemic, institutionalized barriers serve as the root cause of many of the psychological and social difficulties experienced by members of marginalized groups while also encouraging psychologists to become engaged in social justice action (Goodman et al., 2004). The pervasive bias in psychology to privilege intrapsychic and interpersonal explanations over the effects of oppressive environmental conditions serves to maintain the inequitable societal status quo experienced by members of marginalized groups (Prilleltensky, 1997). In other words, a key bias among mental health providers is to conveniently transform societal ills into psychological diagnoses. The liberatory concept of CC may serve as a powerful antidote to these persistent, oppressive forces operating within the mental health professions. We hope that the development of the CCCM-S will serve as a useful tool to assess the development of CC among mental health trainees and practitioners.

## PURPOSE

The purpose of this study was to develop a brief, integrated measure to assess awareness and attitudes related to systemic, institutionalized forms of discrimination associated with racism, heterosexism, classism, sexism, cis-sexism, and ableism. We set out to reexamine the factor structures of the CCCM and CCCMII using confirmatory factor analysis (CFA). We also sought to explore the factor structure of the combined scales using exploratory factor analysis (EFA). Based on the findings from the CCCM and CCCMII scale development studies, we hypothesized that the combined shortened scale would represent an underlying general factor of CC, as well as six orthogonal group factors: racism, classism, heterosexism, cis-sexism, ableism, and sexism.

## METHOD

### Procedures and Participants

We recruited a total of 564 participants using the online Mechanical Turk (MTurk) service. MTurk is a service provided by Amazon that allows "requesters" to hire "workers" for Human Intelligence Tasks (HITs). In this study, we recruited workers to complete a HIT titled "20 minute academic survey on social identities." Once workers clicked on the HIT title, they were taken to a page that described the HIT as a "20 minute survey asking about [workers'] beliefs regarding certain social identities." Once workers accepted the HIT, they were invited to participate in our study by clicking a link that referred them to a Qualtrics survey. Participants who completed the HIT were eligible for 50¢ in compensation. Although 564 participants accessed the survey, a total of 475 participants completed the survey and passed our validity checks.

These participants were paid 50¢ in compensation, a retention rate of 84%. The HIT for the CCCM-S survey was available to any MTurk worker older than 18 and located in the United States. Because the HIT was available to any workers that fit those parameters, we were not able to determine how many workers saw the HIT, nor could we calculate a response rate for it.

The average age of the sample was 37.5 years of age. Most of the sample identified as cisgender (85.7%), with cisgender women comprising approximately half of the total sample (51%), followed by cisgender men (34.5%). The remainder of the participants identified as transgender (14.3%); specifically, transgender women (4.6%) and men (8.2%), as well as agender (0.6%), nonbinary (0.4%), genderqueer (0.2%), or gender neutral (0.2%). Participants identified as white (65.1%), Black/African American (12.8%), Asian American and Pacific Islander (8.4%), Native American/Indigenous American (3.8%), Latino/a/x (3.4%), and Middle Eastern (0.2%).The majority of respondents identified as heterosexual/straight (78.7%), and the remainder identified as bisexual (12.8%), lesbian/gay (3.8%), asexual (2.3%), queer (0.9%), questioning (0.9%), or pansexual (0.6%). Approximately 34.8% of the sample identified as having a disability. In terms of political identity, participants identified as liberal (23.2%), moderate (18.9%), and conservative (16.2%), while others identified as very liberal (11.6%), moderately liberal (10.1%), moderately conservative (9.9%), very conservative (8.6%), or other (1.3%).

## INSTRUMENTS

### Contemporary Critical Consciousness Measure (CCCM)

The 19-item CCCM (Shin, et al., 2016) was developed to assess participants' awareness of and attitudes related to systemic, institutionalized forms of discrimination. The CCCM measures general CC as well as CC specifically associated with racism, classism, and heterosexism (for sample items, see Table 11.1). For each item, participants rated their level of agreement on a 7-point Likert scale ranging from 1 (*strongly disagree*) to 7 (*strongly agree*). Sample items include "All Whites receive unearned privileges in US society," "Most poor people are poor because they are unable to manage their expenses well," and "Discrimination against gay persons is still a significant problem in the United States." In the initial scale development project, acceptable levels of reliability were documented for the general ($\alpha$ = 0.90), racism ($\alpha$ = 0.79), classism ($\alpha$ = 0.88), and heterosexism ($\alpha$ = 0.85) scales. There was also support for convergent validity, having shown significant predictive relationships between the CCCM and its subscales with existing measures of racism, classism, and homophobia.

TABLE 11.1 CCCM and CCCMII item description

| **Item** |
|---|
| CCCM: Racism Subscale |
| 1. All White individuals receive unearned privileges in US society. |
| 2. The overrepresentation of Black and Latino/a/x individuals in prison is directly related to racist disciplinary policies in public schools. |
| CCCM: Classism Subscale |
| 6. Poor people without jobs could easily find work but remain unemployed because they think that jobs like food service or retail are beneath them. (R) |
| 7. Social welfare programs provide poor people with an excuse not to work. (R) |
| CCCM: Heterosexism Subscale |
| 14. Anyone who openly identifies as lesbian, gay, or bisexual in today's society must be very courageous. |
| 15. Gay, lesbian, and bisexual individuals are just as effective parents as their heterosexual counterparts. |
| CCCMII: Cis-sexism Subscale |
| 1. It is appropriate for elementary school curriculum to teach children that there are more gender identities than man and woman. |
| 2. Buildings that only have "male" and "female" bathrooms are a form of discrimination |
| CCCMII: Ableism Subscale |
| 16. Discrimination against people with physical disabilities is a major problem in US society. |
| 17. Focusing on helping people with disabilities adjust to the barriers in our society, instead of breaking down barriers themselves, maintains ableism. |
| CCCMII: Sexism Subscale |
| 30. Discrimination against women is still a significant problem in the United States. |
| 31. Some women choosing to have babies is not the cause of income inequality between men and women in the United States. |

*Note.* (R) = Reverse-coded Items. Items displayed are the first two items of each subscale.

## Contemporary Critical Consciousness Measure II (CCCMII)

The 37-item CCCMII (Shin, et al., 2018) was developed to assess participants' awareness of and attitudes related to systemic, institutionalized forms of discrimination. The CCCMII measures general CC as well as CC specifically associated with sexism and ableism (Table 11.1). For each item, participants rated their level of agreement on a 7-point Likert scale ranging from 1 (*strongly disagree*) to 7 (*strongly agree*). Sample items include: "Discrimination against women is still a significant problem in the US" and "Our society should be transformed to better accommodate the needs of people with disabilities." Acceptable levels of reliability were observed for the general ($\alpha = 0.96$), sexism ($\alpha = 0.92$), and ableism ($\alpha = 0.92$) scales. Convergent and criterion evidence for construct validity was demonstrated through significantly predictive relationships between the CCCMII and existing measures of sexism, ableism, and social dominance orientation. Evidence from the original scale development project also suggested that responses to the CCCMII are not strongly influenced by socially desirable responding.

## RESULTS

### Data Analysis Plan

To develop a brief, integrated measure combining the CCCM and CCCMII, analyses were carried out in the following steps. First, we re-examined the factor structures of the CCCM and CCCMII using CFA. In the previous scale development projects for the CCCM and CCCMII, bifactor structures were confirmed by conducting EFA and CFA with two independent samples for each measure (Shin, et al., 2016, 2018). Bifactor models refer to a type of multidimensional structure in which a general factor contributes common variance directly to the indicators of the model, and some indicators share additional common variance with each other due to group factors (Reise, et al., 2010). In our conceptualization, an individual may have a general level of CC that reflects their attitudes and knowledge about manifestations of power and privilege, broadly. An individual may also be particularly high in awareness and knowledge regarding one dimension of oppression, such as racism, and have relatively low CC in another dimension, such as ableism. In other words, an individual's level of overall CC is independent from their levels of racism-specific CC, cissexism-specific CC, and so on. We thus hypothesized that the original bifactor models for both the CCCM and the CCCMII would be validated and would yield superior fit than other competing models (e.g., one factor, oblique three factor), as this structure best aligned with our conceptualization of CC.

Once we independently confirmed the bifactor structure of each scale, our next step would be to combine responses to the CCCM and CCCMII items and test a bifactor structure with six group factors using CFA. This step ensures that any observed model misspecification would not be due to model-data misfit of the individual scales. We imposed a bifactor structure with six group factors in a confirmatory fashion because of the aforementioned conceptualization of CC. We hypothesized that the combined scale would fit a bifactor structure with six group factors, which would support the independence of CC in the six dimensions. In the case that this bifactor structure could be validated in the combined scale, we would proceed to item selection for the abbreviated scale based on item performance.

Because the CCCM and CCCMII were developed in independent studies, it is possible that the group factors would differ when the two scales were combined, even if a bifactor structure could be identified. If the bifactor model with the original six group factors could not be confirmed, we would proceed with exploratory first-order and bifactor analyses with all the items from the CCCM and CCCMII to uncover the best-fitting bifactor structure. Subsequent item selection for the abbreviated scale would be based on item analysis from the exploratory factor analyses as well as expert reviews.

## Missing Data Analysis and Data Inspection

As noted, 564 participants consented to taking the online survey. After deleting 48 participants who did not provide any data, variables had missingness ranging from 0.4% to 1.6% and appeared to be missing completely at random, Little's MCAR test = 10725.21, DF = 11295, $p > 0.99$. Ten participants recommended their data not be used, and 31 participants failed both attention check questions, so their data were excluded from the subsequent analyses. The final sample had 475 participants.

Data overall showed negative skewness, with 29 items approximately symmetrical (skewness = [−0.49, 0.39]), 25 items moderately skewed (skewness = [−0.85, −0.51]), and 2 items severely skewed (skewness = [−1.10, −1.00]). Kurtosis estimates fell within ± 2 range, [−1.29, 1.03], which suggested that CCCM and CCCMII items had distribution height and sharpness that did not significantly deviate from that of a standard bell curve. We modeled the data using robust maximum likelihood estimation (MLR), which is robust to violations of multivariate normality (Satorra & Bentler, 2001).

## Confirmatory Factor Analysis of CCCM

We tested the bifactor structure of the CCCM based on results from the original development and validation study (Shin et al., 2016). Specifically, we modeled the general factor of CC, which reflects individuals' general awareness and attitudes related to systemic and institutionalized forms of discrimination, as well as three orthogonal group factors: racism, classism, and heterosexism. Because chi-square tests for model fit are sensitive to large sample sizes, we evaluated model fit using fit statistics. A model has adequate to good fit to data when the root mean square error of approximation (RMSEA) is less than 0.06, the comparative fit index (CFI) is greater than 0.90, and the standardized root mean square residual (SRMR) is less than 0.08 (Hu & Bentler, 1999). Results indicated that the bifactor model was a parsimonious model that explained adequate sample covariance as compared to the null model, $x^2(133) = 372.74$, $p < 0.001$, RMSEA = 0.062 (95% CI [.054, 0.069]), CFI = 0.93. However, SRMR = 0.11 was short of the fit criteria, which suggested that the bifactor model did not capture some residual correlations that might be important.

The modification indices suggested that at the item level, only items 14 ("Anyone who openly identifies as lesbian, gay, or bisexual in today's society must be very courageous") and 16 ("Discrimination against gay persons is still a significant problem in the United States") had exceptionally high residual correlation, MI = 18.98. However, no method effect or conceptual reason justified that these two items would share additional variance beyond their underlying factor. Because the modification indices did not reveal conceptually meaningful modification, we retained the bifactor model without post hoc model modification.

## Confirmatory Factor Analysis of CCCMII

Using the same analytical procedure, we tested the bifactor structure of the CCCMII based on results from the original development and validation study (Shin et al., 2018). We retained the bifactor model because it had good model fit, $x^2(592) = 1280.00$, $p < 0.001$, RMSEA = 0.049 (95% CI [0.046, 0.053]), SRMR = 0.075, CFI = 0.93.

## Confirmatory and Exploratory Factor Analysis of Combined CCCM-S

After separately validating the bifactor structures of the CCCM and CCCMII, we combined the two scales and tested the bifactor structure in the same sample. Specifically, we hypothesized that the combined scale would represent an underlying general factor of CC as well as six orthogonal group factors: racism, classism, heterosexism, cis-sexism, ableism, and sexism. The bifactor model showed inadequate model fit, $x^2(592) = 1280.00$, $p < 0.001$, RMSEA = 0.051 (95% CI [0.049, 0.054]), SRMR = 0.085, CFI = 0.88.

To derive the best-fitting model from the data, we ran EFA to determine the factor structure. First, we ran common factor exploratory factor analyses using MLR extraction and oblique rotation (geomin). Parallel analysis suggested that seven factors should be extracted, whereas the conceptual model suggests that six factors should be extracted. As a result, we ran five models extracting three to seven factors. The six-factor model had the best model fit, and yielded a pattern of loading that confirmed our conceptual framework, RMSEA = 0.049 (95% CI [0.046, 0.054]), SRMR = 0.024, CFI = 0.93 (Table 11.2). We employed the item retention rule that a scale with simple structure would consist of items with primary loadings larger than 0.50 and cross-loadings less than 0.25. In the six-factor model, all but one racism item loaded onto the first factor; all but one classism item loaded onto the second factor; three of the six heterosexism items and four cis-sexism items loaded onto the third factor; nine of fourteen ableism items loaded onto the fourth factor; and eight of the ten sexism items loaded onto the sixth factor. Interestingly, the fifth factor had four cis-sexism items with large primary factor loadings, but they all had substantial cross-loadings on the third factor and thus could not be retained. These four cis-sexism items had similar content about one's attitudes toward enforcing the gender binary through the use of pronouns and bathroom rights. Hence, of the six factors, the fifth factor was removed. In summary, we retained a five-factor structure based on the first-order exploratory factor analyses, in which most items loaded onto their respective conceptual factors, yielding factors of racism, classism, ableism, and sexism that were consistent with the original CCCM and CCCMII factor structures. However, there was considerable cross-loading for the heterosexism and cis-sexism items, and many cis-sexism items did not meet the item retention rule.

Second, we ran exploratory bifactor analyses using MLR extraction and geomin rotation to explore whether a bifactor structure captures scale structure. We ran three exploratory bifactor models, extracting four to six group factors. In a bifactor model, an item's largest factor loading may be on the general factor or its respective group factor. As a result, we employed the item retention rule that a simple bifactor structure would consist of items with primary group factor loadings at least 0.15 larger than group factor cross-loadings, after accounting for the general factor. The model with the CC general factor and five group factors yielded conceptually consistent patterns of factor loadings (Table 11.2). Three group factors corresponded with the racism, classism, and sexism factors from the CCCM and CCCMII. Similar to the results from the common factor exploratory factor analyses, the cis-sexism and heterosexism items had considerable cross-loading, with four cis-sexism items loading on one group factor and four cis-sexism items loading on another group factor with the heterosexism items. No ableism group factor emerged, and no ableism item met the item retention criteria. Overall, confirmatory and exploratory factor analyses suggested that after combining the CCCM and CCCMII items, a bifactor structure with one underlying CC factor fit the data. However, there was considerable overlap among the heterosexism and cis-sexism items and thus the conceptual six group factor structure could not be retained.

## Item Selection for CCCM-S

The primary goal of this study was to develop a combined and shortened CCCM with strong psychometric properties. We selected items for the combined CCCM-S based on expert review and exploratory bifactor analysis. First, three counseling psychology researchers with considerable expertise in

TABLE 11.2 Pattern matrix with factor loadings of EFA six-factor and bifactor models and final EFA bifactor solution

| | Initial Exploratory Six-Factor Model | | | | | | Initial Exploratory Bifactor Model | | | | | | Final Exploratory Bifactor Model | | | | | |
|---|---|---|---|---|---|---|---|---|---|---|---|---|---|---|---|---|---|---|
| | F1 | F2 | F3 | F4 | F5 | F6 | GF | F1 | F2 | F3 | F4 | F5 | GF | F1 | F2 | F3 | F4 | F5 |
| CCCM1 | **0.76*** | 0.03 | 0.05 | −0.04 | −0.02 | 0.16* | 0.62* | 0.03 | **0.57*** | 0.00 | 0.03 | 0.07 | 0.59* | **0.60*** | 0.02 | 0.02 | −0.08 | 0.09 |
| CCCM2 | **0.54*** | 0.03 | 0.08 | 0.18* | 0.04 | 0.04 | 0.64* | 0.02 | **0.38*** | 0.00 | −0.02 | −0.02 | 0.60* | **0.41*** | −0.01 | −0.09 | −0.01 | 0.01 |
| CCCM3 | **0.71*** | −0.06 | −0.03 | 0.10 | 0.15* | 0.00 | 0.60* | −0.07 | **0.51*** | 0.11 | −0.10 | −0.04 | 0.52* | **0.60*** | −0.10* | −0.08 | −0.03 | 0.05 |
| CCCM4 | 0.45* | 0.12* | 0.17* | 0.17* | 0.03 | 0.17* | 0.74* | 0.12* | **0.30*** | −0.02 | 0.04 | 0.06 | 0.72* | **0.36*** | 0.10* | −0.04 | 0.11 | 0.01 |
| CCCM5 | **0.69*** | −0.14* | −0.02 | 0.04 | 0.04 | 0.02 | 0.49* | −0.14* | **0.51*** | 0.03 | −0.04 | −0.02 | 0.41* | **0.56*** | −0.19* | 0.01 | 0.02 | −0.01 |
| CCCM6 | -0.10 | **0.83*** | 0.02 | 0.08 | 0.11 | −0.05 | 0.12 | **0.82*** | −0.10 | 0.07 | −0.03 | −0.04 | 0.22* | −0.05 | **0.77*** | −0.04 | −0.04 | −0.04 |
| CCCM7 | 0.09 | **0.85*** | 0.12 | −0.02 | 0.07 | −0.07 | 0.19* | **0.85*** | 0.06 | 0.06 | 0.06 | −0.06 | | | | | | |
| CCCM8 | −0.05 | **0.78*** | 0.01 | −0.01 | 0.01 | 0.05 | 0.07 | **0.77*** | −0.05 | 0.01 | 0.01 | 0.03 | 0.19* | −0.02 | **0.82*** | −0.02 | −0.02 | 0.01 |
| CCCM9 | −0.05 | **0.77*** | −0.05 | 0.02 | −0.07 | 0.10 | 0.04 | **0.76*** | −0.05 | −0.07 | −0.02 | 0.07 | | | | | | |
| CCCM10 | 0.04 | **0.67*** | 0.15 | 0.02 | −0.21* | 0.00 | 0.10 | **0.67*** | 0.02 | −0.18* | 0.13 | 0.00 | 0.21* | −0.02 | **0.70*** | 0.08 | 0.04 | 0.00 |
| CCCM11 | −0.11 | **0.70*** | 0.01 | 0.16* | −0.06 | −0.01 | 0.10 | **0.70*** | −0.11 | −0.09 | −0.02 | −0.02 | | | | | | |
| CCCM12 | 0.33* | 0.64* | −0.02 | −0.10 | 0.00 | 0.10 | 0.23* | **0.64*** | 0.25* | 0.02 | 0.01 | 0.06 | | | | | | |
| CCCM13 | 0.24* | **0.66*** | −0.03 | −0.01 | −0.06 | 0.05 | 0.17* | **0.65*** | 0.18* | −0.05 | −0.01 | 0.02 | 0.24* | 0.23* | **0.68*** | 0.04 | 0.03 | 0.03 |
| CCCM14 | 0.13 | −0.09 | 0.36* | 0.15 | 0.00 | 0.22* | 0.67* | −0.09 | 0.05 | −0.04 | 0.17* | 0.10 | | | | | | |
| CCCM15 | −0.08 | 0.04 | **0.70*** | 0.00 | −0.02 | 0.08 | 0.57* | 0.04 | −0.08 | −0.03 | **0.41*** | 0.02 | 0.65* | −0.03 | −0.01 | **0.38*** | −0.04 | 0.04 |
| CCCM16 | 0.00 | 0.09* | 0.44* | 0.13* | −0.05 | 0.32* | 0.70* | 0.09* | −0.05 | −0.09 | **0.24*** | 0.16* | | | | | | |

| | | | | | | | | | | | | | | | | | | |
|---|---|---|---|---|---|---|---|---|---|---|---|---|---|---|---|---|---|---|
| CCCM17 | 0.03 | 0.04 | **0.68*** | −0.04 | 0.01 | 0.16* | 0.67* | 0.04 | 0.00 | 0.01 | **0.41*** | 0.06 | 0.76* | 0.01 | −0.01 | **0.28*** | −0.07 | −0.01 |
| CCCM18 | −0.06 | 0.09 | **0.67*** | −0.06 | −0.22* | 0.09 | 0.39* | 0.09 | −0.06 | −0.18 | **0.46*** | 0.03 | 0.50* | −0.02 | 0.05 | **0.59*** | 0.03 | 0.04 |
| CCCM19 | 0.31* | −0.07 | 0.15* | 0.17* | 0.12 | 0.18* | 0.68* | −0.07 | 0.19* | 0.05 | 0.01 | 0.07 | | | | | | |
| CCCMII1 | 0.06 | −0.05 | 0.47 | −0.09 | 0.43* | 0.13* | 0.69* | −0.05 | 0.02 | **0.36*** | 0.20* | 0.05 | | | | | | |
| CCCMII2 | −0.04 | −0.03 | 0.28 | 0.03 | 0.71* | 0.06 | 0.69* | −0.04 | −0.08 | **0.56*** | −0.01 | 0.00 | | | | | | |
| CCCMII3 | 0.15* | 0.02 | 0.51* | −0.01 | 0.42* | −0.08 | 0.70* | 0.01 | 0.09 | **0.35*** | 0.20* | −0.09 | | | | | | |
| CCCMII4 | 0.10 | −0.06 | 0.46* | −0.04 | 0.20 | 0.12 | 0.61* | −0.06 | 0.06 | 0.16 | 0.23* | 0.04 | | | | | | |
| CCCMII5 | −0.08 | 0.00 | 0.49* | 0.17 | 0.12 | 0.24* | 0.76* | 0.00 | −0.12* | 0.05 | 0.21* | 0.10 | | | | | | |
| CCCMII6 | 0.10* | −0.03 | **0.66*** | 0.01 | 0.31 | −0.02 | 0.76* | −0.04 | 0.04 | 0.24 | 0.31* | −0.07 | | | | | | |
| CCCMII7 | 0.10* | −0.01 | 0.28 | 0.02 | 0.61* | 0.02 | 0.68* | −0.01 | 0.04 | **0.49*** | 0.02 | −0.03 | | | | | | |
| CCCMII8 | 0.26* | −0.13* | 0.19 | 0.11 | 0.30* | −0.03 | 0.56* | −0.13* | 0.16* | 0.22* | 0.00 | −0.06 | | | | | | |
| CCCMII9 | 0.00 | 0.05 | 0.30 | 0.10* | 0.62* | 0.02 | 0.73* | 0.04 | −0.05 | **0.48*** | 0.00 | −0.03 | | | | | | |
| CCCMII10 | 0.01 | −0.01 | 0.37 | −0.01 | 0.53* | 0.11 | 0.70* | −0.01 | −0.03 | **0.43*** | 0.09 | 0.03 | | | | | | |
| CCCMII11 | 0.02 | 0.00 | **0.78*** | 0.09 | 0.16 | −0.11* | 0.74* | 0.00 | −0.02 | 0.11 | **0.39*** | −0.12 | 0.82* | −0.02 | −0.03 | 0.02 | −0.07 | **-.28*** |
| CCCMII12 | −0.05 | 0.02 | **0.75*** | 0.05 | 0.24 | 0.02 | 0.77* | 0.01 | −0.08 | 0.17* | 0.37* | −0.04 | 0.86* | −0.08 | −0.02 | −0.04 | −0.12 | −0.24* |
| CCCMII13 | 0.09 | 0.02 | **0.78*** | 0.11* | −0.03 | −0.02 | 0.76* | 0.02 | 0.03 | −0.06 | **0.43*** | −0.07 | 0.83* | 0.05 | 0.02 | 0.15 | 0.04 | −0.21 |
| CCCMII14 | 0.03 | 0.05 | **0.79*** | 0.08 | 0.05 | −0.02 | 0.74* | 0.04 | −0.02 | 0.02 | **0.43*** | −0.07 | 0.83* | −0.03 | 0.02 | 0.08 | 0.02 | **-.23*** |
| CCCMII15 | 0.30* | −0.12* | 0.08 | 0.06 | 0.46* | 0.04 | 0.60* | −0.12* | 0.19 | 0.36* | −0.08 | −0.01 | | | | | | |
| CCCMII16 | 0.11* | 0.03 | 0.19* | **0.53*** | −0.01 | 0.06 | 0.76* | 0.03 | 0.00 | −0.12 | −0.03 | −0.03 | | | | | | |
| CCCMII17 | 0.16* | −0.07 | −0.02 | **0.57*** | 0.12 | −0.05 | 0.63* | −0.08 | 0.03 | −0.01 | −0.19* | −0.09 | | | | | | |

TABLE 11.2 *(cont.)*

| | Initial Exploratory Six-Factor Model | | | | | | Initial Exploratory Bifactor Model | | | | | | Final Exploratory Bifactor Model | | | | | |
|---|---|---|---|---|---|---|---|---|---|---|---|---|---|---|---|---|---|---|
| CCCMII18 | 0.18* | 0.04 | −0.01 | **0.59*** | 0.13* | −0.02 | 0.70* | 0.03 | 0.04 | −0.01 | −0.20* | −0.08 | | | | | | |
| CCCMII19 | 0.27* | −0.05 | −0.02 | 0.64* | 0.06 | −0.09 | 0.70* | −0.06 | 0.11 | −0.08 | −0.20* | −0.13 | | | | | | |
| CCCMII20 | −0.06 | 0.02 | 0.16 | **0.60*** | −0.18* | 0.10 | 0.61* | 0.02 | −0.14 | −0.28 | −0.02 | 0.00 | 0.56* | −0.06 | 0.03 | −0.02 | **0.44*** | 0.03 |
| CCCMII21 | 0.08 | 0.07 | −0.10 | **0.69*** | 0.13* | 0.08 | 0.74* | 0.07 | −0.05 | −0.04 | -.27* | −0.02 | 0.63* | 0.05 | −0.01 | −0.23 | 0.34* | 0.03 |
| CCCMII22 | 0.07 | −0.02 | 0.07 | **0.65*** | −0.01 | 0.09 | 0.75* | −0.03 | −0.05 | −0.15 | −0.13 | −0.01 | 0.66* | 0.02 | −0.05 | −0.15 | **0.33*** | 0.05 |
| CCCMII23 | −0.07 | −0.01 | 0.28 | **0.61*** | −0.24* | 0.04 | 0.62* | −0.02 | −0.14 | −0.33* | 0.06 | −0.04 | 0.58* | −0.03 | 0.00 | 0.10 | **0.58*** | −0.05 |
| CCCMII24 | 0.05 | −0.03 | 0.12 | **0.67*** | −0.05 | 0.01 | 0.72* | −0.03 | −0.07 | −0.18 | −0.10 | −0.07 | | | | | | |
| CCCMII25 | 0.06 | −0.20* | 0.10 | 0.48* | 0.04 | 0.04 | 0.60* | −0.20* | −0.03 | −0.06 | −0.08 | −0.03 | | | | | | |
| CCCMII26 | 0.05 | 0.01 | 0.01 | 0.29* | 0.23* | 0.12 | 0.54* | 0.00 | −0.02 | 0.12 | −0.12 | 0.04 | | | | | | |
| CCCMII27 | 0.02 | 0.04 | 0.00 | 0.44* | 0.15* | 0.18* | 0.65* | 0.03 | −0.07 | 0.02 | −0.15 | 0.06 | | | | | | |
| CCCMII28 | −0.02 | 0.06 | 0.06 | **0.59*** | −0.07 | 0.18* | 0.67* | 0.05 | −0.11 | −0.19* | −0.10 | 0.05 | | | | | | |
| CCCMII29 | −0.03 | 0.01 | −0.01 | **0.58*** | 0.10 | 0.18* | 0.70* | 0.01 | −0.12 | −0.05 | −0.18* | 0.06 | | | | | | |
| CCCMII30 | 0.10 | 0.10* | 0.03 | 0.16* | 0.06 | **0.58*** | 0.73* | 0.10* | 0.02 | −0.01 | −0.04 | **0.33*** | 0.74* | 0.00 | 0.01 | −0.02 | −0.01 | **0.38*** |
| CCCMII31 | −0.06 | −0.13* | −0.06 | 0.15 | 0.02 | 0.47* | 0.42* | −0.12* | −0.09 | −0.04 | −0.08 | **0.28*** | | | | | | |
| CCCMII32 | 0.23 | 0.04 | −0.03 | 0.03 | 0.19* | **0.56*** | 0.71* | 0.05 | 0.14 | 0.13 | −0.07 | **0.32*** | | | | | | |
| CCCMII33 | 0.31 | 0.01 | 0.09 | −0.01 | −0.01 | **0.60*** | 0.72* | 0.01 | 0.20* | −0.04 | 0.05 | **0.35*** | 0.73* | 0.18 | 0.00 | 0.03 | 0.01 | 0.29* |
| CCCMII34 | 0.00 | −0.07 | 0.00 | 0.15* | −0.19* | **0.53*** | 0.43* | −0.07 | −0.04 | −0.21* | 0.00 | 0.32* | | | | | | |
| CCCMII35 | 0.12 | −0.03 | 0.08 | 0.14* | −0.06 | **0.60*** | 0.70* | −0.03 | 0.04 | −0.11 | 0.02 | **0.35*** | | | | | | |
| CCCMII36 | 0.12* | 0.04 | 0.05 | 0.06 | 0.04 | **0.67*** | 0.72* | 0.04 | 0.05 | −0.01 | 0.00 | **0.39*** | 0.75* | −0.01 | 0.04 | −0.10 | −0.01 | **0.33*** |
| CCCMII37 | −0.01 | 0.03 | 0.06 | 0.00 | 0.08 | **0.76*** | 0.68* | 0.04 | −0.05 | 0.03 | 0.02 | **0.46*** | 0.71* | −0.06 | −0.02 | 0.04 | 0.02 | **0.44*** |

scale development and social justice issues were asked to rate the content validity and clarity of items based on the construct definitions of the six CCCM factors. Items that were rated high (versus moderate or low) in content validity and clarity by all reviewers were retained, and twelve items were deleted (four classism items, two heterosexism items, two cis-sexism items, two ableism items, and two sexism items).

Next, we applied the item retention rule to select items based on iterations of the exploratory bifactor analyses. We started item selection with the cis-sexism group factor because this group factor had the most items, showed evidence of weak psychometric property in the original scale development study (Shin et al., 2018), and had considerable cross-loading with the heterosexual group factor. We simultaneously considered content representation/duplication and the strength of primary group factor loadings when we deleted items, and we removed one item at a time and repeated the exploratory bifactor analysis. The iterative factor analyses revealed that four cis-sexism items specific to gender-binary pronouns and bathroom rights loaded onto one group factor (e.g., "Information forms that only allow a person to check 'male' or 'female' discriminate against transgender persons"), and four cis-sexism items about transgender rights (e.g., "More laws are needed to make it easier for transgender persons to obtain competent medical or mental health treatment") loaded onto another group factor with heterosexism items. Given the robust advocacy for the use of nonbinary gender pronouns as well as the high profile clashes about bathroom rights, it was possible that these items tapped into individuals' attitudes about these issues and may have been distinct from their awareness of other forms of discrimination against transgender and gender nonconforming individuals. We thus decided to retain the four items about transgender rights, which resulted in a group factor that consisted of four cis-sexism and six heterosexism items.

After the four gender-binary items were deleted, the ableism group factor started to emerge. We proceeded to select items for the ableism group factor using the same item retention rule. The final combined CCCM-S had twenty-four items (Appendix A), which were represented by one general CC factor and five group factors: racism (five items), classism (four items), heterosexism (three items), ableism (four items), and sexism/cis-sexism (eight items). All items loaded significantly on the general factor with factor loadings ranging from 0.19 to 0.85, $M = 0.61$, $SD = 0.20$. Interestingly, in the final model, the four cis-sexism items loaded negatively onto the same group factor with the sexism items rather than the heterosexism items. Because the sexism and heterosexism group factors had a small, nonsignificant negative correlation, $r = -0.15$, we suspected that the negative factor loadings of the 4 cis-sexism items were a statistical artifact, and should instead be conceptualized to load together with the heterosexism items to represent individuals' awareness about discrimination and systemic oppression against LGBTQ individuals.

## DISCUSSION

In the present study, we provided evidence supporting the development of the CCCM-S, a 24-item, self-report measure assessing CC, or awareness and attitudes related to systemic, institutionalized forms of discrimination (Appendix A). The CCCM-S measures general CC as well as CC specifically associated with racism, classism, heterosexism, ableism, and sexism/cis-sexism. Acceptable levels of reliability were observed for each of the scales. Based on feedback from expert reviewers and through the selection of items from iterations of exploratory factor analyses, the results suggest a tentatively stable, multidimensional structure for the 24-item instrument that was best represented as a bifactor model. While results of the current study are promising, CFA with a new sample and additional evidence of construct validity (e.g., convergent, criterion) will need to be conducted before we can determine that the CCCM-S is a psychometrically sound measure. In the following section, we present some potential research, training, and counseling implications associated with the development of the CCCM-S.

## RESEARCH

Due to the predominant single-axis lens in the field of psychology, there is a lack of questionnaires that allow for researchers to examine awareness of different forms of systemic oppression simultaneously and comprehensively. Employing both the CCCM and CCCMII in a study would require participants to answer a total of fifty-six items, which is not ideal considering that researchers would likely include several other measures of interest. The CCCM-S circumvents this issue by succinctly capturing multiple forms of systemic oppression in one cohesive measure. Rapa et al. (2020) have identified two key charges for researchers engaged in CC measurement development. First, they have pointed out the lack of CC measures that incorporate all three subcomponents of the construct. While the CCCM-S is still limited to the critical reflection component, this shortened version will make it easier to couple it with other CC measures that do assess levels of motivation and action. Rapa et al.'s (2020) second charge is for CC measurement researchers to demonstrate measurement invariance for their scales. While the CCCM has demonstrated validity across some samples, the shortened CCCM-S will make it easier for us to establish measurement invariance across additional groups. This is especially important for the CCCM-S, since we have always been interested in assessing levels of CC among those who hold various constellations of privileged and marginalized identities (e.g., wealthy, nonbinary Latinx individual; low-income, cisgender Asian American woman, etc.; see Godfrey and Burson, 2018, for discussion).

## TRAINING

Therapists are expected to engage in continuous processes that allow them to prepare to effectively serve the needs of diverse clients. Multicultural training, specifically education and training focused on CC development, has been shown to increase cultural competency among counseling graduate students (Choi et al., 2015; West-Olatunji et al., 2011). Clients who perceived their therapists to display strong multicultural competencies reported higher levels of satisfaction with therapy and stronger working alliance, and attended more follow-up sessions (Constantine, 2007). Despite ample evidence documenting the benefits of multiculturally oriented counseling practices, training deficits remain pervasive. Curricula lack culturally sensitive material and instead promote a universal application of psychology indicative of ethnocentric monoculturalism (Sue et al., 2019). CC may serve as a precursor for therapists to critically reflect on systemic levels of oppression and thus attend more readily to the refinement of their multicultural competencies. CC trainings may potentially be one method of intervention for therapists to increase their level of CC by metaphorically opening their eyes to existing forms of oppression that exist within society and within the practice of mental health. For instance, therapists who participate in regular CC trainings as part of continuing education (CE) credit, graduate study requirements, or voluntary vocational development may benefit from increased CC and decreased personal biases. We expect therapists with higher levels of CC to have more awareness, knowledge, and skills for addressing systemic barriers and multicultural issues in therapy that influence clients' problems within a social justice context.

## COUNSELING

Racism, sexism, classism, heterosexism, cis-sexism, and ableism continue to be powerful and pervasive forces within contemporary US society. Because therapists are members of society, they are not immune from internalizing the biases and discriminatory beliefs that abound. The multicultural counseling movement, which began more than forty years ago, has urged therapists to improve their multicultural competency by acquiring awareness, knowledge, and skills related to multicultural needs (Sue et al., 2019). Development of multicultural competencies allows therapists to adopt a multicultural orientation (MCO; Davis et al., 2018) where therapists display cultural humility and cultural comfort while attending to cultural opportunities present in session. Adopting multiculturally sensitive and culturally humble therapeutic practices has been shown to have positive effects on therapy outcomes, including strengthening the working alliance between the therapist and client (Davis, et al., 2018). While each of the components of these frameworks is important, the awareness (i.e., critical reflection) pillar has always been considered foundational. We hope that the development of the CCCM-S will allow for more efficient and comprehensive evaluation of mental health practitioners' internalized biases, which may contribute to a more culturally competent workforce in the field.

## CHAPTER 11 APPENDIX
## CONTEMPORARY CRITICAL CONSCIOUSNESS MEASURE-SHORT

The Contemporary Critical Consciousness Measure-Short (CCCM-S) is a self-report measure that assesses general CC as well as CC specifically associated with racism, classism, sexism, heterosexism/cis-sexism, and ableism. Respondents rate their level of agreement on a scale ranging from 1 (*strongly disagree*) to 7 (*strongly agree*). A total scale score as well as subscale scores can be derived from the CCCM-S. To calculate scale scores, sum the items within the respective scale. Higher scores on the CCCM are indicative of greater levels of critical consciousness. When the total scale is used, the score is an index of general CC. When a subscale score is used, the score is an index of CC in that specific domain. The racism subscale is comprised of Items 1–5; the classism subscale is comprised of Items 6–9; the sexism subscale is comprised of Items 10–13; the heterosexism/cis-sexism subscale is comprised of Items 14–20; the ableism subscale is comprised of Items 21–24.

Instructions
Read each of the following statements. Using the 1–7 scale below, please rate your level of agreement with each statement.

1. All white individuals receive unearned privileges in US society.
2. The overrepresentation of Black and Latino/a/x individuals in prison is directly related to racist disciplinary policies in public schools.
3. All white individuals contribute to racism in the United States whether they intend to or not.
4. More racial and ethnic diversity in colleges and universities should be a national priority.
5. Racism against white individuals does not exist.
6. Poor people without jobs could easily find work but remain unemployed because they think that jobs like food service or retail are beneath them. (R)
7. Most poor people are poor because they are unable to manage their expenses well. (R)
8. Overall, white individuals are the most financially successful racial group because they work the hardest. (R)

9. Preferential treatment (e.g., financial aid, admissions) to college students that come from poor families is unfair to those who come from middle or upper class families. (R)
10. Discrimination against women is still a significant problem in the US.
11. Men receive many unearned privileges within US society.
12. Women often miss out on leadership positions due to sex discrimination.
13. US society has yet to reach a point where women and men have equal opportunities for achievement.
14. Gay, lesbian, and bisexual individuals are just as effective parents as their heterosexual counterparts.
15. I support including sexual orientation in nondiscrimination legislation.
16. Gay, lesbian, and bisexual individuals should have all the same opportunities in our society as straight people.
17. More laws are needed to make it easier for transgender persons to obtain competent medical or mental health treatment.
18. The government should make it easier for transgender persons to get identity documents (e.g., drivers licenses) that match their gender identity.
19. There is a need for laws that protect transgender persons from housing discrimination based on their gender identity.
20. Gender identity needs to be added to nondiscrimination laws to protect transgender persons in the workplace.
21. Our society should be transformed to better accommodate the needs of people with disabilities.
22. Lack of funding to support people with disabilities is a symptom of ableism.
23. Employment discrimination towards persons with disabilities is a significant problem within the US.
24. Laws requiring universal design (e.g., replacing stairs with ramps, websites that are accessible for those who are blind) in all major institutions would go a long way toward building a more equal society for persons with disabilities.

## REFERENCES

Barefoot, K. N., Smalley, K. B., & Warren, J. C. (2015). Psychological distress and perceived barriers to care for rural lesbians. *Journal of Gay & Lesbian Mental Health*, *19*, 347–369.

Bowleg, L. (2008). When Black + lesbian + woman ≠ Black lesbian woman: The methodological challenges of qualitative and quantitative intersectionality research. *Sex Roles*, *59*, 312–325. https://doi.org/10.1007/s11199-008-9400-z.

Bowleg, L., & Bauer, G. (2016). Invited reflection: Quantifying intersectionality. *Psychology of Women Quarterly*, *40*, 337–341. http://doi.org/10.1177/0361684316654282.

Choi, K. M., VanVoorhis, R. W., & Ellenwood, A. E. (2015). Enhancing critical consciousness through a cross-cultural immersion experience in South Africa. *Journal of Multicultural Counseling and Development*, 43, 244–261. http://doi.org/10.1002/jmcd.12019.

Combahee River Collective. (2014). A Black feminist statement. *Women's Studies Quarterly*, 42 (3/4), 271–280. (Original work published 1977.) https://doi.org/10.1353/wsq.2014.0052.

Conlin, S. E., Douglass, R. P., Moradi, B., & Ouch, S. (2021). Examining feminist and critical consciousness conceptualizations of women's subjective well-being. *The Counseling Psychologist*, 49(3), 391–422.

Constantine, M. G. (2007). Racial microaggressions against African American clients in cross-racial counseling relationships. *Journal of Counseling Psychology*, 54(1), 1.

Crenshaw, K. (1991). Mapping the Margins: Intersectionality, Identity Politics, and Violence against Women of Color. *Stanford Law Review*, 43(6), 1241–1299. https://doi.org/10.2307/1229039.

Davis, D. E., DeBlaere, C., Owen, J. et al. (2018). The multicultural orientation framework: A narrative review. *Psychotherapy*, 55(1), 89.

Delphin-Rittmon, M. E., Flanagan, E. H., Andres-Hyman, R. et al. (2015). Racial-ethnic differences in access, diagnosis, and outcomes in public-sector inpatient mental health treatment. *Psychological Services*, 12(2), 158–166.

Faloughi, R., & Herman, K. (2020). Weekly growth of student engagement during a diversity and social justice course: Implications for course design and evaluation. *Journal of Diversity in Higher Education*, 14(4), 569–579.

Farook, M. W. (2018). The state of multicultural counseling competencies research. *Psychotherapy Bulletin*, 53(4), 48–58.

Fedewa, S. A., Ward, E. M., Stewart, A. K., & Edge, S. B. (2010). Delays in adjuvant chemotherapy treatment among patients with breast cancer are more likely in African American and Hispanic populations: A national cohort study 2004–2006. *Journal of Clinical Oncology*, 28, 4135–4141. http://doi.org/10.1200/JCO.2009.27.2427.

Flores, G., & The Committee on Pediatric Research (2010). Technical report—Racial and ethnic disparities in the health and health care of children. *Pediatrics*, 125, e979-e1020. http://doi.org/10.1542/peds.2010-0188.

Freire, P. (2000). *Pedagogy of the oppressed.* Continuum.

Godfrey, E. B., & Burson, E. (2018). Interrogating the intersections: How intersectional perspectives can inform developmental scholarship on critical consciousness. In C. E. Santos & R. B. Toomey (Eds.), Envisioning the integration of an intersectional lens in developmental science. *New Directions for Child and Adolescent Development*, 161, 17–38.

Goodman, L. A., Liang, B., Helms, J. E. et al. (2004). Training counseling psychologists as social justice agents: Feminist and multicultural principles in action. *The Counseling Psychologist*, 32, 793–836. https://doi.org/10.1177/0011000004268802.

Heberle, A. E., Rapa, L. J., & Faragó, F. (2020). Critical consciousness in children and adolescents: A systematic review, critical assessment, and recommendations for future research. *Psychological Bulletin, 146*(6), 525–551. https://doi.org/10.1037/bul0000230.

Hu, L., & Bentler, P. M. (1999). Cutoff criteria for fit indexes in covariance structure analysis: Conventional criteria versus new alternatives. *Structural Equation Modeling, 6*, 1–55.

Kugelmass, H. (2016). "Sorry, I'm Not Accepting New Patients": An audit study of access to mental health care. *Journal of Health and Social Behavior, 57*, 168–183.

Lee, M., Han, S., & Thompson, C. M. (2021). Bicultural self-efficacy, bicultural identity integration, critical consciousness, and psychological well-being of people of color in the United States. *The Journal of Psychology, 155*(8), 738–754.

Parent, M. C., & Silva, K. (2018). Critical consciousness moderates the relationship between transphobia and "bathroom bill" voting. *Journal of Counseling Psychology, 65*(4), 403.

Payne, J. S. (2014). Social determinants affecting major depressive disorder: Diagnostic accuracy for Black American men. *Best Practices in Mental Health, 10*(2), 78–95.

Prilleltensky, I. (1997). Values, assumptions, and practices: Assessing the moral implications of psychological discourse and action. *American Psychologist, 52*(5), 517–535. https://doi.org/10.1037/0003-066X.52.5.517.

Rapa, L. J., Bolding, C. W., & Jamil, F. M. (2020). Development and initial validation of the Short Critical Consciousness Scale (CCS-S). *Journal of Applied Developmental Psychology, 70*, 101164. https://doi.org/10.1016/j.appdev.2020.101164.

Ratts, M. J. (2009). Social justice counseling: Toward the development of a fifth force among counseling paradigms. *The Journal of Humanistic Counseling, Education and Development, 48*, 160–172. https://doi.org/10.1002/j.2161-1939.2009.tb00076.x.

Ratts, M. J., Singh, A. A., Nassar-McMillan, S., Butler, S. K., & McCullough, J. R. (2015). Multicultural and Social Justice Counseling Competencies: Guidelines for the counseling profession. *Journal of Multicultural Counseling and Development, 44*, 28–48. https://doi.org/10.1002/jmcd.12035.

Reise, S. P., Moore, T. M., & Haviland, M. G. (2010). Bifactor models and rotations: Exploring the extent to which multidimensional data yield univocal scale scores. *Journal of Personality Assessment, 92*(6), 544–559. https://doi.org/10.1080/00223891.2010.496477.

SAMHSA (2015). *Racial/ ethnic differences in mental health service use among adults.* US Department of Health and Human Services Publication No. SMA-15-4906. Rockville, MD.

Satorra, A., & Bentler, P. M. (2001). A scaled difference chi-square test statistic for moment structure analysis. *Psychometrika, 66*(4), 507–514.

Shelton, K., & Delgado-Romero, E. A. (2011). Sexual orientation microaggressions: The experience of lesbian, gay, bisexual, and queer clients in psychotherapy. *Journal of Counseling Psychology, 58*, 210–221. https://doi.org/10.1037/a0022251.

Shin, R. Q., Ezeofor, I., Smith, L. C., & Welch, J. C. (2016). The development and initial validation of the Contemporary Critical Consciousness Measure. *Journal of Counseling Psychology, 63*(2), 210–223.

Shin, R. Q., Smith, L. C., Lu, Y. et al. (2018). The development and validation of the Contemporary Critical Consciousness Measure II. *Journal of Counseling Psychology*, *65*(5), 539–555.

Shin, R. Q., Smith, L. C., Vernay, C. N. et al. (2021). Seeking counseling services where the rainbow doesn't shine: A heterosexism audit. *Journal of Homosexuality*, *68* (13), 2246–2265. https://doi.org/10.1080/00918369.2020.1734377.

Shin, R. Q., Smith, L. C., Welch, J. C., & Ezeofor, I. (2016). Is Allison more likely than Lakisha to get a call back from counseling professionals: A racism audit study. *The Counseling Psychologist*, *44*(8), 1187–1211.

Shin, R. Q., Welch, J. C., Kaya, A. E. et al. (2017). The intersectionality framework and identity intersections in the Journal of Counseling Psychology and The Counseling Psychologist: A Content Analysis. *Journal of Counseling Psychology*, *64*(5), 458–474.

Singh, A. A., Appling, B., & Trepal, H. (2020). Using the multicultural and social justice counseling competencies to decolonize counseling practice: The important roles of theory, power, and action. *Journal of Counseling & Development*, *98* (3), 261–271.

Sue, D. W., Sue, D., Neville, H. A., & Smith, L. (2019). *Counseling the culturally diverse: Theory and practice*. John Wiley & Sons.

Yip, C. C. H., & Chan, K. K. S. (2021). How sense of community affects sense of self among sexual minorities: Critical consciousness as a mediating mechanism. *American Journal of Community Psychology*, *68*(1–2), 177–186.

Yoo, H. C., Atkin, A. L., Seaton, E. K., Gabriel, A. K., & Parks, S. J. (2021a). Development of a support for Black Lives Matter measure among racially–ethnically diverse college students. *American Journal of Community Psychology*, *68*(1–2), 100–113.

Yoo, H. C., Gabriel, A. K., Atkin, A. L., Matriano, R., & Akhter, S. (2021b). A new measure of Asian American Racial Identity Ideological Values (AARIIV): Unity, interracial solidarity, and transnational critical consciousness. *Asian American Journal of Psychology*, *12*(4), 317.

Watts, R. J., Diemer, M. A., & Voight, A. M. (2011). Critical consciousness: Current status and future directions. *New Directions for Child and Adolescent Development*, *2011*, 43–57. http://doi.org/10.1002/cd.310.

West-Olatunji, C., Goodman, R. D., Mehta, S., & Templeton, L. (2011). Creating cultural competence: An outreach immersion experience in southern Africa. *International Journal for the Advancement of Counselling*, *33*, 335–346. https://doi.org/10.1007/s10447-011-9138-0.

Willging, C. E., Salvador, M., & Kano, M. (2006). Brief reports: Unequal treatment: mental health care for sexual and gender minority groups in a rural state. *Psychiatric Services*, *57*, 867–870.

Worthington, R. L., Soth-McNett, A. M., & Moreno, M. V. (2007). Multicultural counseling competencies research: A 20-year content analysis. *Journal of Counseling Psychology*, *54*, 351–361. https://doi.org/10.1037/0022-0167.54.4.351.

# Conclusion

## Expanding Critical Consciousness Theory and Measurement

### *A Not-So-Slow Train Coming*

LUKE J. RAPA AND ERIN B. GODFREY

As noted throughout the chapters of this volume, critical consciousness scholarship has expanded rapidly in recent years (Heberle et al., 2020). This volume adds to that expansion, with particular focus on theory and measurement. Whether through attention to theory, measurement, or both, the chapters in this book have illuminated complex issues that demand further attention to advance the field, questions regarding the conceptualization and operationalization of critical consciousness along the five axes we described in our introduction: (1) unidimensional–multidimensional; (2) individual–collective; (3) person-focused–systems-focused; (4) domain-specific–domain-general; and (5) singular axis of oppression–manifold axes of oppression.

In Part I, Theory, the boundaries of critical consciousness theory were pushed and new questions were raised about critical consciousness' development and operation. The first few chapters in the volume examined critical consciousness alongside other frameworks, demonstrating the usefulness and promise of integrating critical consciousness with other theoretical perspectives. In Chapter 1, Pinedo et al. made the case for the importance of accounting for the psychological experiences of youth of color as they navigate oppressive societal conditions, especially those tied to inequities due to racial capitalism. The framework proposed offers a new conceptual model for examining how contextual and motivational factors interact with critical consciousness, shaping adaptive development and supporting social mobility among youth of color.

Similarly, in Chapter 2, Suzuki et al. argued for the need to integrate the phenomenological variant of ecological systems theory with critical consciousness, demonstrating that critical consciousness theory can benefit from expansion to more fully consider how critical consciousness is fostered and operates within the context of developmental systems. They also point to new ways to account for the dynamic and collective characteristics of critical consciousness, pointing to novel research questions that, when answered, will deepen understanding of how individuals navigate and resist marginalization within various developmental contexts.

In Chapter 3, Rapa et al. similarly presented a new framework integrating critical consciousness with social empathy, a concept emanating from the field of social work and loosely drawn on Freirean critical consciousness (Freire, 1968/2000). Through this integration, Rapa and colleagues demonstrate how social empathy may complement critical consciousness, in terms of both theory and measurement, and they point to new evidence that social empathy may be a mechanism that interacts with the pathways among the reflection–motivation–action dimensions of critical consciousness, especially, perhaps, for those with relative privilege.

Chapters 4 and 5 similarly pushed theoretical boundaries by asking readers to consider how critical consciousness develops among children and youth. In Chapter 4, Heberle et al. explore the developmental competencies of children in early, middle, and late childhood and argue that these competencies equip them to develop skills associated with and supportive of critical consciousness. While they expand critical consciousness theory by delineating a clear developmental pathway for critical consciousness across childhood, they also provide suggestions for how measurement approaches and instrumentation may need to be adapted to assess critical consciousness during this developmental period. Ultimately, Heberle et al. provide a developmentally grounded blueprint for how critical consciousness might be examined in children. In Chapter 5, Wray-Lake et al. similarly push theoretical boundaries by explicating developmental processes tied to critical consciousness among both youth of color and white youth. Importantly, they examine how youths' contexts for development can lead to variation among youth in their critical consciousness, suggesting that attention to these variations can provide new theoretical insights about the development and operation of critical consciousness among today's youth.

Finally, in Chapter 6 Burson et al. called attention to the ways in which current measures of critical reflection have failed to account for the structural and historical thinking about inequality that is ingrained within critical consciousness theory. They then called for the respecification and expansion of critical reflection instrumentation to include these as distinct subdomains of critical reflection. The authors contend that if critical reflection measures are to be truly critical, then a greater accounting of structural thinking about and historical attributions for inequity must be incorporated into critical reflection measurement.

Through the chapters appearing in Part I, scholars have engaged with some of the most pressing questions in the field: How does critical consciousness develop? To whom does critical consciousness apply: To children? To youth with certain forms of privilege? To all individuals? What theories can be used to complement and enrich our understanding of the development and operation of critical consciousness? Taking on these questions, novel insights have been generated and exciting new directions have been set for future research endeavors. Indeed, a few research priorities clearly manifest from this collection of chapters. One priority is the continued study of developmental pathways and trajectories of critical consciousness over the life course. Knowledge and skills facilitative of critical consciousness surely emerge prior to adolescence, but extant research has primarily emphasized the relevance of critical consciousness among adolescents and emerging adults. The study of critical consciousness in children, as well as in middle-aged and older adults, should be prioritized and theory about its developmental precursors and adult correlates generated. Moreover, longitudinal measurement, using instrumentation designed to measure critical consciousness and its component parts in explicit ways, should be carried out to examine how critical consciousness's development and operation changes over time and occurs across the lifespan. Another priority is the closer examination of mechanisms that support critical consciousness' development and functioning. For example, scholars should continue to examine the roles that individual characteristics (e.g., identity, motivation, empathy, and social empathy) and contexts (e.g., one's developmental system) play in supporting or constraining critical consciousness, and how these also shift in importance and function across the lifespan and for individuals with differing experiences with privilege and marginalization.

The compilation of chapters in Part II, Measurement, engaged in the critical evaluation and interrogation of critical consciousness measurement, considering how current instrumentation aligns with theory and highlighting some of the complexities and intricacies of critical consciousness measurement as it is currently carried out. Perhaps more importantly, new directions were identified in support of continued refinement and expansion of critical consciousness measurement, in order to align measurement more tightly with theory and forge new directions for assessing critical consciousness in ways that capture critical consciousness in all its complexity.

In Chapter 7, Rapa et al. presented a brief history of critical consciousness measurement, contending that it has progressed through four phases: (1) proxy measurement; (2) scale development; (3) scale expansion and (re) specification; and (4) scale refinement and adaptation. Using their review to highlight thorny conceptual, theoretical, and practical measurement issues, Rapa et al. also pointed to a number of new directions for measurement, including more refined intersectional measurement, deeper assessment of structural-historical knowledge and/or thinking, longitudinal measurement, utilization of more intensive measurement approaches, more attention to depth–breadth, domain specificity–domain generality, and more granular measurement, and other novel approaches. In so doing, they set the stage for the remaining chapters in this section, and for other future measurement research.

In Chapter 8, Kornbluh et al. proposed social network analysis as a new approach for studying and measuring the development and operation of critical consciousness among youth, ultimately suggesting it as an effective tool to assess precursors to and specific aspects of critical consciousness at multiple levels: individuals, dyads, and settings. As such, they push the field to consider how to move beyond individual-level measurement of critical consciousness and toward collective and setting-measurement, in line with aspects of critical consciousness theory and addressing key limitations to current measurement approaches.

Similarly, in Chapter 9, Tyler et al. outlined a new approach to studying critical consciousness via daily diary methods in order capture more fine-grained, "micro" assessments of critical consciousness. This approach, they argue, aligns with the likely temporal nature of critical consciousness's development and provides avenues to better capture intraindividual variability – issues that are not well addressed through current critical consciousness measures.

In Chapter 10, Johnson et al. articulated complexities with critical consciousness measurement as tied to "systems" and "selves" in order to push boundaries of measurement (and theory) beyond individual-level assessment of critical consciousness and to account for the dynamic interaction between individuals and their setting-level contexts. Johnson et al. provide new insights and offer clear recommendations for how measurement approaches can be advanced in order to account for more complexity in critical consciousness measurement.

Finally, in Chapter 11, Shin et al. presented a new intersectional measure of critical consciousness, the Contemporary Critical Consciousness Measure-Short, which offers both a general measure of critical consciousness and measures critical reflection on five specific forms of modern-day oppression: racism, classism, heterosexism, ableism, and sexism/cis-sexism. Through this work, Shin et al. continue to advance the field by pushing boundaries of intersectional critical consciousness measurement, providing tools to assess multiple forms oppression and measure understanding of the sociohistorical and sociopolitical foundations of oppression that shape the experiences of many within contemporary American society.

Through these chapters, scholars have engaged with some of the other most pressing questions in the field: How do various measurement approaches align with or diverge from theory? How might new directions in theory and measurement further enhance what is known about the development, operation, and effects of critical consciousness? Are there ways to expand critical consciousness measurement to move beyond individual-level measurement and toward collective and/or setting level measurement? Answers to these questions are beginning to be formulated, and attending to these answers will surely continue to push the field forward, toward further refinement and expansion of critical consciousness theory and measurement. To be sure, from these chapters, clear priorities for future research have already emerged. For example, research should (continue to) prioritize the examination of alignment between extant critical consciousness measures and critical consciousness theory. Where lack of alignment, specificity, or precision is identified, scholars should engage in efforts to enhance or refine instrumentation. Specific efforts are needed to refine measures to account for the multidimensional, intersectional, collective, and dynamic nature of critical consciousness. Specific efforts are also needed to attend more fully to reflection–motivation–action praxis as it relates to the systemic, structural, and historical nature of inequities that exist.

Through this collection of chapters, advances in both theory and measurement have been presented and pursued. At the outset, we noted that our hope was that this compendium might provide novel insights about critical consciousness theory, establish new links between critical consciousness and related developmental theories and frameworks, foster deeper understanding of and appreciation for critical consciousness, and provide new empirical evidence about how critical consciousness develops and operates over the life course – all the while highlighting the complexity of the field and offering innovative ways that critical consciousness might be theorized about and measured. Our aim was to examine and expand critical consciousness theory and measurement in order to bring to light critical issues in the field and to set new directions for future research. The chapters within this volume present a broad range of theory- and measurement-related complexities that manifest today within critical consciousness scholarship and, we hope, will guide future work. Critical consciousness theory and measurement are expanding, as the chapters of this volume demonstrate; like critical consciousness scholarship in general, the critical consciousness theory and measurement train is on the move, and it is gaining speed. We hope that, through your engagement with this volume, that momentum will continue, and critical consciousness theory and measurement will continue to expand as a result.

## REFERENCES

Freire, P. (1968/2000). *Pedagogy of the oppressed*. Continuum.

Heberle, A. E., Rapa, L. J., & Faragó, F. (2020). Critical consciousness in children and adolescents: A systematic review, critical assessment, and recommendations for future research. *Psychological Bulletin*, *146*(6), 525–551. https://doi.org/10.1037/bul0000230.

# INDEX

Ingram Content Group UK Ltd.
Milton Keynes UK
UKHW021531250423
420667UK00019B/58